How Economics Should Be Complicated

Albert Hirschman's Legacy
Works and Discussions

Luca Meldolesi

Series Editor

Vol. 1

The Albert Hirschman's Legacy series is part of the Peter Lang
Political Science, Economics, and Law list.
Every volume is peer reviewed and meets
the highest quality standards for content and production.

PETER LANG
New York • Bern • Berlin
Brussels • Vienna • Oxford • Warsaw

Albert O. Hirschman

How Economics Should Be Complicated

Edited by
Luca Meldolesi

PETER LANG
New York • Bern • Berlin
Brussels • Vienna • Oxford • Warsaw

Library of Congress Cataloging-in-Publication Data

Names: Hirschman, Albert O., author. | Meldolesi, Luca, editor.
Title: How economics should be complicated / Albert O. Hirschman;
edited by Luca Meldolesi.
Other titles: Come complicare l'economia. English
Description: New York: Peter Lang, 2020.
Series: Albert Hirschman's legacy: works and discussions; vol. 1
ISSN 2576-9723 (print) | ISSN 2576-9731 (online)
Includes bibliographical references and index.
Identifiers: LCCN 2020004988 | ISBN 978-1-4331-7300-4 (hardback: alk. paper)
ISBN 978-1-4331-7301-1 (ebook pdf)
ISBN 978-1-4331-7302-8 (epub) | ISBN 978-1-4331-7303-5 (mobi)
Subjects: LCSH: Economic development. | Economics.
Classification: LCC HD75 .H56913 2020 | DDC 330—dc23
LC record available at https://lccn.loc.gov/2020004988
DOI 10.3726/b17245

Bibliographic information published by **Die Deutsche Nationalbibliothek.**
Die Deutsche Nationalbibliothek lists this publication in the "Deutsche
Nationalbibliografie"; detailed bibliographic data are available
on the Internet at http://dnb.d-nb.de/.

29 Broadway, 18th floor, New York, NY 10006
www.peterlang.com

Contents

Introduction: Five Theses and an Excursus

1. The title of this collection brings to mind the title of an article the reader will find further on: "Against Parsimony: Three Easy Ways of Complicating Some Categories of Economic Discourse" (1984).[1] In any case it is not difficult to understand that, sometimes perhaps in a latent or interrogative form, the need to renew the discipline long absorbed the attention of Albert Hirschman.

Going back in time, we can ask, for example, how the problem was manifest in the change in the author's research interests at the end of the 1960s; how the need to meet the challenge of the political disasters in some Third World countries and to pursue detours and forays into other fields (in voice and exit, in passions and interests, in changing involvements)[2] led Hirschman to think "more and more" that parsimony in the construction of economic theory could be carried too far, and that "something is sometimes to be gained by making things more complicated" (cf. below, p. 354). Furthermore, if we go back even further and look, for example, at *National Power and the Structure of Foreign Trade* (1945), it

1. For bibliographic references to the writings of Hirschman cited here, see the bibliography of his works at the end of the present volume.
2. *Essays in Trespassing: Economics to Politics and Beyond*, 1981; p. VI and 23.

immediately becomes clear that here too the author is seeking to combine economics and politics and to thus make economics "less isolated and self-enclosed".

2. These observations are in themselves enough to clarify the direction of the present introduction. We will deal first with some theses concerning the reform of the discipline and will then proceed to an intellectual excursus whose intent is to show points of contact—generally unnoticed—among some of Hirschman's works. These elements are useful both as an aid to understanding the author's sources of inspiration and as a starting point for exploring the contribution of these works to our topic. "How Economics Should Be Complicated" can thus represent both the endpoint of a long work project and one of its central and recurring themes.

This is not to deny, however, that its message may at first sight appear incomprehensible: isn't economics, after all, already a sufficiently complicated discipline? Clearly, the point is not so much to make often difficult analytical processes even more complex, as to understand that conceptual elaboration of the discipline—giving it more "structure" even in its basic categories—can make it more useful as well as more accessible.[3] The point is to call into question the highly parsimonious paradigm traditional economics is based on: of the isolated individual, moved by material self-interest, who freely and rationally chooses among alternative lines of action after having calculated the costs and expected benefits. Hirschman contests this approach and proposes incorporating into economic discourse a series of natural human characteristics and tensions that have until now been forgotten.

3. Back in the early seventies, however, in two linked essays—"The Search for Paradigms as a Hindrance to Understanding" and "Political Economics and Possibilism" (included in the present collection)—he cast doubt on the role generally assigned to paradigms in contemporary social science.

3. It thus happens—as a result of paradoxical but valid reasoning—that complicating economics means making it less simplified but more simple. "Le simple", as Bachelard said, "n'est jamais que le simplifié": this was recalled by L. J. D. Wacquant: "'Compte rendu' de Albert Hirschman 'Vers un'économie politique élargie'", in *Cahiers Internationaux de Sociologie*, vol. LXXXIII, p. 432.

The search for economic and social regularities must of course retain its leading role; nevertheless—Hirschman argues—there is a problem of cognitive style when it comes to the type of paradigms utilized, the way we connect them, and the interpretive power we attribute to them. Specifically, we need to be wary of parsimonious and all-encompassing paradigms, rigid constructions superimposed on reality (and carrying with them anti-democratic implications), and clear and definitive predictions. Every outcome must instead be qualified, delimited, and linked back to its true dimension. In addition, it is essential to leave room—equal room, Hirschman argues—for analysis of the unexpected; along with the repeatable (that is, the probable), we need to study the unique, the possible—learning from the actual history of events.

This "possibilism" is an attitude of mind that favours the search for rare constellations of favourable events, narrow paths, and partial improvements that could be followed by others: it does not respect the boundaries of disciplines and leads, in itself, to a widening of the limits of what is possible (or is considered to be so). This gives rise to an analytical pathway that is at once cautious and brisk, that analyses the reality of proposals for change. In each case, attention is focused on examining a specific feature in depth, while many directions for further analysis are kept open. Proceeding in this way, over time the author progressively explores a vast field of economic-political themes and creates an output that in retrospect seems surprisingly unified.[4]

I

1. Why Complicate Economics?

4. I would like to focus on several aspects of this work. First of all, in 1977 Hirschman published *The Passions and the Interests*, an important essay on the history of ideas that aims to investigate theoretical conjectures concerning the political consequences of economic development before the triumph of capitalism, when social scientists could reason freely on such topics as "commercial expansion for peace, or of industrial growth for liberty" (p. 3). He identifies several important propositions that can help us come to grips with particularly difficult economic/

4. Cf. *A Bias for Hope: Essays on Development and Latin America*, 1971, p. IX, and *Essays in Trespassing*, 1981, p. V.

political issues;[5] this inevitably includes a severe critique of established knowledge and the clean division between economics and politics that lies behind it.

The text reconstructs a long sequence of ideas that began with Machiavelli and led to the eighteenth century argument that coping with passions requires recourse to material interests. In the second part the author concentrates on several salient points—such as Montesquieu and Steuart's concept of 'doux commerce'—to conclude in the end that with Adam Smith the traditional analytical distinction between passions and interests was lost.

In *The Theory of Moral Sentiments*, the father of political economy had placed non-economic impulses, with all the energy they carry, in the service of economic ones, stripping them of the autonomy they previously had enjoyed. Thus, the analysis in *The Wealth of Nations,* in spite of its many political elements, is based on the idea that people are motivated solely by the wish to improve their condition. This was the moment of the birth of the discipline of economics: a great intellectual conquest that at the same time brought with it a significant narrowing of the field of inquiry.

5. The history of ideas reconstructed in *The Passions and the Interests* shows, in a certain sense, the "progressive impoverishment of the prevailing concept of human nature over a period of some three centuries",[6] culminating in the birth of political economy. From this it is clear that there is an opposing need to gradually complicate the discipline, because (in the first place) it was founded on postulates that are over-simplified. This critique is mainly directed at traditional theory, but it also includes the critical schools of economics—the Keynesian school, the institutionalist, Sraffian, Marxist schools, etc.

Starting with his earliest writings—this is my opinion—Hirschman (usually) manages to avoid the choice that has faced economic critics in the last century—that is, either speaking from within the prevailing way of thinking—like Keynes and Schumpeter, or appealing—like Sraffa and (in part) Joan Robinson—to a different tradition. Hirschman instead creates a political focus of interest (economic, social and general policy) outside the discipline and, often starting with fieldwork, develops aspects of economic theory for his own purposes, combining

5. See *Essays in Trespassing*, 1981, p. VI.
6. Ibid., p. 288.

them (sometimes) with modified analytical elements from other social sciences. In this way he obtains new and often surprising results.

Among other things, it allows him to avoid committing himself on every aspect of a theory (on its so-called internal coherence: even in the case of the *General Theory*—cf. below, sec. 16) nor even to limit himself to a verification or a practical application of the theory itself. Instead, in the fashion of the early Renaissance, he is able to freely re-utilize ancient capitals and columns and other materials for purposes that are specific and limited, but useful. And in doing so, he uncovers new architectonic perspectives.

6. An ongoing characteristic of Hirschman's work, then, is his lack of respect for the traditional limits of the discipline, and this in time becomes "the art of trespassing" beyond the limits of the social sciences.[7] This points to a second topic I would like to call attention to.

There is no need to mention here the ups and downs of the concept of interest (which the reader will find later). For our purposes, it is enough to briefly recall the history of political economy, which for two centuries embraced the well-known thesis of Adam Smith according to which it is not the benevolence of the baker or dairyman that we have to thank for our breakfast, but rather their personal interest.

As early as 1820—as Schumpeter, Downs, Olson and many others would do in the twentieth century—James Mill proposed an economic theory of politics assuming that actors follow their own interests in this field as well. But the possibility that a significant gap exists between a citizen's real interests and an individual's perception of them gave Macaulay an opening to denounce the doctrine of interest as tautological, a criticism that would only acquire importance as the concept was diluted to make room for motivations extraneous to material interests in the narrow sense. This happened both by means of concepts of enlightened, forward-looking, real interest, and through the lack of rehabilitation of the eighteenth century distinction between interests and passions: even the initiatives of the Schumpeterian entrepreneur and the animal spirits of the Keynesian capitalist were proposed as manifestations of their interests.

7. Which, together with development and democracy, forms the title of the *Festschrift* in Hirschman's honour (cf. *Development, Democracy and the Art of Trespassing: Essays in Honor of Albert O. Hirschman*, A. Foxley, H. McPherson and G. O'Donnell, eds., Notre Dame, University of Notre Dame Press, 1986).

7. In this way, rather than deducing economic behaviour from the pursuit of material interest, political economy tended increasingly to move in the opposite direction, attributing to economic behaviour—whatever it might be—the quality of conforming to interest. This latter became "the engine of everything people do or want to do" (and eventually other key concepts of economic analysis, such as utility and value, were replaced by more neutral terms such as revealed preferences and constrained maximization).

How to interpret this development? The text offers the hypothesis that the positivist and formalist direction of economic analysis during the past century and a half is linked, in opposition, to the extraordinary interest in the non-rational—in instinct, the unconscious, the customary, etc.—that held sway in philosophical thought at the end of the nineteenth century. Based on the rational pursuit of interests, economics could not incorporate the new discoveries into its analytical apparatus. So it reacted "by withdrawing from psychology to the greatest possible extent, by emptying its basic concepts of their psychological origin" (see below p. 382).

8. This hypothesis seems to me important for (at least) two reasons. In the first place, the dilution of the concept of interest serves to highlight the intellectual turnabout in the discipline at the end of the nineteenth century, which involved the well-known rise of marginalist economics. This can in turn be linked to the economics of "appearance" of Say, Senior or Bailey (rather than to the classical thinking claimed by a long, "orthodox" tradition). Additionally, its arrival was presented as an intellectual revolution happening at the same time in different countries and supported by progress in physics and mathematics. Finally, in some of its basic concepts—balance, efficiency, harmony of interests—neoclassical economics is an offspring of positivist thinking: by contrast, it seemed that its success was favoured by the development of social conflict.

Added to this interpretive picture is the hypothesis that the development of economic analysis in a positivist and formalist direction is linked to the development of other social disciplines. Instead of an immersion—following tradition—in the history of economic thought, here there is an effort to understand the evolution of economics as a part of the overall history of ideas. The end of the nineteenth century thus witnessed a great change: the birth of some new social sciences—psychology, sociology, anthropology; the reformulation of ancient sciences—geography, philosophy, politics, history; the extraordinary attraction for the non-rational prevalent in many disciplines. Positivist culture, which gives a great boost to the natural sciences, is indeed expressed in physics and mathematics in the deductive method, but in medicine and biology it is through experiment and induction. While economics is inspired by the former, the other social sciences turn primarily to the latter: for this reason the separation of content also becomes a separation of method and of research mentality.[8]

9. The interesting thing about Hirschman's hypothesis is clearly in the implicit suggestion it contains. The isolation of economics—in method and content—that took place as a reaction at the end of the nineteenth century is also a legacy of the past, an historical wound that might gradually heal. This also helps us understand the meaning of the author's intellectual proposal. His art of violating the boundaries of disciplines finds here its general raison d'être.

In time a specific opportunity presented itself: the invasion of many research fields by economics in recent decades, mainly in the United States. The central core of these developments, argue Francesco Forte and Elena Granaglia,[9] consists of three trends in the literature: economic analysis of the collective decision-making processes of political bodies and the bureaucracy; microeconomic analysis of judicial-social institutions with regard to ownership and a company's internal and external relations; and the extension of the economic paradigm to fields habitually studied by other sciences, such as non-profit associations, the family, illicit activities and even the associations and dissociations between animals and plants (economics of biology).

Predictably enough, voters, "servants of the state", jurists, philanthropists, lovers, parents, criminals—heretofore considered prey to complex passions—and even animals and plants (who should be inspired by mother nature) are all described as committed to laboriously pursuing the "constrained maximization" of their material interests. In this way, the "economic paradigm, like it or not, invades the most 'sacred' and seemingly distant spheres."[10]

8. Cf. L. Meldolesi, "Per una nuova ipotesi interpretativa sulla storia del pensiero economico moderno", in *Quaderni di storia della economia politica*, 1987: 1–2.
9. *La nuova economia politica americana*, F. Forte and E Granaglia, eds., Milano Sugarco, 1980, p. 7.
10. F. Forte and E. Granaglia, op. cit. p. 43. This "invasion of the field" corresponds to a proposed general paradigm for the social sciences. Hirschman's big idea, says L. J. D Wacquant in the review cited (op. cit. p. 423), "is that the vaunted [micro] economic approach, which today some no longer hesitate to propose as the undisputed

10. The question, Hirschman maintains, has two aspects. On one hand, these analyses activate the mechanism of the scandalous paradox common to so much of social research: their aim is to show that behind the halo of veneration, ignominy, etc. that surrounds these activities lies simple individual material interest. This creates a moral trauma which is the basis for the analyses success.[11] On the other hand, however, as this procedure repeats itself and invades new spheres of life, it becomes predictable and triggers a spiral of decreasing (cognitive) returns.

Moreover, this almost suggests the possibility of an opposite logical process because it reveals some intrinsic weaknesses in the mode of interpreting social reality inherent in the economic paradigm. "As a result, it has become possible to mount a critique which, ironically, can be carried all the way back to the heartland of the would-be conquering discipline" (cf. below, p. 353).

Thus Hirschman achieves a critique of economics that belongs to a broader current of thought. He tells us in a note[12] that he considers *The Passions and the Interests* and the essays linked to it as part of the progressive intellectual initiatives that got started in the United States with the publication of *A Theory of Justice* by John Rawls.[13] His line of reasoning connects above all with the micro and macro analyses (of Kenneth Arrow and John Goldthorpe) which, contrary to the view of Adam Smith, show in different ways the need for "benevolence" in a well-functioning economic system.[14]

A few years later Hirschman likened his work to that of Schelling, Sen and other authors—like Boulding, Collard, Margolis, McPherson, Phelps and Pizzorno—who had begun to take seriously human actions and behaviours not traceable to the traditional concept of interest: "actions motivated by altruism, by commitment to ethical values, by concern for the group and the public interest, and, perhaps most important, the varieties of non-instrumental behaviour" (cf. below, pp. 353–354 and p. 383). In the meantime, he wrote *Shifting Involvements* (1982)

paradigm for all the social sciences (see the imperialist proliferation of theories of rational action in sociology and political science in their conservative versions, such as the economic approach of Becker or the rational choice of Coleman, or in those who self-define as Marxists, like the Analytical Marxism of Roemer and Elster) presents a mutilated image of reality which, without delay, needs complicating".

11. *Essays in Trespassing*, 1981, pp. 298–299.
12. *Essays in Trespassing*, 1981, pp. 287–288.
13. J. Rawls, *A Theory of Justice*, Cambridge (MA), Harvard University Press, 1971.
14. *Essays in Trespassing*, 1981, pp. 299–302.

an important monograph on the oscillation of human involvement between the private and public spheres: it is here, probably, that the final maturation of his position should be sought—above all in a key chapter on reasoning (the fifth, included in the present volume) that opens with a radical critique of *The Logic of Collective Action* by Mancur Olson.[15]

2. The "Free Ride", the "Invisible Hand", the Heart and the Mind

11. As mentioned, the economic theory of politics has a long history behind it; but in recent decades it has taken on a more definite connotation, giving rise to the theory of "public choice".[16] A point of reference for this material is undoubtedly the "free ride" concept (primarily in its application to collective action, as proposed by Olson) which has gained favourable attention from all the finance manuals and many sociology and political science texts.

For an economist, the thesis is more than predictable. The logic of collective action, Olson argues, has to be "exposed" through the postulate of individual interest. Groups of people with common interests do not act in the name of such interests. It is instead the case that the people who make up the groups are pursuing their individual interests and that as a result they have no real reason to participate personally in the activity of the group, since they can get the result they want leaving it to others to make the commitment to collective action, thus enjoying the benefits without incurring costs—the free ride.

But if everyone behaved this way, collective action would be impossible, so how can its existence be explained? Olson's answer is that, with the exception of small groups, collective action is in reality based on constraint and inducement to participate (through economic benefits): the "closed shop" of Anglo-Saxon trade unions, where jobs go only to union members; taxation enforced by the state;

15. "The journey which I undertook", Hirschman writes in the preface to *Shifting Involvements* (1982, p. VII) "permitted a number of elaborate side trips which yielded, among many other observations, a critique of conventional consumption theory, a better understanding of collective action and a new interpretation of the universal suffrage". Second chapter, "Varieties of Consumer Disappointment" (cf. below) begins his critique of the theory of consumption, while the fifth, "From Private Concerns into the Public Arena", contains as mentioned some central aspects of the analysis of collective action.
16. Cf. for example, D. C. Mueller, *Public Choice*, Cambridge, Cambridge University Press, 1979.

farmers' organizations held together by government agencies and cooperatives; professional associations that rely on subtle forms of coercion and the offer of services.

12. As we can see, this conception excludes the existence of a non-instrumental component in the life of trade unions (and political parties) and completely overlooks the great majority of collective actions, such as interest in political activities and participation in demonstrations and elections, along with the back-and-forth discourse of everyday life. So why do people mobilize, follow politics, vote, argue? Olson's theory only suggests that they shouldn't, which leaves it open to the critics.

Hirschman was long occupied—as we shall see—with the different kinds of relations that exist between economics and politics. In *Shifting Involvements* he studies the movement of personal involvement from the private to the public sphere (and vice versa) through the pursuit of happiness and the product of its frustration: disappointment. (The second chapter, included in the present collection, concerns a phenomenology of the disappointments that come from consuming merchandise.) The experience of disappointment in the private sphere thus gives rise to greater participation in the public sphere. Increased collective action is a consequence of such a decision (and the rebound effect that goes with it): it is not supported by a simple assessment of costs and benefits because here participation has a positive meaning (it is not—or not only—a cost).

This "Adam's rib" is probably what lies behind "Against Parsimony". Indeed, the explanation of political action in *Shifting Involvements* is developed here in such a way as to highlight the existence of two types of activity: instrumental and non-instrumental. Alongside these, Hirschman goes back to the book's analysis of consumer disappointment (and the self-reflection it entails); and adds, finally, his thesis on "love" (civic spirit). Thus, to begin his line of reasoning on the reform of the discipline, he now suggests complicating economic discourse through two fundamental human qualities—voice (communication, persuasion, and protest, well-known long-term concerns of the author's[17]) and self-evaluation—along with two tensions of the human condition—between instrumental and non-instrumental modes of behaviour, and between personal interest and public morality (see below, pp. 366–367).

17. The starting point of this interest—the first chapter of *Exit, Voice, and Loyalty* (1970)—is included in the present collection, chap. 11.

13. Thus, the analytic framework of economics would lose the cold pole star of material interest so as to begin moving in a number of directions. But if this is possible and necessary, what then is the true significance of the traditional concept of economics?

Here another central point in Hirschman's reasoning comes into play. One important aspect of the different forms of non-instrumental behaviour is that they are subject to wide variation. In politics, as mentioned, there is a whole range of such activities—from active commitment to simple everyday chatter—which change continually both in quantity and quality. But a higher level of participation in different forms of public action entails a reduction in citizens' dedication to their private interests (and vice versa). And all but total privatization is to be found only where there are particularly authoritarian governments, who seek to suppress even private expressions of disagreement with official policy.

An arresting conclusion follows. "That vaunted ideal of predictability, that alleged idyll of a privatized citizenry paying busy and exclusive attention to its economic interests and thereby serving the public interest indirectly, but never directly, becomes a reality only under wholly nightmarish political conditions!"

A fine outcome, it must be said, for a concept—the Invisible Hand—that represented the keystone of a doctrine of interest which at first probably "served to assuage any guilt feelings that might have been harboured by the many Englishmen who were drawn into commerce and industry during the eighteenth century but had been brought up under the civic humanist code enjoining them to serve the public interest *directly*" (cf. below, pp. 384 and 373).

14. On the other hand, in the face of an intellectual earthquake of these proportions, the reader might at this point appreciate some additional investigation. I would recommend the essay "Morality and the Social Sciences: A Durable Tension",[18] which argues that by birth and vocation the social sciences—beginning with political science and economics—have an inflection that goes against moral instruction. By birth, because they originated from a process of emancipation from traditional moral teachings.[19] By vocation, because just by living in society

18. In *Essays in Trespassing*, 1981, p. 294.
19. On this see F. Braudel, *Civilization matérielle, économie et capitaisme (XV–XVIII siécle). Les jeux des exchanges*, Paris, Colin, 1979 and L. Meldolesi, "Gli spiriti del capitalismo", in *Stato e Mercato*, n 15, 1985.

we have a notable ability (based on common sense and collective morality) to understand problems pertinent to the social sciences which, in their effort to add something to our knowledge, are typically led towards shocking and paradoxical conclusions that often run counter to traditional morals. This is true in economics for the rehabilitation of luxury by Mandeville as well as the parsimony paradox by Keynes. This is also true for the expeditions of conquest we have mentioned.

How then to breech this "existential" incompatibility between moralizing activity and scientific analysis that presents itself simply as a "fact of life"? It is not enough to be aware, *pace* Adam Smith, that a substantial output and distribution of "benevolence" is essential to the functioning of our society; nor is it sufficient to mount a "frontal attack" concentrating, for example, on altruism, almost to counterbalance the previous worry about personal interest.[20] Hirschman suggests that it is instead a matter of setting to work on a careful and long-term project that moves ahead artfully, case by case, concerning itself with the many aspects of human nature hitherto neglected, to be undertaken by economists open to the moral dimensions of reality (and to the analytical contributions of other human sciences).

15. But it is a path fraught with difficulty. The mutual exclusion between heart and mind is deeply rooted in our culture: once trained as a "scientist", the economist's battle to enter this new order of ideas is all uphill. Their "trained incapacity" (Veblen) is so strong that they may not even confess to themselves the moral source of their own research (which happened to the author in *Exit, Voice, and Loyalty*).

But at the same time—the text continues, in a typical about-face—being unaware moralists is not necessarily a bad thing. Given present cultural arrangements, if a morally alive social scientist unconsciously inserts moral considerations into her work, this might turn out to be "peculiarly effective".[21] But there is also

20. As we shall see later (sec. 28 e 54) the argument that a "frontal attack" is insufficient or erroneous plays an important role in Hirschman's inspiration.
21. This observation also concerns *Exit, Voice, and Loyalty*. It is well known that Hirschman became aware only later of the subterranean source of inspiration for this text (which he wrote about in the preface to the German edition of 1974). Reflecting on the book's success, he recently added: "it was probably fortunate that I was not aware of those deep moral stirrings when I wrote the book; otherwise the presentation of my argument might have been less general, less balanced [...] and less scientifically persuasive". (*Essays in Trespassing*, 1981, p. 305).

the opposite problem: once aware of our intellectual traditions, we have already taken the first step in repairing the deep laceration between mind and heart and its less-than-beneficial consequences; and thus also a first step in beginning to think about a science of the future that is at once social and moral.

We must therefore proceed—as I understand it—along the narrow road that runs between these two aspects of the question; following a gradual, difficult (but not impossible) path that climbs between respect, sometimes unconscious, for the pre-existing rules, and the creation of pathways that are new. Since the issue concerns ways of "reconciling the traditional posture of the economist as a 'detached scientist' with his or her role as a morally concerned person",[22] it would be useful to keep these pathways in mind—as I intend to do—as we approach some aspects of the debate on the work of Albert Hirschman.

II

3. *A Methodological Break*

16. As mentioned at the outset, it is possible to interpret the title of the present volume—which intends to "represent" the entire span of the author's work[23]—as dictated by the simple observation that it is precisely this "opera omnia" that contains important indications about what to do (or what ought to be done) to complicate economics. Although unable (not least for reasons of space) to fully argue this statement, I hope to be able to give an idea of the tractable and lively problem that it refers to.

To this end, I would like to begin my brief experiment with the "break" that exists between Hirschman's first writings and those from after the war. As known, the author got his degree at Trieste in 1938 and worked initially in demographic statistics and the Italian economy, writing:[24]

22. Ibid., p. 294.
23. Hirschman's first article appeared in *Giornale degli Economisti* in January 1938 with the title "Note su due recenti tavole di nuzialità della popolazione italiana" (Notes on two recent marriage tables for the Italian population).
24. "Les finances et l'économie italiennes, Situation actuelle et perspectives;" 1938 in *Supplémant au bullettin quotidien*, n. 123 du 1er Juin, Société d'études et d'information économiques, Paris.

> "Italian finances and its economy are increasingly impenetrable. Published data are rare. To get a rough idea of what might be the financial situation of the Realm one is forced into a meticulous compilation of occasional official communications of the Council of Ministers and the Grand Council of Fascism, the reports, anything but explicit, from the Ministry of Finance [...], and some very discrete studies that have appeared in the peninsula's newspapers and magazines".

This job of comparing and reconstructing, which produced "a picture, or rather an outline" of the Italian economic situation, concerned finances (the budget, coverage of the deficit, the tax on public companies' capital), along with monetary and banking policy, prices and consumption, production and the state of the economy, foreign trade, the trade balance.

With a hint of self-irony, Hirschman later declared:

> I liked this "detective" work, especially when I managed to discover things that the fascist authorities wanted to hide [...]. Not only had I somehow acquired a métier of sorts, but it was a great relief to realize that one could do tolerably competent work in economics without having to resolve whether Keynes, whose *General Theory* I had bought in London in the year of its publication (1936) and then taken along to Italy for study, had all the right answers.[25]

17. The work he had done then allowed Hirschman to "set up shop" in Paris as an expert on the Italian economy (and to prepare quarterly reports for the Institut de Recherches Economiques e Sociales di Charles Rist e Robert Marjolin—1939). In this role he was entrusted by John Condliffe with writing the Italian section of a research program on new regimes of exchange control in Europe initially organized under the aegis of the League of Nations;[26] subsequently obtaining a fellowship at the University of California at Berkeley, where he had been forced to take refuge in 1940.[27]

25. "Io, "detective" dell'economia fascista", in *Il Corriere della Sera*, 13 November 1987.
26. *Mémoire sur le contrôle des changes in Italie*, Paris, Société des Nations, June 1939; It., trans., "Memoria sul controllo dei cambi in Italia", in *Potenza nazionale e commercio estero. Gli anni trenta, l'Italia e la ricostruzione*, P. F. Asso e M. de Cecco, eds., Bologna, Il Mulino, 1987, pp. 161–255.
27. L. A. Coser, *Refugee Scholars in America; Their Impact and Their Experiences*, New Haven, Yale University Press, 1984, pp. 163–164.

Now to the point. In their introduction to a collection of Hirschman's writings—*Potenza nazionale e commercio estero. Gli anni trenta, l'Italia e la ricostruzione* (1987)—Pier Francesco Asso and Marcello de Cecco argue that between his early and post-war texts there is a methodological break.

They focus their attention mainly on *Mémoire sur le control des echanges en Italie* (Memoir on exchange controls) and *National Power and the Structure of Foreign Trade* (the first of Hirschman's books, written at Berkeley in 1941–1942 and published in 1945). The *Mémoire* is a very careful documentation of the Italian situation at the time—on the origins of exchange control, its administrative organization, the mechanism of payments, trade and trade policy, currency, the internal economy and current trends.[28] *National Power*, on the other hand, deals

28. Hirschman wrote in "A Dissenter's Confession" (in *Rival Views of Market Society and Other Recent Essays*, 1986, p. 6) that he had come out of the Italian and French experience of the 1930s with a "distrust (based on watching Fascist economic policy in the second half of the decade [from which *Mémoire* emerged]) of peacetime controls, allocations, and grandiloquent plans" and with "a healthy respect (based on watching the misadventures of the French economy) for the efficiency of the price system, particularly with respect to the effect of exchange rate changes on the balance of payments". A late product of these reflections is "Devaluation and the trade balance: a note", published in the present collection (chap. 3).
    The occasion for this rethinking came at the end of 1946 when Hirschman—as we shall see, below, sec. 25—was an "employee" of the Federal Reserve Board of the United States, charged with following the evolution of the situation in Italy and in France. In this capacity, he wrote a comment in the *Review of Foreign Developments* (a sort of internal bulletin) on the paradoxical statement by French finance minister Robert Schuman that "it would be foolish to devalue the franc due to the huge surplus of imports over exports in France's balance of payments". Working on this subject in general terms and in national currency, he initially came to the conclusion that Schuman's argument should not be put aside. But he immediately changed his mind and wrote a "mathematical note" in early 1947 that dealt with the problem of re-balancing the balance of trade payments in terms of foreign currency, as necessary. He proved the validity of the fortunately optimistic proposition that the higher the trade balance deficit, the more likely it is that devaluation will lead to a positive result. This note, which initially appeared in the *Review of Foreign Developments*, was then written and published in the *Review of Economics and Statistics* in 1949.
    So the "healthy respect" for the market that came from his experience in the 30s in the end led to a new analytical result: in spite of the breadth of the literature on the subject, economic theory had not yet got around to a study of the effects of

(in the first section) with theoretical and historical aspects of the relationship between national power and the structure of foreign trade, with explicit reference to the policies of Nazi Germany.

18. Asso and De Cecco maintain (p. 23) that comparison of the two texts "yields a fascinating collection of variations on the theme of mercantilism". But *National Power* has a general aim. It intends to show that[29] "power elements and disequilibria are potentially inherent in such "harmless" trade relations as have always taken place, for example, between big and small, rich and poor, agricultural and industrial countries—relations which could be fully in accord with the principles taught by the theory of international trade".

In this way, the two scholars observe, Hirschman takes a critical position right from the start regarding some of the basics of the dominant economic theory; but at the same time he develops his reasoning through this same analytical structure, almost as if he wanted to show orthodox economists that their own instruments could play a different tune. (It should be noted that the use of elements of the theory as part of the analysis is not what is in question—this typically recurs in Hirschman's work[30]—but rather the fact that, as the reader can personally verify—cf. *Foreign Trade as an Instrument of National Power*, included in the present collection, chap. 1—he offers a theoretical solution that mirrors the traditional one.)

devaluation on the trade balance when total imports and exports are unequal (or had only discussed it in terms of national currency: cf. J. Robinson, *Essays in the Theory of Employment*, Oxford, Oxford University Press, 1947². pp. 142–143). This result did not go unnoticed: cf. G. Haberler, "Adjustment through Changes in Exchange Rates", in *Kyklos*, 3, 1949 (and in *International Finance*, edited by R. Cooper, London, Penguin, 1969) and J. Meade, *The Theory of International Economic Policy*, vol. I, *The Balance of Payments*, London 1951. It was taken up once again by H. W. Arndt ("Yen Appreciation: J-Curve and Valuation Effects", 1987, and "The Valuation Effect of Changes in Exchange Rates: Preliminary Report on the Literature Survey", 1988, typescript) in a discussion of the scale of the Japanese balance-of-payments surplus.

29. *National Power and the Structure of Foreign Trade*, 1945, p. 40.
30. The use of some aspects of economic theory, often as starting points—Giacomo Becattini noted at the conference in Torino on Hirschman's work (13–14 Nov. 1987)—involves economists, whether they like it or not, in a line of reasoning that aims at a broader sort of explanation.

19. Furthermore, in the book's preface[31] the author himself provides some historical and autobiographical reasons to explain the differences between his pre- and post-war writings, beginning with the initial need to get his work into the fight against fascism and Nazism and therefore to "always come to definite conclusions able to inspire action". (To this it should perhaps be added that when Hirschman arrived in California early in 1941, he decided to run the risk of not enrolling in a doctoral course in economics, and instead to write *National Power*, attributing to the book—among other things—a technical-professional purpose.)

This was undoubtedly the sign of a difficult change (perhaps having to do with "trained incapacity"; sec. 15). But my impression is that—just as in the case of another well-known "coupure méthodologique"[32]—the debate will (probably) end up leading the issue into a more congruent dimension. In fact, examined from a general point of view, *National Power* contains other elements that are fully entitled to be part of our expedition to reform the discipline.

20. As has been mentioned, the book deals with the political use of international trade; or how the very nature of commercial relationships can be used to create relations of influence between countries. The solution it proposes starts with Marshall's conception of gain-from-trade and shows that, assuming the existence of asymmetries between the trading partners, the concept can explain the effect of the influence that arises from the possible interruption of trade: for the smaller partners the continuation of the exchange has a value such that the dominant power can force concessions (political, economic, military) in exchange for their gain from trade.

In 1971, looking back at his work, Hirschman saw *National Power* as a study of the political dimensions of economics, or a work of political science *and* economics. This kind of relationship, as he stated in the introduction to *A Bias for Hope*, had been analysed in its most obvious manifestations—as political power springing from private wealth or the reduction of consensus produced by inflation. Little attention was given to the "finer" manifestations of the economic landscape. His first discovery in this field in fact came with *National Power*.

31. *National Power and the Structure of Foreign Trade,* cit., pp. 41–42; cf. below, sec. 25.
32. I refer of course to L. Althusser, *Pour Marx*, Paris, Maspero, 1965, to L. Althusser ed. E. Balibar, *Lire le Capital*, Paris, Maspero 1965 and to the debate that followed.

> "It occurred to me that there is a straightforward connection between the old established economic concept of the gain from trade that country B achieves by trading with A and the influence which A can insert in B as long as the trade is foreign and is therefore subject to interruption or termination on A's will. The entire theory of the gain from trade and of its distribution became therefore relevant for an understanding of the influence and power relationships that arise out of trade" (cf. below, p. 274).

21. This leads to the following conclusion: on one hand, Hirschman undoubtedly utilizes the orthodox analytical apparatus from a different angle of vision and gets different results—in the manner of Keynes and Schumpeter; but on the other, his work is situated in a different theoretical perspective—one that connects economics and political science—and opens the way to a change in thinking that goes beyond the traditional limits of the discipline.

While the liberal and protectionist schools of economics had often studied commercial trade for the purpose (more or less explicit) of reinforcing their countries' power, Hirschman reverses the situation and focuses attention on national power itself. In this way he creates a centre of political interest outside the discipline and from here questions traditional economics for a response to his problem.

What is more, this line of reasoning appears to have been confirmed by successive developments. *National Power* was "rediscovered" in the 1960s, reprinted in 1969 and again in an expanded edition in 1980.[33] The reason, Hirschman explains in the new introduction,[34] is "that the political dimensions and side effects of foreign trade and investment are still very much with us—two obvious examples are the relations of the United States with Latin America and of the Soviet Union with Eastern Europe".

Moreover, it was in this introduction that Hirschman suggested re-establishing the ties of economic and political influence between countries as mutually

33. Along with, as noted, the new introduction—"Beyond asymmetry: Critical Notes on Myself as a Young Man and on Some Other Old Friends"—the 1980 edition also contains "The Paternity of an Index", first published in 1964, which claims the paternity of the commercial concentration index used by the author in Chapter 7 and in Appendix A of *National Power*.
34. In *Essays in Trespassing,* 1981, p. 28.

beneficial and in constant evolution.[35] In this way even today *National Power* maintains a significant role in the author's intellectual output; its role is emblematic as well, because it testifies to the difficulties—along with (fortunately) the possibilities—for development opened up by the intellectual reform movement that has been launched.

4. Undermine, Transgress, Build

22. In addition,—as the introduction to *A Bias for Hope* explains—*National Power* contains only the first of the "finer" political dimensions of the economic phenomena identified by the author. There are many others that can be deduced from additional aspects of his output and from some linked historical experiences; the conclusion is that there is no general key that will systematically reveal the political dimensions of economic relations; each emerges from specific research which, when it leads to a positive result, increases the probability of success of further research. "For what is required is a certain turn of mind, the desire to speculate and to search in a certain direction, rather than the application of any infallible and objective technique" (cf. below, p. 277).

How to explain the existence of such an attitude? This text is from the period of eighteen years (1952–1970) spent (almost entirely) on problems of economic development. It is well known that Hirschman re-examined some of his experiences in two essays—"The Rise and Decline of Development Economics" (1981) and "A Dissenter's Confession" (1984)—which follow, respectively, objective and subjective paths and are primarily related to *The Strategy of Economic Development.* For my part, also taking account of these essays, I will try and clarify a different aspect of the question.

The reason is clear. To work towards reforming a discipline, the economist has to be open to understanding other aspects of reality, which means "violating" the borders of economics. In the preface to *Essays in Trespassing* (1981, p. V),

35. Note that this happens from within the asymmetrical relations brought to light by *National Power and the Structure of Foreign Trade.* The placement of "gain from trade" at the centre of the analysis (in such a way that this gain may mean the dependence of the country that receives it on the country that grants it) implies the possibility of a historical evolution of the asymmetry relation even in the opposite direction from the one first indicated. This line of reasoning can thus continue uninterrupted, as long as it isn't held hostage by "non-dialectical" or "anti-possibilist" thinking—or by economic theory.

Hirschman states that while economics "became progressively more narrow at precisely the moment when the problems demanded broader, more political, and social insights" (Russell Sage Foundation, 1979), the essays gathered ignore completely the narrow confines of disciplines. The problem is that these confines exist—first and foremost in the consciousness of the various researchers.

23. In this way the debate over the author's work runs the risk of being led almost inadvertently back inside the various professional beehives: the economists appreciate Hirschman mainly for his ideas on economic development,[36] the sociologists think his key book is *Exit, Voice, and Loyalty*,[37] the political scientists take an interest in the problem of morality,[38] and so on.

Of course, I do not mean to deny the importance of concentrating (from time to time) on a limited topic and contributing to the debate from one's professional experience. But we should keep in mind that Hirschman's subject matter requires openness to new sorts of knowledge and implies that there is no single thread that will undo the tangled knot of reality. The idea is rather to look for a series of limited "transdisciplinary" results that are linked to one another. In the past, critics have sometimes tried to re-absorb into economics some of the results achieved, purging them of their non-economic meanings and outside connections (e.g. the reception of *The Strategy*, which led the author to ask that more attention be given to some chapters, such as the first (!), on motivations. Cf. the preface of 1961, p. IX).

It does seem legitimate, however, to look at the results in their entirety and at the connections between them (also to lend weight—as a by-product—to the invitation to readers to come out of their shells). Thus I will explore an element of contact between the development of the relationship between politics and economics, and the evolution of possibilism (the two methodological—and perhaps "philosophical"—perspectives discussed in the introduction to *A Bias for Hope*) and then to identify the connection between the genesis of *The Strategy* and that

36. Cf. for example, T. Cozzi, "Albert Hirschman", in *La Stampa*, 14 November 1987.
37. A. Pizzorno, "Sul confronto intertemporale delle utilità", in *Stato e Mercato*, 16 April 1987; L. Gallino, "Hirschman e le scienze sociali. 'Tra lealtà e critica' ", in *La Stampa*, 6 January 1988.
38. J.Q. Wilson, "The Rediscovery of Character: Private Virtue and Public Policy", in *Public Interest*, 1986, n. 1; S. Kelman, *Making Public Policy. A Hopeful View of American Government*; New York, Basic Books, 1987.

of *Journeys Toward Progress* (an important book that has not received the attention it deserves).

24. At the same time, such a point of view cannot help but come naturally to someone like the present writer,[39] who has tried to make sense of the influences of the political and cultural experiences of the young Hirschman on the process which formed his ideas. In "A Dissenter's Confession",[40] overcoming long reluctance, the author himself began to "tell a more complex story" about the formation of his own point of view. Moreover, also in the light of many additional texts,[41] it is possible to arrive, in my view, at several simple observations.

In the first place: we have seen up to now the not so easy establishment of a distance from economic theory (in favour of applied economics and statistics), followed by its critical re-use; and secondly, in the presence of a political option that orients research (on the Italian economy just as on world trade) and interacts with the analysis until it brings to light a first political dimension of the "finer" economic phenomena. But after the war this intellectual process finds a new way of "settling" on both sides; in symbiosis, you might say, with a third characteristic, possibilism.

25. The reason, Hirschman explains,[42] is the relaxing of the political tension that marked the end of the war and favoured the search for new directions. To this an important autobiographical element may be added. His work as an economist with the international division of the Federal Reserve Board that began at the end of 1946 placed the author in the peculiar position of an ex political refugee

39. L. Meldolesi, "Alle origini del possibilismo: Albert Hirschman 1932–1952", in A. O. Hirschman, *L'economia politica come scienza morale e sociale*, Napoli, Liguori, 1987.
40. In *Rival Views of Market Society*, 1986, p. 3.
41. I refer to the pre-war Italian writings already cited, to the five "Italian" essays published in *Potenza nazionale e commercio estero*, cit., numerous unpublished texts that appeared in typescript in the *Review of Foreign Developments* of the Federal Reserve Board between December, 1946 and September 1951 (along with the retrospective writings already cited, brief but insightful: the preface to *National Power* and "Io, 'detective' dell'economia fascista").
42. *Potenza nazionale e commercio estero*, cit., p. 42.

who had suddenly risen to a "surprisingly influential" position. "My reaction", he writes,

> perhaps occasionally excessive, was to repress the use of any sort of power I might have; but above all I worked hard to undermine the convictions of my colleagues (be they pro-market or pro-planning), many of whom saw nothing wrong with using their power to the full in the service of their opinions and convictions.

To perceive the genesis of this attitude (which would then become a "methodological attitude") we turn to the texts from the "Washington period" and note, behind the inevitable professional formality, a duality of behaviour: on one hand there is a sense of responsibility for the work and a determination not to "swim with the current", while on the other—because of this, you might say—a great openness, a willingness to gradually reshape his own point of view to correspond (as much as possible) to concrete developments, even at the cost of revisiting the same theme from different angles.[43]

26. This intense work—Hirschman wrote over forty texts in less than five years—undoubtedly left him in a new frame of mind. He had been entrusted to "follow events" in France and Italy: perhaps the "Italian" essays of 1947–1948[44] and the first part of "Disinflation, Discrimination, and the Dollar Shortage", included in the present volume, are the texts where his new attitude is most visible.

To strengthen the idea, it seems useful to point to a truly surprising page from "Italian Economic and Financial Conditions". Almost as if to condense a thought he had long been "chewing over" Hirschman writes:

> the remaining continuing task of the Italian economy is to lift itself to higher levels of economic activity and investment. Here as always, action implies the taking of certain risks. Even when the national accounts of a country are known with good approximation, it is not easy to indicate the "correct" amount of investment. In Italy a priori deductions, while instructive, can only yield extremely rough guesses and are not able to replace as yet the method of trial and error.[45]

43. It is likely in any case that the roots of this behaviour are earlier; cf. for example, sec. 55.
44. Now published in *Potenza nazionale e commercio estero*, cit.
45. In *Potenza nazionale e commercio estero*, cit., p. 331.

27. The controversy over the doctrinaire use of Keynesian macroeconomics is barely hidden. The text continues:

> While the diagnosis of Italy's position is difficult, the therapy to be prescribed is thus quite likely to be unorthodox. […] The necessity to walk on a very narrow path between deflation and inflation may suggest new methods of using both foreign aid and counterpart funds. Finally, it must be realized that we cannot possibly hope to solve Italy's problems within three or four years. ERP aid can avoid a deterioration in Italy's position and point the way toward economic development. Unless the Italian problem is seen in this light much time may be lost in looking for a simple formula that will 'set things right'.

And so we have before us a mental position—an attitude—inspired by the wish to investigate in a certain direction rather than apply an objective technique, which the author spoke about later (cf. above, Sec. 22). It involves a new visual angle, much less trusting, regarding economic theory (to which Asso and de Cecco called attention); a need for continuous interaction between thinking and historical reality that prepares the way for the discovery of unusual and hidden relations; a need for adaptation and engagement with concrete conditions; and at the same time a search for new and better solutions.

In reality, economic phenomena live in symbiosis with many others. In spite of the professional character of the texts, there is something that emerges here once again, in my opinion, a peculiarity already present in the writings on Italy from before the war (especially in "Mémoire su le control des exhanges")—which is to refer from time to time, in building an analysis, to non-economic aspects of reality—historical, political, administrative, social, and so on—and then calling these into question in a simple, direct, non-systematic way, almost as if it were something "natural".[46] Finally, this broadening of economic analysis in the direction of political science and beyond now goes hand-in-hand with a search for

46. Just one example: the conclusions of "France and Italy: Two Models of Reconstruction" (1947, It. trans. in *Potenza nazionale e commercio estero*, cit., p. 302) contain the following passage (which recalls the motivations concentrated on the group or the individual in the first chapter of *The Strategy*). "It may be that the idea of a national economic goal appeals strongly to the French people because of the frustrating lack of direction from which they suffered during the interwar period. Italy, on the contrary, emerged cruelly disillusioned from a long period of excessive "dynamism," and the considerable progress achieved in Italian reconstruction has resulted largely from the confluence of individual ventures, with or without encouragement from the State".

solutions that do not follow in the tracks of economic theory; that tread the roads of the possible.

28. There are three aspects to this—the interaction between thought and reality that takes both inductive and deductive forms, which keeps a distance from the "cogency" of economic theory and starts making liberal use of its different parts; the expansion of the field and the search for interactions between economic, political and social phenomena; and possibilism: three dimensions linked to each other by dual relations, in such a way that they can operate from analysis to policy, but also vice versa.

In this regard, to complete the line of reasoning, we need to take into account the development of Hirschman's political inspiration and his protractedly tumultuous life experience—from the cultural and political activities in Berlin in the early '30s, to his anti-fascist activity in Spain, Italy and France in the second half of the decade, up to the "American turnaround" of the early '40s—the source (definitive, in my opinion) of the democratic-progressive view that has guided his work down to the end.[47]

"Dependency Theory Reassessed": this was the title of the 1976 session of the Latin American Studies Association that was the origin of the new introduction to *National Power*. It was here that Hirschman declared himself the "avo fondatore" [founding father] of "dependencia", only to distance himself later not from the related literature, but from his own *jugendschrift* proposing a "frontal attack" on national sovereignty. This was the last step, in retrospect ironic and almost didactic, in the separation from his previous "theoretical consciousness".

III

5. Genesis of a Rebellion

29. We have referred a number of times to possibilism—a cognitive attitude that privileges the study of the creative disorder of the human adventure rather than regularity and uniform sequences. It should be noted that this was already at work in the "Italian" writings of 1947–1948 and in the first part of "Disinflation, Discrimination,

47. L. Meldolesi, "Alle origini del possibilismo", cit., parts II and III.

and the Dollar Shortage". Indeed, the search for an unorthodox therapy that would include "walking on a very narrow path" (sec. 27) is typical of this mindset and its efforts to identify escape routes from apparently dead-end situations.

Such reasoning often opens a road—in practice and in theory—that runs between opposing solutions; in this case between inflation and deflation and between the conclusions of two different schools of thought: it is a problem that already appears, completely worked out, in "Disinflation" (cf. below, p. 75). This is thus a pioneering text, introducing a line of reasoning present in many successive essays—such as "Invitation to Theorizing About the Dollar Glut" (1960), "The Welfare State in Trouble: Systemic Crisis or Growing Pains?" (1980), "In difesa del possibilismo" [In Defense of Possibilism] (1985).

This period also saw the emergence of a second form of possibilism, characterized by a specific proposal for change, reasonably and competently constructed, which is intended among other things to create the "optical illusion" of its immediate applicability (also theorized in the introduction to *A Bias for Hope*: see below, page 290).[48]

At the end of the 1940s Hirschman was involved in several European integration projects and took part in the negotiations that led to the European Payments Union. His arguments were usually aimed at getting specific results within this process. But there is also a text—"Proposal for a European Monetary Authority" (1949)—circulated in only a few copies among "insiders", that did not have this purpose. Its aim, rather, was to point out that it would be possible to coordinate "the economic and fiscal attributes" of the countries of Europe and to build new institutions in the "interstices of national prerogatives". This was the basis of the proposal to create a monetary authority that could gradually acquire the power to coordinate the economic policies of the different countries.

30. Moreover, in June of 1951 Hirschman took part in a conference at the University of Chicago (the 27th "Institute of the Normal Wait Harris Memorial Foundation") where he presented "Effects of Industrialization on the Markets of Industrial Countries" (1952); "a topic", he wrote,[49] "far removed from development economics as such". And yet it is this essay—along with the contemporary

48. This refers to (among others) "Foreign Aid—A Critique, and a Proposal" (1968, written with Richard Bird), included in the present volume.
49. In *Rival Views of Market Society*, cit., p. 5.

piece "Industrial Nations and Industrialization of Under-Developed Countries" (1951)—that foreshadows the change in this very field of research.

While the experience of the Marshall Plan was coming to a close, in the United States "the interest of social scientists in the problem of economic development and related cultural changes"[50] was growing. This was the origin of the Chicago conference ("which was notable primarily for the active participation of some eminent anthropologists; and because this was the occasion for Alexander Gerschenkron to unveil his masterpiece 'Economic Backwardness in Historical Perspective' "[51]).

This was also the genesis of two of Hirschman's essays from 1951–1952, which can be read as the conclusion of the previous period and the introduction to the commitment that followed. In fact, continuing the search he had begun for possible paths towards "a better world", Hirschman went back to the theme of international trade and industrialization (to which he had dedicated the second part of *National Power*—cf. in particular, chap. VII), to argue that the industrialized

50. *The Progress of Underdeveloped Areas*, B. F. Hoselitz, ed., Chicago, University of Chicago Press, 1952, p. V. "Of course", Hirschman would write in the preface to *Toward a New Strategy for Development*, K. G. Hill, ed., New York, Pergamon Press, 1979, p. XVII, "the success of the Marshall plan led the economists, policy-makers and Western enlightened public opinion to believe that the problem of underdevelopment was more or less of the same nature as post-war reconstruction, that a capital injection supported by the right kind of investment planning would gradually lead to the growth and well-being of the whole planet [...]. But wasn't this a good thing? If the extent and difficulty of the problem had been identified from the beginning it is very likely that the significant intellectual and political mobilization that occurred would not have happened and that we would be even further away from an acceptable world". (A similar argument regarding Keynesianism and development economics is found in Hirschman, "How the Keynesian Revolution was Exported from America, and other Tales", typescript, 1988, p. 20–21. Cf. also, on the subject, "A Dissenter's Confession", in *Rival Views*, cit., pp. 30 and 33–34.
51. "A Dissenter's Confession", in *Rival Views*, cit., p. 5. The meeting with eminent anthropologists and Gerschenkron's essay both left their mark. "Following Gerschenkron", Hirschman later recalled, referring to the years that followed (ibid., p. 15), "I saw originality and creativity in deviating from the path followed by the older industrial countries, in skipping stages, and inventing sequences that had a "wrong way around" look. It was surely this attitude that permitted me to ferret out the backward and forward linkage dynamic and to acclaim as a dialectical-paradoxical feat what was later called [...] import-substituting industrialization".

countries had nothing to fear—and had much to gain—from the industrialization of countries that were less developed.

31. Implicitly, this idea thus posed the problem of how to pursue development at the other extreme of the hierarchy: in the countries of the Third World. Thus, early in 1952, instead of continuing with his work in Washington (or moving to some comfortable international agency) Hirschman set out for Colombia, where he worked as economic and financial adviser to the National Planning Council.

Of this experience, certainly crucial for the author, his wife Sarah and their daughters Katia and Lisa, we do not know enough. The world, Sarah remembers,[52] expanded. Once the initial difficulties had been overcome, their interest in the cultural, social and anthropological aspects of their new world, in its thousand surprises, its people, the almost incredible beauty of the natural environment never ceased to grow in the four and a half years they were there.

It is also clear that in spite of work problems (cf. sec. 32), the overall conditions of the experience represented an extraordinary tropical greenhouse for the ideas Hirschman had brought with him. Perhaps the commitment required by his new position (very secluded compared with the "limelight" of international economics culture) and the family's gravitation towards the European community created a favourable atmosphere—and protected the author from too traumatic an impact with a social reality that was passing through a period of tragic violence[53]—(which would represent a specific case of the "hiding hand"; an idea proposed in the first chapter of *Development Projects Observed* (1967)—included in this volume).[54]

52. From a private conversation, November 1986.
53. This was made clear by a group of young Colombian historians: Carlos Ortiz, Gonzalos Sanchez, Ricardo Pañaranda and Arturo Alape (cf. on the subject, Hobsbawm, "In Murderous Colombia", in *New York Review of Books*, 20 Nov. 1986, and the books reviewed in the article).
54. At the Turin conference (13–14, Nov. 1987) Hirschman maintained that when he decides to begin a new job he is often protected by a "hiding hand"—that is, by the impression (in part illusory) that what he is trying to accomplish is very different from what was done in the past. This helps him in his work—because there is no interference from what has already been done and because it pushes him towards new goals—up to the point where, when he has got the result he was looking for, he realizes that some of the ideas are not original, while others are and can be connected with the pre-existing ones. As mentioned in sec. 3, the repetition of this process

32. The "Colombian" writings can be divided into two groups. The first concerns specific topics—"Guía para el análisis y la confección de recomendaciones sobre la situación monetaria" [Guide to the analysis and preparation of recommendations on the monetary situation] (1954), "Colombia: Highlights of a Developing Economy" (1955) and "Demanda de energia eléctrica para la C.V.C." [C.V.C. electrical energy demand] (1956) (written, like the previous article, with G. Kalmanoff). The second group, on the other hand, includes two analytical essays that are especially significant for our purposes: "Economics and Investment Planning: Reflections Based on Experience in Colombia" (1955) and "Economic Policy in Underdeveloped Countries" (1957)—which in a certain sense represent the first steps in the construction, respectively, of *The Strategy of Economic Development* (1958) and *Journeys Toward Progress* (1963).

In "A Dissenter's Confession", reconstructing the personal background and principal motives that led to *The Strategy*, Hirschman recalls how, during the Marshall Plan experience, the economists who were innovators tended "to take themselves and their ideas too seriously";[55] especially when it came to balance-of-payments predictions (whose projected deficit was the basis of aid increases). He goes on to say that in Colombia he soon found himself facing the same problem because the headquarters of the World Bank (which had recommended his recruitment) made it clear that he would have to formulate an (ambitious) development plan specifying investments, internal savings, and growth, as well as the level of foreign aid. "All of this was alleged to be quite simple for experts mastering the new programming technique".[56]

As we know, it was here that the revolt against his assignment originated; along with the decision, in 1954, to open a private consulting office in Bogotà (because a development plan built on "heroic" estimates was the last thing Colombia needed; and especially because, as had happened with the Marshall Plan administrators, drafting such a plan would inevitably have turned into external interference). "It all seemed to be an affront to the Colombians", Hirschman adds, "who were, after all, struggling or tinkering with their problems [...]. My instinct was to try to understand better *their* patterns of action".

(conscious and unconscious) gradually gives rise to a broad intellectual structure that (ex post) is surprisingly coherent. (An example of a collective "hiding hand" may be found in note 50).

55. In *Rival Views of Market Society*, cit., p. 6.
56. Ibid., p. 8.

33. With this in mind, we turn to "Economics and Investment Planning": it is not difficult to follow the logic of his rebellion. The essay was written for a conference on investment criteria and economic development organized in October 1954 by the Centre for International Studies at MIT, where the author was faced with a group of economists who identified with Max Millikan and Walt Rostow's *Proposal* to give American foreign policy an expansionist orientation regarding the Third World by means of aid and development planning.

Understandably, the essay begins with the "very interesting" efforts made by individual economists and international institutions to connect various macro-quantities of the economic system to the aim of providing an orientation to the economic policies of underdeveloped countries.[57]

But Hirschman immediately adds that the generalizations that can be drawn lack applicability and goes on to argue that too much importance has been given to development programs at the expense of a search for "a body of principles and meaningful generalizations which would permit the economist to be concretely helpful in the location and elaboration of promising, specific investment projects".[58] Overall planning requires a very limited amount of creative effort. Moreover, the economist has very little to offer here, even in the (unlikely) case that existing statistics allowed such reasoning.

"The elaboration of 'overall integrated development programs' is not essential, and in fact might be harmful". If the economist applies his skills mainly to overall programs of investment, projecting everything at a distance of ten or twenty years, there is a risk of bringing into the economic sphere a state of affairs observed in the political sphere: "The contrast between fine theory and wretched practice".[59] What is instead required is a commitment to developing well-designed sector-based projects. Underdeveloped countries show a low rate of investment and (especially) low efficiency for most investments. It is important to act on both

57. For example, through national income, population increase, capital-output ratios (average and marginal), the propensity to save, and a statistical study of parameter values it is possible to estimate how much foreign capital is required to reach the desired rate of increase in per capita national income. It was believed at the time, Hirschman explains (ivi, p. 8), that it was possible to have an idea, "even without close study of local surroundings, of the likely ranges of savings and capital-output ratios, and those estimates, joined to the country's latest national income and balance of payments accounts, would yield all the key figures needed".
58. *A Bias for Hope*, cit., p. 44.
59. Ibid., pp. 46–47.

of these at the same time, focusing on the tensions and scarcities that show up in the development process and not on the "political" priorities of either the government, the international institutions or economists themselves. It is furthermore essential not to lose sight of generally "forgotten" sectors such as education, small-scale industry, or improvement of production methods in agriculture.

6. *Aquí en el trópico hacemos todo al revés [Here in the Tropics We Do Everything Upside Down]*

34. On closer inspection, this road leads to a greater distance from the traditional formulation for all three aspects of the new approach: detachment from the doctrinaire use of economic theory and the invention (or reformulation) of certain theoretical arguments; the interaction between economics, politics and other aspects of reality; and possibilism. Let us proceed gradually.

In the first place, if we compare the reasoning here with that of "Italian Economic and Financial Conditions" (discussed in sec. 26–27), a surprising correspondence emerges. While the article on Italy maintains that a priori inferences about the "correct" amount of investment only lead to conjecture, the "Colombian" essay argues that projections and overall development plans should be abandoned. While the former supports the need to focus primarily, from within the situation, on the main sectors in difficulty (such as heavy industry, mechanical industries, construction, etc.), the latter urges economists to undertake sector-based projects, prioritizing the points of tension that emerge once development is under way.

On the other hand, in dealing with the realities of the sectors, the economist has to have access to some guiding propositions. It was the effort of identifying this body of generalizations that opened the way to the birth of *The Strategy*.

35. "Economics and Investment Planning" in fact proceeds to propose some specific investment criteria based on the observation of basic characteristics typical of developing economies. From the simple acknowledgement that these countries suffer generally from an insufficiency of capital maintenance points to the criterion by which priority must be accorded to investments, industries and technical processes that require little or no maintenance, or that need a specific level of maintenance (as in the case of the airlines). In addition, contrary to the commonly held idea that backward countries need to develop industries to process their own basic products, it should be noted that often the reverse is the case: the

industries that are potential purchasers of domestic agricultural products initially import these products, and only later replenish their supplies from the domestic market (once—thanks to having a market outlet—such products have been standardized).

Although these observations seem episodic, they are, on the contrary, decisive "findings" that develop into two key propositions destined to exert great influence in the literature.[60] The first concerns the margin of tolerance for poor performance (and as such belongs to the important chapter VIII of *The Strategy*—"Efficiency and growth of the individual firm"—included in the present collection). It explains (at least in part) the preference in developing countries for advanced technology and capital-intensive industry with a flow process—and also emphasizes an intrinsic feature of all productive tasks that can be used to induce behaviour consistent with these tasks.[61] The second gave rise to the concept of the "backward linkage" and thus to "linkage"—one of the main ideas of development economics. Hirschman developed this concept in *The Strategy* (chap. 5) and then in important essays such as "A Generalized Linkage Approach to Development, with Special Reference to Staples" (1977) and "Linkages in Economic Development" (1986).

36. More generally, during the "Bogotà period" the author sought (firstly) to identify some principles of action, established by trial and error, of which the actors themselves could know very little—principles considered erroneous by outsiders, which had instead proved effective; principles that (like the two discussed above) acted in convoluted or inverted "ways" or backwards according to common sense. "Far more fundamentally than the idea of unbalanced growth", he writes, "this search for possible *hidden rationalities* was to give an underlying unity to my work".[62] It is a

60. Cf. "A Dissenter's Confession", in *Rival Views of Market Society,* cit., pp. 15–22.
61. The concept of margins of tolerance for poor performance was later developed on "how one firm or productive operation can be made to *endure* as an efficiently performing unit of the economic system": The third chapter of *Development Projects Observed* (1967), entitled "Latitudes and Disciplines", examines a great variety of pressures for action, such as spatial or localization margins, time constrains in construction, margins for corruption, margins for replacing quantity with quality. Furthermore, the idea of narrow or wide margins for poor performance may be compared to the successive concepts of voice and exit as well as to the seventeenth–eighteenth century problem of curbing passions by means of interests (ibid., pp. 18–22).
62. Ibid., p. 9.

challenging statement, which makes it possible to clarify both the method and the construction phases of *The Strategy*.

As mentioned, progressive detachment from concepts of theory and economic policy constructed a priori and imposed on reality had led Hirschman to look for ways out of specific situations (for post-war Italy and the European payments system), while now in Colombia this same attitude was put to work to identify generalizations that would be useful to a practical economist engaged in sector-based planning.

It may then be concluded that the anti-doctrinaire inclination, in opposition to the a priori (and anti-democratic) cogency of the theory—the willingness, that is, to speculate in a certain direction rather than to verify a pre-established thesis (paragraph 22)—is the basis of the search for exit routes and specific proposals (of uniqueness), as well as of general propositions—and therefore of regularities and paradigms. Of course, both may be pursued separately; but just as a general proposition can be deduced from the examination of a specific situation (as in the case of the two "Colombian" propositions) the reappearance of a certain regularity in a concrete setting should "automatically" prompt the researcher to qualify the analysis on the basis of the multiple unique features of the situation as well—which of course should be done in applying the "Colombian" propositions to Colombia (in a way that identifies pathways and proposals for change).

37. This research mentality undoubtedly shows up in the construction of *The Strategy*: the preface guides our understanding of it. "The elucidation of immediate experience is the sole justification for any thought; and the starting-point for thought is the analytic observation of components of this experience". Hirschman says he drew encouragement from this statement of Whitehead's[63] both because he was committed to clarifying his own immediate experience, and because his reasoning began with the analysis of some components of this experience. In the course of this attempt, he writes,[64]

> the various observations and reflections I had gathered began to look more and more like variations upon a common theme. So I undertook to discover this theme and then used it in reinterpreting a variety of development problems.

63. *Process and Reality*, New York, Macmillan, 1930, p. 6.
64. *The Strategy of Economic Development*, 1958, p. v.

Thus it happened that thinking about generalizations for sector policies had pushed the author to look for a "general economic principle" that would link them to similar propositions. It was from here that the idea of "pressure mechanisms" or "pace-setting devices" originated, and with it the so-called slack paradigm, put forward by Hirschman for developing countries (and proposed by other authors—Simon, Cyert and March, Rosenberg and Leibenstein—to explain various aspects of developed countries).[65]

Having arrived at the conceptual scheme of the book, Hirschman was able to develop his starting propositions and to identify many others. Dissent from prevailing doctrines had been a "concomitant factor" in this effort: in part—as we have seen—it was pre-existing; and in part it was a product of the studies undertaken on his return to the United States. The new analysis could thus be proposed in opposition to the dominant literature on economic development; and had at the same time found useful points of support in other disciplines, anthropology first and foremost.[66]

38. This led in the end to the admirable opening section of *The Strategy*: the "Search for the Primum Mobile"—that is, for the factors, conditions, obstacles, etc. indicated here and there in the economic, historical, sociological, and psychological literature as prerequisites for economic development.

Luckily, Hirschman argues, it is precisely the multiplicity of attempts at explanation that can lead to a radically different conclusion because, when a new explanation is proposed, the previous one comes into question. This is how it was discovered that development is possible even where natural resources are scarce; that in the appropriate conditions productive capacities can be acquired by all

65. In other words, Hirschman explains in the manner of the anthropologists in *Essays in Trespassing*, cit., p. 9 —"a feature I had presented as being specific to the situation of one group of economies was later found to prevail in others as well. Whereas such a finding makes for reunification of our science, what we have here is not a return of the prodigal son [...]. Rather, our understanding of the economic structures of the West will have been modified and enriched by the foray into other economies".
66. Upon returning to the United States, Sarah Hirschman, scholar of philosophy and French literature, decided to pursue the social sciences and to follow relevant academic courses. The "efficient guidance" she provided in the study of the anthropological literature permitted Albert Hirschman "some forays into a territory whose rich resources are too often left unutilized by the economist" (*The Strategy*, cit., p. VI).

peoples; that savings are not chronically insufficient; that entrepreneurship is not absent by any means; that modern behaviour and value systems are not a prerequisite to development. It is true rather that development depends on the ability to muster and make profitable resources that are "hidden, scattered, or badly utilized".

In developing countries there is no spare capacity as in developed countries in time of crisis; but there is a savings capacity that could be activated, a latent or misdirected entrepreneurial capacity, a wide variety of work skills, an under-utilization of labour in agriculture—not to mention the modern industrial techniques that are waiting to be transferred into those countries. The task, therefore, is to combine all these ingredients by means of linking agents, inductive mechanisms, and pace-setting devices, in such a way as to gradually modify the picture of change that prevails in the consciousness of the protagonists. Once again, Hirschman's economic analysis shapes itself and interacts with the social and political aspects of the reality being examined.

IV

7. Planning and Experimenting

39. It is not my intention, however, to reconstruct the lines of thinking that take shape in *The Strategy* (and which also include "The Political Economy of Import-Substituting Industrialization in Latin America" and "Obstacles to Development: A Classification and a Quasi-Vanishing Act", included in this volume). I would rather call attention to a second approach in the work which represents the political counterpart of the first—and therefore also an important complement to it.

Until now, for a number of reasons, this second line of reasoning has remained in the shadows. It does not have a precise disciplinary reference (in economics, in political science,[67] or in the history of ideas) and was developed in

67. In the introduction to *Journeys*, 1963, p. 5, Hirschman writes that "political scientists typically view good government as resulting from certain institutions and capacities such as an adequate bureaucracy, public participation in the governmental process, legitimacy, ability of a political elite to mediate conflicts and so on. Hence the political scientist's advice to countries with a defective political process is to acquire these institutions and capacities much as economists advise them to step up capital formation or to generate a group of entrepreneurs".

successive "spurts", rather than taking shape gradually along internal lines. In building it, moreover, the author responded to his own need to explore: moving ahead on his own path, concentrating alternatively on the economics or politics of development. And if it is true that economists are unfamiliar with the study of the effect of economics on politics (see below, p. 267), it is even more true that looking at things from the opposite angle, how politics affects economics, seems downright problematic in their eyes, not to say unnatural. Thus, paradoxically, interest in this second line of reasoning can acquire the flavour of forbidden fruit—a new intellectual adventure in search of another side of reality.

40. Let us move into the subject itself. In "Economic Policy in Underdeveloped Countries", Hirschman writes with surprising frankness that economists, at the beginning of their mission, usually think that the "principal problem they are going to be confronted with will be that of determining what ought to be done [...] But soon they realize that they have little trouble in deciding what to do or rather what to advise to do, while by far the largest portion of their time is devoted to energy-consuming and often frustrating efforts to put their ideas and proposals across".[68]

The moral is simple: careful observation of the behaviour of the governments of developing countries cannot be avoided.

Thus begins the first "political" text on underdevelopment, written in 1956 when Hirschman returned from Colombia. It is a text that acts as a "counterweight" to "Economics and Investment Planning": while the latter made sense of his revolt against his assigned mission, the former ushered in an interest (that would grow with time) in government authority, and more generally in the cultural and political ambiance of a developing country. As Hirschman declared,[69]

> "On the one hand, I reacted against the visiting-economist syndrome; that is, against the habit of issuing peremptory advice and prescription by calling on universally valid economic principles and remedies [...] after a strictly minimal acquaintance with the "patient". But, with time, another objective was assuming even more importance in my mind: it was to counter the tendency of many Colombians and Latin Americans to work hand in glove with the visiting economist by their own self-deprecatory attitudes".

68. In *A Bias for Hope*, cit., p. 255.
69. "A Dissenter's Confession", in *Rival Views of Market Society*; cit., p. 11.

41. The author is referring to the period following the writing of *The Strategy*; but the origins of this attitude were earlier—as may be deduced from "Economic Policy in Underdeveloped Countries".

Although these countries had already made significant progress, there were still investment projects available, along with fiscal and monetary reforms and certain institutional changes that would obviously be useful. Thus the history of technical assistance missions was inevitably linked to their capacity to achieve such results. "The huge difficulties of this task", Hirschman writes,

> are not always appreciated, partly, I suspect, because, in order to do so, one must catch the experts themselves during their unguarded moments rather than rely on their reports to headquarters; and partly, because the whole tale here is in terms of personalities and human passions, frailties, and frustrations which the experts, once they are "back home," are liable to forget as easily and completely as physical pain. And if they reminisce, it seems to them that they were facing fortuitous circumstances which do not lend themselves to any kind of generalized analysis. Here they could be mistaken.[70]

The point of departure was still economists grappling with their difficulties, but the pole star of the argument was no longer the undue interference of the World Bank. In its place was an effort to understand the governmental actions of underdeveloped countries, searching in the direction of "hidden rationalities", which (at the same time) represented a first step in what Hirschman would go on to call "*an understanding of the understanding* Latin Americans' have of their own reality".[71] The point of the article was to show in a series of examples—concerning development plans, recurring inflation, foreign exchange cycles, fiscal and administrative policies—that some useful generalizations about the conduct of governments in underdeveloped countries could in fact be identified.

42. For our purposes, we can limit ourselves to the first example—attitudes towards planning—which allows us a close comparison with "Economics and Investment Planning".

70. *A Bias for Hope*, cit., p. 156.
71. *Latin American Issues*, New York, Twentieth Century Fund, 1961, p. 4.

First of all, it is easy to see that with respect to the earlier article, the logic of the argument seems here to be reversed. It will be recalled that after having recognized "the worth of aggregate analysis", Hirschman argued that integrated development planning was a "myth", that it was unnecessary and could be harmful. Here the problem is re-examined from the point of view of government of the underdeveloped country.

The reasons for adopting development plans, the author maintains, are well known: the plan is an expression of the desire to improve living conditions (and is therefore a source of popularity); it is often a necessary (or auxiliary) condition for receiving assistance from abroad; it is a useful tool in requests for domestic financial sacrifices and to "displace" the timing of spending requests. The plan is a useful constraint that allows the central government to move forward with its development projects. This function is not generally the main reason for its approval, but an awareness of it often becomes one of the main reasons for continuing with it.

Clearly this is an important step forward in the line of reasoning. There is no prejudicial attitude towards planning as such. On the contrary, if we compare this point of view with that of the earlier article, a double position emerges: rigid with regard to "visiting economists" (with their tendency—not terribly edifying—to exploit, even unconsciously, the weaknesses and difficulties of underdeveloped countries); open, on the other hand, to an understanding of the political and administrative problems of these countries.[72]

43. Here a more complex logical interaction begins to present itself. The consulting economist is asked, on one hand, to do a good job with sector-based projects and identify useful generalizations; and on the other to become aware of the country's management problems and how they develop: this is the origin, in my view, of *Journeys Toward Progress*, which is above all a journey into how the governments of underdeveloped countries deal with problems.

An anticipation of this appears in the attitude towards development plans, instruments which, once introduced, limit governments' freedom of choice, but which—we must now add—can do so in a way judged excessive.

72. To this may be added (cf. sec. 50 and note 88) a positive evaluation of the role the plan can have as a tool in benign ideological operations aimed at calling attention to "forgotten" problems of economic policy.

The interesting thing about this issue is the duality of the attitude expressed and how it can be utilized to move things forward. Referring to the 1955 essay, the author explains that plans often claim to establish overall investment programs despite the inherent weaknesses of the investment criteria and the very wide differences in the validity of the estimates for the different sectors. Once more detailed studies have been carried out it is very likely that some elements of the plan will have to be re-examined. Therefore, in the initial plan it ought to be made clear which of the projects are already ready and which instead need further study (perhaps building a scale, ordered according to the quantities and qualities of the planning work).

44. But this is not the only point. After so much experience with national economic planning, Hirschman continues, it is time to recognize that, along with a "propensity to plan", the governments of underdeveloped countries show a "propensity to experiment and improvise": this is a strength which, directed the right way, could play a beneficial role in the development process.

> "In underdeveloped countries, many dynamic growth sectors remain to be discovered; many patterns of social organization conducive to economic progress remain to be identified; and much flexibility in programming economic development must be preserved to allow governments and investors to take advantage of changing trends in world markets".[73]

With the later evolution of the author's work in mind it is not difficult to imagine how governments might gradually rely more on either the "propensity to plan" or the "propensity to experiment" by developing an unbalanced development sequence.[74] This kind of thinking was discussed at length in development economics; but it is eminently appropriate for politics as well, as was already clear in the concluding page of *Journeys* (cf. below, pp. 157–158), where Hirschman argued the

73. *A Bias for Hope*, cit., p. 260.
74. Perhaps the author was already thinking of this when he wrote: "Account must be taken of the propensity to change and to experiment so that, when it is indulged in, it does not come as a revolt against intolerable restraints but as an action that is foreseen as well as regulated. Economic policy in underdeveloped countries will then continue to fluctuate, but the limits of these fluctuations should gradually become narrower and the oscillations between those limits slower, as experiences with diverse policies are assimilated" (ibid., pp. 268–269).

need to manoeuvre for change by negotiating with new allies while at the same time continuing to rock the boat. It is a dual function that can be carried out by several actors—like Cavour on one hand and Garibaldi on the other—and which was later taken up in various essays: "Underdevelopment, Obstacles to the Perception of Change, and Leadership" (1968) and "The Search for Paradigms as a Hindrance to Understanding" (1970); and again (under other guises) in "The Turn to Authoritarianism in Latin America and the Search for Its Economic Determinants" (1979) "A Dissenter's Confession" (1984) and "In difesa del possibilismo" (1985).

There are thus several typical types of thinking that can open the way towards a positive solution,[75] just as there are possible (rather than probable) policies. Paradigms, propositions that indicate regularity, typical kinds of solutions, historical uniqueness; the methodological palette is enriched with new shades, and its ability to interpret and advise gradually increases.

8. *The Origin of* Journeys

45. It has been pointed out that "Economic Policy in Underdeveloped Countries", written before *The Strategy*, is an important aid to understanding the significance of the book. Once this article is taken into account, the character of *The Strategy* as a development strategy *proposal* addressed to the governments of the underdeveloped countries becomes much clearer. The book does not, as one might think, presuppose the existence of a benign and powerful authority: it presents a reasonable, practical solution to the problem under discussion; well aware that it will have to come to terms with the reality of the public decision-making process in underdeveloped countries. And since the analysis of the strategy is conducted separately from that of policy-making, it is perhaps useful to try and grasp the link between the two.

With this in mind we should recall that during the winter and spring of 1959–1960 (shortly after the publication of *The Strategy*), Hirschman coordinated a study group on Latin America organized by the Twentieth Century Fund. The participant economists were asked curb their tendency to judge and prescribe solutions, and instead to identify "the reasons for which Latin Americans advocate, adopt and change certain economic policies". This was the origin of the decision to explore the "Latin American style" of constructing economic policy.[76]

75. To this well-known approach we should add the one encountered above (sec. 29) of opening a route between opposing theoretical and practical solutions.
76. Cf. A. Heckscher's Preface to *Latin American Issues*, A. O. Hirschman, ed., cit., 1961.

46. *Latin American Issues: Essays and Comments* is the collection of essays produced by the study group. One of them, "Ideologies of Economic Development in Latin America", may be read as an introduction to the more extensive work that would follow. "It seems to me", Hirschman writes,

> that Latin Americans still have not fully emerged from the stage of self-denigration; they are far too ready to issue blanket condemnations of their own ways and to escape to a dream world of ever-new laws, perfectly designed institutions or scientifically calculated plans.[77] Frequently they do not realize how much they could learn if only they scrutinized the growth that is already taking hold here and there. Instead of yearning for an unattainable simultaneous solution of their problems, they should, in my opinion, train themselves to perceive and evaluate the various possibilities of sequential decision-making and problem-solving.[78]

It is this issue that guides *Journeys.* In fact, having become aware of the problems with generalizing about the decision-making process, Hirschman proposed to the Fund that it conduct a broader study based on close observation of policy-making sequences that had occurred historically concerning certain key economic issues.[79] The result was "a hazardous expedition into the vast no man's land stretching between economics and other social sciences such as political science, sociology, and history".[80]

Together with policy-making expert Charles Lindblom,[81] consultant on the project, and Hirschman's wife Sarah, research assistant, Hirschman set out in the

77. The critique is therefore of ideologism: the essay concludes by contrasting the decline of ideologies in the United States to their reaffirmation in Latin America. This "displacement" between the two hemispheres has been maintained over time, but, Hirschman has later argued, it then turned upside down: the administration of the United States has become doctrinaire and Latin American governments (relatively) pragmatic.
78. *Latin American Issues*, cit., pp. 41–42.
79. Cf. Heckscher's Preface to A. O. Hirschman, *Journeys Toward Progress: Studies of Economic Policy-Making in Latin America*, 1963, p. 9.
80. Ibid., p. IX.
81. The collaboration with Lindblom "had originated in the discovery that working in different areas we had reached strongly related conclusions" (ivi, p. 11). It would lead to the jointly written "Economic Development, Research and Development, and Policy-Making: Some Converging Views" (1962, included in *A Bias for Hope*, cit.).

summer of 1960 on a long trip to five Latin American countries (Mexico, Colombia, Chile, Argentina, and Brazil) where he interviewed numerous government functionaries, political and union leaders, business people, intellectuals and economists who had had significant roles in the events that he was aiming to reconstruct. On his return, this mass of documentary material was re-worked along with material from every possible indirect source.

Of the five histories originally planned, three were developed and then evaluated based on a second trip in the summer of 1962. These concerned northeast Brazil, land use and agrarian reform in Colombia, and inflation in Chile. These "Three Problems in Three Countries" make up the first part of *Journeys*, while the related theoretical generalizations constitute the second part: "Problem Solving and Reform-mongering".

47. It is easy to see that in this work Hirschman made use of his own experience as a "participant observer", first of the US and then the Colombian decision-making process. In a later note[82] he recalled that in the late 1940s and early 50s, many institutions in the United States were carefully studied by the Americans themselves, who were surprised by the great success achieved by the United States and anxious to understand why.

> "In this climate it is hardly surprising that the analysis of public policy and of the policy-making process should have become an important concern of American political scientists. The ensuing studies underlined the distance between the theoretical models and actual practice, but generally found that the latter, however weird, worked quite well, if for reasons heretofore poorly understood".[83]

82. *Essays in Trespassing*, cit., pp. 139–140.
83. "Unfortunately", the note goes on, "as soon as this reassuring research result had been proclaimed in the early or mid-sixties, the American style of policy-making stopped operating in its accustomed satisfactory manner". In the meantime, however, Walt W. Rostow ("The National Style", in *The American Style*, E. E. Morrison, ed., New York, Harper, 1958, and *The United States in the World Arena*, New York, Harper, 1960) had advanced the idea of an American "style" (that is, the "acutely pragmatic national style": M. F. Millikan, preface to W. W. Rostow, *The United States in the World Arena*, cit.) to which the Hirschman analysis of the Latin American style is (critically) linked (Cf. *Journeys*, 1963, p. 228).

Of course, the Latin American decision-making style was noticeably different from that of the United States. However, despite some reservations, *Journeys* wanted to make it clear that even the style of Latin American countries could at times produce positive results. "My purpose", Hirschman writes, "was twofold: to demonstrate to the North Americans that their style is not uniquely effective and to convince Latin Americans that by scrutinizing their own experience they can attain some confidence in their own problem-solving capability".

48. This aim was then pursued in a reconstruction of three contemporary histories with deep roots, patiently traced back into the nineteenth century (and for land use in Colombia even much further back). These were actually three short monographs on the history of economic policy, which later suggested to the author further articles.[84]

The book is dedicated "to Celso Furtado and Carlos Lleras Restrepo, *Master Reformmongers*" in Brazil and Colombia. It intends to show "how a progressive change can unexpectedly be smuggled into societies long dominated by traditional social forces and how some collective learning is acquired, in spite of many affirmations to the contrary, when a stubborn policy problem is encountered and tackled over a long period" (*Essays in Trespassing*, p. 143 cf. below, p. 300).

To this end, Hirschman explains ("Policy Making and Policy Analysis in Latin America—A Return Journey", 1975, included in the present volume), the choice to work on more than one problem yielded good results. It made the work more varied and interesting, it permitted more general conclusions and, unexpectedly, allowed the features of each problem—and thus its linked decision-making process—to be better identified through comparison with the others (e.g. by comparison with the periodic droughts in northeast Brazil, Chilean inflation is a human calamity and can provoke political conflicts; moreover, seen in comparison with the bad distribution of Colombian land, it sends regular signals that attract the

84. The study on northeast Brazil was followed by "Industrial Development in the Brazilian Northeast and the Tax Credit Scheme of Article 34/18" (1968); the study of agrarian reform in Colombia led to *Getting Ahead Collectively* (1984), and the study of inflation in Chile to "The Social and Political Matrix of Inflation: Elaborations on the Latin American Experience" (1981).

attention of the government as soon as it goes beyond a certain threshold, and so on).[85]

49. Let us come to the point. Economic development, the author argues in the introduction, confronts government authorities with a multitude of problems; success in promoting development depends to a great extent on how these are addressed. If it is true that the speed, strength and direction of producers' reactions to a change in market conditions have a lot to do with their ability to take advantage of them, it is also true that for governments, the origin, persistence or worsening of economic policy problems and the speed, strength and continuity of their reactions has enormous importance.

The book, as mentioned, attempts to identify a "Latin American style":[86] the study of the three cases allows the respective identification of their structural characteristics. Through them "it is possible to understand and perhaps predict alternative paths of decision-making" (*Essays in Trespassing*, p. 146, cf. below, p. 303). This means that, depending on the problems faced, different characteristics and alternative pathways may present themselves (the reconstructed histories are only part of a greater reality). Yet through them we already "get a feel" for the nature of problems involved.[87]

85. The point of view developed in this way would later influence the book *Crisis, Choice, and Change, Historical Studies of Political Development*, Gabriel Almond et. al., eds., Boston, Little, Brown & Co., 1973).
86. "Our inquiry", Hirschman writes in the introduction to *Journeys*, cit., 1963, p. 5, "takes the existing political framework with its defects for granted and explores whether and how the weight and urgency of certain economic policy problems can nevertheless lead to constructive action. Our basic working hypothesis must be that, within rather broad limits, the existence of defects in political structure does not constitute an absolute impediment to progress in dealing with economic policy problems; by the same token, it is likely that problem-solving will under these conditions follow quite unfamiliar paths whose possible efficiency and hidden rationality we must try to appreciate".
87. By comparing the issues raised with those concerning the funeral rites studied by anthropologists, Hirschman concludes that "before inquiring *how* these problems are analysed and attacked, it is important to realize that societies may differ greatly in the *kind* of problems that their policy-makers decide to tackle seriously" (*Journeys*, cit., p. 229). But even here, on balance, the distances turn out to be less great than one might initially think: the "political-anthropological" process leads to (among other

In the first place, we would do well to distinguish between real, pressing problems and those chosen by the political authorities: the solutions proposed for the former are evaluated according to whether they produce some relief, while this does not happen for the latter. In addition, the relationship between the two kinds of problems is an index of the degree of autonomy the authorities have under various types of pressure. More generally, all this leads to a conception of the state which, while taking account of traditional *étatisme*, answers to collective and category needs. The public authorities in *Journeys* are thus mainly committed to tackling problems they have not chosen, pressing problems, which often take on the characteristics of emergencies (drought, violence, economic crises, etc.).

50. A second important distinction is between problems that are privileged and those that are neglected. Mechanisms available to citizens and pressure groups for attracting the attention of the government, Hirschman explains, are very different from one society to another (e.g. violent demonstrations occur more in response to price increases than to high levels of infant mortality). This means that if the only existing mechanism is demonstrations, many problems will be put aside.

On the other hand, in many underdeveloped countries a network linking the public and the authorities (electoral mechanisms, political institutions and labour unions, an independent press, and so on) simply does not exist. This means that other ways must be found of bringing to light "forgotten" problems. One possible way—which shows up in all three of the studies in the first part of *Journeys*[88]—is to link them to the problems the authorities want to solve.

It is this benign function of ideology, Hirschman argues, that comes into play when the aim is to construct a point of contact between different kinds of problems, often utilizing the conceptual tool of the "overall plan".[89] An example

things) the identification of some characteristics of developed countries that (by analogy with the economic concept of "market-failure") could be seen as showing a failure of the proper functioning of democracy.

88. In Chile, repeated attempts to fight inflation (with little success) led to an investigation of the underlying causes, which brought attention to the "structural" problem of land ownership. In Brazil the inability of dams to solve the drought problem on their own led to an examination of other elements in the region. In Colombia, balance-of-payments concerns strengthened research into reliable ways of increasing agricultural production.
89. In this way, the plan rejected as foreign interference (sec. 32–33) and later accepted as a mechanism of underdeveloped countries' self-discipline (sec. 42) here becomes a

illustrating this is the *Rapporto Furtado* (1959) which draws attention to the monoculture of sugar cane in the Zona da Mata: a long-neglected central issue (see *Journeys*, 1963, p. 72). It argues that the pressing problem, the drought, cannot be solved without an adequate development plan: the argument is presented in such a way as to also propose—along with the irrigation of the basins surrounding the existing dams and the cultivation of other nearby lands—a way of solving the "taboo problem" of the use of the most fertile lands.

Associations of this type generally also require that the privileged problem should continue to weigh on the authorities. This way, after a certain time it becomes tempting to argue that the problem can only be resolved indirectly—that is, by dealing with another problem that has long been neglected (and perhaps using different and more adequate means of intervention).

51. Finally, a third distinction concerns motivations and the comprehension of problems. When motivations systematically take precedence over understanding, mistakes are easily made. Thus it happens that in developing countries, the revolution in expectations and the desire to resolve all the problems of underdevelopment as quickly as possible leads to failure and thus, paradoxically, to a complicated developmental path, paved with exaggerated requests for definitive solutions and institutions that are "shiny and new".

This "mania to wrap things up",[90] often supported (and sometimes instigated) by foreign experts of few scruples, is certainly not conducive to the process of understanding and solving problems. In any case, in spite of the frequent "derailment" of the policies pursued—and the failure complex (or "fracasomania") associated with them—; in spite of the often harmful role of ideologies,[91]

useful instrument of ideological mediation; of an ideology that is not superstructure but rather "in-between-structure" (*Journeys*, 1963, p. 232)—so that it serves to construct plausible causal links between distinct problems (a variant of this "pseudo creative" answer is contained in "The Principle of the Hiding Hand": cf. below, p. 173).

90. From Flaubert's wonderfully apt expression (*Correspondance*, Paris, Conard, 1929) "la rage de vouloir conclure".
91. I refer of course to Hirschman's long polemic against "fracasomania", which already appears in "Ideologies of Economic Development", in *Journeys*, and (above all) in the above mentioned "Policy Making and Policy Analysis", and is taken up again in "On Hegel, Imperialism, and Structural Stagnation" (1976), "Beyond Asymmetry" (1978), "The Turn to Authoritarianism in Latin America" (1979), and "The Rise and Decline of Development Economics" (1981).

Journeys arrives at some conclusions that past vicissitudes have not caused to fade in the least.

These spring (once again) from the search for hidden rationalities. Along the first stretch of the road, Hirschman maintains, the tortuous and uneven pathways[92] can encourage a peculiar process of learning because the detours from one policy to another can help bring the problems into focus, because obvious errors can serve as a lesson, and because policies subsequently attempted may leave elements on the field that can be used later for a positive solution. The "failure complex", moreover, can (for a while) have useful implications, since the expectation of drawing a complete blank reduces resistance to change, and the ultra-negative assessment of the past encourages the view that a real effort still needs to be made.

In conclusion, then, an understanding of how to deal successfully with problems *can* make effective headway, and with it the idea of how, almost by accident, it is possible by working outside the usual channels to get new wine into old casks; perhaps linking pressing problems with others that have been unjustly put aside, while at the same time exploiting the avenues of reaction to social demands and the unilateral initiatives of the authorities. But all this depends on the ability—that is to say, the art—of getting reforms passed. This is what the author has called "reformmongering", a term coined to indicate political behaviour that goes beyond the distinction between reform and revolution present in the Western political tradition since the Bernstein-Kautsky debate at the end of the nineteenth century (cf. on this subject, chapter V of *Journeys*, included in this volume).

9. *In Conclusion*

52. This is where my experiment ends. Its purpose has not been to identify the essence of "how to complicate economics" or to put together a model in which such a problem could be posed. On the contrary, I thought it worthwhile to look at some of the connections within Hirschman's elaborations and to try and bring the problematic issues into focus. Undoubtedly, much could still be achieved by continuing this research (both regarding the content of *The Strategy*, *Journeys*, and related essays, and concerning successive developments: moving in the directions

92. These "journeys toward progress" are exemplified in a painting by Paul Klee, *Highway and Byways*, reproduced at the author's suggestion as the frontispiece to the first edition, which "reveals perhaps better than words the manifold and often ambiguous ways in which he sees nations 'journeying' toward their goals". (Heckscher, Preface to *Journeys*, cit.).

indicated by the author[93] and in others as well). But, for the moment, the argumentation is perhaps sufficient to propose some concluding considerations.

In the first place, anyone approaching the problem of reforming economics obviously cannot avoid mastering the main relevant principles; but it is also important, in my view, to enter into Hirschman's own intellectual experience to gain an understanding of the method of construction, the different stages of development, and the variety and relevance of the results. This requires adequate professional training along with a willingness to take an interest in aspects of reality (and intellectual outcomes) that are different from those we are familiar with. So that rather than "capturing" this or that aspect of an overall formulation from an established disciplinary point of view, it seemed to me necessary to look outside the box at part of Hirschman's work, exploring various texts and arguments, and concentrating on some connections that might throw light on interesting elements that had until now remained hidden.

53. In this regard, it is perhaps useful to recall some points of contact between *The Strategy* and *Journeys* that exemplify the problem. For most economists, the public decision-making process takes place completely outside the purview of economic analysis; or else it is seen as an automatic by-product of the economic process, in just the way decision-making is generally seen in business. On the contrary, Hirschman states in the introduction to *Journeys*, "the feeling that ebbs and tides of decision-making play a considerable role at *all* stages of development had led me earlier to investigate a variety of mechanisms [...] which make for the tides"—that is, which produce greater amounts of entrepreneurial decision-making during the course of economic development. But the question is not just about private decision-making: the response of public authorities to collective demands[94] is not necessarily or inherently less effective than the response of the

93. Consider the relationship between *The Passions and the Interests*, "The Rise and Decline of Development Economics", and "The Turn to Authoritarianism in Latin America and the Search for Its Economic Determinants" indicated in the preface to *Essays in Trespassing* (1981, pp. V–VI); the relationship between *Exit, Voice, and Loyalty*, *Shifting Involvements*, and "Against Parsimony" (cf. *Shifting Involvements*, cit., 1982, chap IV, and below, p. 353); the connections between *The Strategy* and *Exit, Voice, and Loyalty* by means of the concept of a margin for poor performance in "A Dissenter's Confession" in *Rival Views*, cit., pp. 20–22).
94. Previously asserted in *The Strategy*, 1958, pp. 63–65 and 143.

private entrepreneur to changing market conditions. The desire to document this statement leads directly to the main concern of *Journeys*: the study of the behaviour of public decision-makers in tackling and solving collective problems.[95]

It will be seen that the question is framed as a further development of the same problem. Yet, as we have seen above, the genesis of the two books is intertwined, almost the product of a developmental thought process (unbalanced) in which progress achieved in one area leads to a step forward in the other and vice versa. Not to mention that, viewing this process from the political rather than the economic side, *The Strategy* more clearly reveals its connotation as an economic policy proposal, while *Journeys* suggests multiple escape routes towards solutions and the approval of reforms.

54. Proposals and escape routes, on the other hand, are the two forms of possibilism suggested in the introduction to *A Bias for Hope* (cf. below, pp. 290–291) and already present—as we have argued above—in the writings from the "Washington period". By comparison with that period, the possibilism of *The Strategy* and *Journeys* presents itself in what might be called an inverse but (more) connected relation. Earlier, it was the "Italian" writings that proposed exit routes, while the proposal was institutional (to create a European monetary authority), while we now have before us a proposed strategy for economic development and a series of possible journeys related to the process of decision-making.

But there is more. The theses of *The Strategy* and *Journeys* also represent the full development of the intellectual breakthrough that matured during the war years. An echo of that change can perhaps be seen in a short paper of 1968, where Hirschman summed up development economics by arguing that for two decades economists' analyses of backwardness had often led to requests for radical remedies such as revolutions, massive redistribution or at least a coordinated attack guided by centralized planning. "But what if none of these *dei ex machina* are available [...]?" Hirschman writes. "What if the fortress of underdevelopment, just because it is so formidable, cannot be conquered by frontal assault? In that unfortunately quite common case, we need to know much more about ways in which the fortress can be surrounded, weakened by infiltration or subversion, and eventually taken by similar indirect tactics and processes". Considering that *National Power* called for a "frontal attack" on national economic sovereignty, and that "Beyond Asymmetry" (1978) criticized this precisely because it invoked

95. *Journeys*, cit., pp. 2–4.

a "deus ex machina", the hypothesis is inescapable that here Hirschman is calling into question ways of thinking similar to his own in the past.

55. And yet things are still more complex. Hirschman stated[96] that during his first stay in Italy (1937–1938), in addition to having acquired "that minimum self-confidence that allows one to get along" and a good grasp of the Italian economy, he had another experience that "proved to be even more fundamental". At that time, his brother-in-law Eugenio Colorni and some of his friends "had a strongly anti-fascist political commitment, yet they did not rigidly follow an ideology and in no way claimed to have a solution for every economic, social and political problem of the period [...]. What fascinated me [about them] was the fact that a mental orientation free of ideological commitment was intimately bound to a commitment to an extremely dangerous form of political activity [...]. It was as if they had set out to prove that Hamlet was wrong—as if they wanted to show that doubt could *motivate* action instead of weakening or discouraging it. [...] [They saw political activity as the] simple, natural, spontaneous and almost light-hearted counterpart [to their freedom of thought]. Their attitude has always seemed admirable to me as a way of looking at political activity and of combining public and private life".

Even from today's perspective, this experience bridges the theoretical break between the pre- and post-war periods in an important way. It identifies an element of continuity, a past source of inspiration which, at a distance, continues to offer ideas, as shown in a brief but important essay—"On Democracy in Latin America", *New York Review of Books*, April 10, 1986. Here, in my opinion, there is an echo of the author's retrospective conclusion concerning his Italian experience of 1937–1938: that he had learned that the coexistence of a commitment in public life and great intellectual openness was "the ideal micro-foundation for a solidly democratic society."[97]

Luca Meldolesi

As an entry of a series "I grandi economisti contemporanei", this book was originally published in Italian by Il Mulino, Bologna. Introduction and editing were carried out under the personal supervision of Albert Hirschman. Michael Gilmartin has translated the Introduction into English.

96. "Io, "detective" dell'economia fascista", 1987.
97. Ibid.

Acknowledgments

The entries of this volume:

1. Foreign Trade as an Instrument of National Power (*National Power and the Structure of Foreign Trade*, Berkeley, University of California Press, 1945, ch. 2, pp. 13-34).
2. Disinflation, Discrimination and the Dollar Shortage (*American Economic Review*, 1948, part I, pp. 880-889).
3. Devaluation and the Trade Balance. A Note. (*Review of Economics and Statistics*, 1949, pp. 50-53).
4. Balanced and Unbalanced Growth (*The Strategy of Economic Development*, New Haven, Yale University Press, 1958, ch. III and IV).
5. Efficency and Growth of the Individual Firm (*The Strategy of Economic Development*, New Haven, Yale University Press, 1958, ch. VIII).
6. The Contriving of Reform (*Journeys Toward Progress*, New York, Twentieth Century Fund, 1963, ch. V).
7. Obstacles to Development. A Classification and a Quasi-Vanishing Act (1965, now in *A Bias for Hope*, New Haven, Yale University Press, 1971, pp. 312-327).
8. The Principle of the Hiding Hand (*Development Projects Observed*, Washington, Brookings Institution, 1967, ch. I).
9. The Political Economy of Import–Substituting Industrialization in Latin America (1968, now in *A Bias for Hope*, New Haven, Yale University Press, 1971, pp. 85-123).
10. Foreign Aid: A Critique and a Proposal (1968, now in *A Bias for Hope*, New Haven, Yale University Press, 1971, pp. 197-224).
11. "Exit, Voice, and Loyalty": Introduction and Doctrinal Background (*Exit, Voice, and Loyalty*, Cambridge Mass., Harvard University Press, 1970, ch. I).
12. Political Economics and Possibilism (Introduction to *A Bias for Hope*, New Haven, Yale University Press, 1971, pp. 1-37).
13. Policymaking and Policy Analysis in Latin America. A Return Journey (*Essays in Trespassing. Economics to Politics and Beyond*, Cambridge U.K., Cambridge University Press, 1981, pp. 142-166).
14. Varieties of Consumer Disappointment (*Shifting Involvements: Private Interest and Public Action*, Princeton, Princeton University Press, 1982, ch. II).
15. From Private Concern into the Public Arena (*Shifting Involvements: Private Interest and Public Action*, Princeton, Princeton University Press, 1982, ch. V).
16. Against Parsimony: Three Easy Ways of Complicating Some Categories of Economic Discourse (*Bulletin of the American Academy of Arts and Science*, 1984).
17. The Concept of Interest: from Euphemism to Tautology (*Rival Views of Market Society*, New York, Viking, 1986, pp. 35-55).

1

Foreign Trade as an Instrument of National Power

In this work the term *national power* is used in the sense of power of coercion which one nation may bring to bear upon other nations, the method of coercion being military or "peaceful." In trying to expand its power a nation must take account of many factors—historical, political, military, psychological, and economic. Among the economic determinants of power, foreign trade plays an important part. In order to analyse the way in which foreign trade contributes to a certain distribution of power among the various nations, it must be isolated temporarily from the other determinants; for the purpose of our inquiry these other determinants may be impounded in a vast *ceteris paribus* upon which, for the sake of rendering our analysis more realistic, we shall have to draw from time to time.

It will then be our aim to understand why and how relationships of dependence, of influence, and even of domination can arise out of trade relations. We are not concerned with the opposite line of causation which also exists and which may even have had a greater historical importance: the question of how a given distribution of power influences trade relations. It will, however, be well for the reader to remember that frequently the adoption of certain economic policies leading to greater power for a given nation is possible only if there exists an initial power disequilibrium in favour of that nation.

Colonial trade often gives us the opportunity of observing this type of cumulative effect. An initial power supremacy enables the imperial power to shape the direction and composition of the colony's trade, and the trade relations which are thus established in turn strengthen markedly the original power position held by the imperial power.

The Two Effects of Foreign Trade

Foreign trade has two main effects upon the power position of a country. The first effect is certain to be positive: By providing a more plentiful supply of goods or by replacing goods wanted less by goods wanted more (from the power standpoint), foreign trade enhances the potential military force of a country. This we may call the *supply effect* of foreign trade. It not only serves to strengthen the war machine of a country, but it uses the threat of war as a weapon of diplomacy. Although we have seen that free traders have advised statesmen to rely on the supply effect of foreign trade, protectionists have warned them of the dangers of its cessation during war, which, they say, is precisely when it will be most needed. But this danger might be lessened and the supply effect safeguarded:

1) by securing control of the oceanic trade routes;
2) by a policy of extensive preventive accumulation of stock piles in times of peace;
3) by redirecting trade towards those countries from which the danger of being cut off is minimized.

The attempt to trade more with neighbouring, friendly, or subject countries is largely inspired by this consideration, and it has been one of the most powerful motive forces behind the policies of regionalism and empire trade.

All these points are obvious and hardly need further elaboration. As far as the supply effect is concerned, foreign trade serves as a means of increasing the efficiency of the military pressure which one country might bring to bear upon other countries. But, just as war or the threat of war can be considered in turn as a means of obtaining a certain result, so the supply effect of foreign trade is an indirect instrument of power, the direct instrument being war or the threat of war. In its final result, therefore, the supply effect of foreign trade requires at least the possibility of war.

The second effect of foreign trade from the power standpoint is that it may become a direct source of power. It has often been hopefully pointed out that commerce, considered as a means of obtaining a share in the wealth of another country, can supersede war.[1] But commerce can become an alternative to war also—and this leads to a less optimistic outlook—by providing a method of coercion of its own in the relations between sovereign nations. Economic warfare can take the place of bombardments, economic pressure that of saber rattling. It can indeed be shown that even if war could be eliminated, foreign trade would lead to relationships of dependence and influence between nations. Let us call this the *influence effect* of foreign trade, and, because of its importance, give the greater part of this chapter to its analysis.

The terms dependence and influence have hitherto been used indiscriminately to describe the situation which seems invariably to arise out of the trade relations between two sovereign states. But why does such a situation arise at all? In other words, what is the root cause of the political or power aspect of international economic relations? To answer this question we must concede that the explanation of the great power held in the past by Great Britain was the fact that she possessed strategic bases, such as Gibraltar, Suez, and Singapore. The possession of these bases had two consequences: First, it guaranteed the security of British trade; second, as a welcome by-product, it enabled Great Britain to cut off the trade of other countries passing through these points, be it trade with Great Britain or trade between two other countries. This second consequence gave her considerable direct power over, and influence in, other countries, in that they were always exposed to the potential threat of a sudden stoppage of their trade at Britain's will.

1. This idea, which points to trade as an "economic equivalent to war," appears, for example, in the following characteristic passage from the famous anti-Napoleon tract of Benjamin Constant: "War and commerce are but two different means of arriving at the same aim which is to possess what is desired. Trade is nothing but a homage paid to the strength of the possessor by him who aspires to the possession: it is an attempt to obtain by mutual agreement that which one does not hope any longer to obtain by violence. The idea of commerce would never occur to a man who would always be the strongest. It is experience, proving to him that war, that is, the use of his force against the force of others, is exposed to various resistances and various failures, which makes him have recourse to commerce, that is, to a means more subtle and better fitted to induce the interest of others to consent to what is his own interest."—De *l'Esprit de Conquête et de l'Usurpation dans leurs rapports avec la Civilisation Européenne,* Part I, Chap. II.

But every sovereign nation has some influence of this kind, since through the control of its frontiers and the power over its citizens it can at any time interrupt *its own export and import trade,* which is at the same time the import and export trade of some other countries. The stoppage of this trade obliges the other countries to find alternative markets and sources of supply and, should this prove impossible, it forces upon them economic adjustments and lasting impoverishment. True, the stoppage of trade will also do harm to the economy of the country taking the initiative in bringing about the stoppage, but this is not unlike the harm an aggressive country can do to itself in making war on another. A country trying to make the most out of its strategic position with respect to its own trade will try precisely to create conditions which make the interruption of trade of much graver concern to its trading partners than to itself. Tariff wars and interruptions of trade rarely occur, but the awareness of their possibility is sufficient to test the influence of the stronger country and to shape the policy of the weaker.

That economic pressure upon a country consists mainly of the threat of severance and ultimately of actual interruption of external economic relations with that country was clearly recognized by Article 16 of the Covenant of the League of Nations. The intention of Article 16 was to coordinate and combine the power positions which the various member states of the League had acquired in the aggressor country by entertaining commercial and financial relations with it.

Thus, the power to interrupt commercial or financial relations with any country, considered as an attribute of national sovereignty, is the root cause of the influence or power position which a country acquires in other countries, just as it is the root cause of the "dependence on trade." It should be noted that the only condition for the emergence of these political aspects of trade relations is that of unfettered national sovereignties. It has often been pointed out that central regulation by separate sovereign units leads to a dangerous "politicalization" of trade.[2] Undoubtedly the identification of every private interest with national interest and prestige may add a heavy strain on international relations. But state regulation by no means *creates* the political aspects of international economic relations (as the term politicalization seems to imply). It merely emphasizes them or makes them more apparent and exploitable. For the political or power implications of trade to

2. J. B. Condliffe, *The Reconstruction of World Trade* (New York, 1940), p. 56; Lionel Robbins, *Economic Planning and International Order* (London, 1937), pp. 90 f.; Sir Arthur Salter, "The Future of Economic Nationalism," *Foreign Affairs*, Vol. X (October, 1932), p. 18; Eugene Staley, *World Economy in Transition* (New York, 1939), p. 178.

exist and to make themselves felt, it is not essential that the state should exercise positive action, that is, organize and direct trade centrally; the negative right of veto on trade with which *every* sovereign state is invested is quite sufficient.[3] We shall now examine the conditions making this right of veto or the power to interrupt trade an effective weapon in the struggle for power. To bring these conditions about will obviously be the goal of a nation using foreign trade as an instrument of power policy.[4]

The Influence Effect of Foreign Trade (Section 1)

What we have called the influence effect of foreign trade derives from the fact that the trade conducted between country A, on the one hand, and countries B, C, D, etc., on the other, is worth *something* to B, C, D, etc., and that they would therefore consent to grant A certain advantages—military, political, economic—in order to retain the possibility of trading with A. If A wants to increase its hold on B, C, D, etc., it must create a situation in which these countries would do *anything* in order to retain their foreign trade with A. Such a situation arises when it is extremely difficult and onerous for these countries:

3. The powers of the state with respect to foreign trade conducted by private enterprise may be compared to the powers of a labour union which, though refraining from collective bargaining, would have the power to call a strike and to determine its length. It will probably be granted that, in this case, most of the effects of combination would still obtain.
4. Since the power position of a country will be of importance in its commercial negotiations, the inquiry which follows gives incidentally an analysis of what is commonly called bargaining power. This term, however, for three distinct reasons, is inadequate for our purposes. First, the achieving of tariff and similar concessions is only one of the many uses to which the political power arising from foreign trade might be put; cf. in this connection. 1 Ians Staudinger. "The Future of Totalitarian Barter Trade." *Social Research*, Vol. VII (November, 1940). p. 426. In the second place, bargaining power in commercial negotiations is traditionally associated with a certain position of the trade balance between the two countries in negotiation, a view which will be explained and criticized below (pp. 70 f.). Third, the term bargaining power has a definite meaning in the theory of bilateral monopoly which is markedly different from the meaning which it would assume in our analysis. ….

1. to dispense entirely with the trade they conduct with A, or
2. to replace A as a market and a source of supply with other countries.

The principles of a power policy relying on the influence effect of foreign trade are in their essence extremely simple: *They are all designed to bring about* this *"ideal" situation.*

Our analysis of these principles is divided into two parts. In the first, it is assumed that the countries which are the objects of the power policy have no possibility of shifting their trade with A to each other or to third countries, whereas country A remains free to trade with whatever country it desires. Given this assumption, which will be dropped in the second part of our analysis, we have to pay attention only to the first characteristic of the "ideal" situation.

The difficulty for country B, C, D, etc., of dispensing with the trade conducted with A seems to depend on three main factors:

1. The total net gain to B, C, D, etc., of their trade with A;
2. The length and the painfulness of the adjustment process which A may impose upon B, C, D etc., by interrupting trade;
3. The strength of the vested interests which A has created by its trade within the economies of B, C, D, etc.

Gain from Trade and Dependence on Trade

The influence which country A acquires in country B by foreign trade depends in the first place upon the total gain which B derives from that trade; the total gain from trade for any country is indeed nothing but another expression for the total impoverishment which would be inflicted upon it by a stoppage of trade. In this sense the classical concept, gain from trade, and the power concept, dependence on trade, now being studied are seen to be merely two aspects of the same phenomenon, and this connection can serve as a modern application of the ancient saying *fortuna est servitus.*

The whole theory of the gain from trade and its distribution therefore becomes relevant to our subject. The gain from trade has been defined by Marshall in the following terms: "The direct gain which a country derives from her foreign trade is the excess of the value to her of the things which she imports over the value to her of the things which she could have made for herself with the capital and labour devoted to producing the things which she exported in exchange for them."[5] This definition brings out clearly that the gain from trade cannot be measured either by comparing the satisfaction derived from the consumption of the imports with the satisfaction which could be derived from the consumption at home of the exports or by comparing the hypothetical domestic cost of the imported commodities with their actual cost.[6] If a country was shut off from trade it would normally neither continue to produce the goods formerly exported nor try to produce at home all the goods formerly imported, but, given the reduced resources, an adjustment would take place towards the production of the goods most desired.

Professor Viner has elaborated an even more complex concept of the gain from trade. He has shown that differences in satisfaction between the trade and the no-trade situation might occur not only through a different composition of the goods to be consumed in the two situations, but also because of differences in the occupational pattern or in the general balance between work and leisure in the country concerned.[7]

Provided we keep in mind the qualification arising from these considerations, Marshall's definition still gives a good account of the value of trade to a country or, in other words, of that part of a country's well-being which it is in the power of its trading partners to take away.

The first conclusion which could be drawn from the connection which we have established between gain from trade and dependence on trade is that in order to increase its influence in other nations, nation A should simply bring about an expansion of its foreign trade. In accordance with a general presumption established by theory, a voluntary increase of trade on the part of A's trading partners is indeed indicative of an increase of their gains from trade and, hence, of their dependence on A. But this reasoning overlooks the fact that in this way the influence which the other nations hold in country A would also be increased. Some countries might be able to neglect this consideration because of their geographical position, their military power, or other non-economic elements. But, in general, a country embarking on a power policy will have fixed for the amount of

5. Alfred Marshall, *Money, Credit and Commerce* (London, 1923), pp. 109–110.
6. The latter error was attributed by Malthus to Ricardo. Cf. Jacob Viner, *Studies in the Theory of International Trade* (New York, 1937), p. 528.
7. 'Viner, op. cit., pp. 519 ft.

its trade relations with foreign countries a certain maximum limit which it will think unsafe to exceed.[8]

If we take account of this objection, another method might be proposed: country A, seeking to increase its influence in country B, might have an interest in altering the terms of trade in B's favour. Here, then, it would seem, we have an ideal instance of the opposition between a policy trying to maximize national income and a policy setting out to maximize national power.

This statement, however, needs qualification and elaboration. In the first place, the functional relationship between gain from trade and dependence on trade points to a potential clash, not only between national income or welfare and power, but also between the two different types of power policy, the one relying mostly on the supply effect of foreign trade and the other relying upon the influence effect. It is indeed clear that a policy using foreign trade as its instrument may sometimes have to choose between better terms of trade, that is, more plentiful supply of needed materials for a given quantity of home products, on the one hand, and more influence on the trading partner, on the other.

But is there an inevitable conflict between national welfare and national power, or, within a power policy, between the supply effect and the influence effect of foreign trade? This is a necessary conclusion only if we accept the common conception that a given amount of trade results in a fixed total gain to be distributed between the trading countries according to some ratio determined by the terms of trade. An increase of the gain of A can then only be procured at the cost of a decrease of the gain of B. This view, however, should be suspect if only because of its resemblance to the cruder Mercantilist idea that A's gain is B's loss.

Actually we have here to clear up a terminological confusion which is at the root of the whole matter. What is commonly called total gain from trade is by no means, as one might expect, the sum of the gains from trade as defined by Marshall for the individual participating countries. The term total gain, as used generally, is rather to be understood as the physical surplus of goods made possible by the international division of labour. This physical surplus is indeed fixed under given cost and demand conditions. It might be called the total objective gain from

8. It remains true that complete autarky can hardly be considered as an element of an intelligent power policy. And if the nations which have proclaimed autarky as their ultimate goal have remained far off the mark, this may be due not only to the economic difficulties which they have experienced in trying to dispense with foreign trade, but also because they have found it politically inexpedient to do without trade relations.

trade. But a moment's reflection should show that although this objective gain might be wholly non-existent (as in the absence of any international specialization following the opening up of trade), a substantial *subjective* gain as defined by Marshall might still accrue to the various countries, provided only that they do not produce the same range of commodities.[9]

If, therefore, an objective gain from trade in the form of a physical surplus of goods is not even a necessary condition for the emergence of a subjective gain from trade, the existence of a close relationship between the distribution of the objective and the subjective gains as between the countries trading together may be legitimately doubted. The theory of the terms of trade has succeeded in showing how the objective gain is distributed and how its distribution can be affected by changes in tastes and techniques or by commercial policies. It has generally been thought that the terms of trade give a broad indication of the gain from trade; and in spite of its many limitations pointed out by Professor Viner,[10] this method of approach still seems fruitful if one is interested mainly in knowing when a country increases or decreases the gain from its trade with another specified country, as this can under static conditions—that is, with tastes and techniques constant—occur only through a movement of the terms of trade in its favour. But the method fails us decisively if we are interested, not in the increments of the subjective gain from trade, but in its total amount for any given situation. It is indeed not possible to assert that the respective extents of the subjective gains from trade correspond to the division of the objective gain without assuming for the two countries a similarity of tastes and of the levels of satisfaction prior to trade-in other words, without assuming the whole problem away. In the absence of such assumptions there is no reason whatsoever why a country should not obtain a smaller part of the physical surplus of goods obtained by international specialization whilst deriving a larger increase in satisfaction from trade than its trading partner.[11]

9. Even under the very simplest classical assumptions of two commodities of similar importance, two countries of similar size, constant costs, absence of transport costs, and similar tastes in the two countries, it can be shown that further specialization after the opening up of trade, as required by the principle of comparative cost, is not a prerequisite for the existence of some subjective increase in satisfaction from trade.
10. Viner, *op. cit.,* pp. 555–582.
11. The belief that the position of the terms of trade gives a clue to the respective extent of the subjective gains from trade has been much strengthened by the often-quoted case of two countries of unequal size trading in two commodities. In this hypothesis

The inquiry into the factors which determine the amount of the subjective gain from trade has to be made directly. It has been undertaken with the help of diagrammatical illustrations by the neoclassical writers, Edgeworth[12] and, in particular, Marshall.[13] Marshall's conclusion, which is unaffected by two errors in his method,[14] is that "the surplus (of country G) is the greater, the more urgent is G's demand for a small amount of E's goods and the more of them she can receive without any great movement of the rate of interchange in her favor." In other words, with a given volume of trade the subjective gain is smallest if the supply-demand schedule of a country maintains a high elasticity throughout its relevant part; whereas the gain would be largest if a country's demand, after having been very elastic for small amounts of the other country's goods, becomes inelastic in its later (and relevant) stages.[15]

the larger country specializes only partly, its pre-trade ratio of exchange between the two commodities remains unchanged and the whole physical surplus of production due to specialization accrues to the smaller country whilst the supply in goods of the larger country remains unchanged. But so far from being an illustration of the general correspondence between the position of the terms of trade and the extent of the subjective gains, this is actually the only case in which the correspondence holds—a quite paradoxical case—as trade leads neither to an increase in quantity nor to a change in composition of the goods consumed in one of the trading countries.

12. F. Y. Edgeworth, "On the Application of Mathematics to Political Economy." *Journal of the Royal Statistical Society,* Vol. LI I (1889). pp. 558–560. Edgeworth reproduces in the main the "beautiful reasoning" of Auspitz and Lieben, *Untersuchungen über die Theorie der Preise* (Leipzig, 1889), pp. 413–415. In a later work, "The Theory of International Values," *Economic Journal.* Vol. IV (1894}. Edgeworth deals essentially with the increments in the gain from trade, not with the total amount; cf. Viner, op. cit., p. 576 and footnote 3.
13. Marshall, op. cit., Appendix J, pp. 338–340.
14. As pointed out with respect to the algebraic illustration by Allyn A. Young, "Marshall on Consumer's Surplus in International Trade," *Quarterly Journal of Economics,* Vol. XXXIX (1921), pp. 144–150, and with respect to the diagrammatical exposition by Viner. op. cit., pp. 570–575. Viner also shows that the more general objection of Allyn A. Young against the whole concept of Marshall's "surplus" in international trade (which is nothing but another expression for the subjective gain from trade) does not hold.
15. In this context elasticity means the response of the imported quantity to a change in the terms of trade. Although it is not identical with the ordinary concept of demand elasticity, it is related to it. Cf. T. O. Yntema. *A Mathematical Reformulation of the General Theory of International Trade* (Chicago, 1932), pp. 52–56. Professor

This statement may seem surprising, as a country which finds itself in the latter situation is generally said to be in an inferior strategic position and to be exposed to a manipulation of the terms of trade against it. Actually, however, this is only another aspect of the same situation: A country which gains much from the exchange of its home produce against imports may be manoeuvred more easily into concessions according to the rate of interchange than a country for which trade is only barely profitable under existing conditions.

We have mentioned above the possibility that a country, though obtaining a smaller objective gain from trade, may still enjoy a greater subjective gain; it is now seen that this situation is not necessarily an oddity, but may, on the contrary, be considered as probably true.[16]

Kindleberger has shown the inconsistent use made by various economists of the term urgent demand and has proposed the terms flexible and inflexible demand instead of not urgent and urgent demand; cf. C. P. Kindleberger. "Flexibility of Demand in International Trade Theory," *Quarterly Journal of Economics*, Vol. LI (February, 1937), pp. 352–361, He, however, as our quotation shows, is incorrect in contending that Marshall did not use the term urgent demand; paying attention only to the ordinary Marshallian price elasticity, Professor Kindleberger does not realize that Marshall's elasticity concepts, as developed in connection with his foreign trade curves, can take care of the various situations which arise in international trade and are denoted by the terms urgent or inflexible. It remains true that these special terms are useful in shortening the description of the shape of a Marshallian demand-supply curve which is at first extremely responsive to favourable changes in the terms of trade and becomes inelastic for further changes in these terms. The conflicting interpretations of the term urgent demand derive from the fact that the various writers have considered different stretches of the *same* supply-demand curve. Professor Kindleberger rightly shows the connection between the concept of urgency of demand and that of income elasticity. The two, however, are not identical, since income elasticity means responsiveness of the demand of a commodity to income increases, whereas the elasticity of the Marshallian curve means responsiveness of demand of a commodity to a favourable change of its rate of exchange for another commodity.

16. It seems that J. S. Mill had this situation in mind when he wrote in his *Essays on Some Unsettled Questions:* "If the question be now asked, which of the countries of the world gains most by foreign commerce, the following will be the answer. If by gain be meant advantage, in the most enlarged sense, that country will generally gain the most, which stands most in need of foreign commodities. But if by gain be meant saving of labour and capital in obtaining the commodities which the country desires to have, whatever they may be; the country will gain, not in proportion to its own need of foreign articles, but to the need which foreigners have of the articles which

These theoretical considerations are directly relevant to the twofold object of a power policy by foreign trade which we have described. Country A may possibly increase the gain from trade and therefore the dependence of its trading partners either by a change in the composition of trade or by a change in partners without having to submit to more unfavourable terms of trade. To resolve in this way the conflict between the supply effect and the influence effect of foreign trade which at first seemed inevitable, A has to seek trading partners with an "urgent" demand for its export goods.

In the first place, A will therefore turn to countries which have no possibilities of themselves producing the commodities country A exports. A second and more general case, which has been pointed out by Marshall, is the trade with "poor countries," that is, countries with low real incomes before the opening up of trade. Marshall has applied to this case the "law of the diminishing marginal utility of income" in the following terms: "The rich country can with little effort supply a poor country with implements for agriculture or the chase which doubled the effectiveness of her labour, and which she could not make for herself; while the rich country could without great trouble make for herself most of the things which she purchased from the poor nation or at all events could get fairly good substitutes for them. A stoppage of the trade would therefore generally cause much more real loss to the poor than to the rich nation."[17]

itself produces."—J. S. Mill, op. cit., p. 44; cf. also p. 46. Mill has not reproduced this passage in the *Principles* where he has elaborated only the second concept of gain; indeed, the first one hardly fits in with his value theory. Jevons obviously ignored Mill's earlier writings when, as exposed in the *Principles,* he attacked the concept of gain in the following terms: "So far is Mill's statement (about the distribution of the gain from trade) from being fundamentally correct that I believe the truth lies in the opposite direction. As a general rule, the greatness of the price which a country is willing and able to pay for the production of other countries measures or at least manifests, the greatness of the benefit which it derives from such imports."—Stanley Jevons, *The Theory of Political Economy,* 4th ed. (London, 1911), p. 145.

17. Marshall, op. cit., p. 168. It will be noted that, for Marshall, the case of a rich country trading with a poor country and the case of a country having a monopoly in some article trading with another country having no such monopoly are somewhat intertwined. A conclusion similar to that of Marshall follows from Edgeworth's comment on his own assumption in the analysis of foreign trade that "the hedonic worth of money is the same in both countries"; he conceded indeed that "when we know that one party is much better off than another, the assumption may be illegitimate."—"The

A nation pursuing a power policy may be assumed to export industrial goods and to import mainly those articles for which it has either no substitutes at home or only poor and expensive ones. It must be prepared to incur a certain dependence on foreign countries in order to obtain these articles—or, in our terminology, in order to profit from the supply effect of foreign trade. Its problem is therefore how to induce a maximum dependence of foreign countries, given a fixed dependence of its own. In solving this problem it can avail itself of our findings by determining what to export and by choosing the countries from which to import.[18] It can see to it, first, that it possesses a monopolistic position in its export articles by directing trade to those countries which are relatively poorly suited to produce these or similar articles. In our case this means the agricultural countries; and the prevention of industrialization or even the removal of already existing industries is an important part of a policy of trying to preserve or to increase the influence acquired in these countries by an industrial nation.

Theory of International Values." *Economic Journal*, Vol. IV (1894). p. 436. That the comparison of utilities between two collective groups, such as countries, is less rather than more hazardous than intrapersonal comparisons of utility has been shown by a recent contribution (L. G. Melville, "Economic Welfare," *Economic Journal*, Vol. XLIX [September, 1939], pp. 554–553). The possible exceptions to the case which have been pointed out by Marshall are not likely to arise from the difference in the "capacity for enjoyment" of the citizens of the two countries, but rather from the difference in the effect of foreign trade upon the distribution or income in the two countries. If, indeed, the goods imported into the relatively poor country add mainly to the enjoyment of its wealthier classes, whereas the contrary happens in the relatively rich country, the effect described by Marshall may well be neutralized.—I am indebted to Dr Fellner for this point.

18. We assume here, as stated in the beginning of this section, that only the country conducting a power policy is at liberty to choose its trading partners, whereas the latter have no option but to trade with that country. This assumption will be dropped below. Here we also disregard the fact that the power-seeking nation may prefer to obtain a small influence in a neighbouring state rather than a large one in a distant country. In a sense, our analysis considers every country as an equally interesting object of a power policy. Total influence is for us the sum of the influences secured in the individual countries, whereas actually every influence should be weighted according to strategic or other considerations. But this means only that the role played by

In the second place, the nation conducting a power policy has an interest in diverting its trade to poor countries in which the marginal utility of income is high. Thus, if nation A, embarking on a power policy, has had a certain amount of trade with group B of other rich industrial nations, it might of course try to enlarge its influence in these countries by granting them better terms of trade. But this would interfere with its own production and, in addition, these countries might not value very highly the additional supplies coming from A. If, on the other hand, the nation diverts its trade to group C of poor and agricultural countries from which it can receive the same supplies, the gain from trade obtained by group C will exceed what group B's gain had been, and consequently A's influence in group C will be much greater than it was in group B. Although the real costs of the supplies may be higher in group C than in group B, A will then have little difficulty in manipulating the terms of trade in such a way that she gives no more of her home produce in exchange for her imports than formerly.

Renewed attention has been given recently to the analysis of exploitation, both with respect to the factor of production in the domestic economy and to that of one country by another in international economic relations. For the latter subject it has been shown what conditions and what policies are required for a country to turn the terms of trade in its favour. At the outset this type of inquiry seems to be the exact opposite of our analysis of the influence effect, which depends on the gain from trade of the trading *partners.* The possibility of a conflict between the policy of maximization of national income, on the one hand, and the policy of securing the greatest position of influence with the trading partners, on the other, certainly deserves to be pointed out. But our subsequent analysis has shown that these two types of policies are not necessarily alternatives. The successful pursuit of the one policy may even condition the emergence of the other. The ability to manipulate the terms of trade in one's favour depends, indeed, on the gain from trade derived by the trading partners, and the policies we have described are directed precisely to increase this gain. The monopolistic exploitation of a trading partner can then be considered as one of the uses to which the power secured through the influence effect may be put. We are here concerned only with the methods and conditions leading to this power, not with its possible uses which may be the reaping of advantages of any kind—military and political, as well as economic.

the economic determinants of power must eventually be combined with and be qualified by the other determinants. The reader must judge whether the results reached by our analysis warrant the admittedly artificial isolation of the economic factor.

Adjustment Difficulties and Vested Interests

The threat of an interruption of trade—the ever-present characteristic of commerce between sovereign states—has two main effects upon the economy of the country the trade of which is interrupted: It impoverishes this country and also imposes a process of adjustment, since, when imports are no longer forthcoming, the goods formerly exported will no longer be consumed in the home market. Marshall's definition of the gain from trade: the excess of utility of the imports over the utility of the goods produced by the resources otherwise devoted to exports if there were no imports—compares the utilities of two non-simultaneous sets of goods and thus obviously includes a time element. The immediate loss from the stoppage of trade is much greater than the ultimate loss after resources have been fully reallocated. The classical theory of international trade was aware of this distinction;[19] but it concentrated upon the ultimate loss and considered the time elapsing from interruption of trade to reallocation of resources within the country as a short-run period. Modern theory insists that this is not necessarily true; and even if it were true, our analysis would have to take into account the fact that harassed statesmen generally have a short-run view. Given a certain ultimate loss, the influence which one country exercises upon another through foreign trade is therefore likely to be larger the greater the immediate loss which it can inflict by a stoppage of trade.

For a country cut off from foreign trade the most urgent problem is to produce at home or to find substitutes for goods which were formerly imported and to find new employment for the factors of production formerly employed in export industries. The first problem is definitely connected with the ultimate loss from the interruption of trade, whereas the second is a short-run problem. Nevertheless, the "danger of losing a market" if political conditions deteriorate makes for as much concern as the danger of losing supplies. According to classical theory the active side of the gain from trade derives only from the imports, and the exports are set as a passive item against them. Modern theory, on the other hand, has presented an analysis which, within the framework of a national policy aiming at full employment, considers exports as an incentive to employment and national income, and imports as "leakages" which to a certain degree prevent the

19. Ricardo, in his *Principles of Political Economy,* states it thus at the beginning of the chapter on "Sudden Changes in the Channels of Trade".

working of this incentive.[20] The classical and the modern approaches are of course based on quite different assumptions, and each is valuable in its own field for the explanation of some relevant economic facts. The modern approach, with its emphasis on immobility, overhead costs, and incomplete use of resources, leads to an understanding of why the common belief that the real benefit arising from trade lies in exports rather than imports is more than a mere "popular fallacy."

Obviously, the difficulties arising out of a cessation of exports will be greater the greater the exports (and consequently the imports); and the short-run problem is thus intimately connected with the extent of the long-run gain from trade. But with a given quantity of exports the problem created by an interruption of trade will be the more difficult, (1) the smaller the mobility of resources within the country, (2) the more the economic activities leading to exports have been concentrated in certain lines of production or in certain regions.

The mobility of resources includes the possibility of diverting capital goods to new purposes (i.e. their more or less "specific" character), the geographical mobility of the factors of production, and, above all, the ability of labour to turn to new tasks. The inherent advantage with respect to all these aspects of the mobility of resources lies overwhelmingly with the great manufacturing and trading countries as opposed to countries in which agriculture or mining predominates. Here again the prevention of industrialization would be the aim of a power trying to make the adjustment problem appear insoluble to the countries with which it trades.[21]

The second factor having a definite bearing upon the relative ease of adjustment after an interruption of trade is the extent to which production for export is concentrated in certain products or in certain regions. If most of the exports are made up of one particular product, there is very little probability that any great part of it can be consumed at home if the foreign outlet fails; if the exports all come from certain specialized regions within the country, there will be "distressed

20. For a discussion of the "Foreign Trade Multiplier," see Gottfried Haberler, *Prosperity and Depression*, 3d ed. (Geneva, 1942), pp. 461–473, and literature quoted in that work.
21. We are considering the mobility of resources only so far as it influences the distribution of power created by foreign trade. Of course the mobility of resources has an extremely important *direct* bearing upon political and economic power. This aspect has been pointed out very clearly by Mr Hawtrey, op. cit., pp. 83–92. For a good discussion of the various factors influencing the mobility of resources within an industrialized country with special reference to the trade cycle, see C. M. Wright, *Economic Adaptation to a Changing World Market,* Chapter V (Copenhagen, 1939).

areas" and a need for large-scale relief and resettlement. It is highly unlikely that the pattern of the economic activities devoted to exports will follow closely the distribution of general economic activity among geographical regions and lines of production. But the discrepancy of the two patterns may be more or less pronounced, and, accordingly, the contribution of exports to dependence upon foreign trade will be large or small.

This subject is directly linked with the vested interests created by trade: a greater concern with the maintenance and expansion of trade in certain quarters than in the country as a whole. The actual going volume of trade, indeed, produces its own vested interests, just as does the limitation of trade through protection; and the history of commercial policy offers convincing evidence that the protectionists would have been still more successful than they have been if they had had to contend only with the opposition of the "consumers at large."

If conditions are such that the possible loss from a stoppage of trade would fall with special weight upon certain groups within the country, these groups are likely to form a sort of "commercial fifth column." Aside from the purely commercial groups, such as import and export companies, the influence of which is generally meagre, the vested interests will consist of the producers for export and of the industries using imported raw materials. If exports are concentrated in some region or some industry, not only will the difficulty of adjustment in the case of loss of these exports weigh upon the decisions of the government, but these regions or industries will exert a powerful influence in favour of a "friendly" attitude towards the state to the imports of which they owe their existence. Creation of potential adjustment difficulties and of vested interests is thus the twofold result of a commercial policy which aims at an intensive specialization of the trading partner's economy and which tries to prevent the diversification of the partner's exports with respect to regions and to products. In the social pattern of each country there exist certain powerful groups the support of which is particularly valuable to a *foreign* country in its power policy; the foreign country will therefore try to establish commercial relations especially with these groups, in order that their voices will be raised in its favour.

The Influence Effect of Foreign Trade (Section 2)

We must now drop a simplifying assumption under which we have worked hitherto and allow for the possibility of alternative markets or sources of supply. A country menaced with an interruption of trade with a given country has the alternative of diverting its trade to a third country; by so doing it evades more or less completely the damaging consequences of the stoppage of its trade with one particular country. The stoppage or the threat of it would thus lose all its force. In order to prevent this, the country wishing to conserve the influence derived from foreign trade in the real world of many nations must therefore take some precautions. The principles which we have formulated for power policy through the instrumentality of foreign trade retain their full validity. They were aimed at rendering it difficult for the other countries to *dispense* with foreign trade; but if we wish these principles to be effective in the real world, they must be supplemented by measures which make it difficult for other countries to *shift* the trade conducted with them by the nation trying to increase its power by foreign trade.

Any switching of trade would, of course, be rendered impossible by a monopoly of trade imposed by one nation upon another. In the old colonial system a colony was not permitted to turn to other buyers or sellers, even though the mother country had no obligation at all to provide the colony with goods or to buy from it. Under modern conditions subtler methods must be devised in order to arrive at similar results. A country may still hope to create conditions in which the diversion of trade to a third country will be much more difficult for its partner than for itself.[22]

In a very general way the difficulty of substituting country A as a market or supply source for country B may be said to depend not only on the absolute amount of A's trade with B, but also on the importance of this trade relatively to B's total trade. If, for instance, a country loses 5% of its export trade, it should be able to find additional outlets in the markets which account normally for 95% of its exports and where a sales organization for its products is likely to exist already. Similarly, if the country loses a relatively small fraction of its import trade, it is probable not only that its economic activity is not based to an undue degree upon these supplies, but also that other countries will be able and eager to make up for them. The greater the percentage of exports and imports involved in a dominant market, the more difficult it will be to provide substitute markets and sources of supply.

If a nation with an absolutely large volume of trade imports from, or exports to, a small trading nation, the trade they conduct together will inevitably result in a much higher percentage for the small than for the large trading

22. How important this problem is even in simple commercial bargaining is repeatedly brought out by N. F. Hall, "Trade Diversion—An Australian Interlude," *Economica*, Vol. V, new series (February, 1938).

nation. German-Bulgarian trade in 1938, for example, represented 52 and 59% of Bulgarian imports and exports, respectively, but only 1.5 and 1.1% of the German imports and exports. These figures indicate that although the same absolute amount is involved, it will be much more difficult for Bulgaria to shift her trade with Germany to other countries than it will be for Germany to replace Bulgaria as a selling market and a source of supplies.[23] In the real world of many sovereign states it will therefore be an elementary principle of the power policy of a state to *direct its trade away from the large to the smaller trading states.* This principle must then be added to the one established above, viz., that trade should be directed towards the poorer countries. The two are by no means contradictory, as there are many states which are both poor and small.

Similarly, it will be an elementary defensive principle of the smaller trading countries not to have too large a share of their trade with any single great trading country, so that the integration of their economies with those of the great countries (for which no reciprocal integration is forthcoming) may be kept at a minimum compatible with their economic well-being. The idea that dependence can be diminished by distributing the trade among many countries has been clearly enunciated by Macaulay. [...].

A more specific policy by which a country could try to prevent its trading partners from diverting their trade to other countries would consist in the creation of monopolistic or monopsonistic conditions with regard to certain products.[24]

With respect to exports, country A may try to change the structure of country B's economy so as to make it highly and artificially complementary to A's own economy. First, A may encourage the production of products having but little demand in other countries. This amounts to the creation of what might be called "exclusive complementarity" between the economy of country B and country A.

Furthermore, country B may have a comparative advantage in the production of a certain commodity with respect to country A, but not with respect to countries C, D, E, etc. If by some preferential treatment, A induced B to produce this commodity for export, A becomes B's only market, and the dependence of B upon A thus created may be well worth to A the economic cost involved in not buying

23. Not only is it more difficult for Bulgaria than for Germany to shift trade, but it is also harder for Bulgaria to *dispense* entirely with the trade conducted with Germany, because this trade is much more "essential" to her. This is, however, not a consequence of her comparative smallness, but of factors pointed out in section 1 of this chapter.
24. Cf. H. K. Heuser, *The Control of International Trade* (London, 1939), pp. 250–251.

in the cheapest market. In general, any attempt to drive the prices of exports from trading partners above world prices, whether by the direct encouragement of production contrary to the comparative cost principle or by general monetary manipulations, will fit in with the policy of increasing their dependence.

The paying of a higher price is only the most obvious way of rendering more arduous the diversion of a trading partner's exports to third markets. The offer of some special advantage relating to the conditions of the contract other than the price works towards the same effect. Firms often reward loyalty on the part of their customers by rebates and other devices.[25] The economies of regularity and the considerations of risk which explain this practice play an even greater role in foreign trade; with prices uniform, exports will therefore be directed preferably to those countries which are able and willing to guarantee stable prices for a prolonged period.

With respect to imports, the substitution of the imported products from any country will be more difficult in the absence of a natural monopoly the more highly differentiated are the products. Such products tend to create fixed consumption habits and production techniques, and difficulties arise when these products have to be replaced by similar but not identical products from other countries. Hence, it is generally easier for an industrial country to change the source of its supply of foodstuffs and raw materials than it is for a country producing foodstuffs or raw materials to change its traditional supplier of industrial goods.[26]

Under conditions of incomplete use of resources, however, it will generally be much easier to switch imports than exports, all countries being ready to sell and none ready to buy. This fact has indeed tended to dominate the whole discussion of the determinants of bargaining power between two trading countries. It was held that superior bargaining power is *always* on the side of the country having a passive trade balance with its trading partner. In other words, the difficulty of shifting imports was entirely discounted, whereas in assessing the difficulty of shifting exports no account was taken of the various factors enumerated above. It was thought that the country having the greater absolute volume of exports would automatically experience the greater difficulties of diversion and thereby find itself in an inferior bargaining position.[27] This is, of course, far too great a

25. Cf. W. A. Lewis, "Notes on the Economics of Loyalty," *Economica*, Vol. IX, new series (November, 1942), pp. 333–348.
26. Cf. R. F. Harrod's distinction of A, B, and C goods in his *International Economics*, new ed. (London, 1939), pp. 60 ff.
27. Relatively early the German economist Dietzel attacked this view: "In respect to the question of the strength of the (bargaining) position, it does not matter so much

simplification; but the fact remains that an intelligent power policy must take account of the greater difficulty which is generally experienced in diverting exports.

Let us suppose then that country A buys a percentage of B's exports sufficiently large to render a substitution of these exports well-nigh impossible for B. Is there any means of extending this impossibility to the switching of B's imports as well? We see immediately that the policy of bilateralism is perfectly fitted to take care of this problem. Indeed, under conditions of bilateralism, a real impossibility of switching exports induces a *technical* impossibility of switching imports. In this way the device of bilateralism is seen to be an important link in the policies by which the aim of maximum power through foreign trade may be attained.

In all our analysis we have spoken exclusively of direct import and export trade. *Transit trade* plays a special and somewhat contradictory role when we try to answer the question: Should a country, from the point of view of power policy, aim at a large transit trade? On the one hand it would seem that transit trade can always be replaced by direct trade and that therefore the country handling the transit trade is in a rather weak position. But if the replacement of the transit trade is impracticable for geographical, technical, or contractural reasons, transit trade is immediately seen to be an ideal means of increasing power by trade. Indeed, the economy of the country handling this trade is only superficially affected by the trade; whereas it acquires the influence normally deriving from exports and imports both in the country of origin and the country of final destination of the transit commodities. In other words, provided only that its services are indispensable, the country handling the transit trade acquires from that trade a twofold influence and at the same time evades almost entirely any dependence of its own economy.

which one of the two nations waging a tariff war buys more from the other; it matters more which of the two nations can better do without the market of the other, and is able in the case of loss of this market, to sell nearly as much elsewhere."—Karl Dietzel, *Der deutsch-amerikanische Handelsvertrag und das Phantom der amerikanischen Industriekonkurrenz* (Berlin, 1905), p. 20.

An Illustration: German Trading Methods under National Socialism

The conditions or policies which have been described as being conducive to increased national power by means of foreign trade can be summarized by the following synoptical table:

Principles of a Power Policy Using Foreign Trade as Its Instrument

- I. Policies relying on the *supply effect* of foreign trade and trying to insure its working even in times of war.
  - A. Concentrate imports on goods needed for the war machine.
  - B. Accumulate large stocks of strategic materials.
  - C. Redirect trade to neighbouring politically friendly or subject nations.
  - D. Secure control of the oceanic trade routes.
- II. Policies relying on the *influence effect* of foreign trade.
  - A. Policies designed to make it more difficult for the trading partner to *dispense entirely* with the trade.
    1. Increase the trading partners' gain from trade (without impairing the supply effect).
       - a. Develop exports in articles enjoying a monopolistic position in other countries and direct trade to such countries.
       - b. Direct trade towards poorer countries.
    2. Increase the trading partners' adjustment difficulties in case of stoppage of trade.
       - a. Trade with countries with little mobility of resources.
       - b. Induce a wide discrepancy between the pattern of production for exports and the pattern of production for home consumption.
    3. Create vested interests and tie the interests of existing powerful groups to the trade.
  - B. Policies designed to make it difficult for the trading partners to *shift* trade to each other or to third countries.
    1. In general: Direct trade towards the small trading countries.

2. With respect to the exports of the trading partners:
    a. Import products for which there is little demand in other countries.
    b. Drive prices of the export products of the trading partners above world prices:
        i. By fostering high-cost production.
        ii. By monetary manipulations.
    c. Grant to trading partners' exports advantages not relating to the price of their products.
3. With respect to the imports of the trading partners:
    a. Export highly differentiated goods creating consumption and production habits.
    b. Develop trade on bilateral basis.
4. Develop transit trade.

Practically all the outstanding features of German foreign economic policy since 1933 can be subsumed under this scheme …

2

Disinflation, Discrimination, and the Dollar Shortage

. . .

I. Inflation and Balance-of-Payments Deficit

During the first two post-war years, the need for balance-of-payments assistance of European countries was generally explained in terms of the structural changes in the world economy which were brought about by World War II. The great need for reconstruction and the low level of production in Europe, the loss of invisible income from overseas, and the disruption of traditional trade relations of Western Europe with both Eastern Europe and the Far East—all these were held, and no doubt justly, to provide a sufficient explanation for the need of large-scale aid from the United States. When, however, in 1947, European recovery suffered a relapse, and balance-of-payments equilibrium seemed farther away than ever, "monetary" phenomena were given increasing weight at the expense of the "real" structural factors. The development of the terms of trade was widely discussed; devaluation was no longer entirely brushed aside as an untimely and blunt instrument; and the connection between domestic inflation and external imbalance was increasingly stressed. The latter, in particular, is the central theme of the latest annual report of the Bank for International Settlements which acknowledges that the economic policies of several European governments display an increasing awareness of this connection.

The causal link between inflation, whether open or repressed, and foreign exchange shortages is easily understood. In the case of open inflation, the rise in domestic prices soon makes it unprofitable to export and profitable to import as long as exchange rates remain pegged.[1] In the case of repressed inflation, the pressure of redundant internal purchasing power brings about a diversion of both factors of production and output from export industries to domestic nonpriority uses.

This reasoning is appealing inasmuch as it holds out the promise of a short-cut to the solution of balance-of-payment difficulties: it clearly seems easier to "disinflate" or to stop an open inflationary process than to bring about basic readjustments of industrial structure and of trade patterns.

There certainly is a good deal of validity in the "monetary" explanations of the foreign exchange shortage, but it would be dangerous to rely on "disinflation" alone for securing external equilibrium. The relaxed tension of domestic demand, the greater availability of labour, and some scattered symptoms of depression, all of which have been noted over the past year in a number of European countries, are merely presenting these countries with an opportunity to carry out such readjustments in their productive structure as may help to render them eventually independent of foreign aid. If this opportunity is not seized, there will be either economic stagnation, offering no hope for ever emerging from the condition of external imbalance without a drastic reduction in the standard of living, or a growing public demand for indiscriminate "reflation," which would reproduce the situation prior to "disinflation.'[2]

The need for caution in drawing conclusions from the connection between inflation and balance-of-payments deficit becomes even more apparent when it is realized that *the causal relationship runs both ways.* In the post-war situation, the need for foreign aid often became more imperative as a consequence of internal

1. It may be noted that the existence of a fixed rate of exchange is a limitation on the "openness" of the inflation. During the ideally "open" German inflation of the twenties, there never developed a foreign exchange shortage, one reason being that the fall in the foreign value of the mark in general kept ahead of the increase in domestic prices.
2. See on this problem in the United Kingdom, "Retreat from Austerity," *The Banker* (July, 1948), pp. 12–15.

inflation; but, on the other hand, internal inflation was given a powerful stimulus by reconstruction and investment activities which in turn were rendered possible only by the large volume of raw material and equipment imports financed by U.S. grants or loans. No doubt these imports do eventually result in an increased flow of consumers' goods. In the short run, however, foreign aid shipments can exert, paradoxically, an inflationary effect on the recipient countries. This is true in particular when the net imports, because of their "bottleneck" nature, permit use of large quantities of hitherto unused domestic labour and raw materials in reconstruction and investment activities while individual savings are still at very low levels. In fully employed economies, additional investment resulting from "reconstruction imports" will attract already employed domestic factors of production and will therefore result in an upward pressure on wages and prices.

The effect described here may, of course, be accounted for, along traditional lines, by the juxtaposition of a deflationary effect deriving from net imports and of a larger inflationary effect deriving from domestic investment. But if this investment is made possible by the imports and would most likely not have been undertaken at all in their absence, our analysis gains in realism by an explicit recognition of this link. It may be pointed out that, similarly, United State net exports can have an anti-inflationary effect on the United States economy. For the shipment of raw materials and machinery abroad may result in the postponement of capital expansion projects which might otherwise have materialized; it also makes it impossible for these goods to compete for complementary and already otherwise employed factors of production (labour and materials) through which they would be put to use in the American economy. This anti-inflationary effect of the United States net exports on the domestic economy is the logical counterpart to their inflationary effect on the foreign economies, but in the present situation the actual significance of the effect in the United States is no doubt far smaller than that abroad, and is certainly outweighed for the United States by the aggregate inflationary impact of our foreign aid program.

It would be tempting to classify the various categories of imports according to the inflationary or deflationary impact they are likely to have on the recipient economies, but generalizations in this respect cannot be carried very far. Imports of machine tools will not be inflationary if they are replacements rather than part of the installation of a new plant; imports of foodstuffs, on the other hand, may not have a deflationary effect if they release scarce labour resources which can be used in investment activities. In the present situation, however, the often used distinction between "relief" imports (which merely sustain output and standards of living at existing levels) and "recovery" imports (which permit an expansion in output) is relevant to our discussion. The former are likely to have prevalently a deflationary impact while the inflationary effect described above will ordinarily derive from the "recovery" imports.

In this connection, mention should also be made of the possible use of certain imports such as films and tobacco, which may best be described as "essential luxuries," in domestic monetary policy.[3] Since their demand is inelastic within a considerable range, while their prices do not have to be kept low for reasons of social tranquillity, the imposition of heavy consumption taxes on these commodities will result in the mopping up of internal purchasing power to an extent far exceeding the local currency equivalent of their dollar value. Imports of such items are thus particularly well suited for the purposes of a disinflationary policy since their domestic impact is the exact opposite of that of the so-called recovery items. It has been rightly pointed out that by their contribution to disinflation these imports may result, indirectly, in an actual saving of foreign exchange.[4]

The possible inflationary effect of certain categories of foreign aid shipments on the economies of the recipient countries creates a difficult problem of policy. To press for monetary stability on the one hand, and for inclusion of a maximum amount of "recovery items" in shipments financed through U.S. aid on the other, may mean advocating deflation and inflation at the same time. Should monetary stability be achieved primarily by a reduction in investment activity, the absorption of "recovery items" even on the scale which prevailed during the inflationary phase would become impossible. Such inability to absorb recovery imports[5] is a danger signal since it denotes economic stagnation and failure to proceed with the capital formation which is essential to the achievement of equilibrium in the long run. If disinflation is brought about and is maintained by a reduction in essential investment expenditures, the cure may be worse than the disease; if, on the contrary, it is caused by a curtailment of expenditures for non-essential investment

3. This category overlaps, but is not coincidental, with that of the so-called incentive goods.
4. Sir Hubert Henderson, "Cheap Money and the Budget," *Economic Journal*, Vol. LVH (Sept, 1947), p. 270.
5. During Italy's recent deflationary experience, the Italian government has had considerable difficulties in disposing domestically of the full amount of coal it had imported under the various foreign aid programs.

and consumption, and if the resources thus released are gradually channelled into export industries and essential investments, disinflation can indeed make a considerable contribution to the economic rehabilitation of the areas now dependent on aid from the United States.

3

Devaluation and the Trade Balance[1]

In spite of extensive literature on the subject, one point in the formal theory of foreign exchanges still needs clarification: the effect of devaluation on the trade (or current account) balance when total imports (current payments) are not equal to total exports (current receipts).

Marshall was first to point out that devaluation might produce an unfavourable effect on a balance of trade *in equilibrium* on the condition that "the total elasticity of demand of each country be less than unity, and on the average be less than one half ...." He added that "nothing approaching this has ever occurred in the real world: it is not inconceivable, but it is absolutely impossible."[2] Lerner has restated this theorem in his *Economics of Control*.[3]

The theory was considerably amplified by A. J. Brown who added the elasticities of supply, the marginal propensities to import, and several other factors to

1. The author is an economist with the Board of Governors of the Federal Reserve System; the views expressed in this note are not necessarily those of the Board. Thanks are expressed to Alexander Gerschenkron and George Jaszi for thorough discussion and criticism.
2. Alfred Marshall, *Money, Credit, and Commerce* (London, 1923), Appendix J, p. 354.
3. New York, 1944, p. 378.

the demand elasticities as determinants of the trade balance upon devaluation.[4] The starting point of Brown's investigations remained, however, a trade balance in equilibrium.

This assumption was discarded by Joan Robinson who derived the correct formula for the effect of devaluation on a trade balance which is not in equilibrium, but only for the case of the balance expressed in domestic currency;[5] she ignored the fact that a different expression obtains for the usually more important balance in terms of foreign currency.

Since attention will be focused here on the effect of devaluation for varying positions of the trade balance, the following analysis will be made only in terms of demand elasticities. To the reader of Brown and Robinson this will mean that the elasticities of supply are assumed to be infinite, that is, that exports and imports are supplied at constant costs within the relevant range. This, however, need not be the case if the analysis is made in terms of elasticities of demand for *foreign exchange* rather than for the *volume* of imports from abroad. A short digression may be in order to explain this distinction.

The study of the effect of devaluation on the trade balance can start by considering the demand and supply curves for foreign exchange which have been made familiar by the writings of Bresciani-Turroni, Viner, and Machlup.[6] These curves result from a transposition of Marshall's curves for E- and G-bales, so as to make the ordinate represent the ratio of interchange between E- and G-bales and the abscissa either E- or G-bales. From here it seems quite natural to pass to the foreign exchange diagram in which the abscissa represents quantities of foreign (domestic) currency, while the ordinate denotes the rate of exchange expressing the number of units of domestic (foreign) currency that have to be yielded to acquire one unit of foreign (domestic) currency.

4. A. J. Brown, "Trade Balances and Exchange Stability," *Oxford Economic Papers,* VI (April 1942), pp. 57–75, cf. also J. J. Polak, "Exchange Depreciation and International Monetary Stability," *Review of Economics and Statistics*, XXIX (1947), p. 178, for an adaptation of Brown's formula.
5. Joan Robinson, *Essays in the Theory of Employment* (Oxford, 1947, 2nd Edition), pp. 142, 143.
6. C. Bresciani-Turroni, "The Purchasing Power Parity Doctrine," *L'Egypte Contemporaine,* xxv (1934), pp. 433–464; Jacob Viner, *Studies in the Theory of International Trade* (New York, 1937), pp. 539 ft; Fritz Machlup, "The Theory of Foreign Exchanges," *Economica,* vi (November 1939), pp. 375–397, and vii (February 1940), pp. 1–15.

Great care must be exercised, however, in making this transition. For the new demand and supply curves for foreign exchange and the Marshallian curves as transposed by Viner will coincide precisely only on the assumption of constant costs for the production of both E- and G-bales. Only in this case will a change of the exchange rate result in an exactly equivalent change of the terms of trade. If the elasticities of supply of E- or of G-bales are not infinite so that prices rise in the devaluing country and/or fall in the rest of the world, the change in the terms of trade will be smaller than the change of the exchange rate.

In the following note we shall operate with demand curves for foreign exchange which will be so defined as to take account of supply and cost conditions. If, for example, the shape of the demand curve for foreign exchange indicates at a certain point that the demand will be reduced by 19% as the result of a rise in the price of the foreign currency by 10%, this does not involve any definite assumption as to the foreign supply elasticity. Such a situation may result from a decrease of 19% of the quantity purchased abroad at constant prices or from a decrease of only 10% of the quantity purchased combined with a fall of foreign prices by 10% or from many other combinations of fall in foreign prices and fall in demand. The same considerations hold for foreigners' demand for the domestic currency and, therefore, for the supply of foreign exchange. It is clear, therefore, that an analysis taking into account only the elasticities of demand for *foreign exchange*—as distinct from elasticities of demand for imports and exports in volume terms—does not necessarily rest on the assumption of constant costs or of infinite supply elasticities.

We adopt the following notation:

I and E are the values of imports and of exports of the devaluing country expressed in foreign exchange.

I' and E' are the same imports and exports expressed in domestic currency;

r is the rate of exchange giving the number of units of domestic currency necessary to acquire one unit of foreign currency.

$r' = \frac{1}{r}$ is the number of units of foreign currency necessary to acquire a unit of domestic currency.

We can then define (a) the downward sloping demand functions for foreign exchange (imports) and domestic currency (exports)

$$(1) \quad I = f(r)$$
$$(2) \quad E' = g(r')$$

and (b) the corresponding demand elasticities[7]

$$(3) \quad t_I = -\frac{dI}{dr} \cdot \frac{r}{I} = \frac{dI}{dr'} \cdot \frac{r'}{I}$$

for imports, and

$$(4) \quad t_E = -\frac{dE'}{dr'} \cdot \frac{r'}{E'} = \frac{dE'}{dr} \cdot \frac{r}{E'}$$

for exports.

We also have

$$(5) \quad I' = I \cdot r = r \cdot f(r)$$
$$(6) \quad E = E' \cdot r' = r' \cdot g(r')$$

We shall now express the changes in imports and exports upon a small change in the exchange rate in terms of the elasticities.[8] First, in foreign exchange, we obtain by differentiating (6)

7. Since we can write $\frac{dI}{dr} = \frac{dI}{dr'} \cdot \frac{dr'}{dr} = \frac{dI}{dr'} \cdot [-\frac{1}{r^2}]$ · the second equation of (4) is explained analogously.
8. As point elasticities will be used, our results will be strictly derived only for the case of an infinitesimal devaluation. However, the author has convinced himself that the

$$(7)\quad \frac{dE}{dr'} = r' \cdot \frac{dE'}{dr'} + E'$$
$$= E'\left(\frac{dE'}{dr'} \cdot \frac{r'}{E'} + 1\right)$$
$$= \frac{E}{r'}\,(1 - t_E) \text{ and, from (3)}$$
$$(8)\quad \frac{dI}{dr'} = \frac{I}{r'} \cdot t_I$$

Similarly, in domestic currency, we obtain by differentiating (5)

$$(9)\quad \frac{dI'}{dr} = r \cdot \frac{dI}{dr} + I$$
$$= I\left(\frac{dI}{dr} \cdot \frac{r}{I} + 1\right)$$
$$= I\,(1 - t_I) \text{ and, from (4),}$$
$$(10)\quad \frac{dE'}{dr} = E \cdot t_E$$

From expressions (7) to (10) it is quite clear that, provided the demand curves are negatively sloped, an unfavourable effect of devaluation on the foreign balance[9] can originate only from inelastic exports while an unfavourable effect of devaluation on the domestic balance can only stem from an inelastic domestic demand for imports.

For the foreign balance to improve upon devaluation, the certain decrease in imports must be larger than the possible decrease in exports:

$$\frac{dI}{dr'} > \frac{dE}{dr'};$$

use of the proper arc elasticities leaves the results unchanged for the case of finite devaluation, but makes necessary rather unwieldy algebra.

9. In the following, the terms "foreign balance" or "domestic balance" are used as convenient short expressions for "balance on current account in terms of foreign exchange" or "balance on current account in terms of domestic currency." The terms "imports" and "exports" as used here are defined to include current invisible payments and receipts.

while the domestic balance will improve upon devaluation as long as the certain increase in exports is larger than the possible increase in imports:

$$\frac{dE'}{dr} > \frac{dI'}{dr}.$$

Substituting from our previous result, we obtain

$$t_I \cdot \frac{I}{r'} > \frac{E}{r'}(1 - t_E) \text{ or}$$

$$(11) \quad \frac{I}{E} \cdot t_I + t_E > 1$$

as the condition for the foreign balance to improve upon devaluation,[10] and

$$E \cdot t_E > I(1 - t_I) \text{ or}$$

$$(12) \quad t_I + \frac{E}{I} \cdot t_E > 1$$

as the corresponding condition for the domestic balance.

A third inequality is yielded by the condition that the ratio of exports to imports be increased by devaluation. This condition, which is the same whether trade is expressed in domestic or foreign currency, is fulfilled when we have:

$$\frac{dE'}{dr} \div \frac{dI'}{dr} > \frac{E'}{I'}.$$

Substituting from (9) and (10), we obtain

10. Or, of course, to deteriorate upon appreciation of the exchange rate.

$$\frac{E \cdot t_E}{I(1 - t_I)} > \frac{E'}{I'} \text{ or}$$

$$(13) \quad t_E + t_I > 1$$

as the condition for the ratio of exports to imports to increase upon devaluation.

Our results permit the following conclusions:

(a) The "Marshall-Lerner" condition for devaluation to have a favourable effect on the trade balance (sum of the two elasticities larger than unity) holds only when imports are equal to exports. Only in this case do the two first conditions coincide with the third. When this is not the case, the formula expresses the condition for the *ratio* of exports to imports to improve.

(b) When imports and exports are not equal, two different conditions obtain, one for the balance expressed in foreign exchange, another for the balance expressed in domestic currency. In the case of an import (export) surplus, the sum of the two elasticities can be considerably below (above) unity and a favourable (unfavourable) effect on the trade balance as expressed in foreign exchange might still obtain. The exactly opposite proposition holds for the balance expressed in domestic currency.

(c) When elasticities are considered as given, the effect of devaluation on the trade balance expressed in foreign exchange will be the more favourable, the greater the relative import surplus before devaluation. The opposite holds for the effect of devaluation on the trade balance expressed in domestic currency. When imports exceed exports, the more stringent condition for a favourable effect of devaluation is the one relating to the balance expressed in domestic currency; when exports exceed imports, the more stringent condition is the one relating to the balance expressed in foreign exchange.

(d) It follows from the previous point that when imports exceed exports it is possible for devaluation to have a favourable effect on the foreign exchange balance, but an unfavourable effect on the domestic currency balance; this is intuitively evident, but we can now state precisely when this will happen.

Since (12), the condition for a favourable effect of devaluation on the domestic balance, can also be written

$$\frac{I}{E}t_I + t_E > \frac{I}{E},$$

the necessary and sufficient condition for an unfavourable effect on the domestic balance simultaneously with a favourable effect on the foreign balance is

$$(14)\quad \frac{I}{E} > \frac{I}{E}t_I + t_E > 1$$

which obviously can take place only when there is an import surplus. Similarly, the condition for devaluation having an unfavourable effect on the foreign balance and a favourable effect on the domestic balance is

$$(15)\quad \frac{E}{I} > t_I + \frac{E}{I}t_E > 1$$

which can be true only when there is an export surplus.

(e) The condition for the export-import *ratio* to improve upon devaluation is intermediate between the two export-import *balance* conditions since we have necessarily

$$(16)\quad \frac{I}{E}t_I + t_E \lesseqgtr t_I + t_E \lesseqgtr t_I + \frac{E}{I}t_E,$$

the upper signs applying when imports are smaller than exports and vice versa.

Thus it is possible for the domestic balance to deteriorate upon devaluation, for the foreign balance to improve while, at the same time, the export-import ratio would remain unchanged, as shown in the following example:

	Imports	Exports	Domestic Balance	Foreign Balance	Export-Import Ratio
Before devaluation in both domestic and foreign currency	150	100	50	50	.67
After devaluation in foreign currency	120	80		40	.67
After devaluation in domestic currency	180	120	60		.67

Economic Implications

The conditions which have been derived test the success or failure of devaluation in different fields. There are at least two tasks which devaluation might be and has been called upon to accomplish: to solve balance-of-payments problems and to stimulate domestic income.

It is only the balance expressed in foreign exchange that matters when devaluation is undertaken to meet typical balance-of-payments problems. The habit of evaluating the success of devaluation in this respect by comparing trade or current account balances before and after devaluation in domestic currency can be seriously misleading. It is also reassuring to point out that, insofar as balance-of-payments problems are concerned, the greater the disease (i.e. the pre-devaluation relative import surplus), the likelier it is that devaluation will provide at least a partial cure.

The ratio of exports to imports can serve as a first and very rough approximation to the size of the long-run adjustment problem faced by a country with a chronic balance-of-payments deficit. For the same absolute import surplus will generally be more difficult to eliminate if it represents one-half than if it represents one-tenth of total imports.

While the post-war predominance of balance-of-payments problems requires watching of the balance expressed in foreign exchange and, secondarily, of the ratio of exports to imports, the movements of the balance in domestic currency are not without significance. Income effects of the trade balance depend on its size as measured in domestic currency. An increased import surplus in domestic currency due to devaluation will *ceteris paribus* decrease incomes in the devaluing country, even though the trade balance in terms of foreign exchange might have been improved. It may be noted that in this case, considering two countries A and B, domestic trade balances would become more unfavourable in both A, the devaluing country, and B, the country in whose currency A's balance has become more favourable (and B's own balance therefore more unfavourable). In spite of the improvement of A's foreign exchange position, devaluation would therefore have all-round deflationary income effects.

Expression (12) above shows that inflationary income effects from devaluation are most likely to occur in countries with a surplus on current account. It is true that, because of the availability of more direct and effective devices, devaluation is seldom undertaken merely for its income-generating effect. But when it was so undertaken, the direction of the trade balance again favoured the chances for its success: the balance-of-payments of the one country that has depreciated its currency almost exclusively for purposes of internal pump priming—the United States in 1933–1934—showed a surplus on current account before depreciation.

4

Balanced and Unbalanced Growth

Balanced Growth: A Critique

Is Balance in Demand Required?

The general view of development … must now prove its usefulness in dealing with important issues of development policy. This process can best be started by reviewing some current views and theories.

It is often said that in spite of all our efforts economics has not produced a real theory of development. What is meant by this phrase? Probably that economists have not been able to construct, much less agree on, a single and unbroken chain of causes and effects that would neatly explain the transition from "underdevelopment" to development. While this "failure" is of course only to the credit of economists, it cannot be denied that in comparison with the elaborate constructs of static partial and general equilibrium theory, our dynamics, particularly those dealing with underdeveloped countries, have themselves an "underdeveloped" look. Challenging generalizations and theoretical insights are conspicuously rare in the writings on economic development. Nevertheless, theoretical reasoning has by now been applied to a few closely interrelated problems such as balanced growth and the determination of investment priorities. Both deal essentially with the path to or the design of development, the principal subject matter of the present essay.

Before setting out I think it only fair to warn the reader that I heartily disagree with the "balanced growth" doctrine. In fact, if I may indulge for a moment in some introspective analysis, it was the experience of finding myself instinctively so much at variance with this theory that made me aware of having acquired a distinct outlook on development problems, which it might perhaps be worthwhile to explore systematically.

The theory of balanced growth has several authors and aspects. The principal authors are Rosenstein-Rodan, Nurkse, Lewis, and Scitovsky.[1] In one of its aspects, the theory stresses the need for the different parts of a developing economy to remain in step to avoid supply difficulties. Industry must not get too far ahead of agriculture. Basic facilities in transportation, power, water supply, etc.—the so-called social overhead capital—must be supplied in adequate volume to support and stimulate the growth of industry. We shall have to say something later on about these prescriptions of balance between sectors in the course of growth. But first we shall address ourselves to a version of the theory which is of greater analytical interest.

In this version the requirement of balanced growth is derived from the demand side. It is argued that a new venture—say, a shoe factory—which gets underway by itself in an underdeveloped country is likely to turn into a failure: the workers, employees, and owners of the shoe factory will obviously not buy all of its output, while the other citizens of the country are caught in an "underdevelopment equilibrium" where they are just able jointly to afford their own meagre output. Therefore, it is argued, to make development possible it is necessary to start, *at one and the same time,* a large number of new industries which will be each others' clients through the purchases of their workers, employees, and owners. For this reason, the theory has now also been annexed to the "theory of the big push."[2] A big push could, of course, result from one or a few big projects, or from a large

1. P. N. Rosenstein-Rodan, "Problems of Industrialization of Eastern and South-Eastern Europe," *Economic Journal, 53* (June–Sept. 1943), 205; Ragnar Nurkse, *Problems of Capital Formation* in *Underdeveloped Countries* (Oxford, 1953), ch. I; Tibor Scitovsky, "Two Concepts of External Economies," *Journal of Political Economy*, 62 (April 1954), pp. 143–152; W. A. Lewis, *Theory of Economic Growth,* pp. 274–283. The first two authors stress balance in demand, the latter two balance in supply.
2. Rosenstein-Rodan, "Notes on the Theory of the Big Push," paper submitted to the Rio Roundtable of the International Economic Association, 1957, mimeographed.

number of projects of varying size that dovetail with one another. It is clearly the latter alternative of the "big push" theory that is implied by the theory of balanced growth.

As will be explained below, the theory exists also in a more sophisticated variant, but let us stop here for some basic critical comments.

My principal point is that the theory fails as a theory of *development.* Development presumably means the process of *change* of one type of economy *into* some other more advanced type. But such a process is given up as hopeless by the balanced growth theory which finds it difficult to visualize how the "underdevelopment equilibrium" can be broken into at any one point. The argument is reminiscent of the paradox about the string that is equally strong everywhere and that therefore when pulled cannot break anywhere first: it either will not break at all or must give way everywhere at once. However, as Montaigne pointed out in considering this paradox, its premise "is contrary to nature" for "nothing is ever encountered by us that does not hold some difference however small it may be."[3]

Oblivious of this "difference," the balanced growth theory reaches the conclusion that an entirely new, self-contained modern industrial economy must be superimposed on the stagnant and equally self-contained traditional sector. Say's Law is here made to reign *independently* in both economies. This is not growth, it is not even the grafting of something new *onto* something old; it is a perfectly dualistic pattern of development, akin to what is known to child psychologists as "parallel play." There are indeed instances of this kind of development, but they are usually considered conspicuous failures from both the social and economic points of view: the contrast between the Indian communities of the Peruvian altiplano and the Spanish mestizo economy along the coast comes to mind and so do the much decried enclave-type plantations and mining operations that have been set up in several underdeveloped countries by foreign concerns as perfectly self-contained units, far away from the danger of contamination by the local economy.

Naturally, this is not the picture that was in the minds of the authors of the theory. How can we then explain that they set up so unsatisfactory a model? I suspect the reason is that the very difficulty of the task of development has led them to an escapist solution. How many a Western traveller to an underdeveloped country has been bewildered and dismayed by the ubiquitous poverty and inefficiency, by the immensity of the task, and by the interlocking vicious circles! The

3. *Essays,* Bk. 2, ch. 14.

temptation is strong then to leave all this backwardness alone and to dream of an entirely new type of economy where, in the words of the poet, "tout est ordre et beauté!"

One of the most curious aspects of the theory is the way in which it combines a defeatist attitude towards the capabilities of underdeveloped economies with completely unrealistic expectations about their creative abilities. On the one hand, the conception of the traditional economy as a closed circle dismisses the abundant historical evidence about the piecemeal penetration by industry that competes successfully with local handicraft and by new products which are first imported and then manufactured locally.[4] It also disregards the evidence that, for better or for worse, some products of modern industrial civilization—flashlights, radios, bicycles, or beer—are always found sufficiently attractive to make people stop hoarding, restrict traditional consumption, work harder, or produce more for the market in order to acquire them. But, on the other hand, a people that is assumed to be unable to do any of these things and that is therefore entirely uninterested in change and satisfied with its lot is then expected to marshal sufficient entrepreneurial and managerial ability to set up at the same time a whole flock of industries that are going to take in each others' output! For this is of course the major bone that I have to pick with the balanced growth theory: its application requires huge amounts of precisely those abilities which we have identified as likely to be in very limited supply in underdeveloped countries. It is altogether inconceivable that a one-floor economy could set up such a "second floor" with its own forces or even with limited help from abroad; without thorough foreign colonization the task would seem to be hopeless. As Singer writes: "The advantages of multiple development may make interesting reading for economists, but they are gloomy news indeed for the underdeveloped countries. The initial resources for simultaneous developments on many fronts are generally lacking."[5] In other

4. Viner, in a paper prepared for the Rome Congress of the International Economic Association in 1956 ("Stability and Progress: The Problems of the Poor Countries"), has pointed out that from the demand point of view balanced growth is not required whenever a new activity is either cost-reducing rather than output-increasing, or import-replacing or export-oriented. His first category is actually too restrictive, for output-increasing activities can also be introduced in isolation if the outputs are new and highly desired products so that their availability leads to an increase in the demand for income. See, on this point, J. J. Spengler, "Product-Adding vs. Product-Replacing Innovations," *Kyklos, 3* (1957), 249–280. Cf. also Ch. 7.
5. Singer, "Economic Progress in Underdeveloped Countries," *Social Research*, March 1949, pp. 7–8.

words, if a country were ready to apply the doctrine of balanced growth, then it would not be underdeveloped in the first place.

It is possible that the theory of balanced growth has been inspired by a variant of the Keynesian analysis of the slump.[6] In a situation of underemployment equilibrium, the rationale for government intervention may be put as follows: an isolated act of increasing production by a single firm is not likely to be "validated" by the market since the demand that is generated by the increase in production and its multiplier effects is not going to converge on the output of the firm; what is needed to fulfil optimistic expectations and therefore to bring such expectations about is a simultaneous stepping up of production by many firms. This simultaneity in turn can be achieved only if a substantial increase in consumer spending induced by fiscal policy provides guideposts to manufacturers and leads to a generalized recovery of output.

The balanced growth doctrine is now seen to be essentially the application of underdevelopment of a therapy originally devised for an underemployment situation. During the cyclical upswing, a balanced recovery of economic activity is indeed possible—for the industries, machines, managers, and workers, as well as the consumption habits, are all there, only waiting to resume their temporarily suspended functions and roles. In a state of underdevelopment this is obviously not so, and a simultaneous solution is therefore out of reach whether or not the government lends a helping hand.

The last clause is important. For the balanced growth doctrine is usually invoked to provide a justification for centralized governmental direction and coordination of the development process. But this justification is hardly convincing. A task that private enterprise or market forces are unable to handle does not ipso facto become ideally suited to performance by public authorities. We must recognize that there are tasks that simply exceed the capabilities of a society, no matter to whom they are being entrusted. Balanced growth in the sense of simultaneous multiple development would seem to be one of them.[7]

6. Domar, "Investment and Monopolies" in *Income, Employment and Public Policy* (New York, 1948), pp. 49–57, and W. J. Baumol, *Welfare Economics and the Theory of the State* (Cambridge, MA, 1952), pp. 96–97.
7. See p. 101.

The Paradox of the Internalization Doctrine

According to the theory of balanced growth which we have discussed so far, the role of the state is to assure that simultaneity of investments in a large variety of enterprises which is believed to be needed to ensure the success of the individual ventures. A more sophisticated version of the doctrine and of the role it assigns to state action analyses the anticipations rather than the possible actions of entrepreneurs. It states that, under a private enterprise system, entrepreneurs in underdeveloped countries will invest far less than is profitable from the point of view of society. The reason is that atomistic private producers cannot appropriate the external economies to which their activity gives rise, or that they cannot foresee the repercussions which will eventually make them into recipients of economies external to other firms but internal to their own.[8] Private profit calculations fatally underestimate actual social benefits. In the opinion of Rosenstein-Rodan, the pessimistic anticipations of the entrepreneurs are correct as long as they remain atomistic producers; in that of Scitovsky, they are incorrect since they are eventually going to be recipients of pecuniary external economies. But the conclusions are similar in both cases. Production must be integrated and centrally planned as though it were taking place in a single "trust," for only in that case are the external economies going to be "internalized" with a consequent upward revision of profit estimates.

In one respect, the theory is no more than a variant of the balanced growth doctrine. It says: if ten projects could be undertaken jointly, lending each other mutual support in demand, any one of them would be more profitable than the same project undertaken in isolation. On the premises stated, this is undoubtedly correct. But it is also true that a country cannot undertake any number of projects just because they would turn out to be profitable *if* it undertook them. At any one time the available developmental skills of a country set some kind of a ceiling on the number of projects that can be undertaken simultaneously.

Nevertheless, if we allow a certain degree of flexibility, it is legitimate to inquire whether centralization of investment decisions would tend to be growth-promoting. Is it really true that the wider the area over which internalization takes place the greater the incentive to invest is going to be? This would be the case if *all* the repercussions of a new venture were going to be favourable. However, if the repercussions include losses (pecuniary external diseconomies), they will

8. The former situation is described by Rosenstein-Rodan, the latter by Scitovsky. For references, see p. 92, n. 1.

ordinarily be internalized along with the gains and it is no longer certain where we will come out.[9]

The case for centralized investment planning as growth-promoting per se would of course be entirely convincing if it permitted production to be organized in such a way that *only external economies were internalized* while all the external diseconomies and social costs resulting from new ventures remained strictly external to the central authority or were negligible. In this eventuality we would indeed obtain a highly dynamic system, but the question is: can it be done? Here again, the image that was in the minds of the authors of the "internalization" doctrine must have been that of a backward economic sector which would be left pretty much alone, and a brave new sector to be built from the ground up and in isolation; in this fashion, all those who might possibly suffer losses in the course of the development process are effectively assumed away. We do not exclude the possibility that the picture may be fairly realistic in certain special situations such as the reconstruction of an economy devastated by war, or the development of *undeveloped* regions and open spaces through colonization schemes: here the repercussions on existing productive activities may be a small matter compared to that mutual interdependence of the new activities which makes joint planning essential. But in general economic development means transformation rather than creation *ex novo:* it brings disruption of traditional ways of living, of producing, and of doing things, in the course of which there have always been many losses; old skills become obsolete, old trades are ruined, city slums mushroom, crime and suicide multiply, etc. etc. And to these social costs many others must be added, from air pollution to unemployment, so much so that a whole book has recently been devoted to their detailed analysis.[10]

The paradoxical character of the internalization doctrine is now becoming apparent. Assumption of responsibility by the state in the economic field has most frequently been urged, not to provide more impetus to development through the adding up of all the gains, but to *introduce some of the social costs into the economic calculus* and thus to temper the ruthlessness and destructiveness of capitalist development. Presumably the advocates of this course thought that some sacrifice in the speed of the process of creative destruction would be well worth while if it could be made a bit less destructive of material, cultural, and spiritual values. And, admittedly, a major difficulty for the speedy industrialization of today's

9. In the paper cited on p. 94, n. 4, Viner also makes the point that external diseconomies must be taken into account.

10. K. William Kapp, *The Social Costs of Private Enterprise,* Cambridge, MA, 1950.

underdeveloped countries consists precisely in the fact that they are not prepared to incur those social costs that were so spectacularly associated with the process during the early nineteenth century in Western Europe. They are forcing their young entrepreneurial class (as well as their taxpayers in general) to internalize a good portion of these costs through advanced social security, minimum wage, and collective bargaining legislation, through subsidized low-cost housing and similar "welfare state" measures.

Unbalanced Growth: An Espousal

Is Balance in Supply Required?

We have just criticized the idea that development must take place simultaneously in many activities to provide the element of "mutual support" that alone will make it possible to clear the market of the newly produced goods. Having discarded this "pure" theory of balanced growth we must still consider a far less rigorous version, one that insists that if growth is not to be stunted the various sectors of an economy will have to grow jointly in some (not necessarily identical) proportion; no sector should get too far out of line, not because of demand but because of supply or "structural" considerations. For instance, if secondary industry grows, the food and raw material input needed by the workers and the machines will go up; if some of these requirements are imported, then an increase in exports is necessary, etc. etc.

In this form, the balanced growth theory is essentially an exercise in retrospective comparative statics. If we look at an economy that has experienced growth at two different points in time, we will of course find that a great many parts of it have pushed ahead: industry and agriculture, capital goods and consumer goods industries, cars on the road and highway mileage—each at its own average annual rate of increase. But surely the individual components of the economy will not actually have grown at these rates throughout the period under review. Just as on the demand side the market can absorb "unbalanced" advances in output because of cost-reducing innovations, new products, and import substitution, so we can have isolated forward thrusts on the supply side as inputs are redistributed among users through price changes, and at the cost of some temporary shortages and disequilibria in the balance-of-payments or elsewhere. In fact, development has of course proceeded in this way, with growth being communicated from the leading sectors of the economy to the followers, from one industry to another, from one firm to another. In other words, the balanced growth that is revealed by the two still photographs taken at two different points in time is the end result of a series of uneven advances of one sector followed by the catching-up of other sectors. If the catching-up overreaches its goal, as it often does, then the stage is set for further advances elsewhere. The advantage of this kind of seesaw advance over "balanced growth," where every activity expands perfectly in step with every other, is that it leaves considerable scope to *induced* investment decisions and therefore economizes our principal scarce resource, namely, genuine decision-making.

Classical economics, while not taking so positive a view of the imbalances of the growth process, at least was never particularly concerned about them because it relied on prices to signal, and on the profit motive to eliminate rapidly and reliably, any structural disequilibria that might arise in the course of growth. The critics of classical economics, on the other hand, have always pointed to cases in which these "market forces" would not act with adequate strength and speed. Having thus convinced themselves that the adjustment mechanism is beset with virtually insuperable obstacles, some of the critics naturally enough took the defeatist view that growth has to be balanced from the start or cannot take place at all.

This counsel of perfection is not only impractical but also uneconomical. We need not sacrifice the valuable development mechanisms brought into play by unbalanced growth, especially if we go beyond the overly narrow view of the adjustment process that has long dominated economic literature.

Tradition seems to require that economists argue forever about the question whether, in any disequilibrium situation, *market forces acting alone* are likely to restore equilibrium. Now this is certainly an interesting question. But as social scientists we surely must address ourselves also to the broader question: is the disequilibrium situation likely to be corrected at all, by market or nonmarket forces, or by both acting jointly? *It* is *our contention that nonmarket forces are not necessarily less "automatic" than market forces.* Certainly the almost monotonous regularity with which interventionist economists have come forward—and with which authorities have acted—when the market forces did not adequately perform their task testifies to the fact that we do not have to rely exclusively on price signals and profit-maximizers to save us from trouble.[11]

11. Some traditional equilibrium mechanisms were unable to dispense entirely with help from agents outside the market. Thus, the restoration of balance-of-payments equilibrium and the damping of the business cycle was, for a long time, made to depend on correct manipulation by the central bank of the rate of interest, in reaction to

The case of unbalanced growth provides a good illustration. When supply difficulties arise in the course of uneven progress in sectors—such as education and public utilities—where private enterprise is not operating, strong pressures are felt by public authorities to "do something"; and since the desire for political survival is at least as strong a motive-force as the desire to realize a profit, we may ordinarily expect some corrective action to be taken.[12]

There is no implication here that any disequilibrium whatsoever will be resolved by some combination of market and nonmarket forces. But if a community cannot generate the "induced" decisions and actions needed to deal with the supply disequilibria that arise in the course of uneven growth, then I can see little reason for believing that it will be able to take the set of "autonomous" decisions required by balanced growth. In other words, if the adjustment mechanism breaks down altogether, this is a sign that the community rejects economic growth as an overriding objective.

The inclusion of probable reactions of nonmarket forces not only serves to make economic analysis more realistic. It also protects us against a fallacious chain of reasoning that is fairly common in development economics and of which the doctrine of balanced growth is itself an excellent illustration. In this reasoning, one first selects some objective of economic policy that seems desirable enough; then one proves that the objective cannot be attained through the operation of market forces; and one concludes that state action surely will bring the objective about. But this conclusion is clearly a non sequitur. The fact that private entrepreneurs will be unable or unwilling to do certain jobs which we would like to

developing disequilibria. But this role of the central banker has usually been rationalized as an exception to the rule; and in the minds of many economists, the central banker became a sort of honorary member of the market forces.

12. Sectoral imbalances have of course been a conspicuous feature of Russian economic development. The resulting difficulties have been described in Soviet literature as "nonantagonistic contradictions" which are not only admitted to exist but apparently considered to perform a useful signalling and corrective function: "The characteristic trait of our difficulties and contradictions consists precisely in that they themselves indicate to us the basis and the means for their solution." V. Kozlovsky, *Antagonisticheskie i neantagonisticheskie protivorechiia* (Moscow, Moskovskii Rabochii, 1954), p. 70. These "nonantagonistic" contradictions which are successfully overcome by administrative action of the Communist party and the government are then opposed to the "antagonistic" contradictions which are said to afflict capitalism and which can be resolved only by revolution.

see done does not in itself ensure that the government can handle them. We must examine whether these jobs are likely to be performed satisfactorily by public authorities, which function after all in the same society as the entrepreneurs.[13]

Development as a Chain of Disequilibria

As has been shown, the balanced growth theory results from comparing the initial point of underdevelopment equilibrium with another point at which development will practically have been accomplished. A certain impatience with the process that lies between these two points—that is, with the process of development—is shown by the following quotation from a well-known article by Scitovsky:

Profits are a sign of disequilibrium; and the magnitude of profits under free competition may be regarded as a rough index of the degree of disequilibrium.

> Profits in a freely competitive industry lead to investment in that industry; and the investment in turn tends to eliminate the profits that have called it forth. Thus far, then, investment tends to bring equilibrium nearer. The same investment, however, may raise … profits in other industries; and to this extent it leads away from equilibrium …. The profits of industry B created by the lower price for factor A, call for investment and expansion in industry B one result of which will be an increase in industry B's demand for industry A's product. This in turn will give rise to profits and call for further investment and expansion in A; and equilibrium is reached only when successive doses of investment and expansion in the two industries have led to the simultaneous elimination of investment in both. It is only at this stage that … the amount of investment profitable in industry A is also the socially desirable amount. The amount is clearly greater than that which is profitable at the first stage before industry B has made its adjustment. We can conclude, therefore, that when an investment gives rise to pecuniary external economies, its private profitability understates its social desirability".[14]

To my mind, the first part of this passage is a most pertinent portrayal of how development is set and kept in motion, but Scitovsky, considering the proceedings

13. Much the same point is made forcefully by Bauer and Yamey with respect to governmental promotion of industrial enterprise: "A general lack of enterprise in a country does not in itself set up a presumption of such initiative in the public sector," *The Economics of Underdeveloped Countries* (Chicago, 1957), p. 161. However, I do not follow the authors in the conclusions which they draw for the role of governments in economic development.
14. "Two Concepts of External Economies," cit. pp. 148–149.

he describes unnecessarily laborious, proposes to short-circuit them and to reach in a single jump a new point of equilibrium where the "elimination of investment" has been accomplished. But, actually, development is a lengthy process during which interaction of the kind described by Scitovsky takes place not only between two industries, but up and down and across the whole of an economy's input-output matrix, and for many decades. What point in such a virtually infinite sequence of repercussions are we supposed to shoot at? Which intermediate expansion stages ought we to skip, and which ordinarily successive stages ought we to combine? Some skipping or combining may be possible, but with no more than the modest objective of speeding up development here and there. In general, development policy must concern itself with the judicious setting up of the kind of sequences and repercussions so well described by Scitovsky, rather than with any attempt to suppress them. In other words, our aim must be to *keep alive* rather than to eliminate the disequilibria of which profits and losses are symptoms in a competitive economy. If the economy is to be kept moving ahead, the task of development policy is to maintain tensions, disproportions, and disequilibria. That nightmare of equilibrium economics, the endlessly spinning cobweb, is the *kind* of mechanism we must assiduously look for as an invaluable help in the development process.

Therefore, the sequence that "leads away from equilibrium" is precisely an ideal pattern of development from our point of view: for each move in the sequence is induced by a previous disequilibrium and in turn creates a new disequilibrium that requires a further move. This is achieved by the fact that the expansion of industry A leads to economies external to A but appropriable by B, while the consequent expansion of B brings with it economies external to B but subsequently internal to A (or C for that matter), and so on. At each step, an industry takes advantage of external economies created by previous expansion, and at the same time creates new external economies to be exploited by other operators.[15]

In Scitovsky's example, these external economies are essentially caused by production complementarities of one type or another, and we are thus returning to the complementarity effect of investment as a mechanism that would make investment … decisions particularly easy or compelling. We were then speaking of the investment-promoting character of investment, not indirectly through

15. Note that the private profitability falls short of the social desirability of any venture only when its "output" of external economies exceeds its "input" derived from other ventures.

additional savings out of the incomes created by investment, but through direct contact or "contagion."

Technical complementarity in the strict sense is usually defined as a situation where an increase in the output of commodity A lowers the marginal costs of producing commodity B. This will happen typically as a result of the following situations:

a. because A is an input of B and is produced under conditions of decreasing costs;
b. because B is an input of A and is itself produced under conditions of decreasing costs;
c. because A and B are joint products (or because B is a by-product of A) and are produced under decreasing costs.

Because situations such as these have long been familiar to economists, complementarity is usually associated with economies of scale.[16] But there is no need for so restrictive an interpretation. We can define complementarity as any situation where an increase in the demand for commodity A and the consequent increase in its output call forth an increased demand for commodity B at its existing price. This happens not only when the connection between the two commodities is via the production process. The connection between A and B may also arise because the increased *use* of A leads to greater demand for B. We are not thinking here of situations where A and B *must* be employed jointly in fixed proportions. In this case it would not make much sense to say that demand for A and the subsequent increase in its output provide an incentive for the production of B, as it is rather the demand for the good or service into which A and B enter jointly which explains the demand for both products. This is the familiar case of derived demand. But there are many situations in the course of economic development where the increased availability of one commodity does not *compel* a *simultaneous* increase in supply of another commodity, but *induces slowly,* through a loose kind of complementarity in use, an upward shift in its demand schedule. The phenomenon has been described under the apt heading "entrained want";[17] Veblen observed it

16. W. Fellner, *Trends and Cycles in Economic Activity* (New York, 1956), pp. 199–200. N. S. Buchanan and H. S. Ellis, *Approaches to Economic Development* (New York, 1955), pp. 279–280.
17. The term is used by H. G. Barnett in *Innovation: The Basis of Cultural Change* (New York, McGraw-Hill, 1953), pp. 148–151, with the exact meaning we have in mind here: "The fulfilment of one need establishes conditions out of which others emerge … In most instances it is impossible for people to foresee [these emergent

long ago and effectively summed it up when he said that "invention is the mother of necessity" rather than vice versa.

An example of the rigid type of complementarity in use (best treated as derived demand) is cement and reinforcing steel rods in the construction, say, of downtown office buildings. Examples of the looser, "developmental" type of complementarity (entrained want) can be found in the way in which the existence of the new office buildings strengthens demand for a great variety of goods and services: from modern office furniture and equipment (still fairly rigid), to parking and restaurant facilities, stylish secretaries, and eventually perhaps to more office buildings as the demonstration effect goes to work on the tenants of the older buildings. Here again, failure to arrange for all of these complementary items from the start could be denounced as "poor planning" which ought to be avoided by centralized decision-making. But, just as in the case quoted by Scitovsky, an attempt to telescope the whole process would be futile because of the virtually infinite number of complementarity repercussions, and because of the uncertainty about a good many of them; moreover, such an attempt would miss the point that the profitable opportunities that arise, as a result of the initial development move constitute powerful and valuable levers for subsequent development which are to be carefully nursed, maintained at some optimum level, and if necessary created consciously rather than eliminated.[18]

The common feature of the various complementarity situations is that, as a result of the increase in the output of A, the profitability of the production of B is being increased because B's marginal costs drop, or because its demand schedule shifts upward, or because both forces act jointly.

wants] even if they try ... Entrained wants are a consistent feature of motivational stresses for cultural change" (p. 148).

18. This does not mean that when new buildings are put up one should refrain from planning for new parking facilities. Development itself constantly extends the range of complementarities that are rigidly compelled and necessarily simultaneous: the optional equipment of one period becomes the standard equipment of the next, as a result of social and cultural pressures and needs rather than because of purely technological factors. The process of turning loose complementarities into rigid ones is often called "integrated planning" which is then opposed to "improvisation." These terms, particularly dear to city planners, are quite misleading in their antagonism. "Integrated planning" takes care of *a few* of the *known* repercussions of a development move rather than letting them take care of themselves as best they can independently of that move. But it certainly can never hope to comprehend them all.

Put even more generally, complementarity means that increased production of A will lead to *pressure* for increasing the available supply of B. When B is a privately produced good or service, this pressure will lead to imports or larger domestic production of B because it will be in the *interest* of traders and producers of B to respond to the pressure. When B is not privately produced, the pressure does not transmute itself into pecuniary self-interest, and will take the form of political pressure for the provision of B. This is the case for such public services as law and order, education, satisfactory monetary and banking arrangements, highways, water, electric power, etc. Complementarity then manifests itself in the form of complaints about shortages, bottlenecks, and obstacles to development. Action in this case does not take place through the operation of the profit motive, but through group pressures on public authorities and agencies.

A Definition of Induced Investment

The complementarity effect provides us with a new concept of *induced* investment which is more meaningful for underdeveloped economies than the conventional one, that is, investment that is directly related to past increases in output. For this conventional concept of induced investment has validity mainly for countries with a fully built-up industrial and agricultural structure where increases in demand lead to increases in capacity designed to keep marginal costs from entering the area in which they would begin to rise steeply. The required adjustments may cover many industries, but are ordinarily small in any one year in relation to existing capacity. The big dynamic changes in developed economies are expected to originate in "autonomous" investment.

This is not a realistic picture of the growth process in underdeveloped economies. Here an increase in the demand for beer, for example, may lead not only to the expansion of existing brewing capacity but, at a certain point, to the *start* of domestic production of bottles, of barley cultivation, and to a whole chain of similar repercussions. In other words, the investment that is induced by complementarity effects may help to bring about a real transformation of an underdeveloped economy.

One of the difficulties of the concept of induced investment in its traditional meaning is its precise delimitation. The reason for which investment is undertaken is not that demand has increased in the past, but that the experience of the past is taken as a guide to the future. In other words, investment is undertaken because for one reason or another the ensuing output is expected to find a market.

But looked at in this way, all investment is obviously induced and the distinction between induced and autonomous investment becomes untenable or arbitrary.[19]

At first blush, it might seem that the same flaw, in an even more pronounced form, affects the distinction we have drawn. Is not every investment "induced" in the sense that it complements some other existing investment? With the generously wide definition of complementarity which we have given, cannot every step in the development of a country be considered 'as called forth by the preceding steps in a never-ending series of "inducements"? Have we then perhaps explained too much?

At this point we may, however, revert to our earlier discussion of external economies: it was then shown that new projects often appropriate external economies created by preceding ventures and create external economies that may be utilized by subsequent ones. Some projects create more external economies than they appropriate and therefore their private profitability falls short of their social desirability. It is therefore to be expected that the opposite situation can also be encountered—namely, ventures that have a large "input" of external economies and a much smaller "output." The projects thus favoured represent the class of "easy-to-exploit" investment opportunities which always abound in newly developing economies.

We can then define our concept of induced investment by the provision that the projects that fall into this category must be *net* beneficiaries of external economies.

This definition makes induced investment look very much like the multiplier: each investment is conceived as inducing a series of subsequent investments and there is an element of convergence as the "output" of external economies diminishes at each step. This, however, does not necessarily mean that the investments themselves converge; there is no rigid connection between the size of an investment and its net "input" of external economies, although some association between these two magnitudes may be expected to exist.[20]

Theoretically, our definition of induced investment is, I believe, more satisfactory than the conventional one and it is far more relevant in the context of development problems. Nevertheless it is extremely difficult to give empirical content to the concept and we shall therefore not attempt to give our reasoning more rigor than it possesses; we shall continue to speak of investment inducing

19. Fellner, *Trends,* p. 319.
20. See Ch. 6 [of *The Strategy*], the concept of satellite industries.

other investments and shall simply be aware that, there are widely varying degrees of "inducements."

An ideal situation obtains when, as was pointed out in the last section, one disequilibrium calls forth a development move which in turn leads to a similar disequilibrium and so on ad infinitum. If such a chain of unbalanced growth sequences could be set up, the economic policy-makers could just watch the proceedings from the sidelines. It may be noticed that in this situation private profitability and social desirability are likely to coincide, not because of the absence of external economies, but because "input" and "output" of external economies are the same for each successive venture.

In practice, growth sequences are likely to exhibit tendencies towards convergence or potentialities of divergence, and development policy is largely concerned with the prevention of too rapid convergence and with the promotion of the possibilities of divergence.

One more point. The induced investment defined thus far is a gross quantity. In the previous chapter, we made much of the point that development brings with it external diseconomies as well as economies. The external diseconomies brought into the world by new investments refer primarily to the damage done to existing industrial or handicraft establishments by the introduction of modern methods and products. It must be granted, therefore, that new investments will hold back reinvestment in these establishments while leading to complementary capital formation elsewhere in the economy. The effect is, however, quite asymmetrical, as the greatest damage that new investment will cause to pre-existing equipment consists in failure to maintain and replace that equipment. Thus, inasmuch as the external diseconomies of new investments result in negative investment, this destructive effect is likely to be spread over several years; whereas the positive effect of the external economies leads at once to a demand for the total capital requirements of whatever ventures are going to be "induced." Because of this asymmetry, the investment-reducing effect of new investments resulting from competition and substitution effects seems unlikely to match the investment-creating effects of complementarity except where competitive industries are strong and complementarity effects rather weak. This latter situation may be characteristic of the textile industry and may account for the fact that in several underdeveloped countries the setting up of this industry has failed to provide the necessary spark for further development.

Some Related Points of View

The way in which investment leads to other investment through complementarities and external economies is an invaluable "aid" to development that must be consciously utilized in the course of the development process. It puts special pressure behind a whole group of investment decisions and augments thereby that scarce and non-economisable resource of underdeveloped countries, the ability to make new investment decisions.

The manner in which an investment project affects the availability of this resource is for us the principal measure of its contribution to further development. We shall refer briefly to some development … theories that are related to the point of view presented here.

One of the principal characteristics of our approach has been the direct connection we have established between the investment of one period and that of the next. The complementarity effect "calls forth" new investment; to the extent that savings are determined by this process, they play a perfectly passive role. This situation is very similar to the one recently described by Domar in his analysis of a growth model elaborated thirty years ago by the Russian economist Feldman. The essence of this model is the division of total investment into investment designed to expand the output of consumers' goods on the one hand, and of producers' goods, on the other. Domar shows that once this division is made "the propensity to save has no life of its own so to speak and is completely determined by the relative productive capacities of the two categories."[21] The limit to investment in the Feldman model as interpreted by Domar is not the ability or propensity to save, but the productive capacity of the investment goods sector. Although the model is admittedly unrealistic, especially for an open economy, it is interesting as an attempt to build a sequence where investment of one period is directly related to the investment of prior periods without the intermediary of the savings ratio.

The rather tormented discussion around an article on investment criteria by Galenson and Leibenstein has yielded a similar line of thought: namely, that savings and reinvestment may depend not only on the productivity of capital but on various other characteristics of the projects in which capital is invested.[22]

21. *Essays on the Theory of Economic Growth* (New York, 1957), p. 236.
22. See O. Eckstein, "Investment Criteria for Economic Development and the Theory of Intertemporal Welfare Economics," *Quarterly Journal of Economics, 71* (Feb. 1957), 66. This article sets up a model where the income streams resulting from different investment projects are affected by *project-specific* savings propensities. Cf. W. Galenson and H. Leibenstein, "Investment Criteria, Productivity and Economic

Although savings out of income are here an important intermediate link in the causal sequence, it is the specific nature of the investment, rather than merely the resulting income flow, that is seen as determining subsequent capital formation.

These are attempts to build generalizations about the required kind and composition of investment into development theory and to establish a closer-than-usual connection between investments of successive periods. However, these results are reached through the use of assumptions that, to my mind, are unnecessarily restrictive. Three other studies come even closer to our viewpoint. First, there is Perroux's concept of the "growth poles" and his incisive description of the growth process as something that is called forth by these poles.[23] Second, mention must be made of the introductory remarks in Svennilson's work on the *Growth and Stagnation of the European Economy,* which come very close to our point of view. Here Svennilson mentions the importance of complementary developments and describes his work as an attempt to overcome the "unhappy division between the cost and price theory on the one hand and the theory of growth and employment on the other."[24] Unfortunately the subsequent analysis, while often ingenious and always interesting, does not entirely fulfil these promises.

Finally, the importance of interindustry interactions because of external economies, economies of scale, and complementarities has been fully recognized by Fellner. He states that these phenomena can account for a rise in the yield of capital even when the latter is growing at a faster rate than other factors of production and in the absence of technological improvements.[25] But Fellner relegates the action of these forces to the almost prehistoric phase during which "primitive economies" accumulate the "initial capital stock" required for growth. From then on, the only offsets to diminishing returns to capital that are admitted are organizational and technological improvements. I believe that the concept of initial capital stock, like that of "prerequisites," is not a particularly useful one, and that complementarity effects are extremely important in offsetting diminishing returns from capital during a protracted period. Perhaps an economy is never quite through creating its "indivisibilities," that is, its complex of complementary economic activities!

Development," ibid., *69* (Aug. 1955), 343–370, and discussions in the November 1956, February and August 1957, and August 1958 issues of the *Journal.* See also p. 126, n. 23.

23. Francois Perroux, "Note sur la notion de 'pole de croissance,' "*Economie appliquée, 8* (Jan–June 1953), 307–320.
24. U. N. Economic Commission for Europe (Geneva, 1954), p. 8.
25. *Trends,* pp. 200 and 341 ff.

5

Efficiency and Growth of the Individual Firm

The Need for Built-In Spurs

We explored the ways in which economic progress is communicated by one sector, one industry, or one firm to another. By thus judging the developmental merit of a project in terms of the likelihood that it will induce a series of other ventures, we have taken it for granted that the project itself is "here to stay." This assumption will be dropped in the present chapter, in which we will inquire into some of the conditions under which new ventures, once established, may be expected to prosper as efficient and dynamic units of the economic system. We are still searching for inducement mechanisms: but instead of gauging the probability that project A will call forth project *B,* we will now be concerned with the manner in which the growth of a given project becomes "self-induced," that is, with its own development path.[1]

1. The terms "project," "firm," "venture," "enterprise" are used interchangeably in this chapter. We are thinking not only of private industrial or commercial firms, but of any economic unit which enjoys a considerable degree of autonomy, whether it is publicly or privately owned and managed.

In any underdeveloped country one can always hear many a—duly embroidered—tale about ventures that were so hastily undertaken and so badly planned that they had to be written off as a total loss while still under construction or shortly thereafter. But more demoralizing even than such obvious failures is the spectacle of enterprises that, after a hopeful start, have stagnated and deteriorated. Examples of such deterioration are always at hand: the pasteurizing plant whose milk one is strongly recommended to boil thoroughly before drinking; the first-class hotel that three months after a triumphant opening has become third-rate; the "supermarket" which slowly takes on again the familiar aspects of the much decried open-air affairs.[2]

The difficulties commonly experienced by new enterprises in underdeveloped countries have often been noted and so has the adverse effect of disappointments and miscarriages on entrepreneurial expectations and therefore on further development. However, Western observers, having diagnosed the disorder, have usually not bothered about ways and means of improving the performance of individual ventures from within, but have looked for efficiency-inducing and survival-guaranteeing pressures from without.

This is in fact what we have done ourselves thus far. We could argue that all that is needed to ensure the success of any venture is for it to represent a link in one of our development sequences. It is clear that the projects that are best at calling forth other ventures are also those that are most likely to do well themselves. Paradoxically, a road that is not travelled is likely to deteriorate sooner than one

2. The present-day interest in economic development has led economic historians to re-examine the early stages of tire industrialization process in Western Europe. In such studies the usual focus is on identifying key factors responsible for this unique instance of successful development. But actually industrialization proceeds in many countries today whether or not they are endowed with all of the factors, attitudes, and beliefs found to have been present in, say, eighteenth century England. Therefore, historical studies of the conditions under which efforts at industrialization have turned out to be abortive may yield more valuable lessons. The attempts by Muhammad Ali to implant textile and other industries in Egypt during his reign (1805–1849) would seem to be an excellent instance. For some intriguing data on this episode, see David S. Landes, "Bankers and Pashas" in *Men in Business,* ed. William Miller (Cambridge, MA, 1952), pp. 23–70; Moustafa Fahmy, *La Révolution de l'industrie en Egypte et ses conséquences sociales au 19° siècle (1800–1850),* Leiden, 1954; and particularly Helen Anne B. Rivlin, *The Agricultural Policy of Muhammad Ali* in *Egypt* (to be published), ch. 7.

that has to support heavy traffic: the former will surely be neglected whereas there is some hope that the latter will be maintained. Similarly, once an industry causes other industries to be established through forward or backward linkage, it will be needed by these industries as a supplier or a market and its chances of survival and continuous expansion will be better than before.

That growth *around* a venture creates favourable conditions for the health and growth of that venture can hardly be doubted. But if we let things go at that we would limit ourselves to one side of a two-way relationship. The successful performance of an individual venture is needed for the launching of complementary projects just as much as the coming into existence of the latter is healthy for the original venture. Moreover, in underdeveloped countries a venture may have to live as a lonely outpost for a considerable time before it is joined by others through linkage effects. And even after it has been joined, it remains severely exposed to the investment-corroding forces … and whose action must now be more fully understood and taken into account.

Any attempt at solving the difficulties of new ventures in underdeveloped countries entirely through pressures from without must appeal to some progressive influence that is supposed to be already at work in the society where the venture operates. But this procedure means that the difficulties with which we are concerned are assumed away rather than solved. A striking instance of this procedure is, as we have seen, the balanced growth theory, which holds that a venture will be successful if it comes into the world as a member of a complex of firms lending each other mutual, complementary support.

A similar criticism must be made of the usefulness in underdeveloped economies of the, in a sense, opposite mechanism that is frequently relied on for "placing the managers … under the proper pressures to perform for society":[3] competition. In developed industrial countries competition, actual or potential, is no doubt powerfully conducive to keeping firms efficient and progressive. But in urging underdeveloped countries to rely on this mechanism, we would again assume away some of the most typical difficulties they face and give them the unrealistic advice to jump over an important stage in their growth—the stage where in many lines the market cannot support more than one firm, where regional monopolies abound because of poor transportation facilities, and where collusive

3. Clark Kerr, "Productivity and Labor Relations," Reprint No. 96, Institute of Industrial Relations (Berkeley, 1957), p. 8.

agreements or strongly entrenched custom hold back the emergence of genuinely competitive marketing.

Thus, complementary and competitive relationships with other firms cannot be relied on exclusively or even primarily to set up effective pressures to perform for the individual firm. Such pressures must also be generated within the firm itself. To understand how this may be achieved it is necessary to review the typical shortcomings that undermine the efficient functioning of many firms in underdeveloped countries. A list of such shortcomings, which is meant to be purely illustrative, would contain the following items:

1. Absence of a sufficiently vigorous "growth mentality," reflected in:
   a. failure to plough back profits adequately, tendency towards "milking" firms;
   b. failure to keep up with technological progress abroad;
   c. preference for a stagnating enterprise that stays "within the family" over expansion that is bought at the cost of partial surrender of control.
2. Difficulties in administration, management, and "human relations," shown in such symptoms as:
   a. excessive centralization of decision-making and inability or unwillingness to delegate authority;
   b. ineffective staff work and coordination;
   c. failure to pay adequate salaries to key personnel in spite of high turnover and recognized scarcity;
   d. failure to impart to subordinates a feeling of participation and spirit of initiative;
   e. neglect of personnel relations and morale;
   f. neglect of public relations.
3. Difficulties in carrying out functions not directly connected with the central production process, evidenced in:
   a. defective advance planning (engineering studies, market research, provision for finance);
   b. defective cost accounting and control in general;
   c. defective maintenance.[4]

4. For some evidence on these points, see U. N. Economic Commission for Latin America, *Labour Productivity of the Cotton Textile Industry in Five Latin American Countries*, New York, 1951; S. D. Mehta, *The Indian Cotton Textile Industry: An Economic Analysis* (Bombay, 1953), pp. 72–85; F. H. Harbison and I. A. Ibrahim,

These deficiencies can be accounted for in several ways. In part, they are of course due to inexperience in the management of large-scale organizations. But one wonders if this is all, in view of the persistence of some of these traits. Several among them (e.g. la, lc, 2a, and 2b) are directly related to the analysis of the development process .... The difficulties in cooperative decision-making ... which were shown to be a major obstacle to development, do of course affect the day-to-day administration of existing firms and ventures as much as, if not more than, their actual promotion. The lack of a vigorous growth mentality and of effective staff work and personnel relations can be viewed as natural concomitants of a management whose principal members do not yet quite believe in the possibility of mutual gains—nonzero sums—in social and economic "games."

In the second place, the pattern of values and attitudes with which underdeveloped countries set out today on the path to modernization and industrialization is probably less suited to the successful accomplishment of these tasks than the pattern which prevailed in Western Europe at the beginning of the Industrial Revolution. Without stirring up the old dispute about the primacy of beliefs and attitudes, it will perhaps be granted that certain values and institutionalized behaviour patterns that are conducive to successful development such as Max Weber's rationality and discipline, Parsons' universalism and functional specificity,[5] or McClelland's achievement motivation[6] must be induced in most of today's underdeveloped countries by the process of development itself, whereas it can be argued that in some Western European countries and the United States these behaviour patterns were already strongly entrenched before the start of the process.

"Some Labor Problems of Industrialization in Egypt," *Annals of the American Academy of Political and Social Science* (Philadelphia, 1956), pp. 114–124. Naturally, these shortcomings can also be found in advanced industrial countries. It is merely suggested here that their relative importance is greater in underdeveloped countries.

5. Talcott Parsons, "The Professions and Social Structure," *Essays in Sociological Theory Pure and Applied* (Glencoe, IL, 1950), pp. 185–199; for an application of these categories to development problems, see Marion J. Levy, "Some Sources of the Vulnerability of the Structures of Relatively Nonindustrialized Societies to those of Highly Industrialized Societies" in *The Progress of Underdeveloped Areas*, B. Hoselitz ed., Chicago, 1952, pp. 113–125.
6. I am referring to the work of David C. McClelland and his associates: cf. also Everett E. Hagen, "The Process of Economic Development", in *Economic Development and Cultural Change*, 5 (April 1957), 202–204.

Finally, we have the special problems of the latecomers. Derived development, as Wallich has called it,[7] is less inspiring a task than it was in the pioneering countries or in those that came later but strained to overtake the pioneers in the shortest possible time. Such ambitions are beyond the horizon of most of today's latecomers. All they can do is tread ploddingly a trail that others have blazed long ago. Moreover, industries are usually established only when their technology has already settled down, and, they are often based on the importation not only of all of the equipment, but also of many semi-finished materials and parts, so that the entrepreneurial function of combining production factors appears to be a comparatively routine one. In fact, the task of adaptation always remains, but is often underestimated just because everything *appears* to be so cut and dried. This is one of the reasons why new ventures are often undertaken without adequate planning and attention to specific environmental factors.

It is even possible that derived development is exposed to some additional, subtle obstacles of a psychological nature. While overtly considerable effort is made in a country to introduce modern methods and techniques, a vague resentment may yet exist at the same time against the new ways, a secret hope that the equipment or the methods will not work out in "our milieu"; and these feelings may well lead to actions that will bring about the unconsciously desired result, namely the breakdown of the newly introduced techniques. Anthropologists have noted the phenomenon of "defensive ignorance" or of "rejection pattern" practised by certain communities that are actively warding off foreign influences.[8] Here we are concerned with a subsequent stage in which ostensibly the new techniques are brought in with eager enthusiasm. But in actuality an *ambivalent* attitude prevails: one expects miracles and at the same time one hopes they won't happen, so that one may say, with a sense of relief: "These foreign contraptions are no good after all." This attitude is most obvious with respect to technical assistance programs. The excessive enthusiasm with which foreign missions and experts are greeted at their arrival in a country is part of this ambivalent pattern: when unreasonable expectations are raised about the possible accomplishments of a mission, the let-down and disappointment which one also hopes for are virtually

7. H. C. Wallich, "Notes toward a Theory of Derived Development," paper prepared for the Havana Meeting of Central Bank Technicians, 1952, to be published in *The Economics of Underdeveloped Countries*, A.N. Agarwala and S.P. Singh eds. Indian Institute of Economic and Social Research, Allahabad.
8. E. Wolf, "Types of Latin American Peasantry," *American Anthropologist*, June 1955, p. 459; and Ralph Beals, "Notes on Acculturation" in *Heritage of Conquest,* p. 229.

guaranteed to follow. In effect, instead of a rejection pattern we have here one of acceptance qualified by (unconscious) sabotage. In the case of modem machinery and equipment, it may account for the defective maintenance, for the inadequate efforts to train and retain skilled mechanics to serve the machines, and even for the neglect of the nontechnical aspects of production. For here again there is a tendency vastly to exaggerate the perfection and self-sufficiency of the machine and to overrate the extent to which it solves all production problems—an attitude that leads to many a breakdown.[9]

It turns out that the difficulties besetting the proper functioning of new enterprises are the same as those that affect their promotion, *plus a few more.* Therefore we have met with a new kind of imbalance likely to arise in underdeveloped countries: at a certain stage of their growth, the ability to *promote* new ventures may outstrip the ability to *run* them efficiently. Herein lies a further justification for undertaking a careful search for mechanisms that will induce efficiency and growth within the new ventures and which will help to minimize and, through learning processes, eradicate the failings that have been noted.

The Maintenance Problem and a Suggested Solution

Up to now we have insisted on certain handicaps of the latecomers; but there are compensating advantages. Even though they are constrained by the availability of natural resources, by the narrowness of their domestic market, and by the techniques developed in the advanced countries, today's developing countries can choose from a far wider variety of ventures and techniques than could the industrial nations. In part it has been this situation that has given rise to the search for *investment criteria.* The discussion started out with the hope of producing a workable formula for development planners anxious to know which of the various

9. Psychoanalysis has shown how a situation of ambivalence is characterized by (a) reaction formation, that is, the fact of showing and feeling consciously the opposite of what is repressed and felt unconsciously, and (b) the return of repressed hostility in some, usually disguised, form with the aim of bringing about the defeat or destruction of the object of ambivalence. The attitude here described—exaggerated enthusiasm and the raising of excessive expectations—realizes both these phenomena jointly, as though to kill two birds with one stone. I am indebted to Dr Samuel P. Hunt for discussing this matter with me.

projects should be selected. But … such hopes were soon to be dashed as the subject became increasingly complex with every new contribution.

Fortunately we are able to sidestep this discussion. Maximization of output is for us a final outcome of successful development rather than a proximate objective; and the criteria we are now looking for are those that will permit us to judge new ventures, products, and processes in terms of their probable contribution to "self-inducement."

The most obvious, but also the most platitudinous advice to give to underdeveloped countries in this connection is to pick only projects whose output is assured of a rapidly growing market. Certainly, the increase in demand is a powerful energizing influence that creates a growth mentality even when there was none in existence to begin with and that places strong pressures on managers to improve the organization of the production process. The expansion of demand leads to growth of the enterprise and thus provides an element of "excitement" and opportunities of advancement for all personnel. Finally, it may also cause competition to appear and would thereby provide a further stimulus to performance.

But actually it is clear that this criterion sins against the rule which we had set ourselves in the last section, namely, that our self-inducement mechanisms, to be genuine, must not appeal to progressive forces that act on the firm from the outside and thereby make everything easy. This is exactly what we have done by assuming the existence of a strong and growing demand somewhere. The kind of question we are interested in here is rather: given potential demand of equal strength in several lines, which kind of undertaking will be best able to elicit this demand and develop it further through the quality of its product, the shrewdness of its distribution and publicity, and in general the excellence of its management? More generally, given the difficulties already discussed, *what are the kinds of jobs underdeveloped countries are likely to be particularly good (or bad) at?*

We shall use induction in attempting to answer this question and look closely first at one of the difficulties: the lack of proper maintenance. This is perhaps one of the most characteristic failings of underdeveloped countries and one that is spread over the whole economic landscape. Eroding soils, stalled trucks, leaking roofs, prematurely run-down machines, unsafe bridges, clogged-up irrigation ditches—all testify to the same pervasive and paradoxical trait: the inadequate care for existing capital in capital-poor countries.

The basic difficulty about maintenance of capital—as opposed to operation on the one hand and to repair on the other—is that it is a *preventive* activity which must be performed at fairly long intervals that are neither known with precision nor signalled by the capital itself. In primitive societies the need for imparting temporal precision to tasks that by nature are postponable within rather wide limits is often satisfied through ritual. Thus, the beginning and end of the principal phases of the agricultural work cycle are ceremoniously ordered and routinized by means of seasonal festivals, "first-furrow" ceremonies, and the like.[10] For maintenance to be effective, people must be similarly made to act *as though* it had to be undertaken at precise intervals, suppressing their better knowledge that deferment by a day, a week, or a month may not matter; they must organize this fiction, submit to it, and set up a signalling system to enforce it. In other words, maintenance is predominantly an administrative process if we so define an activity whose performance is not directly invited or compelled by the production process or the product itself, and as such it requires an especially high degree of organizational ability.

Once maintenance is recognized as a special problem, the most obvious course would be to undertake only projects which do not require it. This seems to have been indeed a preferred solution of the great architects and engineers of the past, whether we think of the Egyptian or Aztec pyramids, of the Roman highways, the *caminos reales* in Latin America, the Etruscan, medieval, or Chinese walls.

However, this solution has several drawbacks: in the first place, it is extremely expensive in real resources (even though slave labour be used) and is therefore available only for a few key structures; secondly, it is inapplicable in any event to machines with moving parts that require maintenance; and thirdly, it perpetuates the problem by considering the difficulty of *learning* maintenance insuperable.

An opposite type of solution now suggests itself: instead of rendering maintenance entirely unnecessary, is there not something to be said for enterprises in which maintenance is of supreme importance? We are thinking of industries and processes where lack of maintenance carries stiff penalties in the form of serious breakdowns and accidents instead of simply leading to a slow deterioration in the quality and quantity of output or to brief outages of single machines that do not disrupt the whole production schedule. It is this *compulsion to maintain* that is, for instance, characteristic of the operations of integrated, "continuous-flow" processes such as petroleum refining and other chemical transformations. In transportation, a high degree of compulsion exists for airlines—non-maintenance here means certain disaster—while highways can be left to deteriorate for a long time until they become actually impassable, and even then the consequence is

10. See Stanley Hart Udy, Jr., *The Organization of Production in Non-Industrial Cultures,* unpublished dissertation, Princeton University, Department of Economics and Sociology (1957), p. 224.

inconvenience and impairment of income distributed among many people rather than massive loss of life and property. In the case of railroads, the compulsion to maintain is less strong than for airlines, but probably stronger than for highways, as the accidents resulting from non-maintenance are more serious. Our hypothesis that underdeveloped countries will do best in activities where maintenance is inescapably imposed is in this instance nicely borne out by observation: the performance of airlines in these countries is usually quite creditable, that of the railroads mediocre, and the highway system is frequently in a parlous state of disrepair.

The foregoing observations suggest that underdeveloped countries may well make a surprising success of ventures with a complicated technology which *must* be maintained in top working order. It is in these industries that the *maintenance habit* can be acquired and from there spread to the rest of the economy. On the other hand, the "simple" industries which the poorer countries are often admonished to set up first may be precisely those that will exhibit a strong tendency to deterioration. For while here lack of maintenance does not have immediate drastic consequences (and is therefore likely to be indulged in), it does in the longer run have a serious adverse impact on efficiency and morale.

Developing countries cannot, of course, abstain from building highways or from establishing textile mills on the ground that such ventures are exposed to deterioration. But an awareness of the special risks to which this type of investment is exposed can only be advantageous in that it may lead to the adoption of processes especially oriented towards our difficulty. A good example is provided by road construction in Colombia as explained by the consulting engineer who was in charge of supervising the road construction and rehabilitation program financed by the International Bank:

> We made one major concession in our planning to the recognized maintenance organization problem, and it sounds odd, at first thought. We encouraged the construction of low-type bituminous surfaces on relatively low-travelled routes, where this use would not ordinarily be justified in this country. We assumed that, with the increasing truck and bus industry in Colombia, local pressure would be applied to the Ministry of Public Works to repair the deep holes which will develop in cheap bituminous pavements if maintenance and retreatment is delayed, and that such pressure would be greater than if a gravel and stone road is allowed to deteriorate. Gravel and stone surfaces disappear at the rate of 20 to 40 tons per kilometer per year, and its loss may not be detected until the base is

> damaged. In other words, neglect of a bituminous surface is more obvious than neglect of a gravel or stone surface.[11]

The mechanism invoked here is, in addition, a striking example of reliance on nonmarket forces—pressure by the highway users on the Ministry of Public Works—for corrective action in a disequilibrium situation.

Generalizing the Solution

The reasoning used in the consideration of the maintenance problem can be applied to other problems in investment planning. For instance, if there is a tendency for new ventures to be undertaken without sufficient advance consideration of the technical, economic, and social conditions essential to their success, an argument can be made in favour of enterprises that imperiously require careful advance planning because of the complex nature of the investment and the amount of money and prestige committed. Thus, under certain circumstances, it may be rational for governments in underdeveloped countries to concentrate on "show-pieces": when a government undertakes the construction of a large hydroelectric station or of a steel mill, it simply cannot afford to let such ventures go wrong—it places itself under a far stronger compulsion to "deliver" than if it were to spend the same funds on a large number of small projects. The large ventures are therefore likely to be planned much more carefully than the small ones and this factor ought to qualify any comparison of their respective "marginal social productivities."

Similarly, if it is a fact that enterprises in underdeveloped countries are exposed to forces making for a deterioration in the quality of their output because of lack of competition, lack of maintenance of equipment, or for other reasons, then something may be said for considering seriously the establishment of industries where the latitude or tolerance for such deterioration is particularly low—precision instruments, for instance. The field for this type of action may be limited because of the many other elements, particularly with respect to market size, that enter into investment decisions. But it is interesting to note that the firm requirement of high standards of quality is an element in favour of, rather than, as would usually be believed, against, the introduction of this type of production

11. From a letter to the author from Forrest Green, Professor of Highway Engineering at Purdue University.

into underdeveloped countries. Since they would tend to do badly the jobs that may be done either well or badly, it is clear that these countries would have a comparative advantage in jobs that must be done well if they are to be done at all.

To use a parallel from individual behaviour: a person whose attention is apt to wander is likely to drive quite well in heavy city traffic, but is in great danger of landing in a ditch as soon as he reaches an "easy" country road.[12]

But instead of searching for additional analogous situations, it is perhaps of greater interest to attempt *a generalization of* our analysis. The special problem presented by maintenance resided in its not being directly related to the production process so that its timing and periodicity result from arbitrary arrangements rather than from signals sent out by the process or the product itself. In fact, in order to organize maintenance on an efficient basis, we generally resort to arrangements that *simulate* the sending out of such signals either by the calendar or by the machine itself, as when we have our car lubricated when the speedometer passes a mileage number with three zeros—we act *as though* the car asked to be lubricated at this point. This suggests that efficiency can be reinforced by signals, indications, and hints given off by the production process, and that the absence of such hints creates a special difficulty which will be particularly hard to overcome in underdeveloped countries.

In looking at the production of goods and services from this point of view, the impact on labour efficiency of machine-paced as opposed to operator-paced operations first comes to mind. It appears likely that an untrained labour force will perform better in machine-paced operations, not so much because of a tendency towards slacking when the machine does not compel the work, as because machine-paced operations provide for steadiness of pace and regular brief rest periods which the inexperienced self-paced worker has difficulty in observing.[13]

12. This example makes it clear that what we have in mind is definitely *not* a challenge-and-response mechanism. Our driver does well in city traffic not because of the "challenge" of the task but simply because, given his constitution, it is actually on balance *easier* for him to drive properly in the city than in the country—the city traffic requires greater technical mastery, but this increase in the difficulty of driving is outweighed by the fact that intense traffic helps him in the task of focusing his attention. I suspect that quite a few of Toynbee's challenge-and-response mechanisms can be reinterpreted in a similar way, and, in the process, rendered more intelligible.
13. Cf. U. S. Department of Labor, *Hours of Work and Output,* Bulletin No. 917, Washington, 1947. This bulletin reports on the differential effect on workers' productivity of increases in daily work hours during wartime. One of its conclusions is (p. 11): "Where the workspace is controlled by the machine, thus affording the

In general, it is well known that output per worker varies far more in operator-controlled than in machine-controlled operations.[14] The situation is therefore, once again, similar to the one involved in maintenance: if, for a number of reasons, labour productivity tends to be low in underdeveloped countries, this tendency is given much more room to assert itself in operator-controlled operations. Therefore, these countries will tend to do comparatively better in industrial operations that are primarily machine-paced.

Since machine-paced operations are typically more capital-intensive than operator-paced ones, our argument qualifies the advice to adopt labour-intensive processes usually given to capital-poor and labour-rich countries. This advice rests on the assumption that the productivity of labour in underdeveloped countries will not deteriorate relative to developed countries as technology becomes more labour-intensive. But since the scope for poor performance becomes wider when more labour-intensive processes are used, this assumption may be untenable.

This argument for capital-intensive technology in underdeveloped countries will be considered in more detail later in this chapter. Let us first give it greater generality by moving from the individual factory operation to the production process as a whole. This is necessary in any event to explain satisfactorily why labour productivity is likely to be low in operator-paced operations; for low labour productivity is most typically the result of poor management.[15]

operator some brief rest periods while waiting for the machine to perform its operation, the increase in output is more nearly proportional to the increase in hours [than in operator-paced operations]."

14. Adam Abruzzi, *Work, Workers and Work Management* (New York, 1956), pp. 14, 201; and Bela Gold, *Foundations of Productivity Analysis* (Pittsburgh, 1955), pp. 188 ff. In *The Instinct of Workmanship* (New York, Macmillan, 1914), pp. 306–307, Veblen gave a masterly description of machine-controlled operations: "The share of the operative workman in the machine industry is typically that of an attendant, an assistant, whose duty it is to keep pace with the machine process and to help out with workmanlike manipulations at points where the machine process engaged is incomplete." Veblen opposed this machine worker to the craftsman but did not see that a large area in modem industry is reserved to the self-paced operator with power tools and operator-controlled machines.
15. The close relationship between organizational and managerial skills, on the one hand, and labour productivity on the other, has been shown by Frederick Harbison, "Entrepreneurial Organization as a Factor in Economic Development," *Quarterly Journal of Economics, 70* (Aug. 1956), 364–379; cf. also Tulsi Ram Sharma, *Location of Industries in India,* 3rd ed. (Bombay, 1954), p. 220.

Certain types of modern technology perform a crucial function in aiding management in the performance of new, unfamiliar, and perhaps somewhat uncongenial tasks. By predetermining to a considerable extent what is to be done where and at what point of time, the machines and the mechanical or chemical processes they perform reduce these difficulties immeasurably in comparison with a situation where work schedules depend exclusively on the convergence and coordination of many human wills and actions. The productivity effects of technology have been so spectacular that its role in assisting management and thus enhancing efficiency has gone largely unnoticed. Ever since Adam Smith, it has been realized that the division of labour induces mechanical inventions. But the inverse relationship also deserves to be stressed. The technical processes carried out by machinery provide factory operations with a basic structure and rhythm which in effect deal out functions and determine sequences. If it is correct, as Chester Barnard has said, that "processes of decision … are largely techniques for narrowing choice,"[16] then the use of modern technology in manufacturing is one of the most powerful of such techniques.

The degree to which modern technology facilitates coordination varies from one industry to another. In some industries, the technology consists of a basic process around which work falls into place almost naturally; examples are smelting, petroleum refining, cement, brewing, and many others. In other industries, such as construction and much of metalworking, as well as in most service industries, work is not patterned around one or several key technical processes. As a result, sequences are far less rigidly compelled, it is impossible to identify any one process as central, and tasks are typically defined in terms of their *direct* contribution to the achievement of the goal—the final product—rather than in terms of the roles performed in different phases of the production process. In these "product-centred" industries technology therefore makes much less of a contribution to the coordination of efforts unless it succeeds, by organizing "flow," in imitating the

16. Chester I. Barnard, *The Functions of the Executive* (Cambridge, MA, 1938), p. 14. Note also the following description of assembly problems in M. E. Salveson, "On a Quantitative Method in Production Planning and Scheduling," *Econometrica, 20* (Oct. 1952), 562: "In an assembled commodity, if there are *n* component parts there will be theoretically *n*! different sequences in which the parts can be assembled together …. In any real situation, it would be prohibitive to enumerate all of these different sequences and select the one which is optimum …. Instead an engineering type of analysis is used to select some one sequence of assembly according to which the assembly methods and tooling are laid out."

conditions prevailing in the "process-centred" industries. Thus, the efficiency-enhancing and coordination-promoting property of modern technology tends to be much more pronounced in process-centred than in product-centred industries.

It is possible to classify a plant (or industry) into one or the other category by asking the question whether its physical assets have a definite capacity.[17] If a positive answer can be given, as is the case with a blast furnace, a refinery, or a brewery, we have a process-centred situation: with a certain equipment, it ought to be possible to produce so many tons or gallons per day. In the product-centred industries as, for example, in the case of a construction firm or a repair shop, it is not possible to make this kind of statement: outputs here are often heterogeneous and even if the problem of adding them up can be satisfactorily solved, capacity is far less rigidly set by the physical assets alone or it is a far less useful benchmark because actual output seldom reaches more than a fraction of theoretical capacity. This test illuminates another aspect of the manner in which technology in process-centred industries acts as an aid to management: the rated capacity of the plant provides managers with a performance goal and an objective criterion of failure or success, provided demand is adequate. This is a very valuable mechanism in underdeveloped countries where, as we know, competition is often not a sufficiently strong spur to good performance.

Thus there are various ways in which capital enhances the efficiency of management and therefore of labour. This function of capital is of particular importance in underdeveloped societies where the tasks of coordination and of cooperation in large-scale organizations meet with special difficulties.

That there exists a strong social need for this stimulating and coordinating function is suggested by the fact that, in the absence of modern technology, it is frequently performed, particularly in cooperative work, by other devices such as singing[18] or magic and ritual. Among the Trobriand Islanders, according to Malinowski, "magic is a systematizing, regulating and controlling influence in garden work. The magician, in carrying out the rites, sets the pace, compels people to apply themselves to certain tasks, and to accomplish them properly and in time .... There is no doubt that by its influence in ordering, systematizing and regulating work, magic is economically invaluable."[19]

17. This test was suggested to me by Alan S. Manne.
18. Georges Friedmann, *Industrial Society* (Glencoe, Ill., 1955), pp. 157–159 and sources there cited. Cf. also C. J. Erasmus, "Cultural Structure and Process: The Occurrence and Disappearance of Reciprocal Farm Labor," *Southwestern Journal of Anthropology*, 12 (Winter 1956), 452.
19. B. Malinowski, *Argonauts of the Western Pacific* (London, Routledge, 1922), p. 60.

A particularly striking example of the elaborate way in which the function is performed in a primitive society is given by Raymond Firth in his description of the role of ritual in canoe-building and net-making in Tikopia.[20] He shows in minute detail how "certain types of ritual make for conformity of the work to a time-schedule and so help to safeguard the task from miscalculation and inertia." The ritual acts not only as a "unifying factor for the assembly of labor" and as a "general stimulus to the productive process," but also as a specific guide in the course of this process since "the traditional sequence of rites of necessity involves a corresponding sequence of technical operations."[21]

Finally, Firth shows that "with similar environmental, technical and social conditions, work of this kind (i.e. work involving cooperation in large-scale activities) is performed with less regularity, secures a smaller labour force and is integrated less effectively where it is not accompanied by such ritual." His conclusion is that the extra degree of capital intensity implicit in the time-consuming performance of ritual is fully justified, since without it output would substantially decrease and deteriorate.[22]

The parallel is complete with the special stimulating role which modern technology performs and which because of inexperience in management and difficulties in cooperation is particularly needed in underdeveloped countries. Here also some additional capital intensity may sometimes be well worth while if it "safeguards the task from miscalculation and inertia" and prevents decay.[23]

20. *Primitive Polynesian Economy*, London, Routledge, 1939.
21. Ibid., pp. 183, 179, 125, and 181.
22. Ibid., pp. 182–184.
23. Our argument can be given further support from a different direction, but through closely analogous considerations. Besides inducing efficiency, capital-intensive forms of production are likely to prove stimulating to new capital formation. That some economists have claimed too much in this connection is shown in A. O. Hirschman and Gerald Sirkin, "Investment Criteria and Capital Intensity Once Again," *Quarterly Journal of Economics, 72* (Aug. 1958). But, as is also pointed out in this paper, a presumption exists that "capital-intensive capitalists" are more accumulation-minded than land- or labour-intensive property owners, if only because of the threat of obsolescence of their machines and equipment. In other words, the argument in favour of capital-intensive technology can be strengthened by taking into account the differential effect of various types of technology on *savings out of profits*. In underdeveloped countries, where capitalists must learn to plough back profits, this differential effect is likely to be of particular importance.

Capital-Intensive Technology?

Let us formalize our argument. We have given some reasons for believing that production functions are not the same for developed and underdeveloped countries, even though the underlying technological possibilities are identical. The marginal rate of substitution of labour for capital is larger in underdeveloped countries as, with the loss in managerial and labour efficiency consequent upon the adoption of less capital-intensive methods, more labour is needed than in developed countries to make up for a given decrease in capital.

Employing the usual diagram, with labour and capital measured, respectively, along the abscissa and the ordinate, the constant-product curves for a given output of any good may be expected to coincide for industrial and underdeveloped countries only along their most capital-intensive segments. Thereafter the curves will follow different paths, with the isoquant of the underdeveloped country—curve *AU* in Figure 5.1—lying somewhat to the right of the isoquant *AI* that applies in the industrial country. Only the latter is a genuine technical-possibilities curve.

With this situation, it becomes immediately evident that identical relative factor prices in both countries should result in the adoption of more capital-intensive processes in the underdeveloped country than in the industrial one.[24] This is shown by comparing the points of tangency P_1 and P_2 of the two parallel lines *DE* and *FG*. More realistically, if we assume by drawing the line *MN* that relative factor prices are more favourable to labour in the industrial country, this does not necessarily mean that techniques should be less capital-intensive in the underdeveloped country. In spite of this country's lower ratio of labour costs to capital costs, the point P_1 shows that it should use the same amount of capital as the industrial country which will now aim at the point of tangency of *MN* with isoquant *AI*, that is, at P_3.

Having stated the argument, we must qualify it. In the first place, it is quite possible that Western technology has only a few processes to offer, and that, even after taking into account the factors here discussed, all of them are too capital-intensive for the underdeveloped countries in view of their low wages and disguised unemployment. This would be the case if, in the figure, the isoquant *AU* existed not as a continuous curve but as a limited number of points, all of them located northwest of P_1.

24. Capital intensity is here understood to be measured by the capital-output, rather than by the capital-labour, ratio.

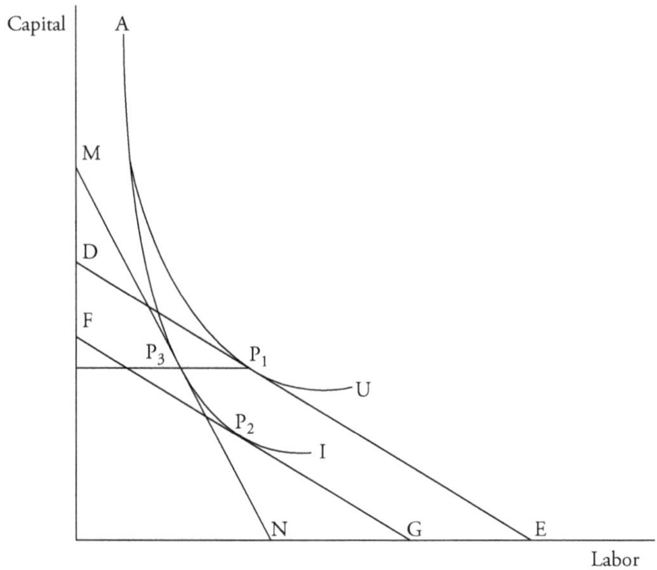

Figure 5.1: Divergent production functions.

Secondly, we have rather arbitrarily equated process-centred industries with capital-intensive technology. This would be correct if process-centred industries were necessarily made up entirely of machine-paced operations. Actually, this need not be the case. A process-centred industry will typically contain a *central* mechanical or chemical process which takes place in a series of machine-controlled operations, but all movements towards and away from that process—of handling materials and internal transportation—could well be man- rather than machine-paced.[25] As long as plant operations *as a whole* are process-centred, the fact that the peripheral operations—which often represent a considerable fraction of total cost—are man-controlled need not affect efficiency since the central process still would indirectly set the pace of *all* operations in the plant.

25. It seems that this is what happens in Soviet industry. See David Granick, "Economic Development and Productivity Analysis: The Case of Soviet Metalworking," *Quarterly Journal of Economics, 71* (May 1957), 205–233, for interesting evidence on the use of labor-intensive methods, principally in auxiliary operations such as handling of materials, inspection, and repair. For similar evidence from underdeveloped countries, see V. V. Bhatt, "Capital Intensity of Industries," *Bulletin of the Oxford Institute of Statistics, 18* (May 1956), 179–194.

Conversely, product-centred processes are not necessarily of low capital intensity. The production of made-to-order machines with the help of highly complex machine tools is a case in point.

Nevertheless, in combination, the criteria developed here do point towards certain highly capital-intensive pursuits as particularly well suited for underdeveloped countries. The list includes thus far: large-scale ventures, activities that must be maintained in top working order, that must observe high quality standards for their output, machine-paced operations, and process-centred industries. For the time being, these criteria can of course be considered only as hypotheses. Empirical verifications should not be too difficult to undertake. If we are correct, labour productivity differentials between an underdeveloped and an industrial country should be much larger in certain industries (e.g. metal fabricating) than in certain others (e.g. cement) even when essentially similar techniques are used in both countries.[26]

Production versus Administration Tasks

The new criteria which have been suggested here are designed to help in locating new activities that can be successfully undertaken in underdeveloped countries. In other words, they do not imply any judgment with respect to activities that have long been carried on in these countries, such as handicraft and small industry. …

26. Leontief's celebrated findings about the comparatively high labour content of United States exports could be considered corroborative evidence (see his "Factor Proportions and the Structure of American Trade: Further Theoretical and Empirical Analysis," *Review of Economics and Statistics*, 38 [Nov. 1956], 386–407, and literature there cited). Conversely, our analysis provides an explanation of Leontief's statistics, related to the one he has proposed himself. It has been suggested that underdeveloped countries may find it easier to approach the efficiency standards of the advanced industrial nations in capital-intensive, process centred, than in labour-intensive, product-centred industries. Therefore, as worldwide industrialization progresses, the comparative advantage of the advanced industrial countries may come to lie increasingly with certain types of labour-intensive goods and services. This can best be illustrated by a fanciful hypothesis. Let us imagine that certain labour-intensive services such as maintenance of roads, buildings, and machinery could become objects of international trade at moderate transport costs. I have no doubt that in this eventuality the older industrial nations would specialize in the export of such services, quite possibly importing steel and cement in exchange!

With respect to new activities, our criteria obviously cannot pretend to replace the usual considerations that make up investment decisions: size of market, locational advantages, and the like.[27] But they add a new dimension to these decisions.

Frequently it will be advisable or necessary to establish enterprises that do not meet our criteria. But in such cases something might still be gained from being aware of the handicaps under which these firms are likely to operate, for it should lead to particular care in the selection of management, personnel, and techniques.

Actually, it will be very difficult to classify projects neatly into those that do and those that do not meet our criteria. For the several characteristics that would make up the *ideal* firm from the point of view of our criteria are most unlikely to be found together in more than a very few projects. Therefore, many firms will have split personalities. For instance, manufacturing firms may well combine product centred and process-centred operations, as is the case in certain assembly operations or when large, isolated process-centred plants, such as sugar and petroleum refineries, have their own machine shops.

But wherever production of physical goods takes place at all, the operators are being helped in their efforts by the tangible nature of their task. The help is particularly substantial in the case of process centred and machine-paced operations, but it is also present in product-centred work. Even though the necessary coordination of efforts has here to be "invented" by the production manager without the powerful hints that a basic process provides, the image of the final product still acts both as a spur to everybody's efforts and as an objective test of achievement or failure.

Any production activity has these three assets: the target is clear-cut, we know it can be reached, and success in doing so is subject to an objective test. These elements are, for instance, fully present in such entirely product-centred operations as the repair of a machine or vehicle.

As soon as we move from the sphere of production to that of administration, tasks lose their definiteness and achievement its "testability." It is therefore to be expected and is indeed widely confirmed by observation and experience that efficiency will be higher in the plant- than in the office-operations of industrial

27. The best treatment and practical illustration of these matters is found in W. A. Lewis, "The Industrialization of the British West Indies," *Caribbean Economic Review, 2* (May 1950), 1–61, and *Report on Industrialization and the Gold Coast,* Government Printing Department, Accra, Gold Coast, 1953

firms.[28] By the latter we mean such functions as production control, planning, finance, personnel and public relations, distribution and advertising, and general housekeeping. The comparative elusiveness of these tasks is combined with, a tolerance for poor performance which is unmatched by any production job. It is almost proverbial for production men to complain that they would have been fired long ago if they turned in as poor a performance as some of the people behind a desk. This special tolerance of "desk jobs" for poor performance makes them also the prey and point of penetration of the forces that remain unconvinced of the need for exertion and achievement: friends and relatives find here an excellent refuge from which to make a last-ditch stand for their right to a quiet, incompetent existence.

It is now easy to understand why functions that are completely divorced from the actual production of goods and services tend to be the real stepchildren of progress in underdeveloped countries. National character and history are usually appealed to in explaining the malfunctioning of the political and administrative processes which stands so often in sharp contrast to real achievements in industrial and agricultural production. Seldom is it realized that these processes are intrinsically harder to master than production jobs. On the contrary, amazement is expressed that a country pretends to set up modern industries when basic problems of public administration have not yet been solved. But this is only one of the many instances where what seems a cart-before-the-horse sequence turns out to be the efficient one in underdeveloped countries: efficient public administrators, admittedly so much needed, can perhaps best be trained in the arts of management by being first exposed to the powerful "teaching aids" which are standard equipment in any industrial production process.

28. United Nations, *Labor Productivity of the Cotton Textile Industry in Five Latin American Countries* (New York, 1951), passim.

6 The Contriving of Reform

… The problem-solving process was described in terms of concurrent or sequential advances in understanding and motivation. For an important group of problem-solving situations these two elements are overshadowed by, and indissolubly linked with, a third condition for advance: the ability to enact and carry through certain measures, remedies, or *reforms,* in spite of the resistance which they evoke. We now turn to such situations; they are of special interest in Latin America today and occupy a prominent place in each one of our country studies.

The Reformer's Initial Handicap

Faced with the claims of the Cuban revolution on the one hand, and with the demands and promises of the Alliance for Progress on the other, Latin Americans appear to have been placed squarely before the familiar, if stark, alternative: change through violent revolution or through peaceful reform?

On the basis of the country studies it will be argued in the following pages that this traditional dichotomy does very poorly at catching the reality of social and economic change. But first it should perhaps be explained that, contrary to what might be expected, a strong initial advantage for the advocates of revolution results from formulating the choice facing the developing countries of Latin America in this bipolar fashion.

Social reform and social revolution are usually distinguished by the manner in which a given change is brought about as well as by the extent of that change. But they have in common the nature of the change, since both propose a shift in power and wealth from one group to another. Hence they are varieties of what we shall call *antagonistic* solutions to problems in contrast to *nonantagonistic* solutions which consist of measures that are expected to leave each group better or at least as well off as before.

A proposed change can be thought of as non-antagonistic by its advocates, but may turn out to be antagonistic and to be perceived as such. In fact, any "progress," however non-antagonistic it was meant to be, will almost always hurt the absolute or relative position of *some* social group, at least initially. Anthropologists have shown that all aspects of the status quo, even those that seem wholly undesirable, have their defenders and profiteers who are going to fight the proffered improvements. Unrealistic expectation of universal cooperation with measures which in the mind of their sponsors had no antagonistic component has spelled the failure of many a technical assistance project. Such disappointments have been well documented even in the ostensibly most non-antagonistic field of public health.[1] Thus we tend consistently to *underestimate* the difficulties of change in the case of (subjectively) non-antagonistic measures and we are constantly surprised and chagrined by the resistances which they encounter.

The opposite bias—overestimate of the difficulties of change—frequently affects measures which are openly and avowedly antagonistic. We know and expect that land expropriation, nationalization of industries or progressive income taxation will be strongly opposed by well-entrenched groups.[2] Hence, when it comes to such measures, the revolutionary who is out to ridicule the peaceful reformer

1. Oscar Lewis, "Medicine and Politics in a Mexican Village," in Benjamin D. Paul, ed., *Health, Culture and Community,* Russell Sage Foundation, New York, 1955.
2. It is usual, but no longer justified, to limit discussion of such measures to those that are antagonistic to the interests of the older and wealthier ruling groups. More and more frequently, some Latin American countries such as Argentina and Brazil have found it imperative to tackle pressing problems of efficiency and financial solvency by curtailing the privileges of certain strategically located groups among the middle or working classes. What experience we have with this variety of antagonistic measures shows that they are no less difficult to push through than those directed against the older ruling groups.

has an easy task indeed. He will show that a basic-transformation of existing power relationships is a prerequisite to adopting and enforcing any measure that threatens the interests and privileges of the ruling class. He will deride the argument that the establishment of democratic institutions and of universal suffrage will allow basic reforms to be adopted legally since, so he will argue, democratic trappings will be discarded as soon as the real powerholders find them no longer convenient.

This argument was first deployed at the beginning of the century by orthodox Marxists who disputed the emerging belief of the so-called Revisionists among the German Social-Democrats that the conditions of the working class could be improved through the trade union movement and exploitative capitalism evolve peacefully into a more acceptable economic system. Pitted against Eduard Bernstein, the founder of Revisionism, Karl Kautsky, then the guardian of Marxist purity in the Social Democratic Party, exclaimed: "Does anyone believe that this victory [of the proletariat] is possible without catastrophe? I desire it, but I don't believe it."[3]

This point of view was eloquently and unremittingly reaffirmed by Harold Laski in the thirties when he predicted that even though the Labor Party might come to power legally, it would be unable to carry out its program of nationalizations:

> The central weakness [of the orthodox Labor position] is due to the refusal of the Labor Party to recognize that the state is the instrument of that class in society which owns the instruments of production and that it cannot utilize that state for its own purposes so long as that class remains in possession of those instruments … Unless a Labor government is prepared to meet a crisis of the first magnitude the forces it will encounter will persuade it rather to operate the capitalist system than to move to its transformation.[4]

More recently the argument, a bit battered from successful experience with reform in the industrial countries of the West, has migrated to the less developed areas. Here, it retains greater plausibility, and, on occasion, considerable validity, for these areas frequently lack a solid tradition of progressive political and

3. Quoted in Peter Gay, *The Dilemma of Democratic Socialism,* Columbia University Press, New York, 1952, p. 65.
4. Harold J. Laski, *Parliamentary Government in England,* Viking, New York, 1938, pp. 159–161.

economic change. John Kenneth Galbraith was perhaps the first to refurbish the argument for its new use:

> Unfortunately, some of our current discussion of land reform in the underdeveloped countries proceeds as though this reform were something that a government proclaims on any fine morning—that it gives land to the tenants as it might give pensions to old soldiers or as it might reform the administration of justice. In fact, a land reform is a revolutionary step; it passes power, property, and status from one group in the community to another. If the government of the country is dominated or strongly influenced by the land-holding groups—the one that is losing its prerogatives—no one should expect effective land legislation as an act of grace.[5]

At almost the same time the argument, as applied to underdeveloped countries, was put back into traditional Marxist terms by Paul Baran:

> The alliance of property-owning classes controlling the destinies of most underdeveloped countries, cannot be expected to design and to execute a set of measures running counter to each and all of their immediate vested interests. If to appease the restive public, blueprints of progressive measures such as agrarian reform, equitable tax legislation, etc., are officially announced, their enforcement is wilfully sabotaged. The government, representing a political compromise between landed and business interests, cannot suppress the wasteful management of landed estates and the conspicuous consumption on the part of the aristocracy; … Set up to guard and to abet the existing property rights and privileges, it cannot become the architect of a policy calculated to destroy the privileges standing in the way of economic progress and to place the property and the incomes derived from it at the service of society as a whole.[6]

This point of view is readily accepted in Latin America where a non-Marxist Chilean writer and politician put the same thought quite succinctly some fifty years ago.

5. J. K. Galbraith, "Conditions for Economic Change in Under-Developed Countries," *Journal of Farm Economics,* November 1951, p. 695.
6. "On the Political Economy of Backwardness," *The Manchester School,* January1952, reprinted in A. N. Agarwala and S. P. Singh, eds., *The Economics of Underdevelopment,* Oxford University Press, Bombay, 1958, pp. 88–89.

> Nobody would believe in a law which would injure the interests of the privileged class. It would be the same as if in Russia a law were passed which ordered the Czar to be shot: nobody would believe in the law.[7]

Compared to these reminders of what is and is not credible and feasible when power is distributed in a certain way, the routine of present-day international experts in blandly proposing year-in, year-out essentially antagonistic measures of every description regardless of political realities seems singularly inane or naïve. In fact, the experts themselves, after having absorbed a critical amount of frustration, frequently become converts to the view that, in this or that country, "everything" has to change before any improvement at all can be introduced.[8]

The idea of revolution as a prerequisite to any progress draws immense strength from the very limited human ability to visualize change and from the fact that it makes only minimal demands on that ability. All we are asked to imagine by the revolutionary is the tumbling down of the old regime in a total upheaval which will give birth to the new order. Revolution thus conceived is essentially a quite brief, though cataclysmic interlude between two static societies: one, unjust and rotten, which is incapable of being improved, and the other, rational and harmonious, which has no further need to be improved upon. Sorel, the apostle of the violent general strike as an energizing myth, clearly had this concept of revolution in mind when he wrote:

> … the general strike must be considered as an undivided whole and …; consequently, no detail about ways and means is of the slightest help for the understanding of socialism. It must even be added that there is always danger of losing something of this understanding, if one attempts to split this whole into parts … the transition from capitalism to socialism must … be conceived as a catastrophe whose process defies description.[9]

7. Alberto Edwards speaking in the Chilean Congress in 1909, quoted by Fetter, *Monetary Inflation in Chile*, Princeton, PUP, 1931, pp. 126–127.
8. An extreme illustration of this mood is the Rio cabdriver who, caught in that city's famous rush-hour jam, remarked to us: "What we need here is a Fidel Castro!" He was obviously convinced that traffic flow cannot be improved in Brazil without a prior social revolution.
9. Georges Sorel, *Réflexions sur la violence,* 11th ed., Marcel Riviere, Paris, 1950, pp. 185, 217.

Sorel thus understood perfectly the dual function of the idea of revolution: to gratify the desire for change and to dispense with the need to visualize the process of change in its intricate and perhaps unpleasant details by telescoping it into an "undivided whole."

The neat trick involved in this operation, while intellectually not very respectable, goes far towards explaining the drawing power of the idea of revolution. But the reformers are also to blame. They have made themselves particularly vulnerable to the charge of being unrealistic by failing to explore how social change short of cataclysmic revolution actually happens. Thus they have permitted the revolutionists to set up a caricature of "change via reform" where the latter follows smoothly (and unbelievably) upon the 51% election victory of the Reform Party or, more modernly though even more naïvely, upon the recommendations of international experts or the offer of finance. Actually there are a good many intermediate stations between this kind of effortless and painless reform at one extreme and total revolution at the other and our studies permit us to map out a few of these stations.

Events of recent years have created a somewhat similar continuum between total peace and total war (cold, phony, brushfire, limited war), and political scientists have identified various types of political regimes (tutelary democracy, modernizing oligarchies) filling the void between Western-type parliamentary democracy and totalitarian autocracy.[10] In contrast to these efforts, our observations do not lead to the firm establishment of a typology. Rather, we shall attempt to show how elements of both reform and revolution are present in the sequences of policy-making which we have studied. In the process we hope to provide basic materials for what may eventually go into a "reformmonger's manual"; perhaps it is time that such a text be written and offer some competition to the many handbooks on the techniques of revolutions, coups d'état, and guerrilla warfare.

This section stands in need of an important postscript. Our argument, as developed so far, does not mean to imply that any reform whatever can always be introduced without revolution, that is, without the prior, violent, wholesale overthrow of the current powerholders. Certainly many situations have existed and still exist in Latin America as elsewhere in which power is so concentrated, opposition to change so fierce, and the social and political structure so rigid that any non-revolutionary change is, short of a miracle, impossible, *besides* being

10. Edward Shils, *Political Development in the New States,* Mouton & Co., The Hague, 1962.

inconceivable. The point we have been trying to make is that there are many other, less rigid situations in which change by methods short of revolution is or has become possible, but where, because of the force of habit or some similar cultural lag, change is still visualized primarily as something that requires a prior revolution. This contrast between reality and the widely entertained image of reality seems to the writer to prevail in much of Latin America today. A similar contrast with opposite content characterizes the present intellectual and political climate in the United States where, as a result of positive experience with gradualism, a majority appears to have come to the unwarranted conclusion that any progressive change whatever can and must be achieved exclusively by a succession of moderate reforms or cannot be achieved at all.[11] This can be just as much an illusion as the opposite belief of many Latin Americans that any "real" change can only come through revolution.

Violence as an Ingredient of Reform

Our statement that reform and revolution are not nearly as far apart as language would make us believe holds up well when we consider the role of violence. The received idea is that revolutions are violent and reforms peaceful. But if we applied this criterion for distinguishing between reform and revolution to the history of land tenure problems in Colombia, we would immediately have to conclude that Colombia has passed not through one but through several agrarian revolutions. Yet the historical record knows of no such revolution.

On reflection it will be realized that even if violence is a necessary condition for revolution it is not a sufficient one, and that it is also a common element of reform. To qualify as revolutionary, violence must be *centralized;* it must attack and conquer the central seats of political and administrative power. In Colombia violence has been scattered, local, decentralized. For the past hundred years, peasants have occupied and are still occupying today lands that are not theirs. Sometimes they have used force and force has occasionally been used against them by those who claim ownership. But eventually forcible appropriation of large areas has been sanctioned by the state through *ad hoc* intervention or general legislation.

11. The exasperating slowness of racial desegregation in the United States has led to considerable soul-searching on this score, most forcefully expressed in the writings of James Baldwin. See also Eric F. Goldman, "Progress—By Moderation *and* Agitation," *The New York Times Magazine,* June 18,1961.

Thus, the willingness of the peasants to occupy uncultivated lands—a kind of entrepreneurial spirit—has powerfully contributed to reform legislation. Without the past experience of mass squatting and the threat of more to come, neither Law 200 of 1936 nor the land reform of 1961 would ever have been passed by the Congress.

In Brazil's Northeast, decentralized violence appears in a different guise. It is first unloosened by nature itself which, through its droughts, periodically chases hundreds of thousands of nordestinos from their homes in search of food, water and work. Relief shipments and the organization of emergency public works are an automatic response to the overriding need of social and physical survival so that it may well be said that, whenever a drought strikes, minimal needs of subsistence are "appropriated" by the Northeastern refugees. When the relief funds are not forthcoming with sufficient promptness, looting of food stores in the cities by the drought refugees serves as a reminder. This sudden and forcible appropriation of public monies by the Northeast leads subsequently to a whole chain of attempts to disburse the monies in such a way as to limit the damage that will be wrought by future droughts.

Since violence has in part the function of signalling protest to the central authorities, an improvement in the signalling mechanism serves to increase pressure as much as an intensification of the problem. Something of this kind happened in the Northeast when better and more numerous highways (built largely during droughts) and the availability of trucks permitted the miserable drought refugees to reach the coastal cities more rapidly and in greater numbers and thereby increased the threat to public order consequent upon the droughts.

As though the violent immediate reactions to the violence of nature were not enough, Northeasterners have been casting around for additional stimulants to action in the form of threatened violence. The traditional threat has been that of secession. Yet the threat of this particular violence always remained a bit rhetorical and ineffectual for lack of credibility. For one, it seemed an irrational move since it would cut off the Northeast from the principal source of relief and investment funds. Secondly, the threat is really one of an all-out centralized clash; it cannot be graduated since a region cannot secede "just a little bit." In both respects the Colombian squatter's kind of violence is more efficient, and its Brazilian counterpart has recently come into prominence in the Northeast through the activities of the peasant leagues. The creation of the new development agency in the Northeast (SUDENE) was originally rather a response to the 1958 drought, but the threat implicit in the rise of the peasant leagues strengthened the agency, which could now claim that its reform program represented the only alternative to a violent and disorderly change in the existing power structure in the Northeast.

In addition to being decentralized rather than centralized, the violence we have encountered in Colombia and Brazil is distinguished from revolutionary violence by the fact that it is not immediately countered by the aggrieved party. The violence one meets with is unilateral, sequential, *temporarily unrequited.* Land is "grabbed" by peasants, but ordinarily no immediate resistance follows. There may be action in the local courts and eventually forcible eviction of the squatters by the police and occasionally the army. Or again nothing may happen for a long time; and when the state believes it important that uncertainty be removed, but does not wish to use force to evict the peasants, it may buy the property from the owner and then attempt to sell it back to the peasant who already holds it, but still is ready to pay something for the much-coveted title which, among other advantages, makes it possible to obtain credit.

Thus the violence that is compatible with reform and frequently appears to be part and parcel of it is not the kind of decisive clash—force meets force in the principal square of the capital—which is usually associated with revolutionary violence. Rather it is a violence akin to guerrilla warfare, with the ability of the groups practicing it to now advance, now retreat, now lie low and now come forward with a new thrust.

As shown in the chapter on Chile, the economic behaviour underlying inflation is rather similar to the temporarily unrequited violence practiced by squatting peasants and retaliating landlords. Inflation results typically when demands for additional money income on the part of one social group are not resisted immediately and fiercely, but are countered indirectly and after some time interval by similar demands on the part of other groups. In this perspective, inflation appears as a device for the coexistence of several groups who are not hostile or do not feel strong enough to engage in out- and-out revolutionary battles or civil war over the distribution of the social product, yet are not friendly enough either to agree on any one pattern of dividing up the product among themselves. There is reluctance to agree, but also reluctance to disagree to the point of revolution or civil war. This is at least one interpretation that can be given to the Chilean inflation of the last twenty years.

At the same time inflation is sufficiently unpleasant to lead to a search for its cause and cure, and since nothing is easier than to establish a causal nexus between one social evil (such as inflation) and another (such as maldistribution of land), inflation has served the function of putting additional pressure behind a variety of reforms which were suddenly found to be desirable not only on their own merits but also because they would help set an end to inflation. Just as the squatting actions of Colombian peasants put more "steam" behind agrarian reform projects and the droughts in the Northeast regularly led to new initiatives in favour of that area, so inflationary pressures have served as a kind of generalized, all-purpose "steam" behind any improvement in Chile's economic and social structure that caught the eye of the reformers.

A final characteristic of the violence we have met in our studies is that it is not only *protest* and *pressure* on problem-solving authorities, but also *direct problem-solving activity.* The Colombian peasant satisfies his craving for a piece of land when he squats and the Northeastern drought refugee solves his immediate problem of hunger when he loots food stores in the coastal cities as does the Chilean worker when he wins higher wages through strikes. Hence, these individual decentralized actions not only signal a problem to the central decision-makers, but they reduce the size of the problem that remains to be solved by the authorities. In effect, they therefore make at least this problem more manageable, hence more amenable to reform moves (while quite possibly creating new problems elsewhere). In Colombia, for example, it would have been unthinkable for any non-revolutionary government in the twenties or thirties to carry out through centralized action the splitting up of the large estates which actually took place as a result of decentralized, spontaneous peasant movements. But once these events had taken place the New Deal government of Alfonso López was able after a long fight to convince Congress to legalize the peasants' actions through Law 200 of 1936. Instead of the sequence: revolution (centralized violence)—redistribution of land under conditions of revolutionary legality, the Colombians invented a highly disorderly sequence: decentralized violence and illegal redistribution of land—legalization of redistribution through Law 200. Disorderly though it was, this sequence permitted an improvement in the distribution of land.

The Latin American scene thus appears to be replete with mechanisms and sequences which permit the exertion of powerful pressures and the venting and adjudication of conflicts by means equally far removed from traditional concepts of either reform or revolution. Policy-makers usually act as a result and in the midst of such situations. To paraphrase Marx, decentralized, unrequited violence is frequently found in the role of indispensable midwife to *reform.* To advocate reforms in Latin America without tolerating, accepting and sometimes even welcoming and promoting the only kinds of pressures which have proven to be effective in getting reforms through is to risk being accused of hypocrisy and deception: now that the United States has declared itself in favour of a variety of reforms in Latin

America, it should perhaps be apprised of the circumstances and hazards usually associated with such an enterprise.

Crisis as an Ingredient of Reform

From violence we now move on to a more general concomitant of reform, namely, crisis. Violence is frequently an important cause and a conspicuous element of a crisis situation (a) because the fact of violence shows that a serious problem exists that requires immediate action, and (b) because the violence itself is felt as dangerous by the constituted authorities who will act to suppress it directly.

Crisis has been defined as a "situation in which there is a great stress toward action, toward the resolution of conflict"[12] and, we might add, towards the solution of problems. The reasons for which a developing emergency or crisis is favourable to problem-solving have not received much attention perhaps because the matter seems so self-explanatory. "Crisis concentrates attention," says Lasswell,[13] and it may well be that some problems simply fail in ordinary times to get attacked effectively, not for lack of knowledge, nor even for lack of motivation, but simply for lack of attention. Experience also shows that crisis may make it possible to take required actions against powerful groups which are normally well entrenched and invulnerable; finally, crisis may stimulate action and hence learning on a problem on which insight has been low and which for that very reason has not been tackled as long as it was in a quiescent state.

Yet, can we take it for granted that crisis-induced anxiety about a problem will help insight? Psychological findings hardly permit us to be confident in this regard. Experimental evidence rather appears to indicate that the injection of pressure and tension is not at all certain to improve performance in problem-solving activities. It apparently helps to speed up routine tasks, but turns into a hindrance with problems whose solutions require reflection and insight.[14]

12. H. D. Lasswell, "Attention Structure and Social Structure" in *The Communication of Ideas,* Lyman Bryson, ed., Harper, New York, 1948, p. 262.
13. Ibid., p. 262.
14. "Results have indicated that the quality of performance in complex learning situations is inversely related to the subjects' degree of anxiety." I. E. Farber, "Motivation in Verbal Learning and Performance," *Psychological Bulletin,* V. 52, 1955, p. 323. For a cautious summary of experimental results, see Kenneth W. Spence, *Behavior Theory and Conditioning,* Yale University Press, New Haven, 1956, Chapter 7. The following is a very strong statement intended by the author, a psychologist, for generalization

How can the apparent contradiction between the findings of the psychologists and the commonplace attitude of the politician who relies on crisis to produce solutions be resolved? To a large extent by showing that in this case, as in many others known to economists, propositions about individual behaviour cannot be extended uncritically to society at large, however suggestive they may be.

In the first place, it is easy to understand that, in a nation, the *quantity* of decision-making, that is, the total motivation to act, will be increased as a result of the intensification of the problem: certain decision-makers will pay attention to 50% inflation when they were not particularly disturbed by 10% inflation; more important, new dangers or problems—loss of elections, revolution, secession—arise as a consequence of the aggravation of the old problem and some decision-makers will be sensitive to these threats when they were indifferent or opposed to proposed actions on the problems of land tenure, inflation or Northeastern backwardness as such. In other words, new, hitherto indifferent or hostile forces will join to support actions, hence new alignments become possible and the possibility of new moves is perceived. All of this has no counterpart in individual problem-solving.

But what about the *ability* to solve problems, or the *quality* of this quantitatively augmented decision-making? Is there any reason to think that the intensification of the problem will tend to raise the level of insight? In this regard, we can have no certainty and the findings of the psychologists may well hold: we may merely get a spate of decision-making more or less in line with "the state of the arts," that is, with whatever views are already held at the time about the way in which the problem should be tackled. And since the very fact that we had to wait for widespread violence to take any action makes it likely that insight into the problem is at a low level, such decision-making may not improve matters very much.

to societal problem-solving situations: "The basic psychological notion here is that, beyond some optimum level for facilitation, increased motivation serves not only to energize the organism but also to restrict its capacity to select among alternatives at all levels of behavioural organization. The result is that heightened emotion and drive tend to produce stereotypy … [which] reduces capacity to solve problems … A normally intelligent raccoon trying to get out from under a stinging shower will persistently bang its head against a locked door that used to be open, completely ignoring free passageways to left and right." Charles E. Osgood, "Reciprocal Initiative," in James, ed., *The Liberal Papers,* Anchor Books, New York, 1962, p. 190.

Yet, here also the parallel with individual problem-solving can be misleading: in experiments on individual problem-solving anxiety is injected artificially from the outside while the problem itself remains the same whereas in societal problem-solving, anxiety is induced *by a change, an aggravation of the problem itself,* and frequently this very aggravation makes it possible to understand it better. For example, as inflation accelerated in Chile from the 20% rate of 1939–1952 to the 50–90% rate of 1953–1955 it became quite clear, as one commentator put it, that wage and salary increases in line with escalator clauses could not be financed out of profits but were bound to lead to further inflation. Similarly, each successive drought in the Northeast brought out one or several ways in which preceding efforts at strengthening the region's resistance to the scourge had gone awry. The 1958 drought, for example, highlighted and exposed the drastic decline in both technical competence and ethical standards which had been suffered by the agency (DNOCS) traditionally in charge of drought relief and public works in the area; this experience was partly responsible for the establishment of a new agency (SUDENE) with a different approach and organization.

The intensification and aggravation of a problem, frequently accompanied and signalled by certain forms of violence, is therefore one way in which reformers strengthen their own motives, gather new allies and gain new insights. Frequently it will not be possible to distinguish clearly which came first, the new motivation, the new allies or the new insights. The appearance of potential new allies will make the reformmongers change the character of their reform proposals so as to accommodate those allies and the emergence of new ideas leads to a search for groups that may support them.

In spite of the fact that this interplay opens up a wide range of possibilities, one particular way of contriving reform holds a privileged place in the popular imagination: the perception of common dangers resulting from the aggravation of the problem is expected to bring the warring parties "to their senses" and result in an equitable solution of the problem "just in time," that is, just as the revolution was about to take over. Reformers are in this case counting on the danger, the crisis, the emergency, the "brink" to panic everyone into action and their expectations are rather similar to those of revolutionaries: for the latter, the problem is solved by jumping over the brink into an unknown but that much more "transparent region"; for the reformers, the look down the brink is to lead to national reconciliation and rededication through which the overdue reforms are consummated and the problem is finally solved. Both conceptions characteristically assume that a total solution exists, but is sabotaged and held back, either by the "ruling class" which must be destroyed or by misunderstandings, inertia, selfishness and "politics-as-usual" which must be swept away in a great movement towards national union. The idea that national union born out of national emergency is sufficient to solve the country's problems in a comprehensive and integrated fashion is almost as tenacious and powerful a myth as that of "total" change via revolution.

The myth is constantly invoked by policy-makers of every kind, but in only one of our studies did reform or important policy decisions come about approximately in this way. In Colombia in 1960, after renewed concern about unrest and the heritage of violence in the countryside, an attempt was made to bring together all factions of opinion for the purpose of formulating an agrarian reform project once preliminary statements by party leaders had shown a convergence of opinion on the subject. Yet even here "politics-as-usual" was resumed in short order and so vigorously that the Agrarian Reform Bill, elaborated in the fall of 1960 by a special nonpartisan National Agrarian Committee, was bitterly fought in Congress by the opposition, found itself in serious jeopardy several times and had to be considerably watered down before it was finally approved in December 1961.

If we look at the important decisions that were taken in the fight on inflation in Chile or the establishment of SUDENE in Brazil, we find even more that they were marked by bitter and protracted battles, unexpected switches, and narrow margins of victory rather than by the miracle of sudden national unanimity. The reason is precisely that situations do not suddenly change from normal to emergency or crisis. Rather, we have here a gradual ascent in the course of which a *succession of* new reform ideas and possible alliances come into view. Besides, there is always disagreement among different groups as to how serious the crisis really is. Even the kind of violence so noticeable in Latin America, being decentralized and unrequited, does not create immediately a situation of utter emergency, but can rather be compared to what is accomplished in the United States by the sending of protest mail to the White House.

Thus, storms and emergencies gather for a long time and various groups in turn become alerted and sensitized to them gradually and unevenly. Hence, a series of attempts at dealing with the problem through changing coalitions is more likely than a Unique Comprehensive Reform.

This conclusion is strengthened by the fact that a problem such as land reform is in fact a collection of problems each of which is likely to fascinate a different clientele: those who favour, say, aid to progressive farmers in the form of tax incentives are not likely to be the same as those who wish idle estates to be broken up. By combining such measures into a "comprehensive" program, one frequently risks combining the enemies of both into a majority of the decision-makers. In

Colombia the former measure was taken in 1957 under one government, and progress was achieved on the latter in 1961 with a quite different combination of political forces.

The Emergence of New Problems as an Aid to Reform

Moreover, Colombia, Chile and Brazil obviously faced other issues besides the ones we chose to analyse. What does this mean for the possibilities of contriving reform on "our" problems? A first thought could be that, since the energies of decision-makers are limited, the raising of other problems is bound to distract them and to hold back action in the areas of our special interest. However, this kind of distraction, or substitution of one problem by another, is not at all conspicuous in our stories unless one considers the lack of action on our three problems during the Second World War as an instance.[15] To the contrary, the arising or aggravation of an "extraneous" second problem B is frequently seen to help decision-making on problem A, as though action on A were stimulated not only by its own intensification but also by the injection of any new concern.

One way in which such reinforcement can happen is through the familiar mechanism of logrolling. The advocates of land reform might enlist additional support for their project from, say, the advocates of urban low-cost housing projects by promising to support the latter cause by their vote and influence. There is evidence of this kind of mechanism in the story of Brazil's Northeast. We noticed that Kubitschek's support of the SUDENE project was not unrelated to the support for Brasília and Kubitschek's expansionary monetary policies on the part of the SUDENE backers. Inversely, President Epitacio Pessôa attempted to placate opposition to his large-scale spending in the Northeast by undertaking railroad and other projects in the Centre-South as well.

Another type of coalition-building is more prominent in our empirical material. It arises not when two problems merely coexist and the backers of reform trade their votes, but when one problem is seen to be interrelated with the other

15. This may be so because the three problems we have analysed have all been crucial, dominant problems in their respective countries at least during certain periods. A dominant problem could be defined as one that holds back action on a series of other problems because of the general expectation that the latter will largely vanish once the dominant problem is solved. The chapter on inflation in Chile quotes a particularly clear, if naïve, illustration of such alleged dominance (p. 215 of *Journeys*).

so that to solve or attenuate one is expected to improve the other. If this can be shown to be the case, the backers of one reform will support the other *in their own interest* rather than merely in the expectation of having the favour returned to them.

A good example of this way of acquiring new allies is the junction of the land tenure and the balance-of-payments problems in Colombia. Ordinarily those who are interested in improving the conditions of the peons and their access to land ownership or secure tenure are entirely distinct as a pressure group from the officials in the Central Bank and the Ministry of Finance who are concerned with the balance-of-payments. But since balance-of-payments improvements (smaller imports or larger exports of agricultural products) can presumably be realized through better land use we have a potential community of interests between the two groups which came to the fore in Colombia when the country faced a difficult balance-of-payments problem after the end of the Rojas Pinilla regime in 1957. One of the more important steps in the sequence of policy-making around the land problem (Decree 290 of 1958) can largely be traced to this confluence. Thus new allies are secured not only by tire aggravation of the central problem which is the target of reform but also by the aggravation of another problem, if it can be plausibly argued that the cure of the latter is connected with that of the former.

The Northeast of Brazil provides us with another, somewhat more complex instance of this relationship. The natural claimants for federal aid to the Northeast were of course the political representatives of the area itself. They traditionally secured the appropriation of relief funds and were responsible for the establishment of the first federal agencies and for the large public works programs in the area. But in the late fifties an interest arose in reorganizing and reorienting these agencies and programs. This move had only limited support in the Northeast since it was directed against some of the local powerholders. But at the same time the apparent inefficiency of the way in which federal funds had long been spent in the Northeast led to concern *outside* of the Northeast. And on the basis of this interest, Northeastern reformers were able to build a coalition with groups in the Centre and South. The problem of waste of public funds in the Northeast mobilized groups quite different from those who were traditionally the advocates of federal subsidies to the region. But support of the former groups became most valuable when an attempt was made to attack the Northeastern problem through new approaches which were opposed by a number of traditional Northeastern interest and pressure groups.

The possibility of solving local and regional problems by mobilizing forces outside the region is of particular interest to the reformer who wishes to attack problems by methods short of revolution. When, within a sovereign country, the pro-reform and counter-reform forces are solidly arrayed against one another and the latter are solidly entrenched, it may well be difficult to achieve reform without resort to revolutionary violence. But if the same situation is characteristic of a region within a country, the reform forces can form alliances with groups outside of their region and overcome in this fashion the local diehards. This freedom to manoeuvre serves to offset two important disabilities under which regional reform movements labour: the threat of revolution is not available to them since they cannot seize the central seats of power and the threat of secession is usually none too credible.

Reformers would do well therefore to be on the lookout not only for symptoms of aggravation of their own problem. By keeping a watch for the emergence of other concerns they may well be able to pick up new allies and to dispense with some old ones who are no longer available or wanted.

The Switch to the Antagonistic Perspective

As we survey the successive attacks on our problems, as well as the many proposed measures, remedies and solutions, the distinction between measures perceived and intended as either antagonistic or non-antagonistic provides us with one way of organizing that plentiful and seemingly disparate material. Do our country studies give us any clue about the sequence in which each category makes its appearance? Does this sequence depend exclusively on the political situation or also on the evolution of the problem itself?

Such questions are of particular interest to reformmongers, for reform, if conceived as an alternative to revolution, is not just any attack on a problem but one that has at least some antagonistic content: the power of hitherto privileged groups is curbed and the economic position and social status of underprivileged groups is correspondingly improved.

It may be helpful, before entering into this matter, to set out schematically the varieties of conceivable policies or events to which the antagonistic or non-antagonistic label might be attached. The policies or events shown in the cells of the table are purely illustrative and are drawn from our studies. For example, land tax schemes, a mildly antagonistic measure, belong in the third column because they affect landowners adversely, and in the second row because the landless peasants do not perceive them as immediately beneficial to them. Thus they are distinguished from expropriation (first row, third column), that antagonistic measure par excellence, which simultaneously hurts the rich and benefits the poor. The other conceivable varieties of antagonistic outcomes—those that hurt the poor while benefiting or leaving indifferent the rich—are never actually advocated; but they happen, as when during an inflation or a drought the rich get richer and the poor poorer. In the following discussion we shall have occasion to refer to most of the possible policies shown in the table.

One striking observation which emerges from our studies is that frequently the horizon of policy-makers seems to be limited to either antagonistic or non-antagonistic remedies to the near exclusion of the other. Policy-makers act typically as though they were either completely oblivious of the possibility of redistribution of power and wealth or completely fascinated by it. Not that all policy-makers, after having long dealt in non-antagonistic remedies, suddenly favour antagonistic measures; but these measures suddenly "steal the show," become the dominant theme around which conceivable solutions of the problem are discussed. The situation reminds one of the well-known psychological experiments where a subject is shown a composite picture in which he perceives either an elegant woman or an old witch (or: either seven or eight cubes) and can perhaps learn to switch from one to the other and back, but can never perceive both together.

Now, to a considerable extent, the change in outlook which makes people suddenly switch from, say, a non-antagonistic to an antagonistic perspective is tied to general political and historical developments. No doubt the Cuban revolution contributed powerfully to placing the land reform issue in its most antagonistic form on the agenda of Latin American policy-makers. But, while such overriding influences must be recognized, an exploration of the inner dynamics of the problem-solving process can give us a fuller understanding of such switches in perspective.

ALTERNATIVE REFORM POLICIES AND EVENTS ACCORDING TO THEIR PERCEIVED IMPACT ON DIFFERENT SOCIAL GROUPS

		Impact on the upper-income groups, as perceived by them		
Impact on the lower-income groups, as perceived by them		**BENEFICIAL**	**INDIFFERENT**	**DETRIMENTAL**
	BENEFICIAL	NA Northeast: Allocation of Federal funds. Colombia's agriculture: Special credit facilities and technical assistance.	NA Colonization of public lands.	A Expropriation of privately held lands and parceling out to peasants.
	INDIFFERENT	NA Tax rebates and special credits to large landowners introducing mechanized cropping.	—	A Land tax designed to force landowner to cultivate or rent or sell.
	DETRIMENTAL	**A** Profiteering during drought. Ordinary course of events in early stages (specially 1904–07) of Chilean inflation.	A Ordinary course of events during Northeastern droughts.	NA (?) Mutual sacrifices in inflation.

A = antagonistic NA = non-antagonistic.

Take, as a particularly clear example, the droughts in Brazil's Northeast. Here is a natural calamity gravely affecting all the people making their livelihood in a certain region, and among possible remedies thought will quite normally be given first to the securing of relief and investment funds from the rest of the country and to public works which might attenuate the effects of the next calamity and improve the regional economy in general. The region secures a supplement of consumption and investment resources from the outside, and the intention, presumption and general impression are that all major groups in the region will stand to profit in some measure from the transfer. However, as the problem is tackled in this non-antagonistic fashion over a long period and yet remains as far as ever from a satisfactory solution, renewed analysis turns up some antagonistic factors: the differential impact of the drought on the large landowners and the sharecroppers or rural labourers, the enrichment of some groups and the profiteering that come with drought relief and public works, and, perhaps most important, the impossibility of putting to productive use the waters dammed up in the expensive reservoirs because of the obstacles to irrigation under existing systems of land tenure. Some policy-makers become aware of these factors before others, of course; in fact, in the Brazilian case, we encounter the extraordinarily farsighted and crafty Arrojado Lisboa, the first director of DNOCS, who, just because he realized the antagonistic implications of irrigation, decided to soft-pedal that aspect of the problem and to concentrate on the non-antagonistic task of dam construction in the expectation that, once in place, the dams themselves would "cry out" for progress in irrigation.

Such calculating foresight is rare indeed and generally the various facets of a problem are revealed to the surprised policy-makers, or to some of them, as their labours advance. But if, in a first phase, such labours are entirely concentrated in the non-antagonistic area, and if the problem does contain an antagonistic component, then at some point this component will appear as the principal task. Since antagonistic tasks will ordinarily appear after non-antagonistic policies have long been in use, the attraction of the new is reinforced by the discredit of the older set of policies or perhaps simply by boredom with them. Here lies one explanation for the thoroughness with which non-antagonistic policies may suddenly give way to an antagonistic perspective.

The Brazilian sequence is broadly repeated in our Colombian and Chilean stories: in 1959–1960 antagonistic proposals moved to the centre of the stage in both countries. In Colombia, the theme of outright land reform became dominant in 1960 after experiments with colonization and land taxation had turned out to be unsatisfactory and after entirely non-antagonistic policies, such as agricultural credit, storage, extension, etc., had long been in more or less intensive use. In Chile, the idea that deep "structural" changes, largely of an antagonistic kind, were required to deal with inflation, rather than "merely" monetary measures that would leave the relative power and income positions of various, social groups largely intact, appeared around 1958–1959 with the strength of a fundamental new insight.

It could be asked why our stories seem to move primarily from the use of non-antagonistic to antagonistic remedies. Is it because the latter are intrinsically more persuasive? This is hard to believe. The discovery that non-antagonistic remedies are available after antagonistic measures have held sway should in principle be greeted as just as stunning an intellectual discovery as the opposite feat. It requires at least as much imagination and sophistication to perceive that two groups whose interests were universally assumed to be wholly divergent actually have some important interests in common as to notice an opposition of interests between groups that were hitherto thought to be, and thought of themselves as, partners traveling along the same road towards common objectives. To illustrate, we recall the sweeping victory of Free Trade with its doctrine that foreign trade is mutually beneficial over mercantilism's dogma that one trading partner's gain is the other's loss. The similar discovery that Russia and the United States actually share one overriding interest, namely survival, while it has not created international harmony, has nevertheless had a profound effect, not only on the debates about nuclear strategy and disarmament, but on the behaviour of the two super-powers as well.

Some elements of our stories can also be quoted here. In Colombia, Currie's 1961 proposal to accelerate industrialization and urbanization was favourably received in some sectors of public opinion largely because it opened up a non-antagonistic perspective, a way of sidestepping land reform and its traumatisms. In Chile during the early fifties, the long-continued, desperate and futile struggle of each group to secure a favoured position for itself in the course of inflation endowed with considerable intellectual prestige the idea of "mutual sacrifices." This is a special kind of non-antagonistic remedy (see the table, third row and column): it proposes that all parties undergo an immediate loss, proportionate to their economic position, to solve the problem of inflation; but such a remedy is likely and turned out to be particularly difficult to put across.

The difficulty of finding in our material really good and effective examples for a shift from the antagonistic to the non-antagonistic perspective is easily explained. We are dealing with societies where the existing social order had not been seriously disturbed or questioned at the point of departure of our stories.

The remedies then proposed were those advocated by the well-entrenched upper classes who had no doubts about the identity of their own interests with those of society at large. Only later was this assumed harmony questioned, and the discovery that an antagonistic treatment might be required came as a blinding insight after so long a period of firm belief in, and practice of, the non-antagonistic therapy. This must be understood if the depth of antagonistic feeling in Latin America today is to be correctly gauged.

The Reformer—Naïve or Wily?

In principle, the turn towards the antagonistic perspective should give their chance to both revolutionaries and reformers. Revolutionaries will maintain, as we have seen, that the needed changes cannot be effected without a *prior* overthrow of the "system"; reformers, on the other hand, behave like the country or the chess player who exasperatingly fights on when "objectively" he has already lost—and occasionally goes on to win! The reformer sets out after his reforms blissfully unaware that the ruling class will never allow this or that antagonistic measure to pass or to become effective. He is a naïve and pathetic figure at the start, an easy target for the revolutionary's sarcasms, but since he *acts,* he learns from his mistakes and from the resistances he encounters, and he frequently ends up as a wily individual from whom the revolutionary may well learn a trick or two.

This education of the reformer is well brought out in our stories. In Colombia, for example, reformers attempted in the fifties to achieve better land utilization through the mildly antagonistic measure of penalty taxation combined with the non-antagonistic measure of colonization of public lands. But they soon found out that planned colonization can make at best only a marginal contribution to the solution of the agrarian problem and that penalty taxation arouses opposition without generating support, since it is fiercely resisted by the landowners but is not perceived as a direct benefit by the landless farmers. The turn to land reform can in part be explained by these negative experiences; even though it is a more antagonistic measure than taxation, its proponents are sure of support from the campesinos, they do not incur the hostility of the small and medium-sized landowners, and the large ones may actually not fight the reform very hard because any individual owner is liable to think that the reform will either not be applied at all or will not reach down to him. Taking full advantage of such constellations, our "naïve" reformer has by now turned into a master tactician who manages to slip through a workable reform to the surprise and dismay of both landowners and revolutionaries!

A similarly a priori improbable feat is the establishment of SUDENE with its group of determined reform-minded top officials, equipped with considerable finance and power, in the middle of a Northeast still dominated by its traditional elites. Again, this achievement was due to learning from prior non-antagonistic attempts at solving the Northeastern problem and to a judicious exploitation of a crisis atmosphere combined with a remarkable talent for forming temporary alliances.

The reforms which take place in Latin America today are anything but manifestations of sweet reasonableness. Nor are they accurately described as resulting from a "recognition by the ruling class that it has to give up something in order not to lose everything," as the cliché would have it. Rather they are extraordinary feats of contriving in the course of which some of the hostile power groups are won over, others are neutralized and outwitted, and the remaining diehards often barely overcome by a coalition of highly heterogeneous forces.

"Divide and reform" tactics are usually found to be one important ingredient of the manoeuvres making these feats possible. The reason why such tactics may be successful has been well put by one of Latin America's most acute political thinkers:

> The social conflicts existing at present in our country express essentially not so much irreducible class struggles as conflicts that divide, within the domain of each class, its dynamic and static sectors, or the productive and parasitic forces.[16]

When economic development has been underway for some time it may be possible to limit the purely antagonistic portion of one's program to, for example, the "parasitic, reactionary, routine-ridden" landlords while neutralizing and perhaps even enlisting the collaboration of the progressive, modernizing group. This is admittedly an extremely delicate operation both because of the long-standing

16. Hélio Jaguaribe, *O Nacionalismo na atualidade brasileira,* Institute Brasileiro de Estudos Brasileiros, Rio de Janeiro, 1958, p. 50. For a further systematic development of the theme of increasing differentiation of Brazilian society, see his recent *Desenvolvimento económico e desenvolvimento politico,* Editôra Fondo de. Cultura, Rio, 1962, particularly p. 169 ff. Differences in the rigidity of class barriers and traditional power structures in Brazil are also stressed by Celso Furtado in "Brazil: What Kind of Revolution?," *Foreign Affairs,* April 1963, pp. 526–535.

commitment of the pro-reform forces to comprehensive change and because of traditional fears of property owners that any one reform may be followed by another, more radical one. In fact, at the present time it is still uncertain whether a limited, rather than cataclysmic, reform can be successfully carried out in the Northeast of Brazil where the collaboration of the more progressive cane growers and sugar mill owners is sought in diversifying agriculture in the coastal belt or in Colombia where the reform law tends to exempt efficient large-scale producers from the projected land redistribution.

These considerations qualify our earlier remarks on the way in which action on a problem is stimulated. No doubt this happens most regularly as a to-be-remedied condition is aggravated or intensified. The histories of the Chilean inflation and of the Northeastern droughts abundantly illustrate this point. Yet, under certain circumstances, the opposite relationship will also be found: action of either a reformist or a revolutionary nature may be stimulated when the problem begins to *recede!* In recent years the most conspicuous example of this relationship is the fight against colonialism which has increased in ferocity the more clearly colonialism was seen to be doomed. Action intensified because the task to be accomplished by the anti-colonial forces suddenly looked manageable and a favourable outcome of their fight appeared probable. Similarly the generalized fight for agrarian reform in Latin America today may have been stimulated by the fact that old-style latifundismo has not only been eradicated in the countries which have experienced agrarian revolutions but is being eroded elsewhere as well.[17] In Colombia, as we have seen, modern commercialized and mechanized agriculture has been expanding in some erstwhile latifundia while others continue to be broken up by spontaneous colonization and squatting. Thus the problem has become smaller and more manageable: in a way, the animal is already cornered and wounded and the agrarian reformers, as elsewhere the anti-colonialists, are moving in for the kill. In such a situation, the reformers do not face a wholly hopeless task, and what would have required a major social upheaval thirty years ago may be achieved today by methods short of revolution.

17. A counter-example that comes to mind is "poverty in the affluent society." Action on the problem of poverty, once it has shrunk in size, becomes more difficult as the remaining poor tend to belong to a *hard core* of sick, old, "unemployable," etc.; action also becomes less compelling because the problem victims are increasingly scattered or isolated. Whether action on a problem is stimulated or slackens as the problem recedes may well depend on these two questions: (1) Does the problem have a hard core? (2) Are the remaining victims of the problem capable of joint action?

Action is actually stimulated when a problem recedes, not only by the fact that it begins to look more manageable and "lickable," but also because revolutionaries are likely to redouble their energies when they notice that the problem on which they had counted to revolutionize society is fading away. Lenin had exactly this reaction in the face of the transformation of Russian agriculture consequent upon the Stolypin reforms and was clearly worried lest the land measures "so transform the countryside that it would no longer be a revolutionary force."[18]

In fact, it is quite possible that revolutionaries have one of their best chances when some policy-makers begin to convince themselves that the problem is well on the way out and that it can safely be left to fade away. This may happen either because, as outsiders, the policy-makers do not experience the problem in their everyday lives or because they are not interested in policies that "merely" help existing trends along instead of majestically initiating new ones.[19] Thus they will judge that patience is in order at precisely the time when those who do experience the problem will become desperately impatient. Interestingly, patience of the outsiders and impatience of the insiders increase for the same reason, namely, that "the end is in sight."

Much has been made in the preceding pages of the opportunity to gain new allies which becomes available to today's reformmongers in Latin America. But even with those allies, the margins with which the battles for reforms are won are narrow indeed. It is therefore easily understood why reformmongers dare not cut themselves off from any actual or potential group support of substantial size even

18. Bertram D. Wolfe, *Three Who Made a Revolution,* Beacon, Boston, 1948, p. 360. The following passage quoted by Wolfe (ibid., p. 361) from Lenin's writings is revealing: "The Stolypin Constitution and the Stolypin agrarian policy mark a new phase in the breakdown of the old, semi-patriarchal and semi-feudal system of tsarism, a new movement toward its transformation into a middle-class monarchy. If this should continue for very long periods of time … it might force us to renounce any agrarian program at all. It *would be empty and stupid democratic phrase-mongering to say that the success of such a policy in Russia is 'impossible.' It is possible!* If Stolypin's policy is continued … then the agrarian structure of Russia will become completely bourgeois, the stronger peasants will acquire almost all the allotments of land, and agriculture will become capitalistic …" (My italics.) *Proletarii,* April 29, 1908, reprinted in *Collected Works,* Third Russian Edition, Vol. XII, p. 193. This passage also shows Lenin to be far less dogmatic concerning the possibility of reform than today's "Marxist-Leninists."
19. See p. 154 of *Journeys* for an episode in our Colombian story which invites this interpretation.

though they may disagree with the final objectives of that group. Clearly it would be foolish for them to gain allies on the Centre and Right at the cost of losing the Left.

This need to spread his net as wide as possible will make the reformmonger appear to be quite naïve once again, this time about the dangers of Communist infiltration. Often this is so because the most effective reformmongers are to be found amongst erstwhile revolutionaries who notice, much to their own surprise, that some of the social changes they have been seeking can be achieved without that "prior" revolution in whose necessity they had long believed. To turn such private insights into the collective experience of a group that has long remained in a position of pure protest against the established order is perhaps even more important than the achievement of any single reform in itself if Latin American societies are ever to become "integrated." From this point of view also, the effective reformmonger must delay as long as possible, and perhaps avoid altogether, any break with his radical followers. Frequently this will not require any special effort or dissimulation on his part since he is himself still doubtful—quite rightly so until the returns are in—that it is possible to dispense with revolution.

At his best, our reformer-revolutionary will therefore retain the trust of his old followers even as he enlists aid and support from new quarters. He will now have to play to several quite different galleries; he will contrive change by negotiating for new allies while not ceasing to agitate for it. These two tasks are of course so different that they are best performed if they can be dealt out to *several* principal actors who feel quite independent of each other, in the manner of the struggle for Italian unification which was able to draw on the highly diverse talents of Cavour, a master contriver, and of Mazzini and Garibaldi, who filled the roles of conspirators and agitators. But sometimes there is only one chief actor who, to be successful, must combine both roles, appear in the guise of Necker and Stolypin one day and in that of Danton or Lenin the next—a highly risky assignment, though perhaps also rather an entertaining one!

In fine, the roads to reform are narrow and perilous, they appear quite unsafe to the outside observer however sympathetic he may be, *but they exist.* Having become acquainted with their twists and turns throughout this book, we emerge with a heightened consciousness of the difficulties facing Latin American policy-makers; but also and foremost, with a new appreciation of the many unsuspected and unorthodox opportunities for manoeuvre and advance.

7

Obstacles to Development: A Classification and a Quasi-Vanishing Act

One could think of several ways of classifying obstacles: natural (lack of resources) and man-made (lack of law and order, lack of capital), objective (lack of resources or of capital) and subjective (lack of entrepreneurship and risk-taking, lack of a desire for change, contempt for material success), internal (all the factors so far named) and external (exploitation by a foreign power), etc.

I find it useful, however, to adopt a classification which is grounded in the concept of "obstacle" itself and which, in the process, questions its solidity from the outset. It is a principal contention of this note that the concept is far from solid, that it is not possible to identify either a finite number of "reliable" obstacles to development or a hierarchy among these obstacles which would permit us to arrange them neatly into boxes marked "basic," "important," "secondary," etc.

The traditional method of identifying an obstacle to development points immediately to the conceptual weakness we have in mind. The method consists in looking up the history of one or several economically advanced countries, noting certain situations that were present at about the time when development was brought actively under way in one or several of these countries (a temperate climate, a population belonging to the white race, "primitive" accumulation of capital, coal deposits, law and order, widespread literacy, a group of Schumpeterian entrepreneurs, a fairly efficient and honest civil service, agrarian reform, the Protestant ethic, etc. etc.), and then construing the absence of any of these situations as an obstacle to development. This procedure could lead one to conclude that the more countries develop, the more difficult does it appear for the remainder to do the same, for each successfully developing country does so under a set of special conditions, thus lengthening the list of obstacles (i.e. the absence of these conditions) which have to be "overcome."

Fortunately, this conclusion is as implausible as it is dismal. The usual way of escaping from it is by the successive substitution of a newly discovered fundamental obstacle for those that held sway before the latest theoretical or historical insight. In this paper we shall proceed in a more empirical vein and attempt to classify obstacles in the order of their greater or smaller reliability as obstacles, on the basis of what evidence we have been able to collect.

Suppose some specific situation or condition can be shown to have been essential for the development of country X at time t; in other words, the absence of this condition performed as an insuperable barrier to the development of X. Now it is possible that the development experience of other countries confirms that of X; on the other hand, one can think of the following ways in which the barrier or obstacle would fail to perform as such in other countries:

1. The obstacle does not constitute an absolute barrier in the case of country Y; certain forward moves are available to this country, and the obstacle, while still exerting a negative influence on development, can be dealt with, perhaps more easily, at a later time.
2. The alleged obstacle, in view of another set of circumstances, turns out not to be an obstacle at all and therefore does not need to be removed, either now or later.
3. The alleged obstacle, in view of yet other circumstances, turns into a positive advantage and asset for development.

In justifying each of these possibilities—and, in the process, discovering several other variants—we shall invert the order in which they have been cited and thus start with the extreme case.

Ambivalence: Alleged Obstacles That Turn into Assets

How difficult it is to classify certain concrete situations as unequivocally hostile or favourable to economic development is well illustrated by the institution of the extended or joint family.[1] Several Western economists belonging to quite different schools of thought have taken the position that the extended family dilutes individual incentives and that its demise and replacement by the nuclear family is required for dynamic development to occur.[2] This is, of course, a highly ethnocentric argument. Westerners who hold this view find it difficult to imagine that anyone would want to exert himself if the fruits of his labours accrue largely to what they consider as distant relatives; implicit in the idea that the extended family is a bar to economic progress is therefore the judgment that no one in his right mind can really care for the welfare of his third cousin.

But suppose "they" do? In that case the argument against the extended family not only falls to the ground, but one can immediately conceive of several advantages in an arrangement in which the basic economic decision-making unit is not the nuclear family, but a wider grouping. For one, the special relationship existing among the members permits them to undertake new tasks requiring co-operation without prior mastery of such complications as hiring labour and keeping accounts.[3] Furthermore, the members may pool their resources not only for consumption, but equally for investment purposes; and thus it may be possible for them to finance business ventures as well as advanced education for the more gifted among them.[4]

Can we save the proposition for the rather special situation where the extended family still exists as a formal behaviour code but can no longer command the full loyalty of the individual member of the society and is perhaps actively resented by him? In that case the strictures of our economists would seem to apply fully.

1. For points similar to those made in this and the following section and for illustrations from India and Nigeria, respectively, see Lloyd I. Rudolph and Suzanne Hoeber Rudolph, *The Modernity of Tradition: Political Development in India* (Chicago: University of Chicago Press, 1967); and C. S. Whitaker, Jr., "A Dysrhythmic Process of Political Change," *World Politics* 19 (January 1967): 190–217.
2. P. T. Bauer and B. S. Yamey, *The Economics of Under-Developed Countries* (Chicago: University of Chicago Press, 1957), p. 66; and Benjamin Higgins, *Economic Development* (New York: Norton, 1959), p. 256.
3. C. S. Belshaw, *In Search of Wealth: A Study of the Emergence of Commercial Operations in the Melanesian Society of South-Eastern Papua* (Menasha, WI: American Anthropological Association, 1955), chaps. 5 and 7.
4. Peter Marris, *Family and Social Change in an African City* (London: Routledge, 1961), p. 138. The importance of kinship ties in the early spread of banking and mercantile enterprise in the West is of course well established.

Yet, such is the variety of possible situations that even here we must tread with care. For example, the very desire to withhold extra earnings from one's family may deflect the more enterprising members of the family from a bureaucratic career (where earnings are fixed and a matter of public knowledge) into a business career (where earnings are uncertain and can be concealed).[5] Moreover, if there is any time lag between the newly won affluence of the individual and the famous moving-in of all the relatives to share in his newly won riches, then the institution of the extended family combined with the desire to escape from it provides a stimulus to ever new spurts of temporarily relative-exempt entrepreneurial activity.[6] Hence, even if the sharing implicit in the extended family system is resented, the obligation to share may act like those taxes that stimulate individuals to greater effort at securing non-taxable gains (and at tax evasion).

Our point is strengthened by the observation that, just as the extended family cannot be held to stunt growth under all circumstances, so the nuclear family will not always promote development. If the economic operator perceives no possibility of common interest, action, or gain with anyone outside his immediate blood relatives, then economic advance is likely to be severely hamstrung, as I have explained elsewhere and as has been documented by several empirical studies.[7]

A more general remark is in order at this point. We have said that an obstacle to development may usually be defined as the absence of a condition that was found to be present in a country which subsequently developed. But in many cases the question that ought to have been asked is how much of this condition was present. Too much may be just as deleterious as too little. It is too much rather than too little individualism and entrepreneurship and too little willingness to work with discipline in a hierarchical organization that plagues much of

5. Ibid., p. 139.
6. "The fact that, under the customary rules of inheritance, individual property was always in process of conversion to family property provided individuals with a great incentive to acquire additional lands, over which they had, for some time at least, unlimited control." Polly Hill, *The Migrant Cocoa-Farmers of Southern Ghana* (Cambridge: Cambridge University Press, 1963), p. 16.
7. A. O. Hirschman, *The Strategy of Economic Development* (New Haven: Yale University Press, 1958), pp. 14–20; Edward C. Banfield, *The Moral Basis of a Backward Society* (Glencoe, Ill.: The Free Press, 1958); Clifford Geertz, *Peddlers and Princes* (Chicago: University of Chicago Press, 1963), pp. 42–47, 73 ff, 122 ff.

Southeast Asia and also other underdeveloped lands.[8] Too much law and order may be as stifling as too little is disruptive. Let us arrange the possible states of society along a horizontal scale with two such extremes at opposite ends. Suppose we measure the chances for development along the vertical scale. In most cases, then, these chances will seriously drop off at both ends of the scale, but they may well be tolerably good during a wide stretch in the middle. In other words, societies that are all individualistic entrepreneurship or that are all hierarchical discipline will both be hard put to develop, but in the real world we are likely to encounter predominantly individualistic and predominantly hierarchical societies that contain some, perhaps well hidden, ingredients of discipline and of entrepreneurship, respectively, hence, they may both be capable of development, even though the paths on which they will set out towards this goal are likely to be very different.

We have dwelt at some length on the extended family, since it illustrates well our notion of ambivalence of alleged obstacles. We shall now give a few more examples, rapidly and at random, to suggest the wide spectrum of situations to which the notion applies.

In Europe the tradition of very high craftsmanship was initially most helpful in the development of new mechanical methods. But the rapid pace of development in the United States in the nineteenth century has been explained in part by the absence of such a tradition in the new continent and by the relative scarcity of skilled labour which stimulated the introduction of capital-intensive, skilled-labour-saving techniques.[9]

Lack of social mobility ranks high as an impediment to economic progress because it sets limits to individual achievement and prevents the best utilization of manpower resources. In Japan, however, the rigid social barriers which kept the merchants and their sons from joining the bureaucracy or from becoming landlords have been hailed as one of the sources of private entrepreneurship and have

8. Malaya probably suffers from an excess of enterprise, since this is a factor which tends to disintegrate existing business." T. H. Silcock, *The Economy of Malaya* (Singapore: Moore, 1956), p. 44.
9. H. J. Habakkuk, *American and British Technology in the 19th Century* (Cambridge: Cambridge University Press, 1962), pp. 116, 128–129.

been contrasted with the harmful effects of the ease with which such transitions were effected by the successful merchants of China.[10]

What could be more inimical to the accumulation of material wealth than the ascetic ideal? Yet, as soon as this ideal extends to combating indulgence in leisure (in addition to indulgence in food, drink, and sex), capital accumulation through self-denying work is a likely, if surprising, result.[11]

Law and order and the absence of civil strife seem to be obvious preconditions for the gradual and patient accumulation of skills, capital, and investors' confidence that must be the foundation for economic progress. We are now told, however, that the presence of war-like Indians in North America and the permanent conflict between them and the Anglo-Saxon settlers was a great advantage, because it made necessary methodical, well-planned, and gradual advances towards an interior which always remained in close logistic and cultural contact with the established communities to the East. In Brazil, on the contrary, the backlands were open and virtually uncontested; the result was that once an excessively vast area had been occupied in an incredibly brief time span the pioneers became isolated and regressed economically and culturally. Jacques Lambert, author of this observation, sums up his remarks in the following sentence: "In contradiction to a deeply entrenched legend, which paints the Anglo-Saxon colonizers as individualists and adventurers and the Iberians as colonial functionaries without initiative, Brazil is now paying dearly for the taste of adventure of the Portuguese and for their excess of initiative."[12]

Alleged Obstacles Whose Elimination Turns Out To Be Unnecessary

We turn now to a somewhat less paradoxical type of situation: the presumed obstacle no longer changes colours and becomes a blessing in disguise; its existence simply leads to the charting of a hitherto unfamiliar path to economic progress, and the resulting, economically more advanced society exhibits a profile that is

10. M. J. Levy, Jr., "Contrasting Factors in the Modernization of China and Japan," in S. Kuznets et al., eds., *Economic Growth: Brazil, India, Japan* (Durham, NC: Duke University Press, 1955), pp. 496–536.
11. Karl F. Helleiner, "Moral Conditions of Economic Growth," *Journal of Economic History* 11 (Spring 1951): 97–116.
12. Jacques Lambert, *Os dois Brasís* (Rio: Ministerio da Educação, 1959), pp. 116–117.

"different" because of the survival of certain institutions, attitudes, etc., which were originally thought to be incompatible with development. These situations can be difficult to distinguish clearly from the preceding ones; for if the presumed obstacle has at all survived, then one can frequently show that it is not only tolerated, but actually lends strength to the new state of affairs. Nevertheless, there is a difference, at least initially, between an obstacle that is being turned or neutralized and one that turns out not to be an obstacle at all, but a factor that promotes and propels development.

The confusion on this score is due to the somewhat shapeless notion of "challenge." Any difficulty or obstacle can be transmuted by a sort of semantic hocus pocus into a challenge which evokes a response. But these Toynbeean terms are not helpful, for they dissolve the concepts of difficulty and obstacle altogether, instead of permitting the differentiated analysis we are aiming at here. To recall an example from our preceding section, it is incorrect to say that the existence of the extended family is a "challenge" to developers; it is rather a real troublemaker in some respects and some situations and a valuable asset in others, as we have shown. The notion of challenge is similarly ineffectual in the case, now under consideration, of obstacles which have no positive dimension, but which do not preclude development via some "alternate route" (alternate to the removal of the obstacle). Let us take a country which lacks an important natural resource such as coal or whose history has not permitted any sizeable "primitive accumulation of capital"; when such countries substitute hydroelectric energy for coal, or bank credit and state finance for private equity capital,[13] they are not "responding" to a "challenge." They are merely encountering a different way of achieving growth which, of course, they might never have discovered had they been more "normally" endowed. "Believe me," says the Marquise de Merteuil in Laclos's *Les Liaisons Dangereuses,* "one rarely acquires the qualities he can do without." Yet, to acquire these very qualities is less a matter of responding to a challenge than of discovering one's comparative advantage. In doing so a country may not even have been aware of the fact that the lack of a certain natural resource, institution, or attitudinal endowment constituted a special difficulty, an obstacle, or much less, a "challenge."

If a country lacks one of the conventional "prerequisites," it can overcome this lack in two distinct ways. One consists in inventing its own substitute for the prerequisite; as just mentioned, Gerschenkron has given us an exceptionally rich and

13. Alexander Gerschenkron, *Economic Backwardness in Historical Perspective* (Cambridge, MA: Harvard University Press, 1962), chaps. 1 and 2.

convincing account of such substitution processes for the Marxian prerequisite of primitive accumulation of capital. The other possibility is that the purported "prerequisite" turns out to be not only substitutable, but outright dispensable; nothing in particular needs to take its place, and we are simply proven wrong in our belief that a certain resource, institution, or attitude needed to be created or eradicated for development to be possible. In other words, the requirements of development turn out to be more tolerant of cultural and institutional variety than we thought on the basis of our limited prior experience. Recent research shows this to be the case in various parts of the world. A revealing study of the Japanese factory by Abegglen has shown in considerable detail how "rationalization and impersonalization are not necessary to the adoption from the West of an industrial economy."[14] Here we are admittedly only one step away from our previous category, where the negative factor is transmuted into a positive one. A study of Argentine entrepreneurship takes this step explicitly.

> Analysts of entrepreneurship hold certain of the Latin American characteristics to be deterrents to success in the development of industry. Granting that [Di Tella, the founder of the firm under study] neither could nor wanted to break the emotional patterns of an inward-looking individualism, a reliance on *personalismo,* or the claims of the family … he skillfully neutralized these assumed deterrents or turned them into positive assets. He used themes and relationships such as *personalismo, dignidad, simpatia, confianza,* and the patron-client relation for the development of [his firm].[15]

In a somewhat different vein, a study of Indian village life has shown that the social, political, and cultural changes that come with development may be of sharply different dimensions depending on the precise way in which economic opportunities arise. The study deals with two villages and the way in which they have taken advantage of irrigation. Change is shown to be more extensive and

14. James G. Abegglen, *The Japanese Factory* (Glencoe, IL: The Free Press, 1958), p. 141.
15. Thomas C. Cochran and Reuben E. Reina, *Entrepreneurship in Argentine Culture: Torcuato Di Tella and S. I. A. M.* (Philadelphia: University of Pennsylvania Press, 1962), pp. 262–263. Abegglen also occasionally takes this step, arguing that certain elements of traditional Japanese culture are not only compatible with the new order, but actually lend strength to it: "the principle of family loyalty and cohesion, when successfully symbolized and incorporated into military, industrial and financial organizations, may have become an important source of energy and motivation for the transition to industrialization" *(Japanese Factory,* pp. 136–137).

comprehensive in the dry village whose lands are close to, but not right in, the irrigation district than in the wet village. In a perceptive introduction, Sir Arthur Lewis remarks: "What we need to know is just how powerful a solvent the love of money is. The answer seems to be that it dissolves what stands in its way, but nothing more. How much is changed depends partly on how much is compatible, and partly on how closely interrelated the various institutions are."[16] It appears from the studies here surveyed that a variety of non-Western institutions are either more compatible with economic development (Sir Arthur's "love of money") or less interrelated with those that are incompatible than has been believed by those who look at each social situation as an "interrelated whole."[17]

Obstacles Whose Elimination Is Postponable

We are now ready for those obstacles which we come closest to recognizing as such, those that refuse to turn mysteriously into assets or to be accommodated in an unexpected fashion within an economically progressive society. They stubbornly remain factors detrimental to development which ought to be eliminated. In many cases, however,—and this is the point of the present section—the priority which this task commands can be shown to be less rigidly defined than had been thought.

I am returning here to a theme which I have set forth at length in my previous writings. I have drawn attention to "inverted" or "disorderly" or "cart-before-the-horse" sequences that are apt to occur in the process of economic and social development; and I have argued that, under certain circumstances, these sequences could be "efficient" in the sense of making possible the achievement of stated

16. T. S. Epstein, *Economic Development and Social Change in Southern India* (Manchester: Manchester University Press, 1962), p. x.
17. "...[Various] studies suggest that the impact of economic modernization upon the total social system is not necessarily as revolutionary and all-embracing as it has sometimes been described; or, put somewhat differently, a modern economic system may be compatible with a wider range of non-economic cultural patterns and social structures than has often been thought." Geertz, *Peddlers and Princes,* p. 144. For an interesting essay on the compatibility of certain traditional values (as distinct from "traditionalism") with progressive economic development, see Bert F. Hoselitz, "Tradition and Economic Growth," in Braibanti and Spengler, eds., *Tradition, Values and Socio-Economic Development* (Durham, NC: Duke University Press, 1961), pp. 83–113.

goals of economic expansion within a briefer time period or at a smaller social cost than would be possible if the more orderly sequence were adhered to.[18]

The implication of this approach for the notion of barrier and obstacle is evident. While it grants that insufficient electric power, inadequate education, or the absence of agrarian reform are serious defects, it is suspicious of theories that erect the elimination of such defects into prerequisites for any forward movement; in addition to the head-on assault on these defects, it will evaluate, look for, and scrutinize ways in which the economy can be moved forward elsewhere and how thereby additional pressure can be brought to bear on the acknowledged obstacles. If they are truly hindrances, then any forward move that can be instigated in spite of them is going to make it even more imperative than before to get rid of them; if, on the other hand, this additional pressure is not generated, then perhaps these obstacles are not to be taken quite so seriously, and they belong, at least in part, in our second category (alleged obstacles that, as it turns out, can be accommodated into an economically progressive society).

Rather than repeat my earlier argument and cite a series of examples to which it applies, I shall limit myself here to one particular type of inverted sequence which seems to me of considerable interest and with which I have not dealt before.

As the search for the conditions of economic development has been unremittingly pursued by social scientists over the past years, increasing attention has been given to the role of attitudes, beliefs, and basic personality characteristics favourable to the emergence of innovation, entrepreneurship, and the like. While these theories, with their expeditions into psychology and psychiatry, are frequently fascinating, the message they leave behind is almost as dismal as that of the very first theories of development which attributed a decisive role to such unalterable factors as race, climate, and natural resources. Rooted, as they are purported to be, in childhood experiences and transmitted unfailingly from one generation to the next, the deplored attitudes or personality structure appear to be similarly refractory to any but the most radical treatment.

We have already seen, in our first two sections, that a good many attitudes which, on the basis of some previous experiences, had been believed to be detrimental to development can, in different settings, be neutralized or even be put to positive use, as the case may be. But let us accept now the premise that some residual attitudes, beliefs, and personality characteristics are really and truly

18. See Hirschman, *Strategy*, pp. 80–81, 93–94, 154–155; and *Journeys Toward Progress*, p. 260.

incompatible with sustained economic advance—must we then accept the conclusion that *all* our efforts should be concentrated on extirpating them, and that no other road to progress is available?

Fortunately, while the behavioural scientists have become depth psychologists, the psychologists have come up with the discovery that attitudinal change can be a *consequence* of behavioural change, rather than its precondition! From a variety of approaches exploring this nexus, I shall single out the *Theory of Cognitive Dissonance,* which was originated in 1957 by Leon Festinger in a book bearing that title. Since then the theory has been widely investigated, tested, and discussed; much of the empirical evidence which has been gathered, together with a chapter on the applicability of the theory to problems of social change, can be found in a volume by Jack W. Brehm and the late Arthur R. Cohen, *Explorations in Cognitive Dissonance.*[19]

Briefly and in nontechnical language, the theory states that a person who, for some reason, commits himself to act in a manner contrary to his beliefs, or to what he believes to be his beliefs, is in a state of dissonance. Such a state is unpleasant, and the person will attempt to reduce dissonance. Since the "discrepant behaviour" has already taken place and cannot be undone, while the belief can be changed, reduction of dissonance can be achieved principally by changing one's beliefs in the direction of greater harmony with the action.

The theory thus predicts significant shifts in attitude consequent upon commitment to discrepant behaviour, and its predictions have been verified empirically. In a classic experiment, for example, college students are asked to write an essay supporting the side opposite to their private view on a current issue. It turns out that after writing the essay (and to some extent even right after committing themselves to write it and before actually writing it), the students' attitude shifts away from what they used to consider their position on the issue. An interesting refinement of the experiment consists in varying the reward given to the students for writing the essay: it then appears that, in contrast to the usual ideas about reinforcement, highly rewarded students change their opinion much less than the lowly rewarded ones, the reason being that dissonance and hence the extent of the shift is highest when the discrepant behaviour cannot be explained away and dismissed by the ego as having at least some pleasurable result.

19. It should be pointed out that the theory is by no means universally accepted. For a highly critical appraisal, see. N. P. Chapanis and A. Chapanis, "Cognitive Dissonance: Five Years Later," *Psychological Bulletin* (January 1964): 1–22.

This theory has been of practical use in helping us understand the processes of "thought reform" or "brainwashing" as applied, for example, to U.S. prisoners of war by their Chinese captors during the Korean War; in a more constructive vein, the theory has contributed to illuminate the psychological processes leading to acceptance of racial integration. A further fruitful field of application of the theory may be the process of attitude change which is required in the course of economic development. The following quotations from the Brehm-Cohen volume are suggestive:

> The theory is different in its essential nature than most other theoretical models in psychology. Where the major concern in other theories has been largely with the guidance of behavior—that is, with what leads to a given behavior or commitment—dissonance theory deals, at least in part, with the *consequences* of a given behavior or commitment.[20]

> Dissonance theory attempts to understand the conditions under which behavioral commitments produce cognitive and attitudinal realignments in persons.[21]

In other words, dissonance theory deals with the possibility of replacing the "orderly" sequence, where attitude change is conceived as the prerequisite to behavioural change, by a "disorderly" one, where modern attitudes are acquired ex post, as a consequence of the dissonance aroused by "modern" type of behaviour which happens to be engaged in by people with non-modern attitudes. One question will, of course, be asked, namely: how can a commitment to "modern" behaviour be obtained from people whose values and attitudes preclude in principle such behaviour? Actually, however, this is not much of a problem among late-coming societies surrounded by modernity and by opportunities to transgress into or try out modern behaviour; at one time or another, it is likely that the latecomer will stumble more or less absentmindedly into such behaviour as pursuit of individual profit, entrepreneurial risk-taking, promotion according to merit, long-term planning, holding of democratic elections, etc.; dissonance will thus arise and will then gradually lead to those changes in attitude and basic beliefs which were thought to be prerequisites to the just-mentioned modes of behaviour. The art of promoting development may therefore consist primarily in multiplying the

20. Jack W. Brehm and Arthur R. Cohen, *Explorations in Cognitive Dissonance* (New York: John Wiley & Sons, 1962), p. 299.
21. Ibid., p. 271.

opportunities to engage in these dissonance-arousing actions and in inducing an initial commitment to them.[22]

One observation will conclude this section. A country which achieves economic advance and modernization through the process just described, that is, where behavioural change paces attitudinal change, is likely to exhibit a personality rather different from the country whose elite right at the outset of the development journey is imbued with the Protestant ethic and saturated with achievement motivation. Because, in the case of the former country these motivations are being laboriously acquired ex post and en route, its path will be more halting and circuitous and its typical personality may well be subject to particularly strong tension between traditional and modern values.[23] While a country can well develop without being endowed at the outset with all the "right" values and attitudes, its development profile and experience cannot but bear the marks of the order and manner in which it accomplishes its various tasks.

This is the end of our exercise in classification. It goes without saying that its purpose was not to destroy entirely the notion of barrier, obstacle, or prerequisite. In the first place, the classification was not meant to be exhaustive, and there may well exist a residual category of obstacles which by no stretch of the imagination can be considered as assets, which cannot be accommodated or neutralized, and

22. If one were to extend the above-mentioned "refinement" of the theory to the development context, one would conclude that the conditioning of foreign aid on internal reform can do positive harm at the stage when an underdeveloped country is about to commit itself to new types of "modern" or reform actions; to reward such perhaps partly dissonant behaviour would lead to less cumulative change than if the behaviour could not be dismissed by the actors as something they did just to get hold of the aid funds. In this way, the theory throws some light on the difficulties of using aid as a means of promoting internal reform which have beset the Alliance for Progress since its inception. Besides many other constructive uses, foreign aid may be helpful in promoting reform and will serve as a reinforcing agent when it is conceived and presented as a means of reducing the cost of a reform to which the policy-makers in the recipient country are already firmly committed; but it is cast in a self-defeating role if it is proffered as a quid pro quo for the reform commitment itself. …
23. In *Journeys Toward Progress*, pp. 235 ff., I have drawn a related difference by distinguishing between societies which, in the process of tackling their problems, let motivation to solve problems outrun their understanding, and those that do not usually tackle problems unless the means to solve them are close at hand. Here also the two styles of problem solving are shown to result in sharply differing development experiences.

whose removal must be accomplished before any other forward step can be usefully attempted. Secondly, if certain alleged obstacles turn out to be blessings in disguise, quite a few factors, hitherto considered as wholly favourable to development, are likely to function in some situations as *curses* in disguise.

Finally, and most important, while our exercise points to many ways in which obstacles can be made into assets or lived with or turned, it says nothing about the ability to perceive these possibilities on the part of the policy-makers in developing countries. If this ability is strictly limited, as is often the case, then this very limitation emerges as a super obstacle, which commands and conditions the existence and seriousness of the more conventional obstacles. And it can now be told that the survey here presented was really aimed at loosening the grip of this central difficulty.

8

The Principle of the Hiding Hand

The karnaphuli pulp and paper mill is one of the earliest large-scale industrial enterprises to have been set up in Pakistan after Partition and Independence. Planned by the official Industrial Development Corporation to utilize the vast resources of the bamboo forests of the Chittagong Hill Tracts along the upper reaches of the Karnaphuli River in East Pakistan, the mill started to operate in 1953. It had perhaps more than its share of technical and managerial teething troubles, but considerable progress had been achieved by 1959 when its management passed into private hands. Soon thereafter, a major upset endangered the very life of the mill: the bamboo began to flower, an event entirely unforeseen and probably unforeseeable in the present state of our knowledge since it occurs only once every fifty to seventy years: given the resulting paucity of observations, the life cycle of the many varieties of bamboo is by no means fully known. In any event, the variety that supplied the Karnaphuli mill with some 85% of its raw material flowered and then, poetically but quite uneconomically, died.

It was known that flowering of the bamboo results in death of the whole plant and in regeneration from the seeds rather than, as normally, from the rhizomes; but it was *not* known that the bamboo that dies upon flowering would be unusable for pulping since it would disintegrate upon being transported and floated down the river. Another unpleasant surprise was the discovery that, once flowering was over, a number of years would have to pass before the new bamboo shoots would grow to a size fit for commercial exploitation. In its seventh year of operation the mill therefore faced the extraordinary task of finding another raw material base.

In a temporary and costly way, the problem was solved by importing pulp, but other, more creative responses were not long in coming. An organization was set up to collect bamboo in villages throughout East Pakistan (the waterways crisscrossing the country make for cheap transportation of bulky cargo), sundry lumber was cut in the tracts, and, most important, a research program was started to identify other fast-growing species that might to some extent replace the unreliable bamboo as the principal raw material base for the mill. Permission was obtained to plant an experimental area of six square miles with several of the more promising species, and plans to cover a much larger area are underway. Thus, the crisis of the flowering bamboo may in the end lead to a diversification of the raw material base for the mill.

Looking backward it may be said that the Karnaphuli mill was "lucky": its planners had badly overestimated the permanent availability of bamboo, but the mill escaped the possibly disastrous consequences of this error by an offsetting underestimate—or, more correctly, by the unsuspected availability—of alternative raw materials.

The question I wish to explore is whether this experience really was a matter of pure luck or whether there are reasons to expect some systematic association of such providentially offsetting errors. A similar phenomenon often occurs in successful irrigation and irrigation-hydroelectric projects: the river that is being tapped is frequently found not to have enough water for all the power, agricultural, industrial, and urban uses that had been planned or that are staking claims, but the resulting shortage can then often be remedied by drawing on other sources that had not been within the horizon of the planners: ground water can be lifted by tube wells, the river flow can be better regulated through upstream dams, or the water of more distant rivers can be diverted. At present such plans are afoot for the San Lorenzo irrigation scheme in Peru, and for the Damodar Valley in India, among our projects; a similar overestimate of the waters available from the to-be-harnessed river which can, however, be corrected by "newly discovered" water from other rivers and areas has been reported for the Bhakra Nangal project in India "though no specific provision was made in the project for the investment on this account."[1]

1. K. N. Raj, *Some Economic Aspects of the Bhakra Nangal Project* (Asia Publishing House, 1960), pp. 53, 58.

It would obviously be silly to expect that overestimates of the availability of a given material resource are always going to be offset by underestimates of alternative or substitute resources; but if we generalize a little more, we obtain a statement that no longer sounds wholly absurd: on the contrary, it is quite plausible and almost trite to state that each project comes into the world accompanied by two sets of partially or wholly offsetting potential developments: (1) a set of possible and unsuspected threats to its profitability and existence, and (2) a set of unsuspected remedial actions that can be taken should a threat become real.

The experience of several of the projects visited fits this very broad proposition. For example, the San Lorenzo irrigation project in northern Peru suffered serious, and at times exasperating, delays caused by political change and second thoughts on the kind of irrigation farming the project should promote. But the considerable economic losses implied by the delays were in part offset by the fact that, as a result of the second thoughts, the San Lorenzo irrigation eventually became a pilot project for the subdivision of land into small but viable family farms and for the granting of credit and technical assistance to previously landless farmers. The project thus set an entirely new pattern for Peruvian agriculture and turned unexpectedly into a breeding ground for administrators who could apply elsewhere in Peru the lessons learned in San Lorenzo.

The Uruguayan livestock and pasture improvement project also experienced extraordinary delays, first because of slowness in political and administrative decision-making and then because the key technical task of improving the natural grasslands by introduction of legumes into the soil turned out to be unexpectedly complex. Yet the solutions that were gradually found through scientific research and practical experimentation and were then applied over an expanding area have now started to make this program into a particularly successful operation and have served to spread the spirit of innovation among a large group of Uruguayan farmers.

Somewhat similar sequences can be found in other projects, although the experience of the Nigerian Railway Corporation serves as an emphatic warning that by itself trouble does not constitute a sufficient condition for a "creative response."

The common structure of the Pakistani, Peruvian, and Uruguayan projects can now be formulated as follows:

1. If the project planners (and this usually includes the World Bank officials involved in financing the project) had known in advance all the

difficulties and troubles that were lying in store for the project, they probably would never have touched it, because a gloomy view would have been taken of the country's ability to overcome these difficulties by calling into play political, administrative, or technical creativity.

2. In some, though not all, of these cases advance knowledge of these difficulties would therefore have been unfortunate, for the difficulties and the ensuing search for solutions set in motion a train of events that not only rescued the project but often made it particularly valuable.

We may be dealing here with a general principle of action: Creativity always comes as a surprise to us; therefore we can never count on it and we dare not believe in it until it has happened. In other words, we would not consciously engage upon tasks whose success clearly requires that creativity be forthcoming. Hence, the only way in which we can bring our creative resources fully into play is by misjudging the nature of the task, by presenting it to ourselves as more routine, simple, undemanding of genuine creativity than it will turn out to be.

Or, put differently: since we necessarily underestimate our creativity, it is desirable that we underestimate to a roughly similar extent the difficulties of the tasks we face so as to be tricked by these two offsetting underestimates into undertaking tasks that we can, but otherwise would not dare, tackle. The principle is important enough to deserve a name: since we are apparently on the trail here of some sort of invisible or hidden hand that beneficially hides difficulties from us, I propose *the Hiding Hand.*

Before relegating the Hiding Hand to the developing countries as its special realm, we shall briefly elaborate the statement that we may be dealing here with a fairly general phenomenon that permits us to understand or reinterpret certain aspects of human behaviour and history. The principle suggests that, far from seeking out and taking up challenges, people typically take on and plunge into new tasks because of the erroneously presumed *absence* of a challenge, because the task looks easier and more manageable than it will turn out to be.

What we are trying to say can be well conveyed by taking Marx's famous sentence: "Mankind always takes up only such problems as it can solve," and by modifying its wording slightly, but its meaning fundamentally, to read: "Mankind always takes up only such problems as *it thinks* it can solve." Addition of the italicized words thoroughly blurs the neat determinacy of Marx's original statement; for, with this version, it is possible that, as a result of various misconceptions about its problem-solving ability, "mankind" will take up either more or fewer problems than it actually can solve at the moment it takes them up. Up to a point, the Hiding Hand can help accelerate the rate at which "mankind" engages successfully in problem-solving: it takes up problems *it thinks* it can solve, finds they are really more difficult than expected, but then, being stuck with them, attacks willy-nilly the unsuspected difficulties—and sometimes even succeeds.

Looking backward on this kind of sequence, an interpretation in terms of some challenge-and-response mechanism seems to be quite consistent with the facts and, of course, it is much more flattering to our ego. Indeed, people who have stumbled through the experience just described will tend to retell it as though they had known the difficulties all along and had bravely gone to meet them—*fare bella figura* is a strong human propensity.[2] While we are rather willing and even eager and relieved to agree with a historian's finding that we stumbled into the more shameful events of history such as war, we are correspondingly unwilling to concede—in fact we find it intolerable to imagine—that our more lofty achievements, such as economic, social, or political progress, could have come about by stumbling rather than through careful planning, rational behaviour, and the courageous taking up of a clearly perceived challenge. Language itself conspires towards this sort of asymmetry: man falls into error, but not into truth.

While some presence of the Hiding Hand may be helpful or required in eliciting action under all latitudes, it is no doubt specially needed where the tradition of problem-solving is weak and where invention and innovation have not yet been institutionalized or routinized. In other words, in developed countries less hiding of the uncertainties and likely difficulties of a prospective task is required than in underdeveloped countries where confidence in creativity is lacking. In the former there are large numbers of achievement-motivated actors who have acquired "the conviction that [they] can modify the outcome of an uncertain situation by [their] own personal achievements";[3] in the latter, on the contrary, new tasks harbouring many unknowns must often be presented as though they were all "cut and dried" in order to be undertaken. Hopefully, the experience that difficulties

2. Exceptions to this behaviour are provided by exceptional men such as Luther who, upon looking back on his life, acknowledged the role of the Hiding Hand most explicitly: "Had I known all in advance, God would have been put to great trouble to bring me to it .... God has led me on as if I were a horse and he put blinkers on me so that I could not see who came running up upon me." Quoted from the *Tischreden* in Wilhelm Pauck, *The Heritage of the Reformation* (rev. ed.; Free Press, 1961), pp. 20–21. This passage was shown to me by Lisa Hirschman.
3. David C. McClelland, *The Achieving Society* (Van Nostrand, 1961), p. 224.

can be successfully handled will eventually permit a more candid appraisal of tasks and projects.

The Hiding Hand principle has several fairly close relatives. The idea that failure fully to *visualize* prospective *internal* costs can be growth-promoting is, in a sense, an extension of the more familiar and more obvious thought that disregard of the costs a new project or industry will inflict on third parties—that is, failure to *internalize external* costs—can serve as a stimulus to enterprise.[4] In both cases, total costs are underestimated and investment decisions activated in consequence. There is, however, an important difference: When internal costs or difficulties are inadequately visualized, the project or firm will find itself in financial trouble unless an offset to these costs is encountered. When external costs are disregarded, on the other hand, the venture can yield a private profit without further ado. Nevertheless, the external costs too require an offset if the venture is to be judged a success from society's point of view."[5]

An even closer approximation to the Hiding Hand principle was formulated several years ago by an economic historian, John Sawyer. Having looked at development projects that were undertaken in the first half of the nineteenth century in the United States, he noted that underestimates of cost resulting from "miscalculation or sheer ignorance" were, in a number of great and ultimately successful economic undertakings—particularly in transport and in the opening up of new resources—"crucial to getting an enterprise launched at all." "Had the total investment required been accurately and objectively known at the beginning, the project would not have been begun." The eventual success of these ventures, in spite of the large initial miscalculation and the consequent financial trouble at various stages, derived from the fact that, once the necessary funds were secured and the project was brought to completion, "the error in estimating costs was at least offset by a corresponding error in the estimation of demand."[6]

4. I discussed this possibility at some length in *The Strategy of Economic Development* (Yale University Press, 1958), pp. 57–61. Failure to internalize external costs is probably most typical of new ventures in product-substituting (rather than product-adding) industries, while the failure fully to visualize internal costs affects the various categories of public and private investment decisions in quite a different pattern. …
5. For the nature of this offset, see ibid., p. 61.
6. John E. Sawyer, "Entrepreneurial Error and Economic Growth," *Explorations in Entrepreneurial History*, Vol. 4 (May 1952), pp. 199, 200.

The resemblance between this idea and the Hiding Hand principle is obvious. There is a double underestimate of both costs and benefits in Sawyer's scheme, while we have observed similarly, if more broadly, a double underestimate of the various difficulties that lie across the project's path, on the one hand, and of the ability to solve these difficulties, on the other. The difference is that Sawyer's model is focused primarily on the underestimate of costs which is presented as being due to the entrepreneur's activity drive and optimism combined with the knowledge that there is a ceiling to the amount that can be raised for the project. The underestimate of benefits is unexplained and acts rather as a *deus ex machina* to save selected projects that turn out to cost much more than expected.

In our Hiding Hand principle, Sawyer's unexplained underestimate of benefits becomes the underestimate, on the part of the project planner, of his own problem-solving ability and, as we have seen, this underestimate has a satisfactory rationale. The principle then goes on to state that in view of this underestimate an offsetting underestimate of the difficulties themselves is required so that perfectly feasible and potentially productive projects will actually be undertaken. We shall now explore in more detail the circumstances under which the Hiding Hand is likely to come into play.

Which are the projects, in other words, that tend to be undertaken because their difficulties are liable to be underestimated? And which ones tend to be systematically neglected because their difficulties are too obvious? These questions make it evident that the Hiding Hand, while permitting an increase in the rate at which projects are taken up, also leads to a bias in project selection.

It becomes clear, for example, that projects derive a crucial advantage from being based on a technique that *looks* transferable even though it may not actually be nearly as copiable as it looks. This is perhaps a principal reason that infrastructural and industrial projects have so large an edge over others: not that the techniques involved are in fact so exceedingly transferable, for time and again industrial projects, particularly those that are not limited to administering "last touches" to a host of imported semi-finished inputs, run into considerable technical and managerial difficulties when they are transplanted to a different environment. But factories look as though they could be picked up and dropped anywhere, whereas in such activities as agriculture and education the need for adaptation and the concomitant problems are immediately obvious. Industry thus lends itself eminently to the operation of the Hiding Hand, whereas agricultural projects suffer from the abandon and sincerity with which they flaunt their prospective difficulties.[7]

This conclusion is reinforced when the principle of the Hiding Hand is viewed in the perspective of time. For its mechanism to work, it is necessary that the operators be thoroughly "caught" by the time the unsuspected difficulties appear—caught in the sense that having spent considerable money, time, and energy and having committed their prestige, they will be strongly motivated to generate all the problem-solving energy of which they are capable.

Just as the Hiding Hand principle states that the to-be-experienced difficulties should be hidden at the moment of the decision to go ahead with the project, so it *implies* that these difficulties should not appear too *early* after the execution of the project has started, for, at least within a certain range, the propensity to tackle the difficulties will be roughly proportional to the effort, financial and otherwise, already furnished. Therefore, a given level of difficulties may be wholly discouraging for the prosecution of the project if it turns up early, while it would be tackled with alacrity and perhaps solved if it arose at a later stage.

In spite of the somewhat paradoxical ring of this assertion—paradoxical only because medical science has impregnated us with the notion that the sooner a malady is recognized and diagnosed the better—it appears to be confirmed by experience with development projects, and it again underlines the disadvantageous position of agricultural as compared with industrial and infrastructural projects. With the (important) exceptions of irrigation and tree-crop projects, agricultural projects have a short-gestation period and therefore production or marketing difficulties unfold rather soon after the projects have been started; hence, attempts to rescue them are often half-hearted and they are readily pronounced failures and abandoned. This is the story of many colonization projects in Latin America and Africa.[8]

7. In the last section of this chapter, we discuss the exaggeration of benefits as an action-inducing mechanism which is an alternative to the Hiding Hand when a project's prospective difficulties are too obvious to be hidden away. But agricultural projects do not lend themselves too well to the operation of this mechanism either.
8. It is difficult to gain an understanding of the history of these projects, for they leave hardly any trace behind as the once-to-be-colonized lands revert to bush and the project planners and operators to silence. One good case study is in K. D. S. Baldwin, *The Niger Agricultural Project: An Experiment in African Development* (Harvard University Press, 1957).

In projects with longer gestation periods and more permanent structures, similar difficulties tend to appear much later, and far more serious efforts are made to overcome them. This difference between projects with short and long-gestation periods is well illustrated by the contrasting fates of the East African Groundnut Scheme and the Owen Falls Hydroelectric Station in Uganda.

Undertaken at the same time (in the immediate post-war period), in the same region, by the same kind of colonial administrators wishing to turn over a new progressive leaf and harbouring similar illusions about the nature of the development process, both schemes were financially unsuccessful during their early years. The Groundnut Scheme was soon abandoned and hardly anything remains of it; the Owen Falls Station, on the other hand, had many lean years, but it endured and finally came into its own and will soon have to be supplemented by new generating capacity. Once it had become clear that the originally anticipated industrial boom in the Owen Falls area was not going to materialize, the Uganda Electricity Board made an effort to tap new markets for its power, building transmission lines to neighbouring Kenya at first and then to a host of smaller industries and towns of Uganda.

By itself, the mere ability of the Owen Falls Station to survive cannot of course be taken as a vindication of the original investment decision. While later administrators were right in considering as bygone the heavy costs that had been sunk into the project in its early years, the project as a whole may still have to be given a poor mark. It is well known that with long-gestation projects one runs the risk that good money will be thrown after bad. We are here pointing out that short-gestation projects are subject to the opposite risk: the failure to throw good money after what looks bad, but could be turned into good, if only the requisite rescue effort were forthcoming. When, as is often the case, the outcome of such an effort is highly uncertain at the time it is undertaken, the probability that the effort will be made increases with the costs that will have been sunk into the project by the time the difficulties appear.[9]

9. This proposition is related to the findings of psychologists that members of a club or group who have paid high initiation fees or gone through severe initiation rites are liable to find the group activities more fascinating than low-fee members. Compare E. Aronson and J. Mills, "The Effects of Severity of Initiation on Liking for a Group," *Journal of Abnormal and Social Psychology,* Vol. 59 (1959), pp. 177–181. In the same spirit, we are suggesting in the text that when there is room for *making* the group activities more interesting, the required initiative is likely to be forthcoming from the high-fee, rather than from the low-fee, members.

The foregoing remarks permit a policy conclusion: Projects whose potential difficulties and disappointments are apt to manifest themselves at an early stage should be administered by agencies having a long-term commitment to the success of the projects. They should be developed as much as possible in an experimental spirit, in the style of a pilot project gathering strength and experience gradually, so that they may escape being classed and closed down as failures in their infancy. The Uruguayan livestock and pasture improvement project followed both these precepts and has thus been able to survive and to achieve maturity and success.

Promoters and developers must long have been dimly aware of the Hiding Hand principle, for they have been remarkably adept at finding ways in which projects that would normally be discriminated against because they are too obviously replete with difficulties and uncertainties can be made to look more attractive to the decision maker.

One widely practiced method consists in pretending that a project is nothing but a straightforward application of a well-known technique that has been used successfully elsewhere. For example, for a number of years after World War II, any river valley development scheme, whether it concerned the São Francisco River in Brazil, the Papaloapan River in Mexico, the Cauca in Colombia, the Dez in Iran, or the Damodar in eastern India, was presented to a reassured public as a true copy—if possible, certified expressly by David Lilienthal—of the Tennessee Valley Authority. Although obviously two river valley development schemes will differ vastly more from one another than two Coca Cola bottling plants, the impression was created, by the appeal to the "TVA model," that clear sailing lay ahead for the proposed schemes. To be acceptable, it seems, a project must often be billed as a pure replica of a successful venture in an advanced country.

It is no doubt a pity that ventures that are 90% indigenous initiative and execution and 10% imitation of a foreign model are regularly presented to the public as though the percentages were, in fact, reversed, but this seems to be the price that must sometimes be paid to "sell" projects that would otherwise look too forbidding.

This attempt at making a project's path look smoother than it is may be termed the "pseudo-imitation" technique. When the novelty or difficulty of the task is too obvious for this technique to be plausible another method is often used. It consists in dismissing previous efforts at solving the task as "piecemeal" and in pretending to more insight than is actually available by drawing up a "comprehensive program." It can be called the "pseudo-comprehensive-program" technique.[10]

10. This technique is a variant of the "pseudo-creative" response which I discussed in *Journeys Toward Progress: Studies of Economic Policy-Making in Latin America* (Twentieth Century Fund, 1963), pp. 239 ff.

An excellent example of this technique is supplied by the Uruguayan livestock and pasture improvement project. It started with the avowed aim of "implementing" a joint mission report issued in 1951 by the World Bank and the United Nations Food and Agriculture Organization. The report's recommendations covered an extremely wide spectrum, as will appear from the following incomplete list of topics: subdivision of pastures by fences, grazing trials, tree plantings on permanent grasslands, introduction of legumes, increased use of lime and phosphate, shrub eradication, works to control runoff water, establishment of fodder reserves through silage and hay, better storage facilities, changes in the cropping system to include legumes, establishment of diversified farming combining harvested crops and livestock, improvement in productivity by irrigation, tillage practices, weed and pest control, erosion control, control of animal disease, improvement in transportation, storage and marketing, organization of research and technical services, appropriate price and other economic policies, etc.[11]

Such a report tends to give the policy-makers and project planners the illusion that the "experts" have already found all the answers to the problems and that all that is needed is faithful "implementation" of these multifarious recommendations. In fact, Uruguayan agriculture had shown prolonged and stubborn resistance to many of the report's proposals which were by no means new; the reason was that considerable and difficult breakthroughs remained to be achieved in technical, organizational, and other realms. But the comprehensive-program technique underplays this need for imagination, insight, and the application of creative energies, and the project planners are, as it were, tricked into undertaking a program whose real difficulties will only gradually become apparent to them.

The comprehensive program whose many components are given equal emphasis and are pronounced to be interrelated in effect covers up the ignorance of the experts about the real cure of the malady they have been summoned to examine; if they knew, they would be proposing a far more sharply focused program. Incidentally, the diffuse kind of program provides at the same time an excellent alibi to the experts in case anything goes wrong: since it is practically impossible to carry out all the proposed actions, any troubles can be blamed on the failure to follow the experts' instructions rather than on the shortcomings of their advice.

11. International Bank for Reconstruction and Development and Food and Agriculture Organization of the United Nations, *The Agricultural Development of Uruguay,* 1951. (Processed.)

Real interdependencies exist, no doubt, and a multipronged attack on a problem is therefore often necessary. But a comprehensive program that stems from real insight into the problem will be easy to distinguish from one that is a smoke screen for ignorance, for in the former the nature of the interdependencies will be clearly spelled out and an effort will have been made, in the interests of feasibility, to limit the number of activities that have to be undertaken concurrently.[12] This sort of *minimization of balanced growth requirements* which has all the marks of insight into the problem was evident in a 1964 plan for the creation of an industrial pole in the Taranto-Bari-Brindisi area in southern Italy: a deliberate effort was made to determine a strictly limited number of establishments producing intermediate goods and providing services, such as tool making, that would have to be available if a certain group of newly planned mechanical industries were to find it attractive to locate at the "pole."[13]

Regional development programs supply additional illustrations that certain comprehensive programs function, in effect, as "servants" of the Hiding Hand. Here also the programs traced out in advance must be as comprehensive and multifarious as possible to build up the morale of the slightly frightened decision-makers; for, in addition to overcoming their ignorance about the path to progress for their region or valley, they must do battle with various powerful contrary interests and must therefore form as broad a coalition as possible by promising something to every important section within the region or valley.

The foregoing is a fairly accurate description of what happened in the case of the development program for Italy's south. The Cassa per il Mezzogiorno was charged with undertaking a vast complex of programs and its activities reached virtually into every nook and cranny of its huge territory. But in the course of undertaking its public works programs, the Cassa soon learned that some were far more efficient and growth-promoting than others. In 1958 a prominent

12. A recent, very interesting attempt to formulate a theory of design has come to a similar conclusion: the correct method for solving design problems when the ultimate solution has to satisfy numerous interdependent requirements is not to treat the system of requirements as an interdependent whole, but to define "isolable subsystems," that is, subsystems among which there is a minimum amount of interdependence, and then to adjust the resulting partial designs to each other. Christopher Alexander, *Notes on the Synthesis of Form* (Harvard University Press, 1964), pp. 40–43 and passim.
13. Italconsult, *Studio per la promozione di un polo industriale di sviluppo in Italia Meridionale* (Rome, 1964), Pt. 2, Chaps. 3–4. (Processed.)

meridionalist, distinguishing between the (unserviceable) "bones" and the (valuable) "meat" of southern agriculture, pointed out that the "meat"—the portion where Cassa investments could be expected to yield high returns—comprised only about half a million hectares of irrigated or irrigable valley lands. Most of the rest of the area where the Cassa had operated—some 11 million hectares—were now dismissed as "bones."[14] The Cassa's proposed concentration of effort on irrigable land became in effect its new agricultural program when the agency's life was extended for a further period of fifteen years in 1965. It was far removed from the all-inclusive approach the Cassa had set out to implement; but just as the managers of Uruguay's livestock program had come to realize that the key to agricultural progress was the introduction of legumes, so the Cassa had found out in fifteen years of "implementation" of its comprehensive program that the larger payoffs of its agricultural program were to be obtained by concentration on the few fertile flat areas that dot the coastal lands of the south.

The two purveyors of the hiding hand—the pseudo-imitation technique and the pseudo-comprehensive-program technique—are nicely complementary: the former makes projects appear less difficulty-ridden than they really are, whereas the latter gives the project planners the illusion that they are in possession of far more insight into the projects' difficulties than is as yet available. Both techniques act essentially as crutches for the decision maker, permitting him to go forward at a stage when he has not yet acquired enough confidence in his problem-solving ability to make a more candid appraisal of a project's prospective difficulties and of the risks he is assuming. The experience of meeting with these difficulties and risks and of being able to deal with them should then enable him to discard these crutches and to achieve a more mature appraisal of new projects. The recourse to the Hiding Hand thus becomes less necessary as development proceeds, and one of the indirect benefits of projects is precisely that the willingness of the decision maker to face uncertainty and difficulty is increased. The Hiding Hand is essentially a mechanism that makes the risk-averter take risks and in the process turns him into less of a risk-averter. In this manner, it opens an escape from one of those formidable "prerequisites" or "preconditions" to development; it permits the so-called prerequisite to come into existence after the event to which it is supposed

14. Manlio Rossi-Doria, *Dieci anni di politica agraria nel Mezzogiorno* (Bari, Italy: Laterza, 1958), p. xix. In this, his original formulation of the meat-bones *(polpa-osso)* dichotomy, Rossi-Doria included 1.5 million hectares suitable for highly productive non-irrigable tree crops and vineyards in the "meat." But in later usage, this term became increasingly restricted to irrigable lands.

to be the prerequisite. In our model, risk-taking behaviour is engaged in actively (though involuntarily) prior to the arrival on the stage of the "risk-taking, achievement-motivated personality"; instead, it is this personality that is fashioned by risk-taking behaviour.[15]

The Hiding Hand model is helpful in understanding the process of growth from yet another point of view. It has often been remarked that what is most needed at an early stage in development is unqualified success for the ventures that are undertaken so that the spirit of entrepreneurship may become strong and widely spread. But this prescription is singularly unhelpful since in the early stages of any development effort numerous disappointments are inevitable, and mere survival is a feat for the innovator. How is development possible then? Perhaps because among many of the ventures that do survive, the Hiding Hand has been at work: in them, the entrepreneurs' experience will have been neither wholly better nor entirely worse than expected, but in a sense *both* worse (getting into unsuspected trouble) *and better* (getting unexpectedly out of it); and even though their financial success is not striking, the resulting infusion of confidence, and perhaps the discovery of a more "exciting" way of life, will strengthen the spirit of enterprise.

In effect, then, the contribution of development ventures depends not only on their—properly discounted—financial returns, but on important side effects which will often be reflected in the time shape of these returns. Specifically, when a venture has gone through considerable teething trouble as a result of the intervention of the Hiding Hand, it is likely to deserve a higher ranking than one with a similar return but no such experience.

We have ended up here with an economic argument strikingly paralleling Christianity's oft expressed preference for the repentant sinner over the righteous man who never strays from the path of virtue. And essentially the same idea, even though formulated, as one might expect, in a vastly different spirit, is found in Nietzsche's maxim "That which does not destroy me, makes me stronger." This sentence admirably epitomizes several of our project histories.

Having achieved, in a roundabout way, a convergence of benefit-cost analysis with the teachings of philosophy and religion, I should probably stop right here. Unfortunately, however, this dramatic effect must be spoiled; for something must

15. For a general argument about this sort of inverted sequence, and an appeal to the theory of cognitive dissonance for explaining it, see my article, "Obstacles to Development: A Classification and a Quasi-Vanishing Act," *Economic Development and Cultural Change,* Vol. 13 (July 1965), pp. 385–393 [ch. 7 above].

be said about the dangers and failures of the Hiding Hand. As noted before, its principal usefulness is in inducing risk-averters to commit themselves to risk-taking behaviour. This commitment permits an acceleration of economic growth; as a result of their experiences, decision-makers are likely to become readier to look newly emerging risk-laden situations straight in the face. The Hiding Hand is thus essentially a transition mechanism through which decision-makers learn to take risks, and the shorter the transition and the faster the learning the better. For this mode of learning about risk is not without grave dangers. One has to be rather lucky to be lured by the Hiding Hand into ventures whose emergent problems and difficulties can be successfully tackled. As long as one needs this "crutch" in order to act, the probability of committing major errors and of undertaking projects that will turn into failures is obviously higher than when he is able to differentiate between acceptable and non-acceptable risk.

Moreover, those servants of the Hiding Hand—the pseudo-imitation and the pseudo-comprehensive-program techniques—have hardly been described in flattering terms. One reason is precisely that while these techniques facilitate decision-making, they can easily be habit-forming rather than self-liquidating. The camouflage they use to disguise pioneering entrepreneurship may go undetected for a long time and may continue to be used when it is no longer needed. Moreover, these techniques have a number of undesirable side effects. The pseudo-imitation technique will not permit a country to reap the full psychological benefit of the ventures successfully launched under its auspices since there will remain a lingering feeling that any achievement is due to the imitation of a foreign model. The pseudo-comprehensive-program technique may, even after a favourable outcome, leave a sense of disappointment and frustration; for, if our description of the process by which insight into the problem is finally achieved is correct, then a number of originally enunciated measures and objectives that were important elements in the "comprehensive program" will no longer be actively pursued once the most promising approach is discovered. As a result, public opinion will tend to lament the abandonment of originally much touted programs and the project, even though a success, will leave behind a vague sense of failure. This is exactly what happened when the Cassa decided to pick the "meat" from the "bones" and when the Damodar Valley Corporation concentrated its work more and more on power generation.

Before concluding it may be of interest to place the phenomenon here described in a wider context. The Hiding Hand is essentially a way of inducing action through error, the error being an underestimate of the project's costs or difficulties. As Sawyer noted for his related theory of entrepreneurial error, the argument smacks uncomfortably of "praise of folly"—a praise that is sometimes deserved but always needs to be narrowly circumscribed.

We bestowed limited praise on the Hiding Hand because, by hiding prospective difficulties and by thus inducing an underestimate of costs, it serves to offset another error that project planners are liable to commit through their propensity to underrate their own inventiveness and problem-solving ability; when this propensity is present, the chances for correct project decisions to be taken will actually improve, up to a point, as the Hiding Hand does its handiwork. Suppose, however, that prospective difficulties stand clearly revealed and that the actors are afflicted by the same lack of self-confidence; the prospective costs will now tend to be *over*estimated, and the only remaining way by which action on perfectly feasible projects can still be induced is through a corresponding *overestimate of the prospective benefits*—we need a magnifying glass for benefits, to take the place of the mechanism that hid the difficulties and shrunk the costs. Thus, the same basic infirmity, namely lack of confidence in one's ability to overcome difficulties, requires correction either by understating the difficulties or by compensating the exaggerated image they project by a similar exaggeration of the project's expected accomplishments.

Exaggeration of prospective benefits is at least as common a device to elicit action as underestimation of costs. This error, specially when it is combined with an underestimate of costs, has of course often led to disaster—history abounds with examples, from bankruptcies and white elephants to lost or ruinously won wars. But just as the hiding of costs, the exaggeration of benefits can occasionally serve to ward off another, less visible, but nonetheless real, disaster: missed opportunity.

This is the case when difficulties in the project's path are unhideable. Take, for example, projects that clearly require from the start the making of politically difficult decisions such as a change in existing administrative structures around which considerable vested interests have gathered. This was the case of the Damodar Valley Corporation whose basic charter meant surrender of important powers of the states of West Bengal and Bihar (and to some extent also of the central government) to the new agency. To justify so unprecedented a move, it became necessary for the promoters of the agency to make such extravagant claims as that it would transform the Damodar Valley into "India's Ruhr" or that it would promote rapid, harmonious, and integrated development of all of the valley's natural and human resources, when in effect its task was rather narrowly limited to flood control, electric power generation, and some irrigation.

Extravagance in promising future benefits can thus often be found and may play a useful role in those development projects that require difficult initial decisions, be it a change in existing institutions or a fiscal sacrifice demanded of some or all of the citizenry. Actually the promise of some sort of utopia is most characteristic of larger-scale undertakings such as the launching of social reforms or of external aggression because they are likely to require heavy initial sacrifices.

Recourse to the utopian vision as a stimulant to action has on occasion been advocated in a sweeping way. The Hiding Hand or, in its absence, the exaggeration of benefits has been considered useful as a means of dealing with a specific and temporary infirmity of some societies, that is, man's inadequate acquaintance with his ability to solve difficulties. A far more generalized pessimism about human nature as weak-willed, routine-ridden, and decadence-prone led Georges Sorel to the belief that humanity required "myths"—inspiring images of battle and triumph—for any substantial forward movement. He was so well aware of the disproportion between the promises of these myths and the ensuing reality that he simply vetoed what is today called project reappraisal: "We should be especially careful," he said, "not to make any comparison between accomplished fact and the picture people had formed for themselves before action."[16] It is strange that Sorel did not realize how unlikely it was that his injunction against looking back would be heeded any more than that of Hades to Orpheus.

A far more appealing and convincing defence of the occasional need for exaggeration of prospective benefits appears in an essay by Kolakowski, the Polish philosopher:

> The simplest improvements in social conditions require so huge an effort on the part of society that full awareness of this disproportion would be most discouraging and would thereby make any social progress impossible. The effort must be prodigally great if the result is to be at all visible .... It is not at all peculiar then that this terrible disproportion must be quite weakly reflected in human consciousness if society is to generate the energy required to effect changes in social and human relations. For this purpose, one exaggerates the prospective results into a myth so as to make them take on dimensions which correspond a bit more to the immediately felt effort .... [The myth acts like] a Fata Morgana which makes beautiful lands arise before the eyes of the members of a caravan and thus increases their efforts to the point where, in spite of all their sufferings, they reach the next tiny waterhole. Had such tempting mirages not appeared,

16. *Reflections on Violence,* trans. T. E. Hulme (Peter Smith, 1941), p. 22.

> the exhausted caravan would inevitably have perished in the sandstorm, bereft of hope.[17]

This fine passage permits two observations. First of all, in contrast to what must have been Sorel's assumption when he issued his injunction against looking back, the Kolakowski image definitely conveys the message that the effort of the caravan was worth the cost and the suffering since it permitted survival. Secondly, the effort would not have been forthcoming had there not been the Fata Morgana, that is, a rather serious overestimate of the benefits.

The similarity to the justification for the Hiding Hand is striking. In Kolakowski's thought (which is of course concerned with large-scale socio-political movements and action rather than with development projects) the exaggeration of benefits is required for precisely the reason indicated earlier: the actors underestimate the strength that is left in them; therefore the to-be-furnished effort is felt as "impossible" until the required social energy is generated by the mirage.

The Fata Morgana image contains one other suggestion, rather different from the use Kolakowski makes of it: there may be special difficulties in visualizing in advance *intermediate* outcomes or *partial* successes such as the "tiny waterhole." In other words, the utopian vision may be necessary not so much to offset the inflated costs of the proposed enterprise as to compensate for an infirmity or man's imagination; for even though costs may not appear unduly high, man may simply be unable to conceive of the strictly limited, yet satisfactory, advances, replete with compromises and concessions to opposing forces, which are the very stuff of "incremental politics"[18] as well as the frequent result of ambitious socioeconomic development moves. The Damodar Valley story furnishes a good illustration for this kind of development: from the early fifties on, the Damodar Valley Corporation was increasingly hemmed in by encroachments on its original powers by the states of West Bengal and Bihar, and little remained in the mid-1960s of the majestic vision of integrated development of the valley's resources under the agency's unified command; yet the contribution of the agency's installations to industrial, urban, and resource development has fully justified the major portion of the investments the agency undertook, and it is doubtful that these investments would have been made without the stimulus of the initial vision.

17. Leszek Kolakowski, *Der Mensch ohne Alternative* (Munich: R. Piper, 1961), pp. 127–128. My translation from the German translation.
18. David Braybrooke and C. E. Lindblom, *A Strategy of Decision* (Free Press, 1963), pp. 71–77.

We have now identified two situations in which overestimates of benefits can play a positive role: (1) when, because of inexperience in problem-solving, the actors have an exaggerated idea of the costs and difficulties of action, and (2) when, because of inexperience with the actual processes of change, the actors are unable to visualize intermediate outcomes and limited advances. As in the case of the Hiding Hand with its underestimate of costs and difficulties, and pending the correction of these various inexperiences, the overestimate of benefits must therefore be recognized as a useful development mechanism for a transitional phase.

But, for the reasons already given, it is much to be desired that this transitional phase be short. The very description-exposé of these mechanisms of self-deception that has been attempted here may persuade project planners to dispense with these crutches as soon as it is possible for them to do so.

...

9 The Political Economy of Import-Substituting Industrialization in Latin America*

"There is now a new school of thought on Latin America which casts the whole matter into a biblical mould and amounts to transposing the doctrine of original sin onto the social terrain. Here is a summary of this thesis: Latin America, with its evil destiny, was forced into the world capitalist system by the European powers right after Columbus and the Conquest. A great many calamities derive from this historical fact, yet they are small if compared to what happens during the next stage when the Continent is fully inserted into the international order organized by the "truly" capitalist nations, with Great Britain at the helm. That stage is reached in the nineteenth century after Independence. Subsequently, with export-led growth really taking hold, the evils become even greater and more numerous. But this is not the end of Latin America's "purgatory in life." Another phase of expiation and, in a way, of even greater degradation was yet to come. It duly arrived with "inward-looking" development and "dependent" industrialization whose adverse repercussions and insuperable limitations have been described ad infinitum.

Such reasoning makes one wonder whether the first and foremost trouble with Latin America was not perhaps the departure of Columbus from the port of Palos … its

*. The opening quotation comes from "Diagnostícos, Estructuras y esquemas de desarrollo en América Latina," mimeographed (Santiago: Escuela lalinoamericana de sociologia, November 1969), pp. 3–5. Unless otherwise indicated, the notes of the present chapter refer to A. O. Hirschman, *A Bias*, cit.

> basic weakness [consists in] the complete failure to understand the contradictory character of every social process".
>
> —Aníbal Pinto Santa Cruz

Disenchantment with Industrialization in Latin America

Not long ago, industrialization ranked high among the policy prescriptions which were expected to lead Latin America and other underdeveloped areas out of their state of economic, social, and political backwardness. In the last few years, however, considerable disenchantment with this particular solution of the development problem has set in. The present paper will survey some characteristics of "import-substituting industrialization" (ISI) in an attempt to appraise its evolution and the principal difficulties it has encountered. Some purely economic aspects of the problem will be discussed, but particular attention has been directed to interrelations with social and political life. The ease with which such interrelations could be suggested—mostly in the form of tentative and untested hypotheses—indicates serious neglect by social scientists of a fertile terrain.

To set the stage for our inquiry it is useful to illustrate, through quotes from Latin America's most prominent economists, the change in attitude towards industrialization as a cure of the area's ills. In his well-known "manifesto" of 1949 Raul Prebisch said:

> Formerly, before the great depression, development in the Latin-American countries was stimulated from abroad by the constant increase of exports. There is no reason to suppose, at least at present, that this will again occur to the same extent, except under very exceptional circumstances. These countries no longer have an alternative between vigorous growth along those lines and internal expansion through industrialization. Industrialization has become the most important means of expansion.[1]

Thirteen years later, Prebisch wrote another basic paper on Latin America, in a sense his farewell message to his Latin American friends upon assuming his new

1. *The Economic Development of Latin America and Its Principal Problems* (New York: United Nations, 1950), p. 6. See chap. 13 for a more detailed account of the Prebisch and ECLA doctrines.

post as Secretary-General of the United Nations Conference on Trade and Development. Here industrialization is presented in a rather different light:

> An industrial structure virtually isolated from the outside world thus grew up in our countries .... The criterion by which the choice was determined was based not on considerations of economic expediency, but on immediate feasibility, whatever the cost of production ... tariffs have been carried to such a pitch that they are undoubtedly—on an average—the highest in the world. It is not uncommon to find tariff duties of over 500 per cent.
>
> As is well known, the proliferation of industries of every kind in a closed market has deprived the Latin American countries of the advantages of specialization and economies of scale, and owing to the protection afforded by excessive tariff duties and restrictions, a healthy form of internal competition has failed to develop, to the detriment of efficient production.[2]

If we take a look at the writings of Celso Furtado, the shift in the climate of opinion stands out even more starkly. In 1960, after a decade or more of rapid industrial advance, Furtado celebrated the resulting "transfer of decision centres" from abroad to Brazil in almost lyrical terms:

> By now the Brazilian economy could count on its own dynamic element: industrial investments supported by the internal market. Growth quickly became two-dimensional. Each new impulse forward would mean an increasing structural diversification, higher productivity levels, a larger mass of resources for investment, a quicker expansion of the internal market, and the possibility of such impulses being permanently surpassed.[3]

Only six years later, after Brazil had suffered a series of political and economic setbacks, a disillusioned Furtado wrote:

2. *Towards a Dynamic Development Policy for Latin America* (New York: United Nations, 1963), p. 71.
3. Celso Furtado, "The Brazilian Economy in the Middle of the Twentieth Century," mimeographed (Israel: Industrial Conference on Science in the Advancement of New States, 1960), p. 5. See also chap. 13, p. 303.

> In Latin America … there is a general consciousness of living through a period of decline … The phase of "easy" development, through increasing exports of primary products *or through import substitution* has everywhere been exhausted.[4]

Considering these two pairs of quotes one could easily conclude that we have here an instance of the acceleration of history. The phase of export-propelled growth (*crecimiento hacia afuera*) in Latin America lasted roughly from the middle of the nineteenth century until the Great Depression; and it took another twenty years, from 1929 to the Prebisch manifesto of 1949, before the end of export-propelled growth became official Latin American doctrine. Then came the next phase of Latin American growth, *crecimiento hacia adentro* or growth via the domestic market. It gathered strength during the Depression and World War II, flourished briefly in both theory and practice during the fifties and was pronounced either dead or a dud in the sixties. It looks, therefore, as though the acceleration of technical progress in the developed countries were matched in the underdeveloped ones by an increasingly rapid accumulation of failures in growth experiences!

As will be seen, there may be considerable exaggeration in the announced failure of import-substituting industrialization just as, in spite of the supposed demise of export-propelled growth, Venezuela, Ecuador, Peru, and Central America achieved notable economic gains in the two post-war decades through rapidly growing exports of petroleum, bananas, fishmeal, and cotton, respectively. While *fracasomania,* or the insistence on having experienced yet another failure, certainly has its share in the severity of the recent judgments on industrialization, the widespread criticism of ISI—in Pakistan and India very similar problems are being discussed—indicates that there is real substance to the concern that is being expressed. But the rapidity of the reversal in the climate of opinion makes one rather suspect that ISI had, from its very onset, both positive and negative aspects, with the latter simply coming into view a few years after the former. Our inquiry will therefore start out with a brief survey of the principal characteristics which set off ISI from other types of industrialization.

4. "U.S. Hegemony and the Future of Latin America," *The World Today* 22 (September 1966): 375. My italics. Detailed critiques of the ISI process in Latin America can be found in two influential articles: Maria de Conceicão Tavares, "The Growth and Decline of Import Substitution in Brazil," and Santiago Macario, "Protectionism and Industrialization in Latin America," both in *Economic Bulletin for Latin America* 9 (March 1964): 1–61 and 62–102.

Four Impulses of Import-Substituting Industrialization (ISI)

Wars and depressions have historically no doubt been most important in bringing industries to countries of the "periphery" which up to then had firmly remained in the nonindustrial category. The crucial role of the two world wars and of the Great Depression in undermining acceptance of traditional ideas about the international division of labour between advanced and backward countries is well known.[5] But industrialization has not only been the response to sudden deprivation of imports; it has taken place in many erstwhile nonindustrial countries as a result of the gradual expansion of an economy that grows along the export-propelled path. As incomes and markets expand in such a country and some thresholds at which domestic production becomes profitable are crossed, industries come into being without the need of external shocks or governmental intervention—a process I have described elaborating *The Strategy of Economic Development* as "import-swallowing"[6] and which has been perhaps more aptly termed industrialization through "final demand linkage," as distinct from the continuation of the process via backward and forward linkage effects.[7] Gradual import substitution in response to the growth of domestic markets accounts for the widespread establishment of industries which have substantial locational advantages because of

5. Apparently even earlier crises had positive effects on industrial growth in Latin America. The following quote is instructive: "There is no ill wind that does not blow some good ... the crisis the country is going through is tremendous—and yet this is a perfect wind for national industry. Many of our industries have had a more or less vigorous protection through customs duties. But all of this would not have been enough had it not been for the crisis of 1875 which gave the impulse to industry and for that of 1890 which strengthened and diffused it." Quoted from *El National* in Adolfo Dorfman, *Desarrollo industrial en la Argentina* (Rosario, 1941), p. 11. My translation.
6. Albert O. Hirschman, *The Strategy of Economic Development* (New Haven: Yale University Press, 1958), chap. 7.
7. See Melville H. Watkins, "A Staple Theory of Economic Growth," *Canadian Journal of Economics and Political Science* 29 (May 1963): pp. 141–158; and Richard E. Caves, "Vent-for-Surplus Models of Trade and Growth" in *Trade, Growth and the Balance of Payments,* Essays in honour of Gottfried Haberler (Chicago: Rand-McNally, 1965), pp. 95–115.

the weightiness of the product (cement, beer) and of those, such as textiles, whose market is large even at low per capita incomes.

Over the past two decades import-substituting industrialization has, of course, no longer been exclusively a matter of natural market forces reacting to either gradual growth of income or to cataclysmic events, such as wars and depressions. It has been undertaken in many countries as a matter of deliberate development policy, carried out no longer just by means of protective duties, but through a wide array of credit and fiscal policy devices, through pressures on foreign importing firms to set up manufacturing operations as well as through direct action: the establishment of state-owned industries or, increasingly, of development corporations or banks which are then entrusted with the promotion of specific ventures.

It is useful to keep in mind these distinct origins of ISI—wars, balance-of-payments difficulties, growth of the domestic market (as a result of export growth) and official development policy—in focusing on the distinctive characteristics of the process.

Clearly, there is not just one ISI process. An industrialization that takes place in the midst and as a result of export growth has a wholly different *Gestalt* from one that feeds on foreign exchange deprivation. For example, in the latter situation it seems much more likely that inflationary developments will accompany the industrialization process than in the former. Or, to proceed to one of the alleged—and often criticized—characteristics of the industrialization process itself, namely its tendency to concentrate on non-essential, luxury-type goods. This tendency to give importance to what is unimportant will be present only when the primary impulse to industrialization arises out of unexpected balance-of-payments difficulties which are fought routinely by the imposition of quantitative import controls. The controls will aim at permitting continued supply of the more essential good traditionally imported at the cost of shutting out non-essentials and will thus cause domestic production of the latter to become especially profitable.

It is easy, however, to make too much of this situation. Of the four motive forces behind ISI—balance of payments difficulties, wars, gradual growth of income, and deliberate development policy—only the first leads to a bias in favour of non-essential industries. The last, deliberate development policy, is likely to produce exactly the opposite bias; and the remaining two causes are neutral with respect to the luxury character of the industry. Wars cause interruption of, or hazards for, all international commodity flows, essential or non-essential, and therefore provide a general unbiased stimulus to domestic production of previously imported goods. The same is true for the stimulus emanating from the gradual growth of markets. It seems likely, therefore, that the role of non-essential goods within the total ISI process has been exaggerated by the "new" critics who, in stressing this role, sound almost like the old-line Latin American laissez faire advocates who were forever inveighing against the introduction of "exotic" industries into their countries.

Characteristics of the Initial Phase of ISI

Industrialization by Tightly Separated Stages

No matter what its original impulse, ISI starts predominantly with the manufacture of finished consumer goods that were previously imported and then moves on, more or less rapidly and successfully, to the "higher stages" of manufacture, that is, to intermediate goods and machinery, through backward linkage effects. The process can and does start here and there with capital or even intermediate goods insofar as such goods are imported prior to any industrialization because they are needed in connection with agricultural or transportation activities. Machetes, coffee hulling machines, trucks and fertilizers are examples. In the textile industry, the crushing superiority of machine spinning over hand spinning, combined with a lesser advantage of machinery in weaving, has made sometimes for the installation of spinning mills ahead of weaving mills, especially in countries where a strong hand-weaving tradition had not been previously destroyed by textile imports from the industrial leaders.

But the bulk of new industries are in the consumer goods sector and as they are undertaken in accordance with known processes, on the basis of imported inputs and machines, industrialization via import substitution becomes a *highly sequential,* or *tightly staged,* affair. Herein lies perhaps its principal difference from industrialization in the advanced countries. This aspect is so familiar and seemingly inevitable that it has not received quite the attention it deserves. It is the basic reason for which the ISI process is far smoother, less disruptive, but also far less learning-intensive than had been the case for industrialization in Europe, North America, and Japan.

This is not the place for renewing the discussion over the advantages or drawbacks of an early or late start in industrialization. Suffice it to point out, however, that those who have stressed the advantages of a late start have often had in mind the ability of newcomers to jump with both feet into a newly emerging dynamic industrial sector (as Germany did with chemicals) instead of remaining bogged down in sectors that had long passed their prime (as England in textiles and railways construction). But the "late latecomers" with whom we are concerned here are not apt to jump in this fashion. Industrialization is here at first wholly a matter of imitation and importation of tried and tested processes. Consider by way of contrast the following description of the establishment of new industries in advanced countries:

> Young industries are often strangers to the established economic system. They require new kinds or qualities of materials and hence make their own; they must overcome technical problems in the use of their products and cannot wait for potential users to overcome them; they must persuade customers to abandon other commodities and find specialized merchants to undertake the task. These young industries must design their specialized equipment and often manufacture it.[8]

Not much of this travail occurs when a new industry is introduced into the "late late" starting countries. It is in this connection that one must be on guard against studies purporting to show that the history of industrialization is substantially the same in all countries, working its way from light consumer goods industries, to heavy and capital goods industries, and eventually to consumer durables. The apparently similar pattern of the earlier and "late late" industrializers in this respect conceals an essential qualitative difference. Even when the earlier industrializers were predominantly in the light consumer goods stage (from the point of view of labour force or value added), they were already producing their own capital goods, if only by artisan methods. As Marx wrote: "There were mules and steam-engines before there were any labourers whose exclusive occupation it was to make mules and steam-engines; just as men wore clothes before there were tailors."[9] But the "late late" industrializers will import, rather than make, their clothes until such time as they are able to set up a tailor in business all by himself. This situation forecloses, of course, for a considerable time any fundamental adaptation of technology to the characteristics of the importing countries, such as the

8. George Stigler, "The Division of Labor is Limited by the Extent of Market," *Journal of Political Economy* 59 (June 1951): 190.
9. *Kapital,* 1 (Vienna-Berlin, 1932), p. 399. This passage and the previous one by Stigler were brought to my attention by Nathan Rosenberg's article "Capital Goods, Technology, and Economic Growth," *Oxford Economic Papers,* 15 (November 1963): 223–224.

relative abundance of labour in relation to capital. Whether and to what extent such an adaptation is desirable is an idle question under these circumstances; given the sequential pattern of industrialization, there is remarkably little choice. ISI thus brings in complex technology, but without the sustained technological experimentation and concomitant training in innovation which are characteristic of the pioneer industrial countries.

"Late" vs. "Late Late" Industrialization

The "late late" industrialization sketched so far may be contrasted not only with that of the presently advanced industrial countries in general, but particularly with that of the so-called latecomers among them. The "late" industrialization of countries like Germany, Italy and Russia has been depicted by Gerschenkron through the following propositions:

1. The more backward a country's economy, the more likely was its industrialization to start discontinuously as a sudden great spurt proceeding at a relatively high rate of growth of manufacturing output.
2. The more backward a country's economy, the more pronounced was the stress in its industrialization on bigness of both plant and enterprise.
3. The more backward a country's economy, the greater was the stress upon producers' goods as against consumers' goods.
4. The more backward a country's economy, the heavier was the pressure upon the levels of consumption of the population.
5. The more backward a country's economy, the greater was the part played by special institutional factors designed to increase the supply of capital to the nascent industries and, in addition, to provide them with less decentralized and better informed entrepreneurial guidance; the more backward the country, the more pronounced was the coerciveness and comprehensiveness of those factors.
6. The more backward a country, the less likely was its agriculture to play any active role by offering to the growing industries the advantages of an expanding industrial market based in turn on the rising productivity of agricultural labour.[10]

10. Alexander Gerschenkron, *Economic Backwardness in Historical Perspective* (Cambridge, MA: Harvard University Press, 1962), pp. 343–344.

Of these six characteristics only the last one applies unconditionally to the late late industrializers. Special institutions designed to supply capital and entrepreneurial guidance (point 5), became important in most of Latin America after the ISI process had already been underway as a result of private, decentralized initiative for a considerable time. As to the remaining four points, almost the opposite could be said to hold for our late latecomers. Their industrialization started with relatively small plants administering "last touches" to a host of imported inputs, concentrated on consumer rather than producer goods, and often was specifically designed to improve the levels of consumption of populations who were suddenly cut off, as a result of war or balance-of-payments crises, from imported consumer goods to which they had become accustomed. Even though the rates at which new plants were built and at which their output expanded were often respectable, the process thus lacked some of the essential characteristics of Gerschenkron's "great spurt."

As a result, late late industrialization shows little of the inspiring, if convulsive élan that was characteristic of the late industrializers such as Germany, Russia and Japan. This is perhaps the basic reason for the feelings of disappointment experienced by Latin American observers who had looked to industrialization for a thorough transformation and modernization of their societies.

Naturally, the difference between the two types of industrialization must not be overdrawn. At least one experience in Latin America, that of Brazil during the fifties, came fairly close to the picture drawn by Gerschenkron: sustained and rapid progress of steel, chemical and capital goods industries during this decade was here combined with a "special institutional factor designed to increase supply of capital," namely inflation, and even with the flowering of a "developmentalist" *(desenvolvimentista)* ideology.[11] But what looked like the hopeful beginning of a "Brazilian economic miracle" was thrown into disarray by the political crises and related economic and social setbacks of the sixties. The gloom that pervades the Latin American mood at present stems precisely from the convergence of frustrations over the unexciting character of late late industrialization in most Latin

11. While not included in the six points cited above, support by a vigorous movement of ideas has been stressed elsewhere by Gerschenkron as a characteristic of late industrialization. See, for example, his *Economic Backwardness,* pp. 22–26. For a survey of developmentalist-nationalist ideas in Brazil during the fifties, see Frank Bonilla, "A National Ideology for Development: Brazil" in K. H. Silvert, ed., *Expectant Peoples: Nationalism and Development* (New York: Random House, 1963), pp. 232–264.

American countries with the despair felt over the stumblings of the one country whose advance had assumed the more inspiring characteristics of the "great spurt."

The Sources of Entrepreneurship

A number of important characteristics of late late industrialization remain to be surveyed. What has been said so far permits, first of all, some discussion of the sources of entrepreneurship. As industry is started primarily to substitute imports, those engaged in the foreign trade sector are likely to play a substantial role in the process. This is the reason for the industrial prominence of (a) the former importers of Lebanese, Jewish, Italian, German, etc., origin, and (b) of the large foreign firms intent on maintaining their market and therefore turning from exporters into manufacturers. Once again, however, it is useful to distinguish between an industrialization which is brought underway under conditions of expanding income from exports and one that is ignited by deprivation of previously available imports (due to war or balance-of-payments troubles). Only in the latter situation are local importers and foreign exporting firms likely to be the main promoters of industrial enterprise. When foreign exchange income is expanding, one may rather expect industrial opportunities to be exploited by indigenous entrepreneurship. Under such conditions, the importing interests are apt to be well satisfied with their lot and activity; industrial development will run clearly counter to their short-run interests, especially when it requires the imposition of even a moderate level of protection. Some evidence in support of our distinction may be cited: in both Brazil and Colombia, coffee booms in the late nineteenth and early twentieth centuries gave rise to periods of industrial expansion led by domestic entrepreneurs who were in no way tied to the importing interests.[12] The latter, on the other hand, were prominent in these and other Latin American countries during the high pressure drives towards import substitution which marked the world wars and the Great Depression.

The importance of foreigners, of minorities or, generally speaking, of non-elite-status groups in the total industrialization process has on occasion been held responsible for the fact that industrial interests do not wield in Latin America the political influence and social prestige which have been theirs in the older industrial countries. Insofar as the phenomenon is real, it can also be explained by the

12. Warren Dean, "The Planter as Entrepreneur: The Case of São Paulo," *The Hispanic American Historical Review* 46 (May 1966): 138–152; Luis Ospina Vásquez, *Industria y protection en Colombia (1810–1930)* (Medellin: E. S. F, 1955), chap. 8.

kind of industries most characteristic of the first phases of import-substituting industrialization: opinions of the owners of soft drink bottling plants or of cosmetic or pharmaceutical industries are unlikely to command as much attention as those of steel and machinery manufacturers. In addition, the industrialists of the leading industrial countries always gained considerable influence by virtue of being exporters; as such they achieved prestige abroad, acquired contacts and gathered information—all accomplishments that were highly prized by their governments.[13] This source of influence is quite unavailable to the import-substituting industrialists who are usually aiming only at supplying the domestic market.[14]

The Exuberant Phase of ISI and Its Political Consequences

A final characteristic of the early phases of import-substituting industrialization is the growth pattern of the newly established industries. It has been suggested that

> output curves in newly established import-substituting industries have tended to be kinked, rising rapidly when exports are being replaced, but flattening out when further growth of demand has been grounded in the growth of domestic income. Profits have also followed this kinked pattern. Thus industries have moved rapidly from high profit and growth to precocious maturity, at which point they fall back to monopolistic quiescence with lower profit rates, a reduced level of investment, and aging plant and equipment.[15]

13. In Germany, for example, social prestige was granted to industrial entrepreneurs only to the extent that they were active in "fields which made a direct contribution to Germany's economic strength [such as] coal, steel, chemicals, industrial engineering" or that they exploited "the all-important export markets" (William N. Parker, "Entrepreneurial Opportunities and Response in the German Economy," *Explorations in Entrepreneurial History* 7 [October 1954]: p. 32).
14. The proposition that the comparative *lack* of political power of the industrialists can be explained by the *lack* of industrial exports becomes perhaps more convincing when one states its positive counterpart: namely that the continuing political influence of the land-owning interests throughout the period of industrialization in Latin America is explained by the continuing almost total dependence of the capacity to import on exports of primary products. This point is made for Brazil in Francisco C. Weffort, "Estado y masas en el Brasil," *Revista Latinoamericana de Sociologia* 1 (March 1965): 53–71.
15. David Felix, "Monetarists, Structuralists and Import-Substituting Industrialization," in W. Baer and I. Kerstenetzky, eds., *Inflation and Growth in Latin America* (Homewood, IL: Irwin, 1964), p. 384.

The extent to which the kinked pattern of output growth is really a fact rather than an inference from the nature of import substitution remains to be established. After all, newly established industries have to overcome initial production and organization problems, they encounter some sales resistance due to preference for the imported product so that the early portion of their sales data may still approximate the logistic curve which has given a good fit for the time shape of the expansion of many industries in the advanced countries.[16] Nevertheless, it is probably legitimate to speak of a particularly "easy" phase of import substitution when the manufacturing process is entirely based on imported materials and machinery while importation of the article is firmly and effectively shut out by controls. Under such conditions, the early experience of the new manufacturers is likely to be most gratifying. It is this phase of import substitution that gives rise to the often noted exuberance and boom atmosphere during which demand is easily overestimated. In any event, low duties or preferential exchange rates for machinery imports make for lavish orders. As a result, the new industry is likely to find itself saddled with excess capacity as soon as it reaches the kink.[17]

It is tempting to speculate about the psychological-political consequences of this pattern of industrialization. Progressive Latin Americans had long hoped that industry would introduce new, much-needed disciplines into the behaviour of their governments. The very nature of industrial operations—their precision, the need for exact timing, punctuality, reliability, predictability and all-around rationality—was expected to infuse these same qualities into policy-making and

16. Simon S. Kuznets, *Secular Movements in Production and Prices* (Boston: Houghton Mifflin, 1930). Arthur F. Burns, *Production Trends in the United States Since 1870* (New York: National Bureau of Economic Research, 1934).
17. Even if expansion plans of competing firms are known all around and there is no excessive optimism, demand tends to be overestimated for two special reasons: with protection the price of the domestically produced product is going to be higher than that of the imported one; and market studies based on import statistics often overestimate the domestic market for the new domestic industry also because the statistics usually include a fair volume of specialty products which the domestic industry is unable to supply. In the case of intermediate products, however, demand may be *under*estimated for an important reason: by looking primarily at the volume of imports of such products as an indication of the room for substitution, the analyst would overlook opportunities that arise as import substitution is undertaken with respect to products which use the intermediate good as an input. See Samuel A. Morley and Gordon W. Smith, "On the Measurement of Import Substitution," *American Economic Review* 60 (September 1970): pp. 728–735.

perhaps even into the political process itself. This sort of inference was based on the nature—or supposed nature—of industrial operations at the plant level. It disregarded, however, the larger financial and economic aspects of the process which had, of course, a much more direct and determining impact on politics. Thus the ease with which new industries were installed in spite of dire warnings and often in the midst of war and depression, the rapid growth they experienced and the handsome profits they realized during the first phases made import-substituting industry appear as a new incarnation of some primary product that would suddenly erupt with an old-fashioned world market boom. Little wonder, then, that the hoped for achievement of rationality in economic policy-making and in the political process in general failed to occur. On the contrary, the "exuberant" phase of import substitution was accompanied by flamboyant public policies which badly overestimated the tolerance of the economy for a variety of ventures, be they income redistribution by fiat, the building of a new capital, or other extravaganzas. Here we can do no more than touch upon these matters; but it may be conjectured that in their very different ways, Perón, Kubitschek, Rojas Pinilla, and Pérez Jiménez could all be considered victims of the delusions of economic invulnerability fostered by the surprising early successes and rapid penetration of industry into a supposedly hostile environment.

The Alleged Exhaustion of Import Substitution

Then, suddenly, the honeymoon was over and the recriminations began. Import-substituting industrialization was officially added, as we have seen, to the long list of certified *fracasos* in Latin American policy-making. We shall now attempt to sort out and evaluate some of the elements in this reversal of opinion.

Four principal accusations have been levelled against the industrialization process as it has appeared in Latin America:

1. Import-substituting industrialization is apt to get "stuck" after its first successes, due to the "exhaustion of easy import substitution opportunities"; it leaves the economy with a few relatively high-cost industrial establishments, and with a far more vulnerable balance-of-payments since imports consist now of semi-finished materials, spare parts and machinery indispensably required for maintaining and increasing production and employment.

2. Import-substituting industry is affected by seemingly congenital inability to move into export markets.
3. The new industries are making an inadequate contribution to the solution of the unemployment problem.
4. The new industries often tend to be established as branch plants and subsidiaries of foreign firms and thereby foster a new type of "dependency" for Latin America.

In the following we shall concentrate on the first two critiques; the other two cannot be adequately discussed within the limits of the present essay.[18]

A Naïve and a Seminaïve Exhaustion Model

The argument on ISI getting stuck is put forward in several forms. Most frequently and crudely, the assertion is made that the process faces "exhaustion" after a certain period during which the "easy" import substitution opportunities are taken up. Exhaustion evokes the image of a natural resource available in strictly limited quantities which is being depleted; and we must ask now to what extent the image is sensible. One model which could underly the exhaustion concept is an exceedingly simple one: at any one point of time, a country imports commodities *A,* B, C ...; the annual import volumes of these commodities are M_A, M_B, M_C ... Next, one assumes the existence of economies of scale such that the minimum economic sizes of plants which are to produce these various goods can be unequivocally defined. If the annual capacities of such plants are designated by P_A, P_B, P_C ... then import substitution opportunities are limited to those products (say, *A, C, E,* ...) for which imports (the *M*'s) exceed the minimum economic sizes (the P's).

This would be a truly naïve model rationalizing the exhaustion concept, and it is perhaps too much of a caricature of what the critics of import substitution have in mind. The more sophisticated among them, at least, do realize that the first steps of ISI open up new opportunities for the establishment of domestic manufactures through both income and backward linkage effects. In the first place, the domestic production *of A, C,* and *E* creates new incomes which may enlarge the market for a number of additional final demand goods to the point where their domestic production becomes, in turn, feasible. Secondly, domestic production of *A, C,* and *E,* which is *ex hypothesi* set up on the basis of imported inputs, opens

18. See chap. 11 for some observations on the fourth critique.

up new opportunities for the establishment of domestic manufacturing facilities turning out these inputs.

The income effect is likely to result in a convergent series of new investment opportunities. Thus it postpones exhaustion in relation to the naïve model, but does not overcome it. When backward linkage effects are taken into account, however, the exhaustion concept tends to evaporate unless it is bolstered by some additional assumptions.

Again a rather naïve, let us call it "seminaïve," exhaustion model could be built up as follows. Industry *A* requires imported inputs $a_1, a_2, a_3, \ldots a_i \ldots$ industry *C* inputs $c_1, c_2, c_3, \ldots c_i \ldots$ and so on. It seems plausible that imports of any individual input, such as $M_{a1}, M_{a2}, M_{a3}, \ldots M_{ai} \ldots$ should be smaller than M_A had been before domestic production of *A* started. On the other hand, it could be surmised (and frequently is unquestioningly assumed) that minimum economic plant size increases as one ascends to "higher" stages of production. If this is so, then we have $P_{ai} > P_A$ while $M_{ai} < M_A$. Under these circumstances the chances that imports will exceed the minimum economic sizes for any large number of imported inputs for *A, C,* and *E* decrease rapidly as one ascends via backward linkage towards the higher stages of production.

Criticism of the Seminaïve Model: The Importance of Policy

I believe that something like this seminaïve model is indeed in the minds of those who speak of exhaustion. For this reason it is useful to spell it out, for as soon as that is done, it is easy to perceive where such an exhaustion model goes wrong and what are, therefore, the requirements of an industrialization process that would "beat" exhaustion.[19]

19. One way of staving off the exhaustion predicted by the naïve or seminaïve model would be to enlarge total market size, either for *all* products through the amalgamation of several national markets, or for *some* products particularly important for industrial progress, through appropriate income redistribution within a given national market. Accordingly the formation of common markets and a redistribution of income which would result in larger domestic markets for mass-produced articles have held an important place in the discussions that arose after the "exuberant" phase of ISI was over. There can be no doubt that the creation of a larger market through either or both of these moves would contribute much to dynamic industrial growth. But we wish to argue here that they are not the only available instruments or, in other words, that market size is not as rigid and definite a barrier as the exhaustion thesis claims.

Two modifications of the model serve to make it look both more realistic and less exhaustion-prone. In the first place, some of the inputs needed for the initial import-substitution industries are likely to be identically the same (steel, paper, glass are needed as intermediate inputs in a wide variety of final demand products). As a result of this product convergence of industrial processes the *ai*'s are not always distinct from the *ci*'s and *ei*'s, so that imports of a number of intermediate goods may well be larger than the previous imports of final demand goods.[20]

Secondly, it is of course not necessarily true that minimum economic plant size increases regularly as one ascends towards the higher stages of production. I am not aware of any systematic study relating to this point. But it is well known, for example, that automobile assembly plants deal with a number of suppliers and subcontractors for many needed components, just as a single steel plant will draw for its supply of coal on several mines. Large capacity plants do characterize the technology of a few important intermediate and basic products; but at every stage—particularly in the machinery and equipment industries which, in a sense, represent the "highest" stage of production—small and medium-sized establishments are also to be found.[21]

If we put these two considerations together, one particularly favourable possibility appears: minimum economic size could providentially be, and in fact often is, large in those industries for whose products (steel, glass, paper) the convergence phenomenon is important. But even apart from such a happy coincidence, the preceding considerations make the exhaustion concept lose the physical and predictable definiteness it had assumed with the previous models. It appears instead that the difficulties that may well dog the backward linkage process are to a considerable extent a matter of economic environments and policies, instead of being determined exclusively by objective quantities such as market and minimum economic plant sizes.

20. Moreover, because of this product convergence the opportunities for import substitution are much greater, in the case of intermediate goods, than appears from a look at the import statistics. See n. 17 in this chapter.
21. For striking evidence on the smallness of the typical machine tool firm in the United States and on low concentration ratios in the industry, see Murray Brown and Nathan Rosenberg, "Prologue to a Study of Patent and Other Factors in the Machine Tool Industry," *The Patent, Trademark and Copyright Journal of Research and Education* 4 (Spring 1960): pp. 42–46. One reason for this situation is that capital/labour ratios are typically low in the machinery industry.

We have a few more words to say on the latter topics before we turn to the economic and socio-political reasons for which the backward linkage process may or may not get stuck. It must be recognized that one implication of the above considerations is to stress even more the importance of market size. In the seminaïve exhaustion model, market size sets definite limits to the number of industries which a given country can set up. With increasing market size, an additional number of industries, all of larger size than could be accommodated previously, become possible. But if one gives up the idea that minimum economic size and stage of production are closely correlated, the advantages of market size can become larger rather than smaller, for a larger market permits the installation not only of an industry requiring that market, but, in its wake, of a host of other plants supplying that industry; the required market size of these plants may be much smaller, but they could not be established without the prior establishment of the industry requiring the larger market and which might therefore be called the "bottleneck industry."

These considerations make us understand better the tremendous importance of market size (so well illustrated by the exceptional achievements in Latin America of Mexico and Brazil) if the backward linkage process is to be vigorous. But they also lead to some interesting policy conclusions: with the seminaïve model, the industrialization process is bound to stop at a given point. It can be likened to the ascent of a mountain which gets steeper all the time; the country is the mountain climber and the larger it (or rather its market) is, the higher up the mountain it gets. If this were really so, there would not be much point in pushing it up a bit higher through special incentives or promotion of public enterprise, and any infant industry protection should be uniform. But if we abandon the seminaïve model, the mountain alters its shape; at one point its slope does become forbiddingly steep, but then it flattens to turn up again only much later. Under those conditions it becomes exceedingly important to climb the forbidding portion (the bottleneck industry) of the mountain as then the traveling can be continued with ease for some time. In other words, the existence of the bottleneck industries is a powerful argument for special protection, or direct promotion, and even better, for efforts to export the portion of the industry's output that cannot be accommodated by the domestic market. In any event, public policy is very much back in the saddle with this view of the industrialization process.

A further remark along similar lines. The phenomenon of product convergence can also be utilized to help a country negotiate the steeper slopes of its bottleneck industries. When an intermediate product industry faces inadequate domestic demand and cannot therefore be established on an economic scale, it is possible to canvas possibilities for setting up industries which might generate additional demands for the bottleneck industry's output. While this may be difficult in practice, the argument leads to a counsel of caution in policies directed against so-called non-essential industries: the demands for intermediate products emanating from these industries can be very precious in permitting *essential* intermediate product industries to be established.

Economic, Political and Technological Determinants of Backward Linkage

While the preceding considerations ended up by stressing the importance of policy, they were still focused on the *mechanism* of industrialization through backward linkages. We must now address ourselves directly to the political economy of the process.

The importance of market size and of an adequate supply of foreign exchange in setting some limits to the process is undoubted; nevertheless, the industrialization processes of countries which are not too dissimilar with respect to these constraints still display considerable variation so that curiosity is aroused about the role of other factors, such as the behaviour of private industrialists and of public authorities.

As is well known by now, the setting up of an industry based on imported inputs has two contradictory effects: it becomes possible, and in some to be defined ways attractive, to set up industries producing inputs for the initial industry; but at the same time, the very establishment of that industry sets up resistances against backward linkage investments. Several reasons for such resistances had already been noted in my *Strategy of Economic Development:*

> The industrialist who has worked hitherto with imported materials will often be hostile to the establishment of domestic industries producing these materials. First, he fears, often with good reason, that the domestic product will not be of as good and uniform quality as the imported one. Secondly, he feels that he might become dependent on a single domestic supplier when he could previously shop around the world. Third, he is concerned about domestic competition becoming more active once the basic ingredients are produced within the country. Finally, his location may be wrong once the source of supply of the materials he uses is thoroughly altered. For all these reasons, the interests of the converting, finishing, and mixing industries are often opposed to the establishment of domestic sources of supply for the products that they convert, finish, or mix.[22]

22. Hirschman, *Strategy*, p. 118. I am quoting myself here because the critics of ISI have sometimes taken me to task for having overrated the power and automaticity of the backward linkage process.

Another powerful factor making for resistance has since received much attention: high tariff protection for the initial industry combined with low or zero tariffs or preferential exchange rate treatment for the industry's inputs.[23] The greater the difference between the level of protection accorded to the import-substituting industry and that applying to its imported inputs, the more will the profit margin of the industry depend on preventing domestic production of the inputs. For it is a fair assumption that the backward linkage industries would, once established, be eligible for a level of protection similar to that benefiting the initial import-substituting industry, and it is at least doubtful whether the initial industry can obtain a compensatory tariff increase for its own output or, in general, whether the resulting increase in costs can be passed on to the consumers without loss in sales volume.

For those various reasons, the newly established industries may not act at all as the entering wedge of a broad industrialization drive. The high customs duties on their outputs, combined with low (or negative) duties on their inputs, could almost be seen as a plot on the part of the existing powerholders to corrupt or buy off the new industrialists, to reduce them to a sinecured, inefficient, and unenterprising group that can in no way threaten the existing social structure. Indeed, like the workers' aristocracy in Lenin's theory of imperialism, these pampered industrialists might go over to the enemy—that is, make common cause with agrarian and trading interests which had long been opposed to the introduction of "exotic" industries.

The possibility that the industrialists who first appear in nonindustrial countries may not be all that much in favour of dynamic industrial development leads to an interesting socio-political puzzle. Sociologists and political scientists have frequently deplored the weakness of the middle class and particularly of the industrialists in Latin America, its lack of self-assertion and its failure to influence

23. See, for example, Santiago Macario, "Protection and Industrialization," and R. Soligo and J. J. Stern, "Tariff Protection, Import Substitution and Investment Efficiency," *Pakistan Development Review* 5 (Summer 1965): pp. 249–270. A general critique of import substitution on the grounds that the concentration on, and strong protection of, consumers goods it usually implies make for misallocation of resources, for obstacles to further industrial growth, and for a bias in favour of consumption is in John H. Power, "Import Substitution as an Industrialization Strategy," *Philippine Economic Journal* 5 (Second Semester 1966): pp. 167–204.

public affairs. Earlier we have tried to account for this phenomenon by some characteristics of late late industrialization. But at this point, one begins to wonder whether it would really be a good thing if the new industrialists were much more self-assertive and powerful than they are—perhaps they would then really be able to choke off further industrialization, something which generally they have not been able to do! Considering what we called the tightly staged character. Of late late industrialization it may in fact be preferable for the governments of the late late industrializing countries to be run by *técnicos,* by groups of planner-technicians, rather than by the new industrialists themselves. It has been in fact due to the regulations issued by the *técnicos* of the Kubitschek administration that backward linkage was enforced rapidly in the Brazilian automotive industry in the late fifties. In Mexico, on the other hand, assembly plants had existed for decades without any progress being made towards the local manufacture of motors and parts until measures similar to those in Brazil were adopted in the sixties. Thus the resistance of the initial industrialists to backward linkage combine with other already noted characteristics of late late industrialization to enhance the potential contribution of public policy to the process.[24]

But we dare not rely on such policies emerging simply because they are needed and because we issue a call for them. Could the resistance to backward linkage be overcome otherwise than by state action? While the resistances of the new industrialists are perfectly rational, one cannot but feel that they are based on a myopic, excessively short-run view of the development process. In this manner, we can supply a concrete justification for the view of a Brazilian sociologist according to which the traditional Western, Puritan-ethic-imbued, rational, profit-maximizing businessman is not really the type that is most needed in the situation of Latin America; what is required, he feels, are entrepreneurs who can identify themselves with the general developmental aspirations of their society, be it even at the expense of some rationality in their everyday business operations.[25]

But, once again, one cannot rest content with issuing a call for the *desenvolvimentista* entrepreneur; it would be more useful to be able to explain his appearance or nonappearance by a series of economic and social factors. This will be our

24. That a policy of forcing backward linkage investments has problems and pitfalls of its own is shown in Leland L. Johnson, "Problems of Import Substitution: The Chilean Automobile Industry," *Economic Development and Cultural Change* 15 (January 1967): pp. 202–216.
25. Fernando H. Cardoso, "The Industrial Elite" in S. M. Lipset and A. Solari, eds., *Elites in Latin America* (New York: Oxford University Press, 1967), pp. 96–99.

next task. While it is true that backward linkage meets with certain resistances and obstacles, we have yet to inquire about the existence of other forces working in the opposite direction, that is, in the direction of making backward linkage work. This appraisal of the comparative strength of forces and counterforces is probably the key to understanding why industrialization has been more vigorous and continuous in some developing countries than in others—long before they ran up against any barriers of market size.

As is the case for the start of late late industrialization, so will the continuation of the process through backward linkage be strongly influenced by the industrializing country's balance-of-payments. The opposition of the initial industrialists to backward linkage investments is likely to be considerably reduced if they occasionally experience curtailments, due to foreign exchange shortages, in the flow of imported inputs; on the other hand, the backward linkage investments require availability of foreign exchange for the importation of machinery. Consequently it is likely that some alternation of foreign exchange stringency and abundance would be optimal from the point of view of generating both the motivation and the resources required for the process. I have previously made this point[26] and considerable attention has been paid to the foreign exchange constraint.[27] Hence, it will be more useful to focus here on other forces affecting the process. There surely exist many situations in which some backward linkage investments are neither impossible in the light of foreign exchange availabilities, nor wholly compelled because of previous searing experience with foreign exchange shortages. We are interested here in the conditions that make for vigorous continuation of industrialization in these situations.

In line with our previous arguments, we posit a certain level of resistance of the new industrialists to the manufacturing of currently imported inputs. The resistance, while rational on the part of the initial industrialists, is undesirable from the point of view of the economy in the sense that profitable production of some inputs is assumed to be possible provided some average or normal level of protection is extended to them. In other words, there is room for, but resistance against, further industrialization along reasonably efficient lines of comparative advantage.[28] We now inquire what conditions other than balance-of-payments developments could make this resistance weaken or disappear.

26. *Strategy*, pp. 173–176.
27. See, for example, Carlos F. Diaz-Alejandro, "On the Import Intensity of Import Substitution," *Kyklos* 18 (1965): 495–511.
28. In somewhat more rigorous terms: the established, protected industries are earning excess profits which they would lose if industries supplying inputs to them were to be established with a "normal" level of tariff protection. The excess profits of the first ISI

The principal point to be made here is very simple: the resistance is almost wholly premised on the supposition that manufacturing in the higher stages of production is going to be undertaken by entrepreneurs other than the already established initial industrialists (or other than members of his immediate family). For if he himself undertakes it, most of the listed objections to the expansion of manufacturing via backward linkage fall to the ground. Thus, the fear of unreliability and poor quality of the domestic article should abate and the fear of domination by a monopoly supplier will disappear entirely. True, domestically produced inputs may have to be purchased at a higher price than was paid for the previously imported product which was perhaps obtained duty free or bought at some preferential exchange rate. But even if the increase in input costs that comes with domestic manufacture cannot be passed on, vertical integration would take the sting out of it; for the decrease of profits in one operation of an integrated industrial concern does not seriously matter if that decrease is compensated by the emergence of profits in another, newly established operation. To realize such profits the industrialist who contemplates the manufacture of hitherto imported inputs will usually have to obtain for those inputs some "normal" level of protection. It must be assumed, therefore, that he does not consider existing customs duties and exchange rate preferences as unchanging parameters immune to his will and influence; the opposite assumption is sometimes made in the literature

industrialists thus have an interesting contradictory character: they set up resistances against further industrialization, but at the same time they represent an obvious and attractive source of possible finance for that very process. Protection of the backward linkage industries achieves quite simply the needed transfer: as is now familiar, this protection lowers the level of effective protection of the industries catering to final demand. The numerous studies which have lately been devoted to the topic of effective protection have paid little attention to this important mechanism, presumably because they were rooted in the desire to denounce the evils and inefficiencies of ISI. That some of these evils are possibly self-liquidating as ISI proceeds, that an industry protected by infant industry tariffs can "grow up" not only because those tariffs are reduced, but because supplier industries with their own tariff protection spring up, was specifically suggested by W. M. Corden in his fundamental article, "The Structure of a Tariff System and the Effective Protective Rate," *Journal of Political Economy* 74 (June 1966): 229. But this implication of the theory of effective protection seems to have been forgotten by the many researchers who have followed in Corden's footsteps.

on import substitution (with pessimistic consequences for the prospects of ISI), but it is manifestly unrealistic for most investment decisions.

If the disposition of the initial industrialists themselves to move farther back into the industrial structure is an important element in overcoming obstacles to the backward linkage process, a brief inquiry into the factors making for a disposition of this sort is in order.

The economist can contribute a general reason for which backward linkage investments are likely to be carried on by the new industrialists themselves: the mere fact that they have been earning profits and are therefore presumably looking for new investment opportunities. Once the new industries have reached the point at which imports have been wholly substituted so that horizontal expansion is no longer profitable, vertical expansion into the "higher stages" of production may well offer the best available and, in any event, the most obvious outlet for investment funds that have accumulated as a result of the profitable operation of the existing industries. The availability of profits from the first phase of import substitution thus provides a generalized incentive for the successful import-substituting industrialist to plunge once again, naturally after appropriate modification of the tariff and exchange rate policies affecting the products whose manufacture is to be undertaken. The likelihood that the new industrialist will look in this particular direction, is increased by two interrelated factors: one, by the special difficulty of moving into export markets, to be commented on in the next section; and secondly by what we called the sequential or "tightly staged" character of late late industrialization. The industrialist manufacturing a final demand good during earlier cycles of industrialization was likely to call into life domestic producers of inputs and of the required machinery; therefore, once he was no longer able to expand his domestic sales volume, he found the higher stages already occupied by others and was therefore impelled to look elsewhere, including to exports, for further expansion. The situation is very different when production is undertaken wholly on the basis of imported inputs.

The availability of profits and resulting search for new profitable investment opportunities act, as has been said, as a general counterweight to the hostility towards backward linkage investments on the part of new industrialists. Whether or not this counterweight will outweigh the hostility is difficult to say. Under the worst of circumstances the combination of the two forces may result in a dog-in-the-manger situation: the new industrialists are able to prevent others from entering the backward linkage arena, but are not sufficiently motivated to enter it themselves.

To carry the analysis a bit further and to account for the different degrees of strength which the backward linkage dynamic has displayed in different countries, it is tempting to make a brief foray into the realm of sociology. The eagerness of an industrialist to move into related fields of activity instead of being satisfied with his existing operation based on imported inputs, may, for example, be reinforced if he has the feeling that his sons are locked into his own class and career. If an industrialist's sons are able and eager to enter the professions or the government, there is no need for father to think about finding new industries for the sons to expand into and to manage (preferably one for each son so they won't fight). But if industrialists look down on government and the professions, or if the latter look down upon the former, or, as happens frequently, if dislike and disdain are mutual, or simply, if the social distance between the industrialists and other groups is considerable, then the advantage of providing jobs for the family may fully compensate for the inconveniences, headaches, and even for minor monetary sacrifices that may be entailed by backward linkage investments. It appears once again, although from a rather different angle, that it is perhaps not a bad thing for the initial entrepreneurs to belong to a group of immigrants or of some other outsiders, with no immediate prospects of joining the established upper class or of moving into politics or the professions.

Social distance is bred by geographical distance. For this reason, one might expect that an industrialization process which, at least in its beginnings, is strongly identified with one or several centres other than the national capital stands a better chance to spill over vigorously from one industry to another than one which has its base in the capital city itself. The importance of having a somewhat isolated, inbred and self-consciously proud industrial centre during the early stages of industrialization is demonstrated by the roles played by São Paulo, Monterrey, and Medellín. No similar pioneering centre outside the capital city arose in Chile and Argentina, and it is perhaps not a coincidence that these two countries have provided the critics of the ISI process with far better examples of its alleged irrationality and propensity to exhaustion than Brazil, Mexico, and Colombia.

A final subject of speculation is the differential impact of technology on the comparative strength of the linkage process in different industries. When a backward linkage effect points to an industry which is technologically quite distinct from the one requiring the input, the input-utilizing industrialist is less likely to be attracted to the input-producing industry than if the latter is closely related to processes and techniques with which the industrialist is already familiar. For example, the backward (and forward) linkage dynamic may show more spontaneous vigour in the "inbred" metalworking and chemical industries than in, say, the textile industry whose inputs come in large part from technological strangers such as, precisely, the chemical industry. Thus the backward linkage dynamic may be held back at some point simply by "technological strangeness." This point is of particular importance for the machinery industry since machinery is usually a technological stranger to the industry in which it is utilized. An inquiry into the technological determinants of the differential propensity of different industries towards linkage investments could be of considerable value. To identify and then to remove this sort of bottleneck should be a principal task of public agencies concerned with industrial development.

The purpose of the preceding observations was to convince the reader that there is far more to the vigour or weakness which late late industrialization displays in various countries than minimum economic size of plants, market size and even foreign exchange availabilities. We have left the naïve and seminaïve exhaustion models far behind and have instead generated a highly complex "field" of forces and counterforces. If the reader feels a bit confused, we have achieved our purpose: for essentially we wished to show that the process is not nearly so straightforward and constrained as it has recently been made to look, and that it depends far more on public and private acts of volition than has sometimes been granted as well as on numerous economic, sociological and technological factors which remain to be investigated.

The Inability to Export Manufactures: "Structural" Causes and Remedies

It is hardly necessary to stress how desirable it would be for our late late industrializing countries to become exporters of the outputs of their new industries:

1. Through exports they would overcome whatever obstacles of market size limit their growth or prevent their establishment.
2. Through exports they would loosen the balance-of-payments constraint which may otherwise prevent capacity operation of existing industries as well as establishment of new industries.
3. Finally, by competing in world markets, industries would be forced to attain and maintain high standards of efficiency and product quality and would thereby acquire defences against oligopolistic collusion and decay to which they often succumb in highly protected, small local markets.

Unfortunately, the intensity with which one would wish for exports of manufacturers from the late late industrializers is matched by the solidity of the arguments which appear to foreclose any real prospects of success in this direction.

Once again, the arguments are familiar: the new industries have been set up exclusively to substitute imports, without any export horizon on the part of either the industrialists themselves or the government; the foreign branch plants and subsidiaries, which have taken an important part of the process, often are under specific instructions not to compete abroad with the products of the parent company; even more decisive than these obstacles deriving from attitudes and institutions, is the fact that the new industries, set up behind tariff walls, usually suffer from high production costs in countries that are, moreover, permanently subject to strong inflationary pressures—hence there is no real possibility of these industries competing successfully in international markets even if they were disposed to do so.

These are weighty arguments and they seem to meet the test of a satisfactory explanation in that they put one's mind to rest. But do they? After all, there are many industries which started out producing for the home market and eventually spilled over into foreign markets. Prior, successful acceptance of a manufactured commodity in the home market has even been considered to be a prerequisite for successful exporting.[29] Secondly, foreign firms have been known to be quite adaptable in their manufacturing and export policies. Just as they have been coaxed by national policies to produce or procure domestically a larger proportion of their inputs, so they could be induced to engage on export drives. Finally, even the most impressive explanation of the inability to export—the cost disadvantage of new industries set up under tariff protection—loses some of its persuasiveness when one remembers that protection of industries in Germany and the United States has not prevented considerable success of those protected industries in world markets. Industrialization of the nineteenth century latecomers was in fact frequently accompanied by both tariff protection and a vigorous export drive which threatened the previous dominant position of the old established industrial countries in a number of important markets. Again, the behaviour of the late late industrializers could not be more different and it now begins to appear that we may be in need of some further, perhaps more fundamental explanations of the inability to export that afflicts them. While such a "structuralist" strategy of

29. S. B. Linder, *An Essay on Trade and Transformation* (New York: Wiley, 1961), pp. 87 ff.

problem solving may show the problem to be even more deeply rooted than had been thought it can also uncover new, hitherto unsuspected ways of attacking it.[30]

One additional explanation of the difficulty of exporting has already been given in the preceding section. It was asserted that in view of the sequential character of industrialization, late late industrialists looking for new profitable business opportunities will frequently have the option between investing in backward linkage industries and expanding into export markets, whereas late industrialists had primarily the latter course open to them since the backward linkage industries were already in existence. Little wonder, then, that the late late industrialists decide to stay cosily at home much longer than the late industrialists who were under a far greater compulsion to make the plunge into foreign markets if they were going to expand. It would therefore be unrealistic to expect an industry to become an exporter before it has truly taken root in the country through a variety of the more obvious backward linkage investments. And the expeditious undertaking of these investments is therefore desirable not only per se, but also as a necessary way station to the opening of the export phase.

Another structural reason for the inability to export derives from the circumstances under which resources have been channelled into the industrial sector in many Latin American countries. Industrial investments became attractive not only because of customs protection, but additionally because of the combination of internal inflation, overvaluation of the currency, and exchange controls. In effect, maintaining an overvalued exchange rate meant that the exporters of traditional primary products would receive a smaller real income than with an equilibrium or undervalued exchange rate. At the same time, the overvalued exchange rate permitted the acquisition at favourable prices (in domestic currency) of those imports that were let in by the control authorities. And since machinery and essential industrial materials enjoyed preferential status, the overvalued exchange rate acted in effect as a mechanism to transfer income from the traditional export sector to the new industries.[31]

30. A general plea for "structuralist" analysis of Latin American economic problems along with a good bibliography is to be found in Osvaldo Sunkel, "El trasfondo estructural de los problemas del desarrollo latinoamericano," *Trimestre Economico* 34 (January–March 1967): 11–58. For an interpretation of structuralism as a strategy for problem solving, see my *Journeys Toward Progress* (New York: Twentieth Century Fund, 1963) pp. 210–216 and 231–235.
31. Alexandre Kafka, "The Theoretical Interpretation of Latin American Economic Development," in H. S. Ellis, ed., *Economic Development in Latin America*

At the same time, however, the overvalued exchange rate acted as a bar to exports from these industries. This probably was not a serious drawback and certainly was not felt as such during the earlier stages of import-substituting industrialization when exports on the part of the nascent industries were not a real prospect. But as a vigorous industrial establishment grew up in various countries one may well ask the question why a different institutional arrangement was not chosen. For example, why not tax the export sector, subsidize the new industries and do away with the overvalued exchange rate so that industrial exports are encouraged? To ask this question is to answer it: in most Latin American countries such a course would have been politically impossible. The power of the groups tied to the primary export sector would hardly have permitted so direct an assault, as is attested by the strong, permanent and occasionally successful pressures that were exerted against the indirect squeeze of the sector which Latin American monetary authorities had more or less inadvertently stumbled on. The great advantage of die inflation-cum-overvaluation arrangement was in fact not only that it resulted in an indirect rather than direct squeeze of politically and socially powerful groups, but that this mechanism was an unintended and, for a long time, an unnoticed by-product of a course of action which had the perfectly respectable objective of "defending the national currency against depreciation."[32]

Viewed in this way, the inability to export manufactures appears as the price which had to be paid for building up an industrial sector under adverse socio-political conditions. Should we then perhaps be simply gratified that industrialization was contrived at all, and be happy to pay the price? Not necessarily. As industrialization proceeded, the desirability of the overvaluation device became increasingly questionable from the point of view of industry itself. For overvaluation not only impeded exports, but interfered, in ways already analysed, with the vigorous exploitation of the backward linkage dynamic. Moreover, in several countries, industries became sufficiently vigorous and integrated so that the help stemming from the procurement of a few imported inputs at bargain prices (via

(New York: St. Martin's Press, 1961), p. 21; and Celso Furtado, "Industrialization and Inflation," *International Economic Papers* 12 (1967): pp. 101–119.

32. The policy originated, ironically enough, in an attempt to *defend* the export interests, for example, in the case of Brazil, to maintain the cruzeiro price of coffee in the face of falling world market prices during the Great Depression. This policy led to an increase in the money supply, and thereby caused domestic inflationary pressures which would eventually result in the inflation-cum-overvaluation arrangement. Cf. Furtado, *Industrialization and Inflation,* p. 103.

the overvalued exchange rate) was bound to be more than offset, for an increasing number of firms, by the loss of potential profits that could have been realized through the exports at a non-overvalued rate of exchange. It could thus be suggested that, at a certain point, overvaluation of the currency turned from a stimulus to industrial progress into a drag on it.

It appears that the much advertised non-competitiveness of Latin American industry may be rooted more in the failure to modify institutions than in any inability to bring down real costs. The question then arises why the industrial interests have not vigorously pressed for institutional arrangements—export subsidies, preferential exchange rates, or more radically, an exchange rate that is undervalued rather than overvalued—that would make exporting profitable. Are there some grounds on which industrialists could be basically *reluctant* to commit substantial resources to an export drive?

This question leads to a third structural reason for—or speculation about—the difficulties of exporting. It has to do, once again, with the distribution of power in Latin American societies. To stage an export drive, an industrialist must frequently make special investments in research, design and packaging; he must assemble a specialized sales force, delegate considerable authority, launch an entirely different advertising campaign; in short, he incurs special risks and new overhead costs which will be recoverable only over a comparatively long period of successful exporting. Therefore, an industrialist will consider exporting only when he can be sure either that the basic institutions and policies which vitally affect his foreign operations are highly stable or, as a minimum, that his interests will be given the most serious attention when these institutions and policies are altered.

In effect, we have just spelled out a "prerequisite" for a determined and successful export drive for manufactures: to undertake such a drive with all its risks and special costs, the industrialist class must feel reasonably sure that it can control certain crucial fiscal and monetary policies of its government. Differently put: only a cohesive, vocal, and highly influential national bourgeoisie is likely to carry industrialization beyond relatively safe import substitution to the risky export-oriented stage. It will be noted that this assertion—the industrialists do not export because they are not influential—completes the second half of a vicious circle whose first half asserted that the ISI industrialists are lacking in influence because they are not "conquering foreign markets" (see p. 97 above). Obviously we should not take inordinate pride in having fashioned a new vicious circle or in having identified a new prerequisite to the economic progress of the developing countries. Rather, we shall consider in a moment ways of breaking out of the circle and of doing without the prerequisite or of finding, à la Gerschenkron, a substitute for it. But we must nevertheless pause at this point in our reasoning and take notice that conditions for a strong export drive by the private sector are highly unfavourable in Latin America: in no country of that continent do the industrialists feel securely in control of vital economic policies affecting them. Policy-makers positively cultivate unpredictability and distance from interest groups; at the same time, they are highly manipulative. Changes in fiscal, monetary, and foreign exchange policies are therefore frequent while communication about these changes with the affected interest groups is infrequent. These are the socio-political traits that account, perhaps more fundamentally than the cost-price structure of the new industries, for their poor export performance.

Having uncovered ever more cogent reasons for the inability to export, have we encountered by the same token a "fundamental" remedy? One way of staking such a claim would be to expect that, as a result of our analysis, Latin America will change the nature of its politics and that its powerholders will henceforth become less manipulative and more communicative. Unfortunately analysis is not likely to act as so powerful a solvent. But is it really necessary to wait until a trusting and intimate relationship between the industrialists and the policy-makers emerges or is it conceivable that countries which find it difficult to establish such a relationship could travel an alternative road?

A radical reaction to the problem would be for the state itself to take over the foreign merchandising function. The spectacle of the state rendering difficult or impossible the performance of an important function by the private sector and then taking over that function because the private sector is ostensibly falling down on the job, is by no means uncommon. If this course of action has not been taken so far for the export of manufactures, one reason is that the importance of this function is only beginning to be appreciated. Also, state enterprise is hardly likely to be at its best in selling a wide variety of manufactures in foreign markets; for, by its nature, this task requires levels of initiative, flexibility, risk-taking and decentralized decision-making which it has been difficult for state enterprise to attain.

A less radical and more promising solution would be for the state simply to take an active role in promoting exports by private enterprise. As already mentioned in connection with exports from foreign-owned branch plants and subsidiaries, the state could very well tie the granting of tax and other incentives to the attainment of export targets in a manner analogous to that with which backward linkage has been enforced in the Brazilian automobile industry. From the point of view of the industrialists, such a policy would have the advantage that one sector of the bureaucracy would become committed to the export drive and could then be relied on to do battle with those sectors whose policies interfere with the success of the drive.

Quite a different solution consists in leaving alone, at first, the obstacles to exporting that derive from the actions of one's own government and in concentrating instead on those that are caused by other governments. This is in fact what is being attempted at present through the United Nations Conference on Trade and Development and its campaign for preferences for the manufactures of developing countries in the markets of developed countries. Perhaps this request can be viewed more sympathetically than it has been if it is considered as a compensation to the exporters of the newly industrializing countries for some of the extra burdens they must bear because of the policies and frequent policy changes of their own governments. In this reasoning, one may also discern a hope that such preferences would be temporary: once exports in volume would have been achieved, the first half of the vicious circle we have identified—industrialists are not influential because they do not export, and they do not export because they are not influential—would have been shattered. There would then be hope that government policies would become more finely attuned to the needs of the exporting industrialists who might therefore dispense in due course with the special privileges obtained from other governments.

The need for common markets among developing countries can also be better appreciated from this perspective. The common markets would not only provide preferential treatment for the industrialists of the participating countries; for these mutual arrangements to be durable, monetary and foreign exchange policies would have to become more uniform and stable than they have been; and such a development would be even more important than the customs preferences themselves in promoting exports from the common market countries, not only to each other, but also to third countries. It is, however, precisely the prospect of less freedom of movement in monetary and foreign exchange policies which makes national governments so skittish about entering effective common market commitments.

Finally our problem could be alleviated by developments in the structure of international trade in manufactures. According to some observers, countries of recent industrialization should be acquiring a comparative advantage in certain types of highly standardized industrial products.[33] To sell such goods abroad may

33. Raymond Vernon, "International Investment and International Trade in the Product Cycle," *Quarterly Journal of Economics* 80 (May 1966): pp. 202–207.

not be possible, in a number of lines, without special international market and firm connections, but it does not require either expensive advertisement campaigns or any special adaptation to foreign tastes and conditions. As a result, the overhead cost of exporting would be cut and the risks deriving from the instability or unpredictability of official economic policies would be correspondingly reduced.

In the preceding pages an attempt has been made to describe the varieties and characteristic features of import-substituting industrialization, and to derive from them socio-political consequences which in turn affect the process. Among the characteristics of ISI the possibility of proceeding sequentially, in tightly separated stages, because of the availability of imported inputs and machinery, plays, as was shown, a particularly commanding and complex role, direct and indirect, positive and negative.

Thus, the sequential or staged character of the process is responsible not only for the ease with which it can be brought underway, but also for the lack of training in technological innovation and for the resistances to both backward linkage investments and to exporting that are being encountered. The most important consequence of sequentiality, however, is the fact that it has become possible for industrialization to penetrate into Latin America and elsewhere among the late latecomers without requiring the fundamental social and political changes which it wrought among the pioneer industrial countries and also among the earlier group of latecomers. The repercussions of this situation on the industrialization process itself are ambivalent: on the one hand, the lack of political power of the new industrialists means, as we have just seen, that exporting meets with political and institutional, rather than purely economic, obstacles; on the other hand, this very lack of power neutralizes in various ways some of the possible adverse effects of sequentiality, for example, the resistance of the new industrialists to backward linkage.

In addition, the fact that import-substituting industrialization can be accommodated relatively easily in the existing social and political environment is probably responsible for the widespread disappointment with the process.[34] Industrialization was expected to change the social order and all it did was to supply manufactures! Hence one is only too ready to read evidence of total failure into any trouble it encounters.

34. See below, chap. 15, pp. 331–333, for an elaboration of this point.

This paper has by no means denied the various difficulties which the ISI process is apt to experience; in fact, they have on occasion been shown to be more deep seated than had been thought. At the same time, our exploration of the characteristics of the process has made it possible to discern avenues towards continued industrial growth that remain open to the late latecomers.

10

Foreign Aid: A Critique and a Proposal

With Richard M. Bird

Foreign aid is as Janus-faced an institution as can be found. It redistributes income from the rich to the poor and can thus serve to speed the latter's development. At the same time, in a world of sovereign nations foreign aid is an instrument of national policy which can be used by the rich to acquire influence and to increase their power.

While foreign aid might never have come into this world without its appeal to both national and transnational interests, it has also suffered from the resulting ambiguity about its "real" function. Unlike pure power instruments such as national military establishments, on the one hand, or overt redistribution mechanisms like the progressive income tax, on the other, foreign aid has never been firmly institutionalized. It has led a precarious existence, bolstered from time to time by cold war conflicts and then flagging again as immediate dangers passed, or the lack of a "domestic constituency" in the aid-giving countries made itself more strongly felt, or certain unpleasant side effects of aid giving became apparent. Lately signals of a new crisis in aid giving have multiplied in the United States; there is disaffection and disenchantment as well in Western Europe and perhaps in the Soviet Union, and foreign aid is none too popular even in the recipient countries.

The first part of this essay attempts a partial explanation of this state of affairs through a critique of basic concepts underlying present aid programs of the United States as well as some multilateral ones. The second part of the paper discusses an alternative mechanism of transferring aid, which would avoid some of the more conspicuous difficulties that have been encountered. The two parts of the paper are not tightly integrated, however: it is quite possible for a reader to agree with our critique while disagreeing with the proposal, and vice versa.

A Critique of Program Aid

Current practice in foreign aid dates from the new principles introduced by the Kennedy administration in the early sixties. Essentially, this country's doctrine moved at that time to embrace what has since become known as the "program approach" to foreign aid.

From Project to Program Aid

The "project approach" had predominated through the fifties. The World Bank had been enjoined by its very statutes to extend loans only on the basis of specific projects (in transportation, power, agriculture, and so forth). The first activity of the United States in the field of aid to underdeveloped countries was technical (Point Four) assistance, which had necessarily a project content and which evolved naturally into capital assistance with a similar content. Important departures from this practice occurred in countries on the periphery of the Soviet bloc. To a number of these countries the United States extended massive military as well as economic assistance, with the latter being usually justified in terms of short-term import or budgetary requirements.

By 1960 criticism of the project approach was widespread. It was easy to show how development depended not on a few specific projects, but on an adequate overall investment effort, with respect to both aggregate size and composition, and how ill-designed fiscal, monetary, and foreign exchange policies could undercut the positive contribution of any individual project to economic growth. Economists further pointed out that the donor country was not really financing the project for which it was ostensibly granting funds, but rather the "marginal" project which the aid recipient would have just given up had he not been handed the additional resources for a project which he probably would have undertaken in any event.[1] For these reasons, so it was argued, a look at the total spending pattern of the recipient country is essential if one wishes to have some assurance that the aid funds are put to productive use. Finally, it was pointed out that project aid necessarily implies a series of biases and perverse incentives: it encourages the aid recipient to prepare large capital projects, to exaggerate the foreign-exchange portion of the total cost of these projects, and to favour public infrastructure projects, which are most easily financed through loans or grants extended from one government to another for project purposes.

While these criticisms of the project approach all contributed to a change in the climate of expert opinion, another important reason for going from project to program aid was the desire to increase the level of aid to some key countries and to provide a solid institutional basis for aid giving at this higher level. Program aid was conceived as aid given "in bulk" on the basis of a general understanding between donor and recipient about the latter's development program and principal economic policies. (Other terms frequently used in connection with program aid are, in ascending order of euphemization, "leverage," "incentive programming," "making sure of self-help.")

As a result of what was then thought to be the model case of India, the accent was at first primarily on achieving agreement on the recipient's development plan, its size, priorities, and the resulting "resources gap" to be filled by aid in its various forms. But, in most developing countries development plans are primarily statements of intention. Further, in the rare country with a highly operational development plan, the fulfilment of the plan's objectives would depend crucially, among other things, on "appropriate" fiscal, monetary, and other economic policies. In Latin America, moreover, program aid under the Alliance for Progress was to be forthcoming not only in connection with a broad agreement on economic development objectives, but was to be premised also on advances in social development that depended on the enactment and implementation of reforms in land tenure, income taxation, educational opportunity, and the like.

The Two Aid Bargains Compared

The general idea of moving from the project to the program approach consisted, therefore, in laying the groundwork for a substantial and steady flow of aid

1. For a critique of this view, see Richard M. Bird, "The Influence of Foreign Aid on Local Expenditures," *Social and Economic Studies* 16 (June 1967): 206–210.

through a meeting of minds between donor and recipient on central economic programs and policies of the recipient country.

When the matter is put in this way, the formidable difficulties of the program approach begin to appear. No doubt, by moving the discussion between donor and recipient from where to build what kind of power station to fiscal, monetary, or agrarian reform policies, one is turning from peripheral to central issues of the recipient's decisions. But is that a good thing? We shall now argue that this move raises at least as many problems as it solves.

To facilitate the discussion, it is useful to attempt at this point a conceptual distinction between "pure" project and "pure" program aid. In the real world this distinction will of course be blurred, as these two archetypes of aid hardly ever appear in their pure forms. Hence it should be understood that our subsequent discussion does not cover every conceivable case of project or program aid, but tries to catch the essential difference between two diverse forms of aid giving. Moreover, we do not aim at extolling project aid, with whose problems and drawbacks we are familiar, but rather at bringing out, with project aid as a back- drop, the heretofore largely neglected political implications and side effects of program aid.

As a starting point for the discussion, we may imagine that aid is given in the form of a check drawn by the donor to the order of the recipient, without conditions or strings of any kind. This unconditional aid can then turn into conditional aid along two principal routes.

First, the donor can insist that the money be spent for certain specific purposes: the result is pure project aid as here defined. Secondly, the donor may require that the recipient country change some of its ways and policies as a condition for receiving the funds: this is our definition of pure program aid.

From the point of view of the recipient, there is a fundamental difference between the two bargains which may conceivably accompany the transfer of aid funds. Pure project aid forces the recipient country to substitute to some extent the donor's investment preferences for its own insofar as the use of the aid funds is concerned. As a result, the recipient country lands in a situation it senses as inferior to the one in which the same amount of aid would be available unconditionally. Nevertheless, the aid permits the country to achieve a position in which it is unequivocally better off than without aid, in the sense that more funds are forthcoming for some purposes while, generally speaking, investments that the country would have made in the absence of aid will not be curtailed. Thus, the conditions attached to pure project aid are not likely to arouse strong hostility in the recipient country and do not require the policy makers to sacrifice any important objective which they would have been able to pursue in the absence of aid.

The situation changes significantly in the case of the bargain characteristic of pure program aid. The commitment a country undertakes in connection with this type of aid is typically of the following kind: to increase investment and decrease consumption, to increase the share of the private sector and decrease that of the public sector, to devalue the currency and thereby alter relative price relationships within the country, to throttle inflation and therefore strike a blow at the particular interest group whose turn it is to benefit from the next inflationary appropriation, credit expansion, or rise in prices or wages; and so on, and so forth. In all these instances, compliance with the conditions attending program aid makes one group within the recipient country worse and another better off than before. The bargain preceding the granting of program aid also implies that the aid-receiving government will alter its previous policy-mix in such a way as to sacrifice in some measure objective A (say, a larger public sector) to objective B (say, growth).

Economists who have discussed the concept of community welfare have long been divided into two groups: those who deny, and those who affirm, that meaningful statements can be made about increases or decreases in collective welfare when, as a result of economic change, one group gains at the expense of another. There is no need for us to enter into this discussion, except to note that its protracted and stubborn nature testifies to the fundamental difference between the two situations that we have just described. With pure project aid, the recipient government can achieve all of its pre-aid objectives (plus some additional aid-financed ones) and no group in the country need be any worse off. With the type of conditional program aid discussed here, the objectives of public policies will be reshuffled and some domestic group is likely to be hurt. Even though the total resources available to the country are increased through the aid, the hurt group cannot be directly compensated, at least in the short run, for its loss, by the very terms of the aid agreement.

We should mention here one particularly important way in which project aid shades off in the real world into program aid. When the project donor spends its funds on, say, a certain kind of power station, it will often have views, and will attempt to have them prevail, on such matters as accounting practices, power rates, administrative autonomy, and perhaps even public versus private ownership of the utility. Project aid may then also involve policy changes that would hurt some groups or individuals. Even in this case, however, an important difference between project and program aid remains. Program aid is usually given in connection with changes in central economic policies of the recipient, whereas the policy changes the donor is liable to insist on in connection with project aid are germane to the construction and operation of the project and are therefore likely to be concerned with matters that are at some remove from the central policy concerns around which the more important group conflicts rage.

The Program Aid Bargain Further Considered

It will, of course, be argued that whatever sacrifice is entailed by the policy changes required by the program aid bargain is more than fully compensated by the other side, namely the aid package itself. The fact that aid is accepted on these terms could be considered as evidence that there is nothing to worry about. After all, the recipient government could have refused aid (as Burma did in general, and Brazil and Colombia at one time or another, in connection with assistance from the International Monetary Fund) if it felt that the conditions were too harsh. But this application of the notion of revealed preference misses several points. In the first place, we were intent on showing the difference between two forms of conditional aid giving and on pointing out that the cost of obtaining aid is of a different nature in the two cases. Secondly, it is a gross oversimplification to treat a government entering the program-type bargain on foreign aid like a consumer buying himself a bag of apples. Since aid, in this case, has as its counterpart a shift in national objectives and in the short-term fortunes of different social groups, the bargain will be considered a bad one by the circles that value highly the objective that has been sacrificed and by those groups whose interests have been hurt. Hence, the very bargain that gives rise to program aid can and will be attacked directly by these circles and groups as being damaging to the national interest as they define it. Pure project aid is ordinarily immune to this kind of destabilizing side effect. Precisely for that reason, those who attack it will often resort to alleging that it is impure and carries some unavowed and excessive cost in terms of general economic or political policy commitments. In other words, to be effective, an attack on project aid will attempt to prove that it is really program-type aid.

The difference between a country or a country's government adopting certain changes in its central economic policies as a quid pro quo for aid and a consumer disbursing cash for a pound of apples goes deeper still. The program aid bargain is effective only if the government is genuinely convinced of the positive value of the policies it has adopted in conjunction with the aid—if there has been, that is, a genuine meeting of minds between donor and recipient about the economic policy measures conducive to development. It is as if the consumer were not only made to hand over the cash, but were asked to positively enjoy this act instead of sensing it as a cost. Moreover, the commitment of the recipient government is ordinarily not just to a single policy action, but to a policy that requires implementation through a practically infinite series of actions. A more correct comparison of the program aid bargain would therefore be to the decision of a person who joins the monastic orders: he does not usually consider his vows of poverty and chastity as a payment for the promise of eternal afterlife, but as something to be valued and perhaps enjoyed directly and independently of that promise.

One matter is already becoming clear: for the commitments entered into in the course of program aid negotiations to be faithfully adhered to, the recipient government ought to be so convinced of the correctness of the policies to which it commits itself that it would have followed these policies even without aid. Paradoxically, therefore, program aid is fully effective only when it does not achieve anything—when, that is, no quid pro quo (in the sense of a policy that would not have been undertaken in the absence of aid) is exacted as the price of aid. (It is ironical that, at least when it is effective, program aid is vulnerable to the very charge that has long been levelled—wrongly, we think—against project aid: namely, that one can never be sure that the project thus financed would not have been undertaken even in the absence of aid.)

In these situations, the donor would set himself the task of rewarding virtue (or rather, what he considers as such) where virtue appears of its own accord.

This is indeed a modest and manageable task, but it is also one that does not usually satisfy the donors. Precisely because the institutional basis and public opinion support of aid are so precarious in the donor country, the proponents and dispensers of aid have quite naturally felt compelled to make extraordinary claims for what aid can accomplish. The most persistent of these claims has been that aid acts as a "catalyst." This term is meant to convey that aid makes the difference between stagnation (or perhaps deterioration) and vigorous economic growth of the recipient country, or between the recipient being hostile and being friendly to the donor country. To these traditional and exaggerated claims for aid, a new variant has been added by the program approach: namely, that aid, properly conditioned, makes the difference between the recipient following the "wrong" and adopting the "right" economic policies.

In this fashion, then, aid is not seen in the role of rewarding virtue, but in the role, infinitely more difficult, of bringing virtue into the world. Now the fact that aid is known to be available *if* certain policies are followed will sometimes serve to strengthen a domestic group genuinely and independently convinced of the correctness of these policies and it is therefore not inconceivable that aid will on occasion help this group to come to power. This is the ideal case in which program aid acts first as a catalyst and then achieves so complete a meeting of minds and so full a sharing of values and objectives between donor and recipient that from then on they will march hand in hand toward a better future.

We have on purpose drawn a caricature, for it is our conviction that this picture of program aid as a catalyst for virtuous policies belongs to the realm of rhapsodic phantasy. At best, situations in which aid helps virtue to triumph in this fashion are the exception rather than the rule. The normal case is far more prosaic: the knowledge that aid is available if certain policies are adopted serves to make these policies more attractive and less costly than they would otherwise be. These policies will therefore often be adopted by aid-hungry governments in spite of continuing doubts of the policy makers themselves, resistance from some quarters within the government, onslaught against the "deal" from the opposition, and general distaste for the whole procedure.

Naturally, doubts and reservations are not voiced at the moment of the aid compact; hence the delusion on the part of the donor that there has been a full meeting of minds. But soon after virtue has been "bought" through aid under these conditions, the reservations and resistances will find some expression—for example, through half-hearted implementation or sabotage of the agreed-to policies—and relations between donor and recipient will promptly deteriorate as a result.

Problems Encountered in Buying Virtue Through Aid

It may be argued that once a government has unequivocally committed itself to certain acts as a condition of receiving aid, there is a good chance that it will convince itself that these acts are truly in the national interest even though previously it may not have thought so. Psychologists have developed the theory of "cognitive dissonance" to analyse individual behaviour in similar situations. The theory teaches that if a person engages in "discrepant behaviour"—in acts, that is, which cannot be reconciled with what he considers to be his beliefs and values—he will attempt to reduce the resulting dissonance by changing his values in such a way that harmony is restored.

However, the theory also stresses another point that is crucial here: if the discrepant behaviour is induced by either carrot or stick, there will be far less consequential value change than if the discrepant behaviour occurs in some accidental, absentminded, or experimental fashion. If the behaviour is rewarded (as it is, in our case, by the granting of aid), dissonance hardly arises, because, in accounting for his behaviour to himself, the actor has a ready explanation and excuse for the fact that he did something contrary to his principles, opinions, or preferences.

(For the same reason, declarations of support for a cause against which one has previously fought are unlikely to change a subject's prior beliefs when such declarations are exacted under torture.) Therefore, the very act of rewarding policy changes through aid undermines the determination with which these changes will be carried out and makes backsliding and sabotage more likely.

These considerations explain why certain types of policy commitments on the part of aid-receiving countries are more workable—and therefore have turned out to be more popular with the donors than others. The more workable and more popular commitments are precisely those that are highly visible, verifiable, measurable and, at their best, irreversible. One thinks of a revision of the customs tariff, of the imposition of credit restrictions in order to curb inflation, or, most typically perhaps, of a devaluation. In the latter case, there would seem to be little possibility of backsliding or of second thoughts. Yet, while devaluation cannot be retracted, its intended effects can usually be frustrated by subsequent monetary, fiscal, and wage-price policies. Hence, even in the case of devaluation, a government which harbours a feeling that it has been pushed into an unwise policy can often administer an "I-told-you-so" lesson to the donor just by omitting to carry out certain complementary policies after the devaluation.

In the case of other economic or social policies that sometimes have stood in the centre of aid negotiations, the continued psychological resistance of the aid recipients to such policies after a formal compact has been sealed can manifest itself more directly and easily. Whether the aid negotiations were concerned with enlarging the private sector of the economy or with establishing the basis for a land reform, the commitments a government has undertaken in these areas can be rendered inoperative through bureaucratic harassment or through lack of administrative energy, respectively. The old Spanish colonial adage "*se acata pero no se cumple*" (one obeys but one does not comply) will thus be widely practiced once again, and properly so. A country which permits its key economic policies to be determined by this type of international negotiation finds itself in fact in a semicolonial situation and is likely to adopt all the time-honoured methods of stealthy and indirect resistance appropriate to that situation.

The fact that certain commitments have less latitude in implementation and are therefore less prone to sabotage than others has naturally led to a preference of aid negotiators for these types of commitments. In this way we can explain the increasing tendency to make program aid depend on the taking of specific monetary and exchange rate measures and on the "appropriate" behaviour of certain fiscal and monetary indicators, while less and less attention is paid to economic growth and social justice, supposedly the principal objectives of aid.

The Hidden Costs of Program Aid

The resistance of the recipient country to some of the policy commitments it has underwritten in the course of the aid negotiations is not the whole story. The general unhappiness about having had its arm twisted can find other outlets than backsliding on these same commitments.

In a simple model of international relations we may assume that, for the sake of independence, self-respect, and defence against accusations of being a satellite, the government of B, a poor country, is determined to maintain a certain average distance from country A, a great power and a potential donor. Country B measures this distance along two dimensions, the extent to which it adopts economic policies suggested by A and the extent to which it takes A's position on the leading issues of international politics. Under these conditions, a success on the part of the great power in having B "do the right thing" in economic policy will result in a strong urge on the part of B to compensate for this move in the direction of A by a move in the opposite direction in international politics. Only in this fashion can the desired average distance be maintained. That this model of international behaviour is not completely unrealistic, in spite of its simplicity, can be shown by recalling a few episodes of the recent past: the attempt of the Quadros government in Brazil to move in the direction of a strongly neutralist posture in international relations after having adopted economic policies long advocated by the United States and the International Monetary Fund; to some extent, Pakistan's rapprochement with China; and, lately, a number of "surprising" foreign policy positions taken by the present Indian government just after it had finally been so "reasonable" in its decisions on domestic economic policy.

In this manner, a "successful" program aid negotiation in the course of which the recipient agrees to a variety of economic policies suggested by the donor may well have hidden, though considerable, costs: first, a direct cost to the donor in terms of the loss of certain diplomatic and foreign policy supports he thought doubly secure because of the aid extended; secondly, a serious loss of public support for the aid program in the donor country, as a result of what will be felt as ingratitude, hostility, and "irresponsible antics" on the part of the recipient. In this indirect fashion, the attempt at maximizing the productivity of aid by exercising "leverage" involves the risk of drying up the flow of aid at its very source.

Other Frictions Created by the Program Approach

Our case can be further bolstered by important differences between project and program aid related to the diplomacy of the aid process. Consider first the donor's claim to have his advice taken seriously on the ground that he contributes substantial resources. This claim is strong in the case of projects, where the donor's contribution often amounts to one-half or more of the total cost of the project. It is much weaker in the case of program aid, for here the donor's contribution is measured against the recipient country's national product or, at best, its total investment or imports. In such comparisons, the aid effort is almost always likely to look disproportionately small in relation to the important changes in national economic policies that are being sought.

Next, we may examine the donor country's implied claim that its own judgment is superior to that of the recipient. In the case of projects financed by the donor, the justification and credibility of the claim is usually quite strong. The donor country is likely to know more about the construction of highways and power stations than the recipient, simply because it is economically more advanced and has specialized knowledge in the areas in which it stands ready to finance projects. When it comes to appropriate economic policies to foster growth along with price stability and an acceptable distribution of income, the claim of the donor country to superiority is far more questionable. Frequently the donor country itself is far from having fully solved these very problems. Even if it has done better at them than the aid recipient, the applicability of its experience to the wholly different economic, social, historical, and political circumstances of another country must be much in doubt. The claim to superior knowledge is therefore fairly credible and innocuous in the case of project aid. It is not credible in the case of program aid—indeed, it is profoundly irritating.

The diplomacy of aid is even more directly involved in our final point. It is in the nature of the aid relationship that comparatively low-level officials of the donor country are paired off in aid negotiations with high-level officials of the recipient countries. This irksome difference in levels is far less pronounced in the case of project aid than program aid. In discussing the layout and specifications of a highway, an engineer of an aid mission or of the World Bank may perhaps exchange arguments at one point with the director of the highway agency of the aid-receiving country. But the matters discussed in conjunction with program aid relate, as we have seen, to central economic policies and issues. Given the centralization of decision making and the thinness of the elite in the typical aid-receiving country, these matters can ordinarily be decided only at the very top of the political structure, by the president and his minister of finance. And who are their counterparts around the negotiating table? At best, the director of the local aid mission and, usually, various mission staff members. In this way, program aid recreates a typical colonial situation in which the rulers of the recipient country have to deal as equals with, and often feel that they have to take orders from, persons who, within their own country, are miles away from the seat of power. There is no need to expand on the resentment created by this situation.

Recapitulation and Some Recommendations

These, then, are some of the disadvantages of the program approach to foreign aid. To recapitulate: the program approach will accentuate old and create new discord within the recipient country and it will erode the government's support; it will lead to attempts at backsliding and reneging on the commitments that have been entered into; it will have a hidden cost for the donor and will diminish public support for aid programs in the donor countries as it impels the recipient to assert his independence by moving away from the donor in areas not covered by the aid agreement; and the negotiations leading to program aid will prove highly irritating to the recipient, both because he will not recognize the claim of the donor to superior knowledge of the questions that are typically the subject of program aid negotiations and because the gap in the respective levels or ranks of those who do the actual negotiating between donor and recipient is painfully wide.

After this indictment of program aid, is there anything good to be said about it? Certainly there is. The main virtue of program aid has been to permit, in the early sixties, a considerable increase in the volume of aid extended to a number of countries. Two questions therefore arise. First, is it possible to change the practice of program aid in such a way as to avoid some of its more unpleasant side effects? Secondly, and more ambitiously, is it possible to go beyond both the limitations of project aid and the liabilities of program aid, and devise a wholly new approach? This question will be taken up in the next section.

The answer to the first question is not particularly difficult. The very analysis of the program approach that we have given yields a partial remedy; for, if the policy makers were fully aware of the political side effects of aid giving under the program approach, they would become more circumspect in its use.

Some specific recommendations also emerge from the preceding pages. Since, in our opinion, the program approach overreaches itself when it attempts grandiosely to bring virtue into the world, the explicit or implicit conditioning of aid on changes in policies of the recipient countries should be avoided. This does not mean that the donor cannot make his opinions and preferences known; but it does imply that elaborate arrangements should be made to divorce the exchange of opinions about suitable economic policies from the actual aid-giving process. The educational virtues of such discussions will be strengthened rather than weakened as a result. Finally, the donor should resist the temptation to measure "performance" of the recipient at frequent intervals by narrow quantitative indicators, when by its very nature such performance can be assessed properly only over a relatively long period of time by a combination of quantitative information and qualitative judgment.

An Alternative Mechanism for Foreign Aid

In spite of these possible avenues of improvement of current practices, the present aid-giving processes are sufficiently defective to warrant a search for new techniques—however utopian they may appear at first sight. To our minds, the basic requirements of a satisfactory aid technique are three in number: (1) it should permit the transfer of a substantial volume of funds to the poor countries, (2) it should not be tied systematically to the achievement of a meeting of minds on central economic policy decisions of the recipient countries, and (3) it should still exert pressure toward the efficient use of the resources that are provided.

We shall now discuss a scheme that gives promise of satisfying these conditions and would have two important additional merits. First, it would place international development more on a people-to-people basis and thereby rekindle public interest in it. Secondly, it would institutionalize more openly and firmly than heretofore the redistribution of world income from the rich to the poor countries.

Like any new scheme, the one to be described here is replete with uncertainties and difficulties. Fortunately it lends itself to being introduced gradually and it could therefore initially supplement rather than replace existing resource flows. Once perfected in one country as a result of experience, the proposed alternative mechanism for transferring aid might largely supersede current bilateral programs and might also spread to other donor countries.

The essence of the plan is to involve the individual taxpayer of the donor countries in the foreign aid program. Instead of paying taxes for a package of government expenditures that includes foreign aid together with all domestic programs, taxpayers could elect to use a limited portion of their income tax obligation for contributions to one or several World Development Funds. These funds would not be administered by any government and would channel financial assistance to various investors, public and private, in developing countries.

For their "contribution to foreign aid" the taxpayers would receive a full tax credit from the Internal Revenue Service. Such a tax credit would require legislation, but not on an annual basis. In the last resort, the government would of course still be the donor to developing countries, in that its tax revenue would be reduced by the amounts that individual taxpayers were earmarking for foreign aid, but the resulting funds would not belong to the government and their allocation and uses—and, to some extent, their amount—would no longer be determined by it.

Before turning to the details of the scheme, a brief justification for handling national expenditures for foreign aid so differently from expenditures for all other purposes is in order. A national decision to extend financial assistance to developing countries must necessarily be made by the established constitutional processes of each donor country and its implementation requires action by existing national fiscal authorities. At the same time, the foreign aid decision must be interpreted as the assumption, on the part of the donor country and its citizens, of an obligation to contribute to world development. But this intent of the foreign aid decision stands in great danger of being jeopardized and perverted if the resulting funds are administered by donor-country governments. Our discussion of program aid is suggestive in this respect. Foreign aid that is supposed to transfer income from the rich to the poor countries becomes all too easily, when it is administered by national governments, an instrument through which the rich impose their will on the poor! The possibility and even likelihood of this unfortunate mutation is a risk peculiar to foreign aid expenditures, and strong institutional safeguards against it are required. Here lies the basic justification for the break with traditional canons of fiscal policy that is implicit in our tax credit proposal. (The establishment of multilateral agencies such as the World Bank has been one response to the need for moving away from the extension of development aid by national governments, but the response has not fully met the need, both because of the limited funds these institutions command and because they depend entirely and directly on governmental contributions.)

The following discussion first outlines the basic mechanism of tax credits and then treats the difficult problem of efficiently allocating the funds thus obtained.[2]

2. The tax credit mechanism and a number of the other points made here were suggested by the remarkable effectiveness of a somewhat similar Brazilian scheme for regional development. See chap. 4 of *A Bias for Hope*, cit..

Finally, some possible objections to the scheme are considered, and it is contrasted to earlier tax incentive proposals. At this stage, the proposal is necessarily quite tentative. We have tried, nevertheless, to be concrete and specific, primarily to explore the feasibility of the idea and to invite further discussion.

The Tax Credit

In more detail, the tax credit mechanism might work somewhat as follows. Individual taxpayers could claim a full tax credit for their foreign aid contributions, up to 5% of their federal income tax or $10,000, whichever is smaller. A hypothetical average taxpayer with an adjusted gross income of $16,000 and a tax liability of $2,030 could, for example, obtain a tax credit of $102 under this scheme. The claim for credit would have to be substantiated by a receipt from the depository bank or other satisfactory documentation. The limits of 5% and $10,000, while arbitrary, are designed to eliminate the possibility of undue influence by wealthy individuals on the operations of the development funds proposed below, and to hold the potential cost of the scheme to the treasury to reasonable dimensions. Corporations would not be eligible for this credit for similar reasons, the danger or suspicion of "private imperialism" being particularly acute in their case.

From *Statistics of Income* data it may be crudely estimated that the maximum amount that could have been made available for development in this way in 1965 was about $2.3 billion, compared with actual public economic assistance from the United States in the fiscal year 1966 of about $2.5 billion. Since incomes are now higher and aid lower, the potential of the tax credit scheme would at present be in excess of current aid levels. The important question of the probable actual yield of this incentive will be taken up later.

Return to the Investor

Apart from the psychic satisfaction of helping the poor of the world become less poor, the benefits which an individual might get from taking part in this scheme should be narrowly limited. For every $100 (or other round figure) deposited, the taxpayer would receive a "Share in Development." To avoid complications, this document should not be a marketable asset. The possibility may be held out, however, for such shares to earn a small return, on the order of 2½% a year for 40 years, until the face value of the "loan" is fully repaid. Whether or not this return is actually received would depend on the nature of the use made of the funds on average, as discussed below. Any such return would presumably be taxable as normal income to the taxpayer.

Another possibility might be to introduce a lottery feature with some such prize as a tourist trip to the less developed country or countries of the winner's choice.

Uncertain and small as these incentives would be, they should serve to make the tax credit option a preferred alternative to simply paying taxes. Their primary purpose is to maintain the interest and involvement of taxpayers in the progress of the less developed world without imposing serious service and transfer problems on the recipient countries.

How to Channel the Funds

One can envisage various ways in which the funds provided by the tax credit mechanism might flow to less developed countries from the United States or from any other developed countries that might adopt this idea. At one extreme, all the tax credit funds might be remitted by the depository banks to a single World Development Fund, which would then allocate them to different activities in different countries. This alternative does not attract us at all, since such a single fund would surely be tempted once again to influence the central economic policies of recipient countries and to engage in the leverage practices which have been criticized above.

At another extreme, every individual investor might search out some qualifying activity in some less developed country into which he would like to put his money. While the option of doing this might well be kept open (given the limits on the tax credit, the possibilities of abuse are negligible), it would clearly be impossible for most of those potentially affected by the tax credit to behave in this way. Nor would it necessarily be desirable, even if they could do so, for those activities in which individuals would prefer to put their money as investors are often very different from those which they would wish to finance to promote world development. Some compromise is needed to avoid monolithic bureaucracy, on the one hand, and self-centred individualism, on the other.

One possibility is for the funds to be channelled in some proportions (which could be reconsidered at periodic intervals) to special sections of the existing multilateral organizations, such as the World Bank and its affiliates, the Inter-American Development Bank, and the other regional banks now in the process of formation. This solution would have the advantage of avoiding the setting up of a new bureaucracy, but there is some question about channelling all available funds to these far from infallible international agencies.

Partly for this reason and partly to explore the possibilities of still more decentralized aid giving, we shall discuss here an alternative: to set up a number (say ten) of independent private organizations called "Development Funds" as agents for disbursing the funds collected through the tax credit. Each Fund would be managed by a small professional and administrative staff. Recruitment would be on an international basis from the considerable body of those in both private and public sectors, in both poor and rich countries, who now have relevant experience in the problems of investment and development.

The principal aim of these Funds would simply be to transfer available funds as quickly and as efficiently as possible to less developed countries. (In the event that the Funds could not invest the amounts provided by the tax credit within, say, three years, the money could revert to the treasury. This three-year rule applies in the Brazilian scheme for the development of the Northeast.) The rules outlined below would offer some guidance in this task, but the main test of success would, in the nature of the operation, have to be something as vague and general as the approval of the board of directors of the Fund. Each Fund might have a separate board of six to eight members, or there might be one general advisory board of sixteen to twenty members for all the Funds. In either case, at least half the membership of the board (or boards) should consist of citizens of less developed countries. No one country should have a majority on any board. The board members would serve in their private capacity and not as representatives of any country or organization. These stipulations are designed to emphasize the international and nongovernmental character of the Funds and to permit drawing as widely as possible on world competence in guiding their operations. How these boards and the Fund managements might be initially constituted and perpetuated is a matter for further study.

Some Operating Rules

The main restriction imposed on the investment policy of the Funds is that any project in which they invest should be partially financed by someone else. The required complementary investor (or investors) might be a local private entrepreneur, a local development bank, the government or a public enterprise, and perhaps also some other international lending agency, or any combination of these.

The requirement that someone else be willing to put up some of his own money for the project in question (probably a specified percentage of the total cost) is crucial to ensure efficient use of funds and to prevent the recipient country's considering the cost of capital to be zero. The percentage of the matching requirement might vary with the country, it might well be set at a lower level for the poorer countries. (In setting such general, though flexible, rules some of the economic criteria derived from the experience of present aid giving agencies might prove very useful.)

It deserves emphasis that the Funds would be institutionally neutral. The degree of their involvement in a country's economic life should not be affected by the way in which that country chooses to draw the borderline between the public and private sectors. The only generally unacceptable partners would be private foreign enterprises and bilateral lending agencies, although there could be exceptions even to this rule, particularly when it is clear that principal ownership and control rest in local hands.

Should the Funds be restricted to the financing of a limited list of certain "productive" or "essential" activities? For a number of reasons, we do not think so. It is up to the recipient countries to determine whether they want to be permissive or restrictive in this respect. Every sovereign country will evidently be able to restrict the access of its nationals to the Development Funds in any way it sees fit and the Funds should be left to use their best judgment, within those limits, without further direction.

The financing provided by the Funds should be flexible—equity, medium-term, or long-term loans, or a combination of these. For non-revenue-producing projects in the public sector the terms might be very soft—for example, a fifty-year loan, with a ten-year grace period and a 2% interest rate. For normally revenue-producing projects, public or private, the terms should be correspondingly harder both to encourage them to produce revenue in actual practice and to provide financing for other activities in the future.

Return Flow

Depending on the nature of the investment, payment of interest, principal, and dividends could be stipulated either in convertible or in local currencies. As most developing countries are at present either too debt-ridden or too poor to shoulder large additional amounts of international indebtedness, the net return flow stemming from the Funds' investments should be strictly limited. Some small inflow of foreign exchange from successful projects would be desirable to cover the administrative expenses of the Funds, and, as noted above, to enable them to pay out a small return of capital to the original individual "investors." Any such repayment to investors would depend on the average return to the Funds, since one taxpayer's money would not be distinguishable from another's. The backflow of dollars from past investments should not normally exceed that needed for these purposes, but if it did so occasionally it would provide a useful reserve and supplement to the ordinary resources of the Funds.

Since the Funds are conceived primarily as channels and should not end up controlling or owning enterprises in the less developed countries, even the payment of dividends, interest, and amortization in local currency requires careful consideration. One suggestion with merit is that the original individual investor might be allowed to designate his favourite charity or other non-profit organization in the developing country as the recipient of such funds. This would, however, require too much cumbersome tagging of funds with individual names. An alternative proposal along similar lines is that each recipient country would designate or set up one or several non-profit organizations which, on approval of the Development Fund concerned, would receive any repayments, stock sale proceeds, or profits and disburse such monies to worthy activities. This feature would offset to some extent the bias toward investment in revenue-producing activities in the private sector that might perhaps be considered inherent in the scheme, no matter how much the Development Funds might be directed to maximize economic development, rather than financial returns alone.

Fund investments in equity require special consideration. Again to avoid permanent entanglement of the Funds in the recipient countries' affairs, all such investment could be in nonvoting stock (as is the present practice of the International Finance Corporation) and one could require the Funds to turn over any such equity after a period of, say, ten years to the non-profit organizations just referred to.

Competition and Coordination

The purpose of creating ten or twelve Funds instead of one is to encourage diversity and competition. It would therefore be best not to assign certain countries or groups of countries or certain types of investments to one Fund rather than another. In time, of course, one might expect the different Funds to acquire their particular areas of competence both regionally and functionally, but there seems no reason to specify in advance what these areas should be. Nevertheless, a few general rules in this regard might be useful to avoid undue concentration or neglect. For example, it might be specified that no Fund could have more than 50% of its total investment in any country or type of activity. In general, more than

The proposed tax credit goes far beyond any tax incentives to investment in less developed countries presently available in the United States. A number of provisions in the present tax law have been advertised as such incentives. Present tax provisions do in fact place direct investment by American firms in less developed countries on a slightly more favourable basis than direct investment by such firms in more developed countries. As a rule, however, investment in the United States is even more favoured because of the 7% investment credit. (The major exceptions to this statement are those investors who can take advantage of the low tax rate applicable to Western Hemisphere trade corporations or of the privilege of tax deferral through tax haven subsidiaries.) Proposals to extend the investment credit to investment in developing countries would simply put such investment on an equal footing with domestic investment in the United States. This is hardly a positive incentive policy, especially when, as is now apparently the preferred approach, the credit is to be extended country-by-country on a tax treaty basis rather than by statute, as with domestic investment.

The most generous tax incentive that has been seriously, though fruitlessly, discussed, a 30% investment credit, would admittedly constitute real favouritism at last. But favouritism to what? To *direct* investment by *American* firms—or to precisely the kind of foreign investment that carries with it all too often a set of problems and opportunities for friction at least as formidable as those accompanying program aid. Our proposal avoids these difficulties, as well as the need for recipients of the tax benefit themselves to hunt down favourable investment opportunities. For these reasons, the proposed tax credit to individuals is totally different from anything that is now in the tax law or that has been contemplated.

Like all tax incentives, our proposal constitutes, of course, a special favouritism to certain activities, but we submit that it is an unneutrality as worthy as fostering private charities, probably more so than many tax-exempt foundations, and certainly more so than percentage depletion in the oil industry. The increased rigidity of budgetary policy implicit in any fiscal measure of this kind could be reduced, if desired, by making the percentage credit in any year variable between appropriate upper and lower limits, say, 3 and 8%. A more basic justification for the special fiscal treatment of foreign aid implicit in our scheme has already been given at the beginning of this section.

Another traditional objection to tax incentives, and a harder one to answer, is that they are usually ineffective. We have no secure basis for estimating the probable flow of funds resulting from this proposal, or the cost to the treasury. For reasons suggested above, it would probably be greater than that under the other tax incentive proposals mentioned, which simply means it would be more effective in achieving the supposed aim. Most of those who bothered to take this option would probably be relatively well-to-do people, but this is hardly an objection, since it means the funding of the program would be more progressive in its incidence than that of the usual aid program. If we assume that the limits suggested above (5% of the income tax, or $10,000) were adopted and that all of those with adjusted gross incomes of over $10,000 took advantage of the tax credit, the potential funding from this source in 1965 would have been on the order of $1.5 billion, but this is only the crudest of guesses. One might expect the initial amount available to be relatively small and to grow with time and success.

Despite all the points requiring further thought, it perhaps deserves reiteration that the proposed scheme avoids the problems of grappling with the "central issues" of economic policy and the consequent detailed interference in domestic economic policies of recipient countries that so mars the present public programs of foreign aid. It also avoids most of the traditional objections to increased reliance on foreign investment, primarily because there is no question of increased foreign "control" either by American corporations or by the U.S. government, nor even by the proposed Development Funds themselves. The scheme may seem overgenerous to the developing countries. For the reasons given in the first part of this paper, however, we are convinced that such generosity is in the best interests of the aid-giving countries themselves.

One most desirable side effect might be felt immediately as a result of a trial adoption. Considering the small and uncertain return the taxpayer might expect, we would have, for the first time, a concrete indication of how many people in the United States care enough about foreign aid to be willing explicitly to divert some of their tax dollars to it. Our initial assumption is that more aid is a good thing. This proposal would, if nothing else, enable us to know how many people agree with us.

11

"Exit, Voice, and Loyalty": Introduction and Doctrinal Background

Under any economic, social, or political system, individuals, business firms, and organizations in general are subject to lapses from efficient, rational, law-abiding, virtuous, or otherwise functional behaviour. No matter how well a society's basic institutions are devised, failures of some actors to live up to the behaviour which is expected of them are bound to occur, if only for all kinds of accidental reasons. Each society learns to live with a certain amount of such dysfunctional or misbehaviour; but lest the misbehaviour feed on itself and lead to general decay, society must be able to marshal from within itself forces which will make as many of the faltering actors as possible revert to the behaviour required for its proper functioning. This book undertakes initially a reconnaissance of these forces as they operate in the economy; the concepts to be developed will, however, be found to be applicable not only to economic operators such as business firms, but to a wide variety of noneconomic organizations and situations.

While moralists and political scientists have been much concerned with rescuing individuals from immoral behaviour, societies from corruption, and governments from decay, economists have paid little attention to *repairable lapses* of economic actors. There are two reasons for this neglect. First, in economics one assumes either fully and undeviatingly rational behaviour or, at the very least, an *unchanging level* of rationality on the part of the economic actors. Deterioration of a firm's performance may result from an adverse shift in supply and demand conditions while the willingness and ability of the firm to maximize profits (or growth rate or whatever) are unimpaired; but it could also reflect some "loss of maximizing aptitude or energy" with supply and demand factors being unchanged. The latter interpretation would immediately raise the question how the firm's maximizing energy can be brought back up to par. But the usual interpretation is the former one; and in that case, the reversibility of changes in objective supply and demand conditions is much more in doubt. In other words, economists have typically assumed that a firm that falls behind (or gets ahead) does so "*for a good reason*"; the concept—central to this book—of a random and more or less easily "repairable lapse" has been alien to their reasoning.

The second cause of the economist's unconcern about lapses is related to the first. In the traditional model of the competitive economy, recovery from any lapse is not really essential. As one firm loses out in the competitive struggle, its market share is taken up and its factors are hired by others, including newcomers; in the upshot, total resources may well be better allocated. With this picture in mind, the economist can afford to watch lapses of any one of *his* patients (such as business firms) with far greater equanimity than either the moralist who is convinced of the intrinsic worth of every one of *his* patients (individuals) or the political scientist whose patient (the state) is unique and irreplaceable.

Having accounted for the economist's unconcern we can immediately question its justification: for the image of the economy as a fully competitive system where changes in the fortunes of individual firms are exclusively caused by basic shifts of comparative advantage is surely a defective representation of the real world. In the first place, there are the well-known, large realms of monopoly, oligopoly, and monopolistic competition: deterioration in performance of firms operating in that part of the economy could result in more or less permanent *pockets* of inefficiency and neglect; it must obviously be viewed with an alarm approaching that of the political scientist who sees his polity's integrity being threatened by strife, corruption, or boredom. But even where vigorous competition prevails, unconcern with the possibility of restoring temporarily laggard firms to vigour is hardly justified. Precisely in sectors where there are large numbers of firms competing with one another in similar conditions, declines in the fortunes of individual firms are just as likely to be due to random, subjective factors that are reversible or remediable as to permanent adverse shifts in cost and demand conditions. In these circumstances, mechanisms of recuperation would play a most useful role in avoiding social losses as well as human hardship.

At this point, it will be interjected that such a mechanism of recuperation is readily available through competition itself. Is not competition supposed to keep a firm "on its toes"? And if the firm has already slipped, isn't it the experience of declining revenue and the threat of extinction through competition that will cause its managers to make a major effort to bring performance back up to where it should be?

There can be no doubt that competition is one major mechanism of recuperation. It will here be argued, however (1) that the implications of this particular function of competition have not been adequately spelled out and (2) that a major alternative mechanism can come into play either when the competitive mechanism is unavailable or as a complement to it.

Enter "Exit" and "Voice"

The argument to be presented starts with the firm producing saleable outputs for customers; but it will be found to be largely—and, at times, principally—applicable to organizations (such as voluntary associations, trade unions, or political parties) that provide services to their members without direct monetary counterpart. The performance of a firm or an organization is assumed to be subject to deterioration for unspecified, random causes which are neither so compelling nor so durable as to prevent a return to previous performance levels, provided managers direct their attention and energy to that task. The deterioration in performance is reflected most typically and generally, that is, for both firms and other organizations, in an absolute or comparative deterioration of the *quality* of the product or service provided.[1] Management then finds out about its failings via two alternative routes:

1. For business firms operating in situations of monopoly or monopolistic competition, performance deterioration can also be reflected in cost and resulting price increases or in a combination of quality drops and price increases. On the other hand, changes in either price or quality are ruled out when both are rigidly dictated by a perfectly competitive market; in this admittedly unrealistic situation, deterioration can manifest itself only via increases in cost which, with price and quality unchanged, will lead straightaway to a decline in net revenue. Under perfect competition, then, managers learn about their failings directly and exclusively from financial evidence generated within the firm, without any intermediation on the part of the customers who remain totally unaware of the firm's troubles. It is perhaps because the whole range of

(1) Some customers stop buying the firm's products or some members leave the organization: this is the *exit option*. As a result, revenues drop, membership declines, and management is impelled to search for ways and means to correct whatever faults have led to exit.
(2) The firm's customers or the organization's members express their dissatisfaction directly to management or to some other authority to which management is subordinate or through general protest addressed to anyone who cares to listen: this is the *voice option*. As a result, management once again engages in a search for the causes and possible cures of customers' and members' dissatisfaction.

The remainder of this book is largely devoted to the comparative analysis of these two options and to their interplay. I will investigate questions such as: Under what conditions will the exit option prevail over the voice option and vice versa? What is the comparative efficiency of the two options as mechanisms of recuperation? In what situations do both options come into play jointly? What institutions could serve to perfect each of the two options as mechanisms of recuperation? Are institutions perfecting the exit option compatible with those designed to improve the working of the voice option?

Latitude for Deterioration, and Slack in Economic Thought

Before setting out to answer some of these questions, I shall now step back briefly and indicate how I conceive the subject of this book to be related to economic and social science thought around us.

Talking with students of animal behaviour (at the Centre for Advanced Study in the Behavioural Sciences) about the social organization of primates I learnt about the smoothness-and efficiency with which leadership succession, a problem human societies have found so intractable, was handled in certain baboon bands. Here is how the process is described for a typical band of Hamadryas baboons lorded over by one male leader:

phenomena here described has no place in the perfectly competitive model that it has not been paid attention to by economists.

> Sub-adult males steal very young females from their mothers and attend them with every semblance of solicitous maternal care. The young female is rigorously controlled, and repeated retrieval trains her not to go away … At this stage there is no sexual behaviour, the female being yet two to three years from child bearing … As these young interlopers mature and the overlord ages, the younger animal starts initiating group movements although the direction of eventual movement is dependent upon the older animal's choice. A highly complex relationship develops between the two animals which, by paying close attention to one another and by reciprocal "notification," cooperate in governing group movement. Old males retain command of group direction but gradually relinquish sexual control over their females to the younger male animal … It seems that eventually old males resign entirely from their original reproduction units but retain great influence within the band as a whole, and young males refer to them continuously particularly before developing the direction of march[2]

Compare this marvel of gradualness and continuity with the violent ups and downs to which human societies have always been subject as "bad" government followed upon "good," and as strong or wise or good leaders were succeeded by weaklings, fools, or criminals.

The reason for which humans have failed to develop a finely built social process assuring continuity and steady quality in leadership is probably that they did not have to. Most human societies are marked by the existence of a surplus above subsistence. The counterpart of this surplus is society's ability to take considerable deterioration in its stride. A lower level of performance, which would mean disaster for baboons, merely causes discomfort, at least initially, to humans.

The wide latitude human societies have for deterioration is the inevitable counterpart of man's increasing productivity and control over his environment. Occasional decline as well as prolonged mediocrity—in relation to achievable performance levels—must be counted among the many penalties of progress. A priori it would seem futile, therefore, to look for social arrangements that would wholly eliminate any sort of deterioration of polities and of their various constituent entities. Because of the surplus and the resulting latitude, any homeostatic controls with which human societies might be equipped are bound to be rough.

2. John Hurrell Crook, "The Socio-Ecology of Primates," in J. H. Crook, ed., *Social Behaviour in Animals and Man* (to be published by Academic Press, London). The passage quoted summarizes research by Hans Kummer, "Social Organization of Hamadryas Baboons," *Bibliotheca Primatologica*, no. 6 (Basle: S. Karger, 1968).

Recognition of this unpleasant truth has been impeded by a recurring utopian dream: that economic progress, while increasing the surplus above subsistence, will also bring with it disciplines and sanctions of such severity as to rule out any backsliding that may be due, for example, to faulty political processes. In the eighteenth century the expansion of commerce and of industry was sometimes hailed not so much because of the increase in well-being that it would make possible, but because it would bring with it powerful restraints on the wilfulness of the prince and thereby reduce and perhaps eliminate the system's latitude for deterioration. One characteristic passage from Sir James Steuart's *Inquiry into the Principles of Political Oeconomy* (1767) will suffice to make the point:

> How hurtful soever the natural and immediate effects of political revolutions may have been formerly, when the mechanism of government was more simple than at present, they are now brought under such restrictions, by the complicated system of modern oeconomy, that the evil which might otherwise result from them may be guarded against with ease …
>
> The power of a modern prince, let it be by the constitution of his kingdom ever so absolute, immediately becomes limited so soon as he establishes the plan of oeconomy … If his authority formerly resembled the solidity and force of the wedge (which may indifferently be made use of, for splitting of timber, stones and other hard bodies, and which may be thrown aside and taken up again at pleasure), it will at length come to resemble the delicacy of the watch, which is good for no other purpose than to mark the progression of time, and which is immediately destroyed, if put to any other use, or touched with any but the gentlest hand … modern oeconomy, therefore, is the most effectual bridle ever was invented against the folly of despotism[3]

This noble hope echoes nearly two hundred years later in the writings of a Latin American intellectual similarly predicting, against all likelihood, that economic progress and latitude for deterioration will be negatively, rather than positively, correlated:

> [In the pre-coffee era, policy makers] are lyrical and romantic because they cannot yet defer to a product whose output is constantly on the increase. It is a time of childhood and play. Coffee will bring maturity and seriousness. It will not permit Colombians to continue playing fast and loose with the national

3. (Chicago: University of Chicago Press, 1966), I, 277, 278–279.

> economy. The ideological absolutism will disappear and the epoch of moderation and sobriety will dawn … Coffee is incompatible with anarchy.[4]

History has cruelly disappointed the expectations of both Sir James Steuart and Nieto Arteta that economic growth and technical progress would erect secure barriers against "despotism," "anarchy," and irresponsible behaviour in general. Yet their line of thought is hardly extinct. It is, in fact, not unrelated to today's widespread belief that a major war is unthinkable and therefore impossible in the nuclear age.

The common assumption of these constructs is simply stated: while technical progress increases society's surplus above subsistence it also introduces a mechanism of the utmost complexity and delicacy, so that certain types of social misbehaviour which previously had unfortunate but tolerable consequences would now be so clearly disastrous that they will be more securely barred than before.

As a result society is, and then again it is not, in a surplus situation: it is producing a surplus, but is not at liberty *not* to produce it or to produce less of it than is possible; in effect, social behaviour is as simply and as rigidly prescribed and constrained as it is in a no-surplus, bare subsistence situation.

The economist cannot fail to note the similarity of the situation with the model of perfect competition. For this model contains the same basic paradox: society as a whole produces a comfortable and perhaps steadily increasing surplus, but every individual firm considered in isolation is barely getting by, so that a single false step will be its undoing. As a result, everyone is constantly made to perform at the top of his form and society as a whole is operating on its—forever expanding—"production frontier," with economically useful resources fully occupied. This image of a relentlessly *taut economy* has held a privileged place in economic analysis, even when perfect competition was recognized as a purely theoretical construct with little reality-content.

These various observations add up to a syndrome, namely, to man's fundamentally ambivalent attitude toward his ability to produce a surplus: he likes surplus but is fearful of paying its price. While unwilling to give up progress he hankers after the simple rigid constraints on behaviour that governed him when

4. Luis Eduardo Nieto Arteta, *El café en la sociedad colombiana* (Bogotà: Breviarios de orientación colombiana, 1958), pp. 34–35. This posthumously published essay was written in 1947, only a year before the outbreak of the sanguinary civil disturbances known as *la violencia*, just as Sir James Steuart wrote about the definitive conquest of despotism not long before the rise of Napoleon.

he, like all other creatures, was totally absorbed by the need to satisfy his most basic drives. Who knows but that this hankering is at the root of the paradise myth! It seems plausible, indeed, that the *rise* of man above the narrowly constrained condition of all other living creatures was frequently sensed, though it can hardly ever have been avowed, as a *fall*; and a radical but basically simple act of the imagination may well have metamorphosed this condition which one was really yearning for into its exact opposite, the Garden of Eden.[5]

But we must leave paradise and return to social thought, for there is another side to our story. The simple idea that the ability to produce a surplus above subsistence makes it possible and indeed likely that occasionally less than the maximum producible surplus will be produced has not gone wholly unnoticed. In fact, next to the traditional model of the permanently *taut* economy, elements of a theory of the slack economy begin to be available. I am not referring now to unemployment and depression economics—the *slack* associated with these phenomena results from malfunctions at the macroeconomic level which frustrate firms and individuals in their supposedly undiminished zeal to maximize profits and satisfaction. Nor is the question of slack involved in the dispute about what it is that business firms, and particularly the large corporations, really do maximize: profits, growth, market shares, community goodwill, or some composite functions of such objectives. The assumption underlying this dispute is that, whatever it is that firms do, they do it the best they can even though the criterion for "best" performance is becoming rather murky. Finally I am not concerned with the large body of writings showing that the actions of conscientiously maximizing private producers and consumers may fail to produce a *social* optimum, because of the existence of monopolistic elements and externalities. Here again the difference between actual and potential output is not due to some "failure of

5. Samuel Johnson intimated this thought in his fable about the Happy Valley of Abyssinia. When Prince Rasselas first analyses the discontent he feels in the paradise-like valley, he compares his condition to that of some grazing goats in the following terms: "What makes the difference between man and all the rest of the animal creation? Every beast that strays beside me has the same corporal necessities with myself; he is hungry and crops the grass, he is thirsty and drinks the stream, his thirst and hunger are appeased, he is satisfied and sleeps; he rises again and is hungry, he is again fed and is at rest. I am hungry or thirsty like him, but when thirst or hunger cease, I am not at rest; I am like him pained with want, but am not, like him, satisfied with fulness." (Samuel Johnson, *Rasselas*, II).

nerve" at the micro-economic level. But of late there has been increasing attention to the possibility of just such a failure.

A seminal contribution in this area was H. A. Simon's suggestion that firms are normally aiming at no more than a "satisfactory" rather than at the highest possible rate of profits.[6] This notion was given considerable underpinning in 1963 by Richard Cyert and James March, who in their book *A Behavioral Theory of the Firm*[7] introduced the concept of "organizational slack." At about the same time, Gary Becker showed that some of the basic and empirically well-tested microeconomic theorems (e.g., that market demand curves for individual commodities are negatively inclined) are consistent with a wide range of irrational and inefficient behaviour on the part of consumers and producers even though these theorems had originally been derived on the assumption of undeviating rationality.[8] The importance of slack was later affirmed in a particularly sweeping form by Harvey Leibenstein.[9] Finally, in a widely discussed polemical essay, Professor M. M. Postan has recently contended that Britain's economic ailments are better understood by focusing on microeconomic slack than on any mistaken macroeconomic policies. He writes:

> For many (perhaps most) of these … ailments the morbid causes will be found not in the malfunctioning of the life processes in the body economic, such as the low rate of savings, or the high level of prices, or the insufficient allocation of national resources to research and development, but in specific failures of its individual cells—management, design, salesmanship, or the behavior of groups of labor.[10]

6. H. A. Simon, "A Behavioral Model of Rational Choice," *Quarterly Journal of Economics*, 69: 98–118 (1952). An early, completely forgotten empirical work with a related theme has the significant title *The Triumph of Mediocrity in Business*, by Horace Secrist, published in 1933 by the Bureau of Business Research, Northwestern University. The book contains an elaborate statistical demonstration that, over a period of time, initially high-performing firms will on the average show deterioration while the initial low performers will exhibit improvement.
7. Richard M. Cyert and James G. March, *A Behavioral Theory of the Firm*, (Englewood Cliffs, NJ: Prentice-Hall, Inc., 1963).
8. Gary S. Becker, "Irrational Behavior and Economic Theory," *Journal of Political Economy*, 52: 1–13 (February 1962).
9. Harvey Leibenstein, "Allocative Efficiency versus X-Efficiency," *American Economic Review*, 56: 392–415 (June 1966).
10. M. M. Postan, "A Plague of Economists?" *Encounter* (January 1968), p. 44.

I feel considerable kinship with this group of writings for I had adopted a similar position in dealing with the problem of development. The basic proposition of *The Strategy of Economic Development* (1958) was that "development depends not so much on finding optimal combinations for given resources and factors of production as on calling forth and enlisting for development purposes resources and abilities that are hidden, scattered or badly utilized."[11] And the term slack actually came under my pen when I summarized later on the essential argument of that book in an article co-authored with C. E. Lindblom:

> At any one point of time, an economy's resources are not to be considered as rigidly fixed in amount, and more resources or factors of production will come into play if development is marked by sectoral imbalances that galvanize private entrepreneurs or public authorities into action … The crucial, but plausible, assumption here is that there is some "slack" in the economy; and that additional investment, hours of work, productivity, and decision making can be squeezed out of it by pressure mechanisms.[12]

Various reasons have been invoked for explaining slack. Leibenstein's emphasis is on the uncertainties surrounding the production function and on the non-marketability of managerial and other skills. Cyert and March refer primarily to the bargaining process that takes place among the various parties whose (shaky) coalition is required for factors to be hired and for output to be produced and marketed. I stressed rather similarly the existence of obstacles to entrepreneurial and cooperative behaviour needed for the making of development decisions.

Those who have found that the individual economic operators and, as a result, the economy are ordinarily far from doing as well as they might, can be expected to react to their shocking discovery along two principal lines. The immediate and most obvious reaction is a determined search for ways and means to take up the slack, to retrieve the ideal of the taut economy. As long as the pressures of competition do not seem to be sufficient, the pressures of adversity will be invoked.[13] Frequent changes in the environment, forcing the firm to be "on its toes," will be identified as one way of inducing performance closer to the firm's

11. (New Haven: Yale University Press, 1958), p. 5.
12. "Economic Development, Research and Development, Policy Making: Some Converging Views," *Behavioral Science*, 7: 211–212 (April 1962).
13. See Leibenstein, "Allocative Efficiency versus X-Efficiency," cit.

potential.[14] Insofar as innovation is concerned, the inducing and focusing virtues of strikes and war have been stressed.[15] My own search concentrated on pressure mechanisms such as intersectoral and intrasectoral imbalances and on production processes that exact high penalties for poor performance or do not tolerate it at all.[16] Finally, the advocates of social revolution have contributed to this line of thought: one of their most seductive arguments has long been that only revolutionary changes can tap and liberate the abundant but dormant, repressed, or alienated energies of the people.[17]

Quite a different reaction to the discovery of slack occurs when the discoverer asks himself, after having got over his initial shock, whether slack may not after all be a good thing, a blessing in disguise. The idea that slack fulfils some important, if unintended or latent, functions was put forward by Cyert and March, who point out that it permits firms to ride out adverse market or other developments. During such bad times slack acts like a reserve that can be called upon: excess costs will be cut, innovations that were already within one's grasp will at last be introduced, more aggressive sales behaviour that had been shunned will now be engaged in, and so on. Slack in the political system has been rationalized in a very similar manner. The discovery that citizens do not normally use more than a fraction of their political resources came originally as a surprise and disappointment to political scientists who had been brought up to believe that democracy requires for its functioning the fullest possible participation of all citizens. But soon enough a degree of apathy was found to have some compensating advantages in as much as it contributes to the stability and flexibility of a political system and provides for "reserves" of political resources which can be thrown into the battle in crisis situations.[18]

The immediate response to the discovery of slack has thus been either to assert the rationality of a certain level of slack or to look for ways of extirpating excessive levels by invoking exogenous forces such as adversity, imbalances,

14. Charles P. Bonini, "Simulation of Information and Decision Systems in the Firm" (unpub. diss. Carnegie Institute of Technology, 1962).
15. Nathan Rosenberg, "The Direction of Technological Change: Inducement Mechanisms and Focusing Devices," *Economic Development and Cultural Change,* 18 (October 1969).
16. Hirschman, *Strategy,* chs 5–8.
17. See, for example, Paul Baran, *The Political Economy of Growth* (New York: Monthly Review Press, 1957).
18. See *Exit, Voice, and Loyalty*, cit., pp. 31–32.

revolution, and so on. Both these approaches look at slack as a gap of a given magnitude between actual and potential performance of individuals, firms, and organizations. This book takes a further, more radical step in recognizing the importance and pervasiveness of slack. It assumes not only that slack has somehow come into the world and exists in given amounts, but that it is *continuously being generated* as a result of some sort of entropy characteristic of human, surplus-producing societies. "There's a slacker born every minute," could be its motto. Firms and other organizations are conceived to be permanently and randomly subject to decline and decay, that is, to a gradual loss of rationality, efficiency, and surplus-producing energy, no matter how well the institutional framework within which they function is designed.

This radical pessimism, which views decay as an ever-present force constantly on the attack, generates its own cure: for as long as decay, while always conspicuous in some areas, is hardly in undisputed command everywhere and at all times, it is likely that the very process of decline activates certain counterforces.

Exit and Voice as Impersonations of Economics and Politics

In examining the nature and strength of these endogenous forces of recovery, our inquiry bifurcates, as already explained. Its breakup into the two contrasting, though not mutually exclusive, categories of exit and voice would be suspiciously neat if it did not faithfully reflect a more fundamental schism: that between economics and politics. Exit belongs to the former realm, voice to the latter. The customer who, dissatisfied with the product of one firm, shifts to that of another, uses the market to defend his welfare or to improve his position; and he also sets in motion market forces which may induce recovery on the part of the firm that has declined in comparative performance. This is the sort of mechanism economics thrives on. It is neat—one either exits or one does not; it is impersonal—any face-to-face confrontation between customer and firm with its imponderable and unpredictable elements is avoided and success and failure of the organization are communicated to it by a set of statistics; and it is indirect—any recovery on the part of the declining firm comes by courtesy of the Invisible Hand, as an unintended by-product of the customer's decision to shift. In all these respects, voice is just the opposite of exit. It is a far more "messy" concept because it can be graduated, all the way from faint grumbling to violent protest; it implies articulation of one's critical opinions rather than a private, "secret" vote in the anonymity of a supermarket; and finally, it is direct and straightforward rather than roundabout. Voice is political action par excellence.

The economist tends naturally to think that his mechanism is far more efficient and is in fact the only one to be taken seriously. A particularly good illustration of this bias appears in a well-known essay by Milton Friedman which advocates the introduction of the market mechanism into public education. The essence of the Friedman proposal is the distribution of special-purpose vouchers to parents of school-age children; with these vouchers the parents could buy educational services that would be supplied in competition by private enterprise. In justifying this scheme he says:

> Parents could express their views about schools *directly*, by withdrawing their children from one school and sending them to another, to a much greater extent than is now possible. In general they can now take this step only by changing their place of residence. *For the rest, they can express their views only through cumbrous political channels.*[19]

I am not interested here in discussing the merits of the Friedman proposal.[20] Rather, I am citing the above passage as a near perfect example of the economist's bias in favor of exit and against voice. In the first place, Friedman considers withdrawal or exit as the "direct" way of expressing one's unfavourable views of an organization. A person less well trained in economics might naïvely suggest that the direct way of expressing views is to express them! Secondly, the decision to voice one's views and efforts to make them prevail are contemptuously referred to by Friedman as a resort to "cumbrous political channels." But what else is the political, and indeed the democratic, process than the digging, the use, and hopefully the slow improvement of these very channels?

In a whole gamut of human institutions, from the state to the family, voice, however "cumbrous," is all their members normally have to work with. Significantly, one major, if problem-plagued, effort presently underway toward better public schools in the large cities is to make them more responsive to their

19. "The Role of Government in Education," in Robert A. Solow, ed., *Economics and the Public Interest* (New Brunswick, NJ: Rutgers University Press, 1955), p. 129. A revised form of this essay was included in Friedman's *Capitalism and Freedom* (Chicago: University of Chicago Press, 1962) as ch. 6 and the cited passage appears unchanged on p. 91. The italics are mine.
20. For a good discussion see Henry M. Levin, "The Failure of the Public Schools and the Free Market Remedy," *The Urban Review*, 2: 32–37 (June 1968).

members: decentralization has been advocated and undertaken as a means of making the channels of communication between members and management in the public school systems less "cumbrous" than heretofore.

But the economist is by no means alone in having a blindspot, a "trained incapacity" (as Veblen called it) for perceiving the usefulness of one of our two mechanisms. In fact, in the political realm exit has fared much worse than has voice in the realm of economics. Rather than as merely ineffective or "cumbrous," exit has often been branded as *criminal*, for it has been labelled desertion, defection, and treason.

Clearly, passions and preconceptions must be reduced on both sides if advantage is to be taken of an exceptional opportunity to observe how a typical market mechanism and a typical nonmarket, political mechanism work side by side, possibly in harmony and mutual support, possibly also in such a fashion that one gets into the other's way and undercuts its effectiveness.

A close look at this interplay between market and nonmarket forces will reveal the usefulness of certain tools of economic analysis for the understanding of political phenomena, *and vice versa*. Even more important, the analysis of this interplay will lead to a more complete understanding of social processes than can be afforded by economic or political analysis in isolation. From this point of view, this book can be viewed as the application to a new field of an argument on which much of *The Strategy of Economic Development* was based:

> Tradition seems to require that economists argue forever about the question whether, in any disequilibrium situation, *market forces acting alone* are likely to restore equilibrium. Now this is certainly an interesting question. But as social scientists we surely must address ourselves also to the broader question: is the disequilibrium situation likely to be corrected at all, by market or nonmarket forces, or by both acting jointly? *It is our contention that nonmarket forces are not necessarily less "automatic" than market forces.*[21]

I was concerned here with disturbances of equilibrium and the return to it. Kenneth Arrow has argued along very similar lines for movements from less-than-optimal to optimal states:

> "I propose here the view that, when the market fails to achieve an optimal state, society will, to some extent at least, recognize the gap, and nonmarket social

21. Hirschman, *Strategy*, p. 63. Italics in the original.

> institutions will arise attempting to bridge it … this process is not necessarily conscious".[22]

These views do not imply, as both Arrow and I immediately hastened to add, that any disequilibrium or non-optimal state whatever will be eliminated by some combination of market and nonmarket forces. Nor do they exclude the possibility that the two sets of forces could work at cross-purposes. But they leave room for a conjunction—which could quite possibly be inadequate—of these two forces, whereas both laissez-faire and interventionist doctrines have looked at market and nonmarket forces in a strictly Manichaean way, it being understood that the laissez-faire advocate's forces of good are the interventionist's forces of evil and vice versa.

A final point. Exit and voice, that is, market and nonmarket forces, that is, economic and political mechanisms, have been introduced as two principal actors of strictly equal rank and importance. In developing my play on that basis I hope to demonstrate to political scientists the usefulness of economic concepts *and to economists the usefulness of political concepts*. This reciprocity has been lacking in recent interdisciplinary work as economists have claimed that concepts developed for the purpose of analysing phenomena of scarcity and resource allocation can be successfully used for explaining political phenomena as diverse as power, democracy, and nationalism. They have thus succeeded in occupying large portions of the neighbouring discipline while political scientists—whose inferiority complex vis-à-vis the tool-rich economist is equalled only by that of the economist vis-à-vis the physicist—have shown themselves quite eager to be colonized and have often actively joined the invaders. Perhaps it takes an economist to reawaken feelings of identity and pride among our oppressed colleagues and to give them a sense of confidence that their concepts too have not only *grandeur*, but *rayonnement* as well? I like to think that this could be a by-product of the present essay.

22. "Uncertainty and the Welfare Economics of Medical Care," *American Economic Review*, 53: 947 (December 1963).

12

Political Economics and Possibilism*

In reflecting on the essays brought together in *A Bias for Hope* I noted two principal common characteristics. In the first place, I frequently encounter and stress the political dimensions of economic phenomena just as I like to think in terms of development sequences in which economic and political forces interact. This focus seems to come almost naturally to me in connection with any problem I happen to be attacking and the first part of this introductory essay is an attempt at identifying the central concepts that underlie this "decentralized" activity of building bridges between economics and politics.

Another pervasive characteristic of the writings here assembled is a preoccupation with processes of social change. Understanding social change is obviously not something that can "come naturally" to anyone; one can only grope for it. Consequently the second part of this essay inquires into the nature of my own gropings.[1] It is necessarily more speculative—and, mercifully, much shorter—than the first part.

*. Introduction to *A Bias for Hope. Essays on Development and Latin America*, Newhaven, Yale University Press.

1. A related attempt is in the second half of chap. 16 of *A Bias*, cit..

Economics and Politics

If demand generated its own supply in the social sciences as it is supposed to do in the marketplace, there would exist by now a number of intellectually satisfying and empirically tested models of the social system based on the intimate interactions and interdependence of economic and political factors. In fact, of course, nothing of the sort is anywhere in sight. Economists continue to identify scientific progress with the elimination of "exogenous" forces from their constructs, while political scientists are similarly most at ease when they have explained political events by appealing to purely political categories.[2] Where the linkage between political and economic forces is too obvious to be disregarded, both categories of scholars have held to the most primitive linkage models in which typically a phenomenon belonging to the "foreign" discipline is introduced as some sort of prerequisite—and can then promptly be forgotten as purely "domestic" or endogenous forces take over. Insofar as economists are concerned, this practice goes back to Adam Smith's dictum that "little else is requisite to carry a state to the highest degree of opulence from the lowest barbarism, but peace, easy taxes, and a tolerable administration of justice." Political scientists, from Montesquieu and Rousseau to Hayek and Holt-Turner, have similarly looked for some unique and permanent economic characteristic—a certain level and distribution of welfare, or a certain organization of economic life—which makes the emergence of some type of political organization possible, probable, or even inevitable. Once again, no allowance is made in such theories for any continuing interplay between economic and political factors.

How is it possible to overcome the parochial pride of economists and political scientists in the autonomy of their respective disciplines and to go beyond the primitivism of the briefly noted efforts at linking them? Rather than issue another clarion call for an integrated social science, I find it more useful to survey the building blocks that have already been assembled, however inadequate they may be for the construction of an imposing or systematic structure. As just noted, I have frequently turned up some mini-building-blocks of the sort, and a classification and evaluation of these finds may be helpful in bringing a more systematic search underway. The following survey will therefore be largely intro- and

2. Note, for example, the success of Samuel Huntington's explanation of political development in terms of "institutionalization" in his *Political Order in Changing Societies* (New Haven: Yale University Press, 1968).

retrospective, but I shall make an effort both to note contributions of other writers and to introduce some new points.

Economic Theories of Politics

A first distinction that is not always clearly made is that between economic theories of politics and theories of political economics (or, better perhaps, theories of economics-cum-politics). The former term has come into use to designate the increasingly numerous and important contributions to political science that have been made, mostly by economists, through the application to political phenomena of modes of reasoning and analytical tools originally developed within economics. The logic of allocation of scarce resources among competing ends, of input-output relationships, and of decision making under uncertainty, to name just a few, should obviously be able to elucidate a great many areas of social and political life other than the strictly economic ones for which that logic was originally devised. Some of the better known efforts of this kind are the *Economic Theory of Democracy* by Anthony Downs and *The Logic of Collective Action* by Mancur Olson.[3] An example in *A Bias for Hope* is the note on the "stability of neutralism" (chap. 9) where I use the apparatus in indifference and transformation curves to explain the behaviour of an underdeveloped country that can choose between two aid givers and wishes both to receive aid and to maintain its independence.

Two general points can be made about these writings. First, while they may throw much new light on politics, they do not normally deal, nor do they set out to deal, with the interaction between politics and economics.[4] Secondly, there are serious pitfalls in any transfer of analytical tools and modes of reasoning developed within one discipline to another. As the economist, swollen with pride over the comparative rigor of his discipline, sets out to bring the light to his heathen colleagues in the other social sciences, he is likely to overlook some crucial distinguishing feature of the newly invaded terrain which makes his concepts and apparatus rather less applicable and illuminating than he is wont to think. As I argue for imported ideologies, the distance between reality and intellectual schema is

3. See also the collection of articles in Bruce M. Russett, ed., *Economic Theories of International Politics* (Chicago: Markham, 1968).
4. This body of writings should therefore not be grandly designated as the "new political economy" as is done in the otherwise very useful survey article by Bruno S. Frey, "Die Ökonomische Theorie der Politik Oder die neue Politische Ökonomie: Eine Übersicht," *Zeitschrift für die gesamten Staatswissenschaften* 126 (January 1970): 1–23.

here likely to be both wider and more difficult to detect than was the case as long as the scheme stayed "at home."[5]

For example, Downs's assumption that parties are uniquely motivated to maximize votes is several notches more unrealistic than the one that entrepreneurs are profit maximizers; the resulting theory is therefore likely to be contradicted by the facts with special vehemence, as I have recently shown.[6]

In the case of my own study on neutralism, I became aware that the ease with which the apparatus of indifference and transformation curves could be transferred from the realm of economics to those of international relations and aid giving was deceptive: in the process, the independence of the indifference map from the production-possibility schedule, so important for the determinateness and normative significance of equilibrium, was largely lost.

The theory of public goods supplies a third example of the care that must be taken when economic concepts are transferred to the realm of politics. It is particularly striking and instructive, and I shall deal with it at somewhat greater length. One of the principal points made by the theory is that the true demand for public goods cannot be ascertained in the market or even by survey methods:[7] since the availability of public goods to an individual consumer is by definition not depleted through consumption on the part of others, each consumer is likely to understate his true preference for the public good as he hopes that others will be willing to pay for all of the supply he wishes to secure; in this manner he would get a "free ride." The free rider problem has thus become a principal focus of the theory and its existence provides the basic justification for the provision of public goods by the government (and for financing through taxes).

This is all very acute and pertinent with respect to the supply of a wide variety of public services under modern conditions. Yet, if taken in the widest possible context, public goods include not only police protection, parks, and similar amenities, but public policies that are felt as right and perhaps even gratifying by large groups of citizens. Such policies could even be considered as specially pure public goods since they can be enjoyed by all citizens at the same

5. See *A Bias*, cit., chap. 15, pp. 335–337.
6. See Albert O. Hirschman, *Exit, Voice, and Loyalty* (Cambridge, MA: Harvard University Press, 1970), chap. 6.
7. See Robert Dorfman, "General Equilibrium with Public Goods" in J. Margolis and H. Guitton, eds., *Public Economics* (New York: St. Martin's Press, 1969), pp. 270–272, and James M. Buchanan, *The Demand and Supply of Public Goods* (Chicago: Rand McNally, 1968).

time, whereas the capacity of parks, police protection, and the like is necessarily limited so that at some point of mass use, their consumption becomes "rival," as is always the case for private goods. Now the "production" of these public policies often requires an effort of advocacy, lobbying, and agitation on the part of the citizens, and here the free rider problem raises its head again: in normal times, with many other needs and interests claiming his time and energy, the average citizen will tend to "let George do it" even though he may be mildly or even strongly interested in the outcome. But the times, like the weather, are seldom wholly normal; on quite a few occasions, lately, they have been abnormal and "a-changin'," and astoundingly large numbers of citizens, far from attempting to get a free ride, have been taking to the streets, to the nation's capital, or to other places where they expect to exert some influence for change. In this connection, it is interesting to note that while economists keep on worrying about the free rider problem, political scientists have become increasingly concerned about the "participation explosion." The latter phenomenon is clearly the obverse of the former: in many cases the individual citizen will insist on being present in a march or demonstration, on participating in a letter-writing campaign, and perhaps even on contributing to an election campaign, although his marginal contribution to the "production" of the public policy he desires to bring about may be close to zero (if not negative at times). To justify his participation in this case, he will perhaps exaggerate to himself the likely importance of his contribution; vis-à-vis others, he may well overstate his "true" preference for the public good in question and will certainly not understate it as he is supposed to according to the theory.

Why would he act in so strange a way? Because he senses his participation not as a cost, but as a benefit, because participation in a movement to bring about a desirable public policy is (and, unfortunately, may be for a long time) the next best thing to actually having that policy. The sudden, historically so decisive outbursts of popular energies must be explained by precisely this change in sign, by the turning of what is normally sensed as a cost that is to be shirked into a benefit, a rewarding experience, and a "happiness of pursuit" in which one simply must share. The possibility of this mutation is fundamental for the understanding of political change and leadership; for achieving change often requires such a mutation and a leader is he who knows how to effect it. Yet the concept of costs turning into benefits is difficult to grasp for the economist trying to reason about "the logic of collective action" by applying tools essentially grounded in the analysis of the market economy.[8] To find someone who knew all about these matters one must go back to Rousseau, who wrote, in *The Social Contract* (bk. 3, chap. 15): "In a truly free country, the citizens … far from paying to be exempted from their duties, would pay for the privilege of being allowed to fulfil these duties themselves."[9]

8. See Mancur Olson, Jr., *The Logic of Collective Action* (Cambridge, MA: Harvard University Press, 1965). In this book, individual participation in collective action to obtain a public good is made to depend on the balancing of the private benefits to be expected from the good against the private costs of participation. At one point in the argument, Olson grants a role to "social pressures" and "social incentives" in the cost-benefit calculus: participation could occur because without it the individual would lose prestige, or the esteem and friendship of his peers (pp. 60–63). In other words, participation is always costly, but on occasion this cost is more than offset by the cost of nonparticipation. This view has much in common with the logic that shows how man always acts out of selfish motives.
   In *Exit, Voice, and Loyalty,* I allowed myself to be imprisoned by the traditional notion that the use of voice is always costly. My case for the potential superiority of voice over exit would have been considerably strengthened had I realized that in certain situations the use of voice becomes acutely pleasurable and should therefore no longer be computed as a cost, but as a benefit.
9. One can also profitably go back to Pascal who was perhaps the first to note the distinction between private and public goods, in the following terms: "[Those] who have come closest to the truth have considered that the universal good which all men desire does not consist in any of the particular things which can only be possessed by a single individual … they have understood that the true good must be such that all can possess it at the same time, without diminution or envy" (*Pensées,* 425). As Pascal intimates here, God is the purest public good imaginable: my possession of Him does not detract in the slightest from that of anyone else. At no point can the possession of God ever become "rival" or "exclusive." Note that for this quintessential public good the free rider problem is totally solved. The possibility of obtaining a free ride through the religious exertions of others is excluded by the personal relationship between the god-seeking individual and God. At the same time, striving for God is not sensed as a cost by the religious person particularly since there is no clear dividing line between striving and possessing, so that a free ride would not be desirable even if it were possible.
   Yet, various carefully circumscribed free rides are perhaps present in the Christian religion through the concept of grace, the possibility of praying for others, and the sacrifice of Jesus. Indeed, Paul's Epistle to the Romans (5: 12–21) contrasts the free

One might suggest, then, that economists setting out to elucidate political problems by wielding nothing but their own tools are likely to stumble. Fortunately, their very stumbles can turn out to be illuminating.

Political Dimensions of Economic Phenomena

In proceeding now from economic theories of politics to political economy (or political economics, or politics-cum-economics) proper, I shall stay away, for the time being, from any semblance of a general theory; rather I shall bring together numerous partial observations with the intent of learning something about the nature and structure of the interrelationship between economics and politics.

The observations I wish to relate here can be characterized as political dimensions (or side effects) of economic phenomena. That such dimensions and side effects exist is of course no great discovery. The trouble is that the search for them has been undertaken primarily by sociologists or political scientists who have naturally focused on the most obvious, large-scale features of the economic landscape, such as economic wealth, growth, industrialization, inflation, mass unemployment, and so on. The effects of such economic macro-features or -events on politics are either evident, and hence uninteresting, or are so complex and depend on so many other variables as to be unpredictable and inconclusive. It is, for example, not a very fascinating discovery that private wealth can often be translated into political power and vice versa; or that a government's public support will ordinarily be eroded by accelerated inflation or mass unemployment. On the other hand, the effect of economic growth and industrialization on, say, political stability in an underdeveloped country is quite unfathomable in the absence of detailed information about economic, social, and political conditions.

Speculation about connections between economics and politics becomes much more profitable when one focuses not on the roughest outline, but on the finer features of the economic landscape. This can of course best be done by the economist who knows about them; the trouble is that his professional interests do not ordinarily lie in this direction. At the same time, the political scientist who has the motivation to look for such connections lacks the familiarity with economic concepts and relationships that is required. Hence the field is happily left to a few mavericks like myself.

ride to salvation available to Christians through Jesus' death with the free ride to sinfulness forced on all men as a result of Adam's fall.

My first discovery of the "finer" kind I am talking about was made almost thirty years ago when I was examining the ways in which a country can acquire political influence through its foreign trade. It occurred to me that there is a straightforward connection between the old established economic concept of the gain from trade which country B achieves by trading with A and the influence which A can exert in B as long as the trade is foreign and is therefore subject to interruption or termination at A's will. The entire theory of the gain from trade and of its distribution became therefore relevant for an understanding of the influence and power relationships that arise out of trade.[10]

A very similar exploration of the political implications of an old established economic concept is undertaken in my most recent book. There it is shown that the famous "consumer surplus" measures not only the consumer's gain from being able to buy a product at competitive market prices, rather than at prices set by a discriminating monopolist, but also the consumer's readiness to react strongly through either "exit" or "voice" should the quality of the product deteriorate. To the extent that voice is chosen, the size of the consumer surplus can be directly related to political action which consumers are liable to engage in to resist and fight deterioration.

Or let us turn to the economic theory of customs unions. For over twenty years now, the analysis of the static economic effects of such unions has been based on the distinction, first suggested by Jacob Viner, between trade creation and trade diversion. It was shown that the trade-creating effects of a customs union had to outweigh the trade-diverting ones for the union to make a positive contribution to the efficient use of world resources. The distinction between trade creation and trade diversion is certainly not one of the more difficult ones in economics. Nevertheless, I have yet to see a political analysis of customs unions which would take advantage of the considerable value of that distinction for an appraisal of the political forces favouring or opposing a union. As a first approximation, it could be said that the political chances of the formation of a union are the exact obverse of its economic effects: the larger the trade-creating effects, that is, the greater the need to reallocate resources in the wake of tariff abolition, the greater will be the resistance to the union among the producer interests of the potential participating countries. On the other hand, trade-diverting effects imply that producers of the member countries will be able to snatch business from their

10. See my *National Power and the Structure of Foreign Trade* (Berkeley: University of California Press, 1945, rev. ed., 1969).

competitors in non-member countries: the trade-diverting effects will therefore be highly popular with them and will provide a needed cement of interest group advocacy for the union. In the appraisal of the political appeal and feasibility of customs unions, trade creation and trade diversion thus turn out to be extremely useful categories; but the signs which they must be given there are opposite to the ones they carry in the economist's analysis of the welfare effects of customs unions.

Other dichotomies which have long been used by economists can be similarly made to yield considerable food for political thought and analysis. Attempts in this direction are made in chapter 11 with the distinction between portfolio and direct investment and in chapter 10 with that between project and program aid.[11] In the latter respect, it is pointed out that a form of aid giving such as program aid which seemed far more rational to the economist than project aid carried severe political side effects and liabilities. These are now widely recognized, but escaped detection, not only at the time when program aid was first proposed, but for a considerable period thereafter.[12]

Hidden political implications thus exist for some theoretical economic concepts, such as gain from trade and consumer surplus, and for categories originally devised for analysing, from the economic point of view, such institutions as customs unions, international investment, or foreign aid. Further examples can be drawn from economic history. Here again it normally takes an economist or an economic historian to do the job of uncovering the political implications.[13] For

11. With respect to the implications of direct as opposed to portfolio investment, see also Hans O. Schmitt, "Integration and Conflict in the World Economy," *Journal of Common Market Studies* 8 (September 1969): 1–18.
12. For an early warning by a politically sophisticated economist, see Thomas C. Schelling, "American Aid and Economic Development: Some Critical Issues" in *International Stability and Progress,* American Assembly (Columbia University, 1957), p. 137. See also chapter 10 of the present book.
13. The work of Barrington Moore, Jr. is an important exception to this norm. In his *Social Origins of Dictatorship and Democracy* (Boston: Beacon Press, 1966), he attributes a major role in the shaping of the political destinies of various nations to the "success or failure of the upper class in taking up commercial agriculture" (p. 459). But he does not stop with this comparatively grand dichotomy and elsewhere points out the vastly different political consequences deriving from land-intensive and linkage-rich sheep raising in England, from labour-intensive grain growing in Prussia, and from the linkage-poor wine trade in France. See his chap. 1 and pp. 45–50, 460–463.

the latter arise out of the characteristic detail of economic events. This is the case, for example, for the pattern of industrialization among twentieth-century latecomers: the early stages of their industrialization are largely concerned with the production of finished consumer goods on the basis of imported machinery and intermediate goods; also, during a prolonged period, this production takes place entirely for the domestic market, to substitute previously imported commodities, with no thought of exporting. In chapter 3 it is shown that such observations on the specific differential nature of industrialization can explain much about the frequently noted lack of political assertiveness and power of the industrial bourgeoisie in the developing countries, particularly in Latin America.

When one focuses on primary production and its history in these countries, purely technical economic characteristics also turn out to be politically relevant. The wide fluctuations of coffee prices are a good example. These fluctuations have long been explained by the large number of producers, by the five-year interval between planting and full bearing of the coffee tree which means that even a strong response of producers to price changes has little immediate effect on supply, and by the tendency of the tree to yield a bumper crop at irregular intervals. But these very economic and botanical characteristics also account for the tendency of coffee growers to join together as a powerful interest group which will exert pressures on the state to undertake price support schemes in times of distress. In response to these pressures, the state can then be led to assume responsibilities with respect to the formulation and direction of national economic policy at a relatively early stage.

The low price elasticity of short-run supply characteristic of coffee has interesting further consequences for public policy making. Once the coffee-growing country becomes ripe for industrialization, that characteristic makes it possible for the state to finance the needed infrastructure and to subsidize the nascent industries by a policy of squeezing the coffee sector by direct or indirect taxation. Such a policy would be far less successful if the to-be-squeezed primary product had a higher price elasticity of short-run supply, as is, for example, the case for cattle or wheat. In that case the policy might soon "kill the goose that lays the golden eggs," a phrase that has often been used to describe the ill-fated attempts of Perón to push industrialization in post-war Argentina at the expense of the agricultural sector. With respect to coffee, however, there appears the possibility of a truly dialectical sequence: first, the special production and market characteristics of coffee make for the formation of a strong pressure group of coffee growers which pushes the state into assuming responsibilities for interference with market forces. As a result, the state becomes aware of its capabilities and duties as the maker of national economic policy for development. At a later stage of growth, such a policy will require that income be redistributed away from the coffee growers and toward other sectors which need to be nurtured. And this redistribution can then be carried out with success because of the very characteristics of coffee that originally made for the vigorous and successful pressures of the coffee planters on the state.

It was necessary to show at some length the way in which political forces and relationships grow right out of specific economic situations and characteristics. For through the variety of instances surveyed, I hope to have established a double proposition. On the one hand, it appears that the number of connections between economics and politics is limited only by the ability of social scientists to detect them. On the other hand, it seems quite unlikely that there exists somewhere a master key which would bring into view the usually hidden political dimensions of economic relationships or characteristics in some more or less automatic or systematic manner. Each time, it seems to be a matter of a specific ad hoc discovery; at the same time, he who makes such a discovery increases his chances of making yet another one. For what is required is a certain turn of mind, the desire to speculate and to search in a certain direction, rather than the application of any infallible and objective technique. At most, our examples point to some practical hints or heuristic devices which might help the researcher to "catch" these elusive connections. One such device is the notion of "blessing in disguise" (or mixed blessing, i.e. curse in disguise) with which I have long been taken.[14] Frequently (but by no means unfailingly) it appears that the political dimensions takes the sign opposite to the one that attaches to the economic concept or characteristic. For example, the "gain from trade" measures also the opportunity for domination. In the same vein, the sluggish response of coffee supply to price changes and, in general, a deficient "ability to transform" which would normally be considered unfortunate characteristics by economists, turn out to be advantageous for the development of the coffee-producing country's political (and industrial) capabilities. This sort of compensatory relationship is now familiar to everyone because of the manifold noxious side effects of technical progress that have come into view. But situations in which the political side effects of economic events do not at all exhibit this contrapuntal character certainly cannot be ruled out—what has been said about late industrialization is a case in point. Here we have rather an example of a cumulative sequence à la Myrdal where an intrinsically none-too-favourable

14. See chap. 7 of the present book, and the introduction to my *Journeys Toward Progress* (New York: Twentieth Century Fund, 1963).

economic event—delayed industrialization—has further adverse political consequences. The notion of cumulative disequilibrium can indeed serve as another heuristic device. But there are good reasons to think that the connections between economics and politics which result from the use of this device are comparatively easy to find; therefore they are apt to be less interesting and have probably been overemphasized in what there exists of political economics today.[15]

In view of the large number of political implications of economic concepts which the politically inclined economist can uncover, I have little doubt that a similarly long list could be manufactured by the political scientist who would focus, to start with, on some political characteristic or event and would then draw attention to its economic side effects. Unfortunately, the inclination to explore such lines of causation seems to be just as weak among political scientists as it is unusual for economists to be interested in the reverse nexus. As an amateur political scientist, I shall give just one example of the potential fruitfulness of political economy speculations that would have their starting point in politics rather than in economics. One important political characteristic of some Third World societies, particularly in Africa and Asia, is the number and seriousness of cleavages along linguistic, religious, and racial-tribal lines. In comparison to Nigeria or Pakistan, countries like Colombia or even Brazil (not to speak of modern England or France) look remarkably unitary and homogeneous. Besides its many consequences for politics, the existence of such cleavages has profound implications for the appropriate strategy of economic development. For example, in countries affected by such cleavages the tolerance for income inequalities arising in the wake of development is likely to be much smaller than it is in more unitary countries. Hence, in the former, a capitalist strategy will be particularly hazardous, and may well either be abortive or lead the country straight into civil war. This is a vast topic which can only be touched upon here; it serves, however, to point up the important contribution that political scientists could make to the body of knowledge we are looking for.

15. See below, p. 294. The two heuristic devices just mentioned—the notion of blessing (or curse) in disguise and the concept of cumulative disequilibrium—do not by any means permit us to discover all the possible connections between economics and politics. A simple reason is that it is impossible, in many cases, to assign an unambiguous positive or negative sign to the socio-political implications of an economic event or characteristic. This point is stressed and illustrated in my *Development Projects Observed* (Washington: Brookings Institution, 1967), pp. 186–188.

Interaction between Economics and Politics

The line of inquiry outlined in the preceding section has intrinsic value since it permits political factors to permeate economic analysis and vice versa; it can also furnish important elements for a systematic economics-cum-politics. Without the prior accumulation of a large number of such elements, any call for a more integrated social science is bound to be futile. We even came close to describing a particular form of mutual interaction between economic and political forces in discussing the political consequences of high fluctuations in coffee prices. I probably derive special pleasure from the almost chance encounters with politics of the last section in much the same way in which I prefer the sudden, unexpected view of the main piazza one comes upon in a medieval city to the elaborate panoramic layout of later periods more given to "rational, comprehensive planning." Nevertheless, I shall now make a brief attempt to examine head-on the possible outline of general models in which economic and political forces would both be treated as endogenous variables.

Long acquired habits of thought interpose enormous obstacles to such an enterprise. The idea of a self-regulating economic system (erected on the basis of some political prerequisite such as law and order, but otherwise perfectly self-sustained) has retained a considerable grip on the economist's imagination; it has in fact been bolstered in recent years by the confection of similarly self-regulating equilibrium growth models. In such constructs, political factors and forces are wholly absent; if they play any role at all it is that of spoilers. Examples of the latter situation come easily to mind. The imposition of a price ceiling in the wake of political pressures feeding on temporary shortages and price rises makes the shortages more serious and protracted than they would be otherwise. Nationalist agitation leads to the imposition of a tariff, and a loss of welfare is the regrettable result. Lately it has been argued that the loss may not be regrettable, that the willingness to bear the loss may be explained and perhaps justified by a "taste" for economic nationalism; but since it is understood that such a taste is exceedingly odd and unenlightened this condescending "empathy" hardly changes the substance of the more old-fashioned—and more forthright—argument. The view of political factors as spoilers is bolstered by the many tales of how "controls beget more controls," how a simple political interference with economic forces will eventually make the whole system bog down in a maze of official regulations, corruption, and "perverse incentives." Clearly the construction of a model of interaction of economic and political forces will not come easily to those who have been brought up to believe that the admission of politically motivated actors into the economic arena amounts to a pact with the devil.

But economists are not alone in casting political forces in the role of spoilers. The inconclusive discussion on the relation between economic growth and political stability is instructive in this regard. The conjecture that economic growth would lead to the lowering of political tensions and to greater cohesiveness has been increasingly disputed by those who hold that growth tends to have destabilizing political effects. On the basis of the latter view it is then of some (but hardly overwhelming) interest to construct an economics-cum-politics replica of the economic demographer's "low-level-equilibrium trap": first there is economic growth, then this growth leads to adverse political developments which in turn cause economic decline so that economy and society revert to the low level from which they started out.

Such models in which economic growth either dispels or generates political storm clouds are really quite primitive. It is odd that they should have been taken so seriously and tested so doggedly when all the while a much superior construct was available: the Marxian concept of the historical process which rests on a far more realistic, if more complex, interaction between economic and political factors. If one replaces—and this does not do undue violence to Marx's thought—his "productive forces" and "relations of production" by economic and political factors, respectively, the representation of this process is somewhat as follows: at any one historical stage, the economy functions within a given political and institutional framework; on the basis of and owing to this framework, economic forces left to themselves can achieve some forward movement, but beyond a certain point further development becomes more difficult and eventually is held back by the unchanging political framework which, from a spur to progress turns into a "fetter"; at that point, political-institutional change is not only necessary to permit further advances, but is also highly likely to occur, because economic development will have generated some powerful social group with a vital stake in the needed changes.

For the economist, this vision has actually a pleasantly familiar look. It reminds him of one of the basic paradigms of his own science, namely the law of diminishing returns. It is strange that the close resemblance of this law to the Marxian concept of historical change should have been overlooked. Generations of economists have been taught that the output of any productive process will increase at a decreasing rate if the quantity of one cooperating factor of production is kept constant while that of the others is increased. Marx essentially affirmed the same relationship: the fixed factor of production causing decreasing returns was for him any given political and institutional order. In Marx's thought, this order is not subject to small incremental changes and improvements. Hence, the need for revolutionary change.

I was not aware how close I was to this generalized Marxian model of interaction between economic and political forces when I wrote in *The Strategy of Economic Development* that "nonmarket (i.e. political) forces are not necessarily less automatic than market forces"[16] and showed repeatedly how such forces are likely to arise when market mechanisms by themselves would cause shortages of social overhead capital, or would lead to regional imbalances or to other types of disequilibria which required—and were likely to entrain—the intervention of political action. Why did I fail to make the connection between one of my principal theses and Marxism? Largely, I think, because I rediscovered the possible alternation of economic and political forces in propelling societies forward in the context of processes that take place on a small scale as compared to the huge canvas on which Marx painted. But much of the fruitfulness of the Marxian scheme may well lie in applying it to slices of reality rather smaller than was intended by the master.

In any event, this is what I have been doing. An example is the description of import-substituting industrialization in chapter 9 of the present book: in combination with import controls, the existence of an overvalued exchange rate is shown to be at first a considerable help in getting the process underway in a certain political environment, but it eventually turns into a hindrance to further industrial development because it holds back both the expansion of capital goods manufacture and the achievement of a substantial volume of industrial exports. I also identify interest groups and political forces that are likely to advocate ever more powerfully the needed institutional changes.

A number of points can be made about such transpositions of the Marxian scheme to smaller-scale processes of economic-political development. In the first place, the political and institutional changes that are needed in any one of these sequences are less likely to be revolutionary than in those that interested Marx. Clearly, passing from a highly overvalued exchange rate to a slightly undervalued one is less likely to require a revolution than the transition from the capitalist to the socialist mode of production. Nevertheless, even such comparatively minor changes in institutional structure require discontinuous decisions which are often difficult and replete with political struggles and risks.

16. New Haven: Yale University Press, 1958, p. 63.

Another way in which the Marxian scheme can be usefully varied is by examining more closely the nature of political change that is supposed to resolve "contradictions" which have arisen in the preceding phase. Marx thought here in terms of revolutions that sweep away all of the institutions of whatever ancien régime needs to be done away with, and that then set up socio-political conditions ideal for the vigorous and unhampered unfolding of the "productive forces" during a prolonged period until such time as a new batch of contradictions emerges. Most of the time, historical reality is, of course, far less neat: socio-political change entrained by the contradictions is often partial, grudging, and with a lot of unfinished business left behind, so that the need for further change makes itself felt once again in fairly short order. The frequently fragmentary character of political-institutional change thus explains why the Marxian scheme is found to be so surprisingly useful on a far smaller historical scale than that for which it was conceived. This reasoning also suggests that the amplitude, length, and frequency of the interaction cycles will vary considerably over time and from country to country. One element in this variation could be the freedom different countries have to undertake large-scale political change. Untrammelled in this respect, the hegemonic powers will often go in for all-inclusive, apocalyptic, and cathartic crises that will be widely spaced in time, thereby conforming rather closely to the Marxian vision. Dependent countries, on the other hand, are kept from having their revolutions or their civil wars by some hegemonic power standing watch over them, always ready to dispatch armies or economic advisers commissioned to forestall a real crisis;[17] they must therefore introduce political change in a more stealthy and imperfect fashion[18] and are likely to exhibit more numerous interaction cycles that will revolve rapidly, so that the "next" required measure of public policy is never very far away. This is one reason why many observers of the reality of the dependent countries have found it so utterly indispensable to think systematically about the interaction of economics and politics.

A real advantage of visualizing growth processes in the manner previously outlined lies in the greater flexibility and realism with which it becomes possible to appraise economic policies and developments. No longer will one condemn any policy that is not immediately directed toward establishing the ideal tax or exchange rate system, or the most advanced agrarian reform legislation. Rather, the observer and policy maker will think in terms of sequences in the course of

17. The role economic advisers play in short-circuiting crises is illustrated in my *Journeys Toward Progress*, pp. 206–210.
18. See *A Bias*, cit., chap. 15, pp. 333–335.

which a forward step in one direction will induce others, perhaps after a period of "decreasing returns" and political-action-inducing disequilibria. It is not just a matter of "[moving] the economy wherever it can be moved";[19] on the contrary, while there will be less need for trenchant statements about uniquely correct policies and absolute priorities, the policy maker will often have to engage in difficult speculations about what I called "efficient sequences" in the *Strategy of Economic Development:* from among the various directions in which it is possible to move, he will have to form a judgment about the one that is most likely to achieve eventually certain objectives which are not within the direct reach of policy making. It is perhaps of interest to note here that the "pure economist" who refuses ever to think in terms of certain second-best policies which, via consequential political changes, could lead indirectly to the achievement of a desired objective, has a counterpart in the revolutionary who asks for the needed political changes right away, as an absolute prerequisite to any forward movement: neither seems ever to think in terms of economics-cum-politics (or politics-post-economics) sequences.

The most difficult and critical problem in thinking about such sequences is an appraisal of the likelihood that the needed political changes will actually take place once the phase of decreasing returns to economic forces acting alone has set in or, in Marxian terms, once the productive forces have entered into sharp contradiction with the relations of production. Reflecting on the role of the bourgeoisie in the French Revolution, Marx thought he had solved the problem, insofar as the societies he analysed were concerned, by identifying the industrial proletariat as the force that would have both the will and the power to make the socialist revolution. While in this respect his vision has turned out to be faulty, the kind of search he engaged in remains an essential part of the enterprise I am advocating here for smaller-scale sequences. There was never an intention on my part to assert that any sort of imbalance would be automatically corrected. Nor is it a question of the right size of the imbalance. The Toynbeean notion of a proper response arising directly from the challenge (provided only it is of the right size) is entirely foreign to my thinking.[20] Whenever I noted the phenomenon of economic forces alone leading to an imbalance or otherwise tension-laden or unsatisfactory state of affairs which needs to be corrected by political action, I have tried to locate specific "agents of change" which, much like Marx's industrial proletariat, would have the motivation and power to bring about that action.

19. Chap. 2, p. 82.
20. See also *A Bias*, cit., chap. 14, pp. 318–319.

Here is one example of this type of concrete search: after describing the economic forces which could make for increasing interregional disequilibrium in the course of a country's economic development, I pointed out that political counterforces might arise from the fact that "the poorer sections of the country, where careers in industry and trade are not promising, often produce, for that very reason, a majority of the country's successful politicians and thereby acquire influential spokesmen in the councils of government."[21] Similarly, in the treatment of import-substituting industrialization (chap. 9 of the present book) I engage in a determined search for forces that might counteract the tendency of industrialization to bog down after the "easiest" import substitution opportunities in the last stages of production have become exhausted.

It is nevertheless tempting to inquire whether there are any general reasons to expect political actions to be forthcoming in the situations that have been described. A very general model could be derived from the observation that many actors in a society can choose, at any one point of time, to engage either in economic or in political action. It has often been noted that an industrialist, for example, has the option of spending most of his time and energy either on improving the efficiency of his production and sales organization or on lobbying in the nation's capital for special tariff protection or other legislation favouring his firm and industry. Disregarding the adverse value judgment that attaches in this example to political action, we may bring this sort of option into contact with the tendency of economic growth to run into decreasing returns when it proceeds within an unchanging institutional framework. Surely, the decreasing returns will somehow impress themselves on the consciousness of the individual economic-political actors. Once they notice that the marginal productivity of economic action is diminishing in comparison to the prospective marginal productivity of political action, there will be a tendency on their part to substitute political for economic action. Hence, it is likely that an effort to carry out the needed political changes will actually be undertaken.

This very general reasoning by no means dispenses the social scientist from engaging in a detailed search for specific "agents" or "carriers" of change. But it is useful in permitting him to get away from one feature of the Marxian system which is still very much on the—conscious or unconscious—mind of numerous contemporary writers: the obsessive search for the vanguard or spearhead of the revolution, for the one or at least the principal class or homogeneous group that

21. *Strategy*, p. 193.

can be counted on to overthrow the existing order or to effect needed changes. The model just sketched makes it quite plausible that the "decreasing returns" phenomenon will impress itself on the consciousness of a wide variety of groups and individuals; if political change comes, then, it may well result from the combined efforts of many parties rather than from the exertions of a single group. I believe that thinking about the likelihood and strategy of currently needed social and political change, in the United States and elsewhere, would considerably gain in realism if it could free itself of the notion that such change is impossible without the discovery of a single, homogeneous vanguard group.[22]

Misperception and Interaction

In the preceding treatment the emergence of "contradictions" or of "decreasing returns" has retained rather an aprioristic character. The notion has been made plausible to the economist by equating any given political framework with the existence of a factor of production in fixed supply, but I will admit that the analogy need not be wholly compelling.

Is it possible to provide a more solid foundation for the assertion that "economic forces acting alone" need to be relayed at periodic intervals by political-institutional changes? Perhaps there is really no need for an elaborate justification of this point, for it is overwhelmingly unlikely that any institutions devised by human minds will be able to accommodate indefinitely and efficiently any new economic and technological change that happens to come along. The specific reasons for which existing socio-political institutions are inadequate in dealing with newly arising economic forces are likely to be vastly different from one case to another, but the emergence of some such inadequacy would appear to be a remarkably safe bet. I shall nevertheless attempt to go a little farther and conclude this part of the introductory essay by pointing to one particular (and perhaps particularly interesting) class of economic-political sequences.

22. The grip of the homogeneous vanguard-group concept is evident in the writings of otherwise highly diverse authors. Thus, Heilbroner in *The Limits of American Capitalism* (1966) and Galbraith in *The New Industrial State* (1967) look to the "scientific elites" or to the "Educational and Scientific Estate," respectively, for accomplishing the social changes they deem desirable, and New Left writers are focusing their search on youth or Blacks. See Massimo Teodori, ed., *The New Left: A Documentary History* (Indianapolis: Bobbs-Merrill, 1969), particularly the selections for chap. 16, "In Search of a Class Analysis."

In market economies, the intervention of government through taxes, subsidies, and direct provision of goods and services has ordinarily been justified for cases of "market failure," the most typical of which is the presence of monopoly or of external economies and diseconomies. Government action in the economic field is thus conceived as a corrective and complement of private action. The picture that emerges from this way of looking at things is that, little by little, all the areas in which the market tends to fail will be ferreted out, and the best possible mix of market and nonmarket decision making will be approached and permanently established.

This "asymptotic" conception of the state's role is unsatisfactory because it leaves unexplained the continuous seesaw action between market and nonmarket forces which has in fact been taking place in all market economies. One way of accounting for the seesaw may be found in the notion that economic decision makers are frequently subject to misperceptions of newly emerging opportunities. Along such lines I have argued that opportunities in underdeveloped regions tend to be seriously underrated by private investors at some stage of their country's development; similarly, at some other stage, the need for continued reliance on capital from abroad will be overrated. In both cases, perception lags behind reality: the economy of the underdeveloped region and the capacity to raise industrial capital domestically have grown, but institutional inertia and past habit make it hard to take advantage of these changes or even to notice them. Decisive acts of public policy—such as the establishment of exceptional incentives for the underdeveloped region or a restrictive policy toward foreign investment—may then be necessary to acquaint economic operators with an emerging reality which they stubbornly ignore. In the case of the underdeveloped region, such acts are essentially designed to "change ingrained attitudes, both of self-deprecation within the region and of prejudices against it, its people, and resources in the rest of the country."[23]

When public policy measures are motivated by this need to change perceptions, the possibility of an optimal, once-and-for-all corrective intervention disappears. Instead, there arises the perspective of a *sequence* of interactions between market and nonmarket forces. For policy measures correctly designed to change expectations and perceptions will no longer be optimal once they have accomplished the mission assigned to them. In the short run, policy measures will thus have to overshoot any long-run goal. To give an example: the incentives essentially

23. See *A Bias*, cit., chap. 4, p. 154.

needed if misperceiving entrepreneurs are to set up their first industrial ventures in an underdeveloped region are bound to be much stronger than those that need or should prevail once a broadly based industrial establishment has come into being and entrepreneurs have been thoroughly cured of their previous misperceptions. In contrast to market failures grounded in objectively existing externalities, the presence of misperceptions therefore creates the need for a series of properly spaced corrective moves, each one requiring of course its own constellation of political pressures, alliances, and other favourable circumstances.[24]

Moreover, the series is not necessarily convergent, for it is quite conceivable, and indeed likely, that new misperceptions arise at each successive stage. As a result, I am tempted to argue that the relentless search for permanently optimal policies and institutions which characterizes much of social science is often misdirected. In many situations, it may be possible to define optimality only with respect to the width and frequency of periodically needed reversals of policies and changes in institutions.

Let me again give an example from the area of international development policy. A discussion has long been raging about whether close contact by means of trade and capital flows with the advanced industrial countries is beneficial or harmful to the less developed countries. Some authors have been able to cite important static and dynamic, direct and indirect benefits that accrue to these countries from close contact. Others have shown that close contact had a number of exploitative, retarding, stunting, and corrupting effects on the underdeveloped countries and that spurts of development in the periphery have often been associated with periods of interruption of contact, such as world wars and depressions. To neither of these two warring parties has it apparently occurred that they may

24. In the case just noted and in a number of others, the need for corrective public policy measures could be obviated by the timely arrival on the scene of creative Schumpeterian entrepreneurs, who are able to perceive the change in circumstances or the new opportunities that go unrecognized by their more routine-ridden and prejudiced contemporaries. My point here is precisely that in some key situations the likelihood of such a providential appearance is infinitesimal.
It should be obvious, incidentally, that misperception and underestimate of newly and gradually emerging opportunities and capabilities is no monopoly of private decision makers. Public authorities are, if anything, even more subject to the inertia that breeds misperception and that can be corrected and overcome only by incentives and ideologies which are excessive from any long-run point of view. The extremes of early laissez faire capitalism can perhaps be interpreted in this fashion.

quite conceivably both be right. In order to maximize growth the developing countries could need an appropriate alternation of contact and insulation, of openness to the trade and capital of the developed countries, to be followed by a period of nationalism and withdrawnness. In the period of openness, crucial learning processes take place, but many are of the latent kind and remain unnoticed and misperceived. They come to fruition only once contact is interrupted or severely restricted: the previous misperceptions are then forcibly swept away. Thus both contact and insulation have essential roles to play, one after the other.

This conclusion upsets deeply rooted modes of thought. Everywhere, not only in relation to the international economic policy of the developing countries, social scientists are looking for optimal policies and states, and that generally means that they are looking for optimal combinations of desirable, but mutually antagonistic ingredients of such states. Thus we look for the correct combination not only of contact and insulation, but of central control and decentralized initiative, of moral and material incentives, of technical progress and social justice, and so on.

It is here suggested that we devote at least a portion of our time and efforts to understanding the possible usefulness of alternation and oscillation, as opposed to optimal combination.[25] In the first place, it is possible, as in the case of contact and insulation, that certain patterns of alternation would yield results superior to the best that could be obtained by stable combination. Secondly, the focus on alternation would permit one to acquire a feeling for the right amplitudes of the many swings that do occur anyway in the real world. Finally, attention to these patterns of alternation would yield a special bonus from the point of view of this essay: it would reveal a good many sequences in which economics and politics relay each other repeatedly as principal actors.

25. While I have only now formulated this idea as a general principle, I have long "applied" it in a variety of contexts. See *Strategy*, pp. 173–175; *Exit, Voice, and Loyalty*, pp. 124–125; and *A Bias for Hope*, chap. 12, passim, chap. 15, pp. 340–341, and chap. 16, p. 349. A similar point of view is expressed by Erik Erikson who exalts the Hindu life cycle scheme which "allows for a succession of pointedly different life styles" over "the almost vindictive monotony of Judean-Christian strictures by which we gain or forfeit salvation by the formation of one consistently virtuous character almost from the cradle to the very grave" (*Gandhi's Truth* [New York: W. W. Norton, 1969], p. 37).

A Passion for the Possible

The intensive practice of economics-cum-politics is no doubt a principal characteristic of the essays here collected. At the same time, however, these essays are pervaded by certain common feelings, beliefs, hopes, and convictions, and by the desire to persuade and to proselytize which such emotions usually inspire. I would not be true to the purpose of this introduction as proclaimed in the preface, if I did not make at least a brief attempt to talk also about these matters.

Most social scientists conceive it as their exclusive task to discover and stress regularities, stable relationships, and uniform sequences. This is obviously an essential search, one in which no thinking person can refrain from participating. But in the social sciences there is a special room for the opposite type of endeavour: to underline the multiplicity and creative disorder of the human adventure, to bring out the uniqueness of a certain occurrence, and to perceive an entirely new way of turning a historical corner.

The coexistence as equals of the two types of activities just outlined is characteristic of the social sciences. In the natural sciences the unexplained phenomenon and alertness to it are also of the greatest importance, but only as a means to an end, as the beginning of a new search for an improved general theory which would subsume the odd fact, thus overcoming its recalcitrance and destroying it in its uniqueness*. In the social sciences, on the other hand, it is not at all clear which is means and which is end: true, most social scientists behave in this respect as if they were natural scientists; but they would be more surprised than the latter and, above all, considerably distraught if their search for general laws were crowned with total success. Quite possibly, then, all the successive theories and models in the social sciences, and the immense efforts that go into them, are motivated by the noble, if unconscious, desire to demonstrate the irreducibility of the social world to general laws! In no other way would it have been possible to affirm so conclusively the social world as the realm of freedom and creativity. But by now there surely is something to be said for pursuing this theme in a less roundabout fashion.

*. As this book goes to press I find that I am here doing an injustice to at least one natural scientist. In his recent book, *Le Hasard et la nécessité* (Paris, Seuil, 1970), pp. 160–161, the biologist Jacques Monod argues in favour of the "disagreeable idea" that the emergence of both life and man may have resulted from unique occurrences whose a priori probabilities were close to zero.

The importance of granting equal rights of citizenship in social science to the search for general laws and to the search for uniqueness appears particularly in the analysis of social change. One way of dealing with this phenomenon is to look for "laws of change" on the basis of our understanding of past historical sequences. But the possibility of encountering genuine novelty can never be ruled out—this is indeed one of the principal lessons of the past itself. And there is a special justification for the direct search for novelty, creativity, and uniqueness: without these attributes change, at least large-scale social change, may not be possible at all. For, in the first place, the powerful social forces opposed to change will be quite proficient at blocking off those paths of change that have already been trod.[26] Secondly, revolutionaries or radical reformers are unlikely to generate the extraordinary social energy they need to achieve change unless they are exhilaratingly conscious of writing an entirely new page of human history.

I have of course not been disinterested in claiming equal rights for an approach to the social world that would stress the unique rather than the general, the unexpected rather than the expected, and the possible rather than the probable. For the fundamental bent of my writings has been to widen the limits of what is or is perceived to be possible, be it at the cost of lowering our ability, real or imaginary, to discern the probable.

The nature of these persistent widening attempts—or of what I shall call my "possibilism"[27]—varies with the public I am addressing. In putting together the essays of this volume, I found that I have been playing to two quite different galleries. The essays of part II criticize policies of the rich and powerful countries toward the developing countries and advocate substantial changes in those policies. In making my proposals, I refuse, on the one hand, to be "realistic" and to limit myself to strictly incremental changes. At the same time, however, these proposals are not presented as being so revolutionary or so utopian that they have no chance whatever to be adopted in the absence of prior total political change. On the contrary, I feel an obligation to make them in concrete institutional detail thereby deliberately creating the optical illusion that they could possibly be adopted tomorrow by men of good will.

This "naïve" disregard of socio-political realities and of vested interests is precisely rooted in my possibilism: I propose fundamental changes in institutions such as international aid and investment, but I am not willing to prejudge

26. See also *A Bias*, cit., chap. 16, p. 358.
27. The meaning I am trying to bestow on this term has nothing in common with the watered-down environmental determinism for which it has stood among geographers.

categorically the extent, much less the modality, of the wider social and political transformations that may or may not be a prerequisite for such proposals ever being adopted. The reason for this agnosticism is in this case the observation that the constraints on policy makers are far less binding in a number of conceivable historical constellations than at "normal" times. Moreover, one important condition for such constellations to yield real change is the prior availability and discussion (followed then, of course, by contemptuous dismissal) of "radical reform" ideas that can be readily picked up when times suddenly cease to be normal.

The essays of part III deal in large measure with ideologies and concepts characteristic of the literature on economic and political development and of the intellectual climate in the developing countries. Here I have found an exceptionally good hunting ground for exaggerated notions of absolute obstacles, imaginary dilemmas, and one-way sequences. The essence of the possibilist approach consists in figuring out avenues of escape from such straitjacketing constructs in any individual case that comes up. But to go about this task efficiently it is helpful to be equipped with a few conceptual tools. In the following I shall therefore describe in general terms how I have come to practice "possibilism," how I have found it possible to increase the number of ways in which the occurrence of change can be visualized.

One handy device is, once again, the notion of blessing (or curse) in disguise. By pointing to the ways in which many presumed "obstacles" to development have in some situations turned into an asset and a spur, one obviously casts doubt on any statements about this or that "obstacle" having to be eliminated if there is to be this or that desirable development.

But the notion of "blessing in disguise" is like a label for a certain class of sense data; it has little explanatory value. An intellectually more satisfying, though more specialized, foundation for possibilism was encountered in the theory of cognitive dissonance. A group of social psychologists has shown through this theory, that changes in beliefs, attitudes, and eventually in personality can be entrained by certain actions instead of being a prerequisite to them (see chap. 7 of the present book). This idea is so congenial to my thinking that I pointed to one such "inverted" sequence even before I had become acquainted with Festinger et al.: in many situations, so I argued, the Protestant ethic is not the cause of entrepreneurial behaviour, but rather arises as its consequence.[28]

28. *Strategy*, pp. 185–186. Somewhat earlier, Pascal had pointed out that religious feelings can be the consequence, rather than the cause, of devotional acts, such as kneeling (*Pensées,* 233, 250).

Similar critiques of widely accepted ideas on the one-way nature of certain sequences can now be found elsewhere in the social sciences. Take the seemingly self-evident notion that a consensus on basic values and political procedures is a precondition for the establishment of a viable democratic system. According to a recent paper which appeals to historical evidence as well as to cognitive dissonance theory, the causation has often run the other way—democracy has come into being as a result of an accidental, but prolonged standoff between forces originally quite bent on crushing each other; and what basic consensus about political decision making is later found to prevail in these cases can be shown to have been the consequence of democracy, rather than its cause.[29]

The idea that beliefs, attitudes, and values can be refashioned and moulded by more or less accidentally undertaken practice is put forward here only for the purpose of justifying the existence of alternatives to certain "orderly" sequences. There is no intention, at least on my part, to claim primacy for the inverted sequence over the orderly one. In fact, I recognize that the former can give rise to special problems and tensions in comparison to the latter [...]. Moreover, I have lately come to criticize certain aspects of cognitive dissonance theory that in turn imply an excessive denial of human choice and freedom.[30] For the theory predicts that once a certain action is engaged in, beliefs will be changed to suit that action, whereupon renewed resort to the same type of action becomes more likely, leading to a further strengthening of the changed beliefs, and so forth, in a cumulative sequence. To show how it is possible to break out of such sequences is an important task of the possibilist, as will shortly be shown.

A third general foundation for possibilism is in the notion of unintended consequences of human action and in its relation to change. An episode from the recent history of Peru will serve to introduce this topic with which I shall deal at somewhat greater length.

The immediate cause of the military takeover of 1968 in that country was a public uproar over a proposed settlement of the long dispute over United States-owned petroleum interests. The expropriation of these interests by the strongly

29. Dankwart Rustow, "Transitions to Democracy: Toward a Dynamic Model," *Comparative Politics* 2 (April 1970): 337–364. This idea also is a rediscovery: Machiavelli noted in a famous passage that the "perfection" of the Roman Republic and "all the laws that were made in favor of liberty" were due to the so often lamented "disunion between the Plebs and the Senate" *(Discorsi,* bk. 1, chaps. 2 and 4).
30. *Exit, Voice, and Loyalty*, pp. 92–96.

nationalistic military was a natural consequence of their seizure of power and served to justify it in the eyes of the nation. But then, in 1969, the military government struck out once again, this time at the powerful domestic "oligarchy," by expropriating the large coastal sugar plantations and in general by decreeing a far-reaching land reform. Yet, not long before, an Argentine sociologist had proved definitively, in a widely reprinted article, that the days of the progressive military coup in Latin America were gone forever! The military, he showed, had turned from being occasional, if unreliable, innovators into staunch and cruel defenders of the socioeconomic status quo.[31]

What went wrong with this prediction in Peru's case? In the discussion of the deeper-lying causes for the actions of the Peruvian colonels and generals, two explanations recur most frequently. First, in the fifties, it was decided that the technical instruction of upper echelon officers should be supplemented by training in citizenship; as a result, a centre for high military studies (CAEM—Centro de Altos Estudios Militares) was established where Peruvian anthropologists and sociologists held teaching positions and exposed the officers to modern ideas and theories of social integration and development. Secondly, these officers had conducted an anti-guerrilla campaign in the early and middle sixties, during which they had efficiently destroyed the guerrilla movement; that experience, it is generally reported, was so searing for them, that they became determined to change the basic conditions which imposed such tasks upon them.

Those who supply or routinely repeat the latter explanation do so generally without realizing what a sensational and paradoxical theory they are propounding. Because this miserable twentieth century has presented psychologists with unprecedented opportunities for studying human cruelty, torture and assorted atrocities, the psychological mechanism of progressive brutalization is now well known: a person may commit his first brutality more or less by accident or on command, but then, having committed it, has to justify it to himself and in this progressive fashion he becomes ever more committed to his inhumanity—the widespread existence of this sort of cumulative movement is, alas, well established.

In the Peruvian case, on the other hand, the experience of one's own brutality appears to have produced not greater brutalization, but the determination to change the state of the world which caused the brutality in the first place—an almost miraculous conversion appears to have taken place for once among the

31. José Nun, "The Middle Class Military Coup," in Claudio Veliz, ed., *The Politics of Conformity in Latin America* (London: Oxford University Press, 1967), pp. 66–118.

perpetrators of cruelty. The reason may lie in the previously noted combination of circumstances: officers who had been taught in the CAEM that it was their mission to forge a united Peru which could be a true fatherland for all of its sons including the most miserable Indian, were suddenly placed in the position of napalming the villages of those very Indians and of killing them, as well as young poets and intellectuals from the cities who had taken seriously those very teachings. As a result, the tension between ideology and actual behaviour as imposed by the environment was exceptionally wide and painful. On the other hand, the military had bred into them a high degree of confidence that the environment is subject to change at their hands. Jointly, then, that painful tension and that confidence may account for their reforming zeal, for their refusal to submit to the cumulative spiral of brutalization.

The story has several points. For example, it contains a nice instance of a blessing in disguise, a part that is played here by the thinness of the country's intellectual elite. This ordinarily much lamented characteristic of Peruvian (or Latin American) society meant that army officers, once they were to be taught sociology and political science, came (unintentionally, of course) under the influence of the very few social scientists and intellectuals whom Peru could muster and who were all strongly oriented toward fundamental changes in the status quo.

A more noteworthy lesson of the Peruvian story is that social scientists may have become overimpressed with the cumulative character of the processes they study. We are by now thoroughly conditioned to explain and anticipate cumulative spirals by Myrdal's process of circular causation, by Merton's self-fulfilling prophecy, and by some just noted aspects of cognitive dissonance theory, not to speak of more routine reinforcement and feedback processes. As a result, any change in the direction of a process—the turnaround or dialectical reversal or *Umschlagen*—takes us by surprise, except, perhaps, for the outbreak of revolution in its classic form.

It is ironic that Myrdal proposed his notion of circular causation in order to get away from the self-equilibrating models in economics and sociology and from their conservative, laissez faire implications. For, in a sense, he threw out the revolutionary baby with the conservative bathwater. According to his analysis, the cumulative processes of discrimination, deterioration, and underdevelopment, disastrous as they are, do not awaken by themselves any counterforces—the only exception is the intellectual who observes things from the outside and somberly predicts that they will get much worse unless some appropriate action is taken. The many insurgent and radical social scientists who have embraced this sort of model have thus fallen unwittingly into a profoundly un-dialectical and, what is worse, unperceptive and unimaginative way of thinking.

One important way of rekindling perception and imagination and of developing an alertness to dialectical, as opposed to purely cumulative, social processes is to pay attention to the unintended consequences of human actions. This is extraordinarily well illustrated by the Peruvian story. Here both the training in citizenship the military received (though not in the actual form it took at CAEM) and the suppression of the guerrillas in the Sierra were activities purposefully designed to ensure the maintenance of the status quo; but in combination they had unintended side effects which led to irreversible social change.

The concept of unintended consequences of human actions has of course a distinguished ancestry. Intimated by Vico and propounded as a paradox by Mandeville, it was developed systematically by Adam Smith and his contemporaries. But the concept was always cast in one particular mould: a set of rather unprepossessing activities, such as the pursuit by everyone of his own material gain, was shown to have edifying consequences because through their unintended side effects these activities would guarantee the overall functioning, stability, and rationality of the existing social system.

Perhaps it is because many of the later critics of this way of thinking were social reformers that its rich potential for understanding and expecting social change, rather than equilibrium, rationality and optimality, has not been actively exploited. The idea that change, particularly major social change, is something to be wrought by the undeviatingly purposeful actions of some change agents is certainly far more widespread than the view that change can also occur because of originally unintended side effects of human actions which might even have been expressly directed toward system maintenance.

The possibilist will not contend that the predominant view of change is wrong; but he will challenge its predominance by collecting evidence supporting the alternative point of view. The Peruvian story was one case in point, but since it is a personal interpretation of still unfolding events, I shall invoke some more authoritative examples.

In the first place, I can refer to two anthropologists who attempted, a few years ago, to give a comprehensive account of the "human revolution" and proposed as their principal theoretical construct the following principle which they called "Romer's rule," "after the paleontologist A. S. Romer who has applied it so effectively … in his own work":

> *The initial survival value of a favorable innovation is conservative, in that it renders possible the maintenance of a traditional way of life in the face of changed circumstances.*

The authors continue:

> Later on, of course, the innovation may allow the exploration of some ecological niche not available to the species before the change; but this is a consequence, not a cause.
>
> One of Romer's examples concerns the evolution of Devonian lungfishes into the earliest amphibians. The invasion of the land was feasible only with strong fins (which in due time became legs). But strong fins were not developed "in order to" invade the land. The climate of the epoch was tempestuous; the water level of the pools in which the lungfishes lived was subject to sudden recessions. There was thus selection for those strains of lungfishes which, when stranded by such a recession, had strong enough fins to get back to the water. Only much later did some of their descendants come to stay ashore most of the time.[32]

In other words, the lungfishes' attempt at system maintenance (the desire to get back to the water and thus to remain amphibians) leads here to system change. A similar view of change and innovation is put forward by an economist in a book on agrarian development under population pressure.[33] Initially, so the author shows, population growth in primitive agricultural communities leads merely to reduction of fallowing and consequently to lower output per man hour. But, at the same time, the intensification of agriculture may cause work habits to become more regular and more efficient, and larger numbers may lead to new forms of the division of labor. These secondary effects can then "set off a genuine process of economic growth."[34]

It should not be inferred from these two examples that change via unintended side effects is in any way restricted to "lower forms of life" such as animals or "primitive people." Efforts to maintain or restore a social organization or a way of life or a standard of living that is threatened or weakened have yielded unintended innovational change in modern societies just as among the lungfish. At the

32. Charles F. Hockett and Robert Ascher, "The Human Revolution," *Current Anthropology* 5 (June 1964): 137.
33. Esther Boserup, *The Conditions of Agricultural Growth* (Chicago: Aldine, 1965).
34. Ibid., p. 118.

threshold of the modern age, the discovery of America originated in an effort at "system maintenance," in the search, that is, to keep *up* or restore maritime contact with India. Many technical inventions which then led to further important transformations of technology, occurred as a result of sudden interruptions of normal trade flows due to war or blockade and the consequent need to maintain prior output levels through the production of substitutes. Industrialization in many countries, particularly among the twentieth-century latecomers, was similarly brought underway not so much by the will to industrialize as by the need to keep up the supply of consumer goods whose importation became suddenly impossible during the world wars and the Great Depression.

In short, history could be viewed as the process of men in general, and the ruling classes in particular, continually outsmarting themselves in their efforts to reproduce and maintain the existing order.

Change that occurs in such manner as a result of unintended side effects can be compared from several points of view to the kind of voluntaristic change that is brought about consciously by some change agent, be he a revolutionary or an agricultural extension officer. In the first place, the unintended change is often likely to be more revolutionary than change brought about by the most revolutionary of change agents, for the simple reason that the imagination of the change agent is severely limited by his immediate experience and historical precedent. More important, unintended change is of course far more difficult to detect and to block by the forces opposed to change; for that matter, these forces often participate unwittingly yet actively in bringing it about. On the other hand, unintended change may be less satisfying to those profiting from it than voluntaristic change, since it "falls into one's lap" without either advance planning or sustained struggle.

Actually these two types of change are little more than analytically useful distinctions; most of the time they will be found to be closely intertwined in the real world. For example, voluntaristic change will often take over after unintended change has done the spadework and created conditions in which the outline of previously hidden possibilities of change can begin to be perceived by an activist change agent. In other situations, such voluntarist activists may be futilely trying to make "the last revolution," as Régis Debray put it, but since they draw all the fire and monopolize the attention of the pro-status-quo forces, they make it even easier for the unintentional processes of change to come to fruition. Elements of both these combined situations are present in the Peruvian story.

Such, then, are some of the devices which the possibilist can use to sharpen the perception of available avenues toward change. There are probably quite a few others. For these devices cannot be expected to trace out by themselves new, hitherto undiscerned avenues; they are only meant to help defend the right to a non-projected future as one of the truly inalienable rights of every person and nation; and to set the stage for conceptions of change to which the inventiveness of history and a "passion for the possible" are admitted as vital actors.

13

Policymaking and Policy Analysis in Latin America. A Return Journey

Latin American economic, social, and political development prospects have become much more uncertain than they seemed a decade or two ago. Even though, at that time, most observers with a sense of elementary prudence did not venture outright predictions, they were fairly confident that the Latin American nations faced some clear-cut alternatives: in one direction lay the road toward greater social justice which would, in turn, lead to economic advance and a more stable and participatory political system (disagreement prevailed on whether revolution was required to open up this road); and there was a second road which led to another combined, but now all-round dismal product: economic stagnation, political decay, and worsened social inequities.

The events of the last decade have shattered this naïve Manichean view. It took its most self-conscious stand in the early sixties with the ideology of the Alliance for Progress, and perhaps its last one in the mid-sixties with the theory of structural stagnation; common to both was the idea that without social progress (to be achieved through various reforms and redistribution of income and wealth), the countries of Latin America were condemned to economic stagnation. While the Alliance for Progress was built on the premise that "All Good Things

Go Together,"[1] the theory of structural stagnation attempted to prove that all bad things go together and was thus the mirror image of the former. Both these ideological structures could not but succumb after the telling blow they received from the reality that unfolded in the late sixties. A glance at developments in Brazil from 1968 on left no doubt about what should have been obvious anyway: economic growth, social progress, and "liberty"—or, more simply, the respect for human rights—do not necessarily advance jointly. In particular, it appeared that some varieties of economic growth are fully compatible with social and political retrogression.

The sense of shock produced by this experience could not fail to have its effect on the intellectual climate: one senses today a new willingness to explore, almost from scratch, the mechanisms of interactions between economy, society, and the state. This is at least how I choose to interpret the current interest in detailed studies of the determinants and consequences of public policies.

To undertake such studies obviously implies a "felt need" to make new discoveries about these interactions. Such discoveries could be about the mechanisms of change or about the mechanisms of resistance to change; they could be about successes in dealing with emerging problems, about failures, or about various intermediate cases. Admittedly, when I wrote *Journeys Toward Progress: Studies of Economic Policy-Making in Latin America*[2] some twelve years ago, I was interested in showing how progressive change can unexpectedly be smuggled into societies long dominated by traditional social forces and how some collective learning is acquired, in spite of many affirmations to the contrary, when a stubborn policy problem is encountered and tackled over a long period. But these biases are not consubstantial with the sort of effort on which I had set out and I shall attempt here to separate my method from my message, for the former may be of service even to those who disagree with the latter. In the first part of this paper, I therefore propose to reformulate some of the basic methodological and conceptual tools and approaches to be found in *Journeys*; in the second part I shall return to my biases and shall reexamine their validity. In both parts, in fact, new reflections will take up the major portion of the argument.

1. See Robert Packenham, *Liberal America and the Third World* (Princeton: Princeton University Press, 1973), pp. 123–129.
2. New York, Twentieth Century Fund, 1963. A new paperback edition with a new preface was issued by W. W. Norton in 1973. Page numbers in the text refer to *Journeys* (page numbers in the Twentieth Century Fund and the Norton editions are identical).

It so happens that this somewhat egocentric approach results in a logical subdivision of our subject matter. The principal methodological contributions of *Journeys* are to be found in various typologies I established for the purposes of understanding *differences* in policy behaviour. These differences depend, in part at least, on the structural characteristics of the various issues which concern policymakers, and my typologies attempted to pick out the more significant among these characteristics. In my biases, on the other hand, I underlined certain features of the policy-making processes in Latin America that seemed to me to be *common* to all of them.

Any comparative study of policy experiences will face the double task of calling attention to significant differences and of bringing out any similarities, obvious and nonobvious. This paper, then, shall offer in turn some conceptual handles for these two tasks.

I. Focusing on Differences

An Observation on Research Strategy

One of the major decisions I had to make at an early stage in my work on *Journeys* was whether I should analyse policymaking around the same problem, such as land reform in different countries, or whether I should select different problems in different countries. The former course was clearly that of prudence, for a minimal degree of comparability would be assured in an investigation of how different countries cope with identical or at least roughly similar problems. One difficulty with that course was that the same problem would normally not have the same salience in several countries and this fact would in turn reduce comparability. More important, to choose different problems in different countries was simply more varied and interesting; it also held out the promise of reaching conclusions at a higher level of generality—I would be able to conjecture about Latin American ways of handling policy problems in general rather than only about Latin American ways of dealing with, say, inflation.

I chose the second course and am still glad I did. I do not wish to imply that everyone should do so and even less that a collective research project should. The advantage of a single researcher carrying on such a far-flung enterprise is that he can constantly keep all comparable elements of the various policy experiences in a single central brain. The solitary researcher will notice an emerging similarity in the middle of his work and can pursue it in detail as soon as he perceives it. A contrasting mode is team or group research, in which different persons are normally in charge of different country studies, and the chances of encountering such similarities are poorer. Either they will be programmed in advance of research and writing through common guidelines that never quite fit, or they can only be established ex post, when the individual studies are already completed, in the course of writing the comparative chapters of the study.

But this is by way of a digression intended for those who are contemplating further comparative research on policymaking. The essential point to be made here relates to an unexpected benefit that accrued from the very heterogeneity of the problems I selected for study: it became easier to perceive those structural characteristics of each *individual* problem that helped in understanding policymaking with regard to that problem. For example, the following characteristic properties of the inflation problem (studied in Chile) stood out in contrast to those of regional underdevelopment (studied in Brazil) and maldistribution of land (studied in Colombia), (pp. 162–163):

(1) In contrast to the periodic droughts afflicting the Northeast of Brazil, inflation is clearly a man-made calamity and lends itself therefore peculiarly to recriminations among groups, to suspicions that one group is gaining at another's expense—in short, to political conflict.
(2) Inflation, in contrast to maldistribution of land, sends out regular signals, is measurable from month to month, and is therefore apt to get special attention from the policymakers as soon as it passes some tolerance threshold.
(3) Unlike regional underdevelopment, inflation is formally rather similar from country to country. It also deals with the arcane and technical subject of money. Therefore, dominant doctrine and international experts play particularly important roles in attempts at solution. But, in view of the previous point, both experts and doctrines are apt to play highly political roles, in spite of their technical garb.
(4) Inflation, unlike the two other problems, is easily "oversolved"—it can suddenly give way to deflation, perhaps an even greater evil than inflation. Fear of deflation may therefore inhibit policymakers dealing with inflation whereas policymaking on regional underdevelopment or on maldistribution of land can ordinarily proceed for a considerable distance without the danger of going too far.

Discovery of such structural characteristics is an important part of the analyst's task; through them it is possible to understand and perhaps predict alternative paths of decision-making. The trouble is that each new problem will exhibit some characteristics of its own that turn out to be critical for the behaviour of policy-makers so that it would be futile and even dangerous to pretend having prepared a finite and definitive checklist of such characteristics that would claim to take care of this aspect of policy studies for future researchers. With this caveat, I shall nevertheless proceed to compile and comment on my favourite list.[3]

Pressing and Chosen Policy Problems

Which, among the many potential and conceivable policy issues, are those on which policymakers act? An obvious first distinction, and one of some importance, is between issues that are forced on the policymakers through pressure from injured or interested outside parties and issues that they have "picked out of thin air" (pp. 254–335). This distinction between "pressing" and more or less autonomously "chosen" policies (my favourite example of the latter is the building of Brasília by Kubitschek) permits right away some prediction about the path problem-solving will take: in the case of a pressing problem that causes acute discomfort to some vocal group, policy actions will immediately be evaluated in

3. The attempt I made in *Journeys* to discover structural characteristics of policy problems that condition different ways of dealing with them within a given political system has much in common with Theodore J. Lowi's dictum "policies determine politics" and his distinction—designed to prove that dictum—between "distributive," "regulative," and "redistributive" policies. While I find this distinction and Lowi's use of it to explain different patterns of policymaking in the United States extremely illuminating, I do not believe it possible to establish once and for all a finite number of distinctions or list of characteristics that will adequately account for all important differences in policymaking behaviour in relation to every conceivable issue. I am making a similar point with regard to the various linkages characteristic of staples in p. 85 of *Essays in Trespassing. Economics to Politics and Beyond*, Cambridge University Press, 1981. Lowi's fundamental article is "American Business, Public Policies, Case-Studies, and Political Theory," *World Politics*, 16 (4) (July 1964): 677–715; he subsequently elaborates and applies his scheme in "Decision Making vs. Policy Making: Toward an Antidote for Technocracy," *Public Administration Review*, 30 (3) (May-June 1970): 314–325, and "Four Systems of Policy, Politics and Choice" *Public Administration Review*, 32 (4) (July-August 1972): 298–310.

terms of its success in relieving discomfort whereas no such immediate feedback occurs in the other situation.

Secondly, the extent to which a country's authorities are able to "choose" problems rather than merely respond to "pressing" ones says something of importance about the activity of pressure groups, and the relative autonomy of policymakers. This is an area, therefore, where policy studies can be quite revealing, in an empirical way, about the relationship between state and society and about the relative autonomy of the state.[4]

The point goes deeper and highlights one important possible bias of policy studies. In what was once the dominant view of political science, the state is endowed with a will of its own, such as the urge to expand its power in relation to other states or the desire to maximize the welfare of all or of a ruling section of its citizens. The state has an *interest*, a *raison d'état*, which it pursues single-mindedly. But if one focuses on "pressing" problems, as policy studies usually do (and as I largely did in *Journeys*), the state loses its august character of a sovereign pursuing its own objectives and initiating policies to this end; rather, it is seen as coping, as best it can, with a variety of emergencies, as constantly plugging holes, and stopping a wheel from creaking by applying a bit of grease in a hurry. Note that this conception of the *coping state* goes farther than the interest-group or even the bureaucratic-politics approaches; these are still concerned with improving our understanding of the state's actions, rather than with affirming that most of the time the state does not act, but reacts. The distinction between the view that sees the state as coping and the older concept according to which the state determines and pursues its interests has much in common with Herbert Simon's well-known distinction between the maximizing and the "satisficing" firm;[5] in fact, "coping" would have been preferable to Simon's unbeautiful neologism.

Both views contain some truth, and the idea of the coping state is a useful counterweight to the more conventional notion of the state as initiating demiurge. But it certainly can be carried too far if the analyst loses sight of the fact that coping takes place within constraints arising out of the maintenance needs of the basic social and political structure. These constraints are least visible when existing social and political structures and institutions are wholly unchallenged.

4. The question of the relative autonomy of the state remains a much debated issue in Marxist political theory. See, for example, Ralph Miliband, "Poulantzas and the Capitalist State," *New Left Review* (November/December 1973): 83–93.
5. "A Behavioral Model of Rational Choice," *Quarterly Journal of Economics*, 69 (1952): 98–118.

An interesting paradox follows: it is precisely when, in this manner, the state is at its strongest that its managers will have and give the impression that they are just coping, that is, forever handling the matters that somehow require immediate attention without pursuing any grand design. In other words, the more firmly established the power of the state, the more its managers feel without power to affect the course of events as they just keep busy "putting out fires." Perhaps it is by virtue of this paradox that the phrase "muddling through" came to characterize British policymaking in the nineteenth century when Great Britain was at the peak of its power, while the concept was given a theoretical underpinning in the United States in the 1950s when it was that country's turn to hold a position of unparalleled power in the world.[6]

On the contrary, when control weakens and the existing social and political structures are under serious attack, then the state, challenged to adapt the old order to new circumstances or to build a new order, is more likely to engage in a spate of autonomous policymaking. Such action is then likely to lead to a host of new problems with which the authorities will have to cope so that in a period of state-initiated structural change, both aspects of policymaking are apt to come to the fore.

The distinction between pressing and chosen problems can be developed in other directions. For example, various dynamic paths might be explored. The pressing problems of one period can become the chosen problems of the next or vice versa. It is conceivable that solutions for a problem become available only when it no longer possesses real urgency, but that, because of the existence, real or imagined, of a solution, it is now tackled anew as a "chosen" problem. An example is perhaps the way Colombia's Lleras Restrepo took up the issue of agrarian reform in 1960 when there was little of the peasant unrest and land invasions that had marked earlier periods (p. 157). Alternatively, a chosen problem can turn into a pressing one if tinkering with the problem has the usually unintended effect of mobilizing those who stand to benefit from the proposed or advertised solution.

6. See C. E. Lindblom, "The Science of 'Muddling Through,'" *Public Administration Review*, 19 (1959): 79–88. Lindblom has commented to me that, in retrospect, he regrets the title of this widely known paper as it does not accurately reflect the nature of the method of decision-making he really advocated and has called "disjointed incrementalism." This method, so he argues, can be used effectively for achieving rapid and substantial change. I agree, but must also point out that the considerable impact of Lindblom's ideas owes much to their having been construed or misconstrued at the time as a theoretical foundation for a policy of muddling through.

This is the "sorcerer's apprentice" dynamic: timid or perfunctory reform moves lead to demands for far more vigorous policies than had been contemplated by the authorities who had initiated action without any visible outside pressures. This dynamic is not unknown on the Latin American political and socioeconomic scene, but it has received less attention than its familiar counterpart: we can all cite the sad story of some reform move that looked hopeful and vigorous at the outset but that was subsequently aborted or coopted.

A further observation on "pressing" problems: in *Journeys* and in this paper so far, pressures originate entirely outside the government. They arise as reactions of citizens and groups of citizens to drought, land hunger, and inflation. But a large portion of the pressures to act that are experienced by governments day-in, day-out is generated from within rather than from without. Appointments for jobs that mean choices between competing candidates have to be made, conflicts between government agencies and between groups composing the ruling coalition of forces have to be adjudicated, demands for public spending on all kinds of government-generated projects have to be dealt with. The relation between outside and inside pressures is complex and worth exploring. On the one hand, outside pressures are translated into and exacerbate inside pressures as when inflation leads to conflicting advice about the best way to restore price stability. On the other hand, when outside pressures decline as a result of, say, the establishment of an authoritarian regime that prohibits meetings and other channels through which citizens can voice their protest, it is possible and perhaps likely that conflict and intrigue within the government increase sufficiently to keep the aggregate pressures experienced by the top decision-makers entirely undiminished. The result is the strange but frequently observed spectacle of an authoritarian government that has its hands full coping with the pressures arising from within its own ranks.

Privileged and Neglected Policy Problems

Another not unrelated way of approaching this subject is to focus on the manner through which policy problems gain access to the policymaker. We are now talking primarily about "pressing" problems, and about degrees of pressure. In this respect, I have distinguished between *privileged* and *neglected* problems (pp. 229–234). I defined as "privileged" those problems whose victims have adequate access to the policymaker so that the latter are obliged to pay attention, for the sake of political stability in general and of their own political survival in particular. "Neglected" problems, on the other hand, do not enjoy this direct access, but they can be brought to the attention of policymakers in various indirect ways. One possible way of gaining access is to forge a link between the neglected and the privileged problem through the demonstration that the former lies at the root of the latter. For example, the problem of land distribution in Latin America, long a neglected problem in the above sense, gained considerably in access to the policymaker and in persuasiveness when it was connected, by the structuralist theorizers, to the problem of inflation which was eminently a privileged problem. The forging of such causal links is the job of intellectuals and of ideology, which is crucial in countries where channels of access for large groups of population are weak or blocked.

Neglected problems are likely to be tackled in a manner very different from the privileged ones. As long as the force behind them is by definition not overwhelming, policymaking on them will often be tentative, desultory and absent-minded. There is, however, the possibility that, however half-hearted, this sort of policymaking will lead to mobilization of those groups (e.g. the peasants, the poor, the aged) in whose favor it is being undertaken so that, as a result of tinkering, the problem turns into a privileged one, with direct access of the problem victims to the policymakers. In this view, the role of intellectuals and ideology is a temporary and transitional one; they extend a helping hand to the problem until such time as it can stand on its own feet.

In *Journeys* I expressed the opinion that the forging of ideological links through which neglected problems could "ride the coattails" of privileged problems is a characteristic feature of policy-making in less developed countries, precisely because of widespread lack of mobilization and access on the part of large groups of people. However, a look at United States and European politics during the last decade convinces one that access in these so-called advanced societies is not nearly as universal as was once thought. In the first place, of course, access is unequally distributed, in accordance with the uneven ability of different groups to achieve organization and influence.[7] Secondly, the advanced industrial societies have evolved ways of reconstituting and even *importing* groups that lack access as formerly deprived groups gain access. Finally, some of the problems characteristic of advanced societies, such as pollution and discontent about work conditions, are more diffuse and less obviously intolerable than earlier problems of misery and oppression, so that a considerable effort of intellectual focusing and clarification is needed for these problems to enter the consciousness of the victims.

7. See, for example, Grant McConnell, *Private Power and American Democracy* (New York: Knopf, 1966).

A further qualification is needed. The distinction between privileged and neglected problems may be unnecessarily rigid and dichotomous. How privileged a problem is depends on answers to such questions as: how numerous and how concentrated are the problem victims, how important is the issue to them, and how much influence do they have? One reason for which policymaking on inflation is more continuously in evidence than policymaking on regional underdevelopment or on maldistribution of land is that inflation is felt by a majority rather than by a minority, that unhappiness over it cuts across class and regional lines, and that it lends itself to mass protest right in the capital city. A great deal depends therefore on visibility, and visibility changes over time, as a result, for example, of technological change. Better transportation and communication have made many previously invisible problems visible, as happened in the case of the droughts of Northeast Brazil: from the thirties on, the drought victims no longer had to accept death by starvation in the parched countryside, but could board buses and trucks to drive to the cities where they proceeded to loot the food stores. Thus the ideological route that has been outlined is not the only one through which a hitherto neglected problem can gain recognition by the policymaker.

Motivation versus Understanding in the Taking-Up of Policy Problems

In the previous section I noted a convergence of behaviour of the less and the more developed countries. A similar convergence will be found to characterize the third distinction concerning policy problems that was made in *Journeys*. Mindful of Marx's famous dictum that "mankind always takes up only such problems as it can solve" and of Lindblom's elaboration to the effect that "perception of a problem or definition of a goal often follows and is stimulated by the identification of a possible policy" (p. 237), I suggested that understanding of a problem and motivation to attack it are two necessary inputs into policymaking and problem-solving, but that the timing of these two ingredients could be significantly out of phase: understanding can pace motivation (as is assumed by Marx and Lindblom), but in other situations motivation to solve a problem may arise in advance of adequate understanding. The latter situation, I argued, is characteristic of Latin American countries to the extent that they import "solutions" from the outside in the form of the most up-to-date central banking legislation, economic planning agencies, or common market schemes. This typically "dependent" behaviour results, of course, in frustration precisely because these institutions are often established without the necessary minimal understanding of the problems they are set up to resolve. It seemed to follow that the incidence of this type of policymaking would be much less frequent in the more autonomous countries, that is, those less influenced by foreign models in the way they decide which problems to attack, how to attack them, and which ones to leave alone pending a gain in understanding.

Already in *Journeys*, however, I pointed to the possibility that the very success in problem-solving that is likely to result from initially following the Marx-Lindblom route "could breed … overconfidence in the solvability of all problems" and hence lead straight into the opposite style (p. 238). As I was writing in the heady days of the Kennedy era, it did not take great powers of prophecy to make this statement. The motivation-outruns-understanding style became in fact dominant in the sixties in the United States and unhappy experience with it has then led to the oft-heard complaint: "If we can put a man on the moon, why can't we solve the problems of the ghetto?"[8] Policymaking on poverty, pollution, cancer, and lately energy ("self-sufficiency in 1980") have all exhibited this style so that policymaking in the United States has now adopted the Latin American style of rushing in with impulsive pseudo-solutions.

Obviously irritated by the policymaking style lately so much in evidence in the United States, Anthony Downs has recently written some perceptive pages about what he calls the "issue attention cycle" in American politics.[9] He distinguishes between the following phases of the cycle:

1. The "pre-problem stage" during which the problem exists all right, but not much public attention is paid to it.
2. Then comes "alarmed discovery and euphoric enthusiasm." The problem is considered a priori fully solvable "if only we devote sufficient effort to it."
3. In the next phase, it is realized that solving the problem may be costly and goes against the immediate interests, of large and influential groups of people.
4. As a result of this realization, there is then a gradual decline of intense public interest, which is helped by the providential appearance of another problem that will occupy the limelight.

8. Richard R. Nelson, "Intellectualizing about the Moon-Ghetto Metaphor: A Study of the Current Malaise of Rational Analysis of Social Problems", *Policy Sciences*, 5 (4) (Dec. 1974): 375–414.
9. "Up and Down with Ecology—the 'Issue-Attention Cycle'", *The Public Interest*, 28 (Summer 1972): 38–50.

5. Finally, there is the "post-problem stage" which differs from the pre-problem stage in that a number of efforts and agencies that have been set up to "solve" the problem in Phase Two continue to exist and may actually make some quiet progress. Moreover, according to Downs, once the problem had passed through the cycle, it will continue to receive a modicum of public attention.

Downs then proceeds to analyse policymaking on pollution and other ecological problems with the help of this conceptual scheme. He does so quite successfully for the obvious reason that his scheme was directly inspired by experience with those particular issues. Nevertheless, it may be of interest to think about the applicability of the scheme to other policies. It seems to me to be particularly relevant to that class of policies for which motivation to solve a problem has pushed far ahead of understanding, but even then the Downs scheme can serve at best as a paradigm: in many situations of this type the actual sequence of policymaking may well exhibit a different pattern.

II. Focusing on Similarities

The principal value of the distinctions that have been drawn in the preceding sections is that they permit some inferences and predictions about differential characteristics of policymaking and problem-solving. If the paths and sequences of policymaking exhibit similarities, within a country or from one country to another, this will often be so because one is looking at problems with the same basic characteristics—for example—they could all be "pressing" problems with motivation outrunning understanding. Nevertheless, one may well entertain the hypothesis that, over and above the characteristics that derive from the *intrinsic* nature of each policy issue that is being tackled, policy behaviour in Latin America reflects some more general and common *environmental* factors, such as culture, history, and the stage of social and economic development. A search for such common characteristics is peculiarly conjectural and it is no accident that it is connected with what I called my biases earlier in this essay. I can plead, however, that the generalizations about the policy-making process I came up with in *Journeys* arose inductively from the close study of the three policymaking sequences rather than from the attempt to deduce the characteristics of Latin American policymaking from history or culture. In fact, I generally called attention to empirically encountered common traits without attempting any explanation. But without explanation or, at least, interpretation[10] such findings retain a fortuitous character and do not carry conviction. To relate them to general features of Latin American societies will be one task of this part of the essay.

Fracasomania and Real Disasters

One of the principal patterns that emerged as a common feature of my three stories was the insistence on the part of each new set of policymakers to decry as utter failure everything that had been done before; consequently the impression was created that one had to start from scratch over and over again. I coined the term "fracasomania" or "failure complex" for this trait. I now return to this theme with a few comments, most of which are not to be found in *Journeys*, but are the result of further reflection and observation.

In the first place, it is of course possible, as in the old story about the inferiority complex (in which the psychiatrist tells the patient "do not worry about having a *complex*, you *are* inferior"), that policymaking actually is a string of failures. As has just been noted, policymaking that is prompted more by motivation than by understanding is particularly failure-prone. But in a good number of cases, I came to the conclusion that the claims of total failure, made with monotonous regularity soon after each new policy move, were considerably exaggerated. I then looked for the possibly hidden rationality of this "fracasomania," for the functions that it may possibly serve. One argument ran as follows: the alleged failure of past policymaking induces the expectation of renewed failure and this expectation—for example, that a land reform will not be vigorously enforced—may make it easier to adopt reform legislation than if there were not a general conviction that such legislation will remain only on paper (pp. 244–245 of *Journeys* for this and other such observations).

Nevertheless, I did point out that fracasomania seemed to me in many respects an unfortunate trait: "It means to shut oneself off from newly emerging cues and insights as well as from the increased confidence in one's capabilities which should otherwise arise" (p. 245). Subsequently, I became more concerned over a closely related but more general phenomenon, namely, the pervasive "obstacles to the *perception* of change," and found that "when there are special difficulties in perceiving ongoing change, many opportunities for accelerating that change and for taking advantage of newly arising opportunities for change will

10. For this distinction see Clifford Geertz, *The Interpretation of Cultures* (New York: Basic Books, 1973), Chapter 1.

surely be missed."[11] In that article I tried to account in various ways for these special difficulties, but I have since come upon some more general explanations that permit me to relate the phenomenon to Latin America's relative backwardness and to its dependence.

As a result of prolonged relative backwardness, a general expectation is that one's country will continue to perform poorly. Hence, any evidence that the country may possibly be doing better or may be emerging from its backwardness in one way or another is going to be dissonant with previous cognitions and is therefore likely to be suppressed; on the contrary, evidence that nothing at all has changed will be picked up, underlined, and even greeted, for it does not necessitate any change in pre-existing cognitions to which one has become comfortably adjusted. The difficulty in perceiving change and any partial forward movement is thus related to the findings of social psychologists who have experimentally shown that persons with a low self-concept feel some discomfort when they suddenly perform well.[12]

The experience of prolonged backwardness, as just described, has much in common with that of prolonged powerlessness. Take situations in which politicians who have spent the largest part of their lives in the opposition suddenly and unexpectedly gain power: all too often their actions seem almost calculated to make them forfeit that power in the shortest possible time. The reason may once again be that they have become used to their earlier role, wish to return to it, and are therefore acting out an unconscious defeat wish.

The insistence on failure of past efforts and the conviction of each new policymaker that he is starting from scratch can also be understood as a result of protracted intellectual *dependence*. Both intellectuals and policymakers have long tended to look abroad for remedies and solutions instead of scrutinizing carefully their country's experiences and the travail that has gone into various proposals and experiments. The usual gap between the old and young generations becomes a gulf when the educated young elite feels, as a result of foreign study and contacts, that they do not need to bother with what their elder compatriots' experience and reflection have to offer. To justify this action, they must, of course, deny that any accomplishment at all can be credited to the older generation. The difficulty of establishing a cumulative intellectual tradition under conditions of cultural

11. *Bias for Hope*, p. 337.
12. Elliot Aronson, "Dissonance Theory: Progress and Problems," in R. P. Abelson et al., eds., *Theories of Cognitive Consistency: A Source Book* (Chicago: Rand McNally, 1968), p. 24.

dependence is thus closely related to the fact that policymaking exhibits so little cumulative learning.

A third reason for the proclamation of failure and for the wilful non-perception of change is almost too obvious to deserve notice. It is standard opposition politics to decry and deny any success on the part of one's adversary and it is standard revolutionary politics to propagate a "sense of being in a desperate predicament"[13] among the masses. My point is that this normal phenomenon of partisan politics is strongly reinforced by the presence of the other reasons for fracasomania. The proclamation of failure is a terrain on which those who are comfortably adjusted to protracted backwardness and dependence can unite with those who advocate total change. Indeed, one wonders sometimes whether they are two distinct groups.

Lack of learning is by no means the most serious consequence of fracasomania and of the inability or refusal to perceive change. In a government intent upon transforming a country's socio-economic structure, these traits can lead to complete mishandling of the political situation, from ignoring and needlessly antagonizing groups that could be won over to underestimating the strength of others that cannot. It is precisely such mishandling that marked the careers of the Goulart and Allende regimes. In the case of the latter, the inability to identify and win over, or at least neutralize, potentially progressive groups was reinforced by the influence of certain theories that specifically proclaimed the inexistence of any such groups and the impossibility of any economic advance or progressive change under conditions of "dependent capitalism." And the inability to gauge correctly the strength and determination of the opposition is also caused by the refusal to perceive that things can indeed change: for the basic belief behind the refusal to heed the most obvious storm signals is always the refrain "aqui no pasa nada"—in other words, the deeply held and, in the event, fatal conviction that this is still a backward and sluggish society where nothing ever happens or changes.

This is obviously not the place to pursue these speculations. But the fact that I was led right into them from seemingly innocuous and abstract reasoning about the characteristics of policymaking sequences shows how studies in the field can serve to illuminate not just how tax or education policy is made—an important enough endeavour in itself, of course—but can contribute something to the

13. Robert C. Tucker, "The Theory of Charismatic Leadership," *Daedalus* 97 (3) (Summer 1968): 75.

understanding of the most important, baffling, and tragic events in recent Latin American history.

On "Surprising" Policy Decisions

One of the topics that interested me most in *Journeys* was what I called "reform-mongering" and, in a subsequent book, the "smuggling in of change."[14] As a result of my studies, I became convinced that the conventional dichotomy of the early sixties, "violent revolution vs. peaceful reform" did poorly at catching the reality of social change in many Latin American countries. Instead of coming out with my own fully articulated theory of socio-political transformation, I brought together a number of significant episodes in the course of which decisions were taken that the pre-existing climate of opinion or the prevailing socio-political structure made a priori rather unlikely. To understand the episodes I asked such questions as:

> What was the role or contribution of crisis in leading up to such decisions? (pp. 260–264)
> What was the role of violence? (pp. 256–260)
> When new problems or crises arose, did they bring additional pressures to solve the older problem or did they divert attention and energy from it? (pp. 264–267)

As a result, I proposed a number of fairly low-level generalizations about the conditions which permit these "surprising" or "out-of-character" policy decisions to be taken. What is really at stake here once again is the question of the relative autonomy of the state. While I may have been excessively intent on making discoveries of the "out-of-character" sort, I was thereby reacting against most previous analysts who seemed to be determined never to be surprised by anything.

I still maintain that the "capacity to be surprised," considered by Raymond Poincaré to be the essence of scientific genius, needs to be cultivated by the policy analyst as well. This capacity may be actively suppressed by the analyst's desire not to upset the comfortable intellectual schema with which he has equipped himself. But even in the absence of such ideological rigidity, policy decisions that should really occasion surprise are often found to be "obvious" or "easy" *because that is how they look in retrospect*. For example, the absence of resistance to a decision

14. In *Development Projects Observed* (Washington, D.C.: Brookings Institution, 1967).

on the part of interested parties which might have been expected to oppose it, is often taken as proof that the decision was easy to take. Thus, I have heard it said that it was easy for Peru's military government to expropriate large coastal sugar plantation owners in 1969 or that it was "easy" for the U.S. State Department in the early sixties to secure the agreement of the large U.S. food-processing corporations to the conclusion of the International Coffee Agreement.[15] The crucial difference here is between what is easy and what proves easy. In both situations, it proved easy to take decisions or to set upon a course that looked quite complex, risky, and daunting at the outset. At the moment and in the circumstances in which they were taken, these policies met with little resistance, but this would not have been the case at some earlier point of time. In other words, the social forces and groups that were expected to offer resistance, *turned out to be paper tigers, but for a long time they had been real tigers.*

To perceive and then act on this mutation (of one species of tigers into another) is an essential attribute of political leadership; to take notice and be appreciative when such leadership is forthcoming in the course of a policymaking sequence is the least one must ask of the policy analyst. We have recently witnessed some disastrous instances of just the inverse kind of policymaking: attacks on interests and social forces in the apparent belief that they were paper tigers, when in actual fact they turned out to be real tigers.

On Indirect and Unanticipated Effects of Public Policies

It must nevertheless be admitted that Latin American analysts have developed a remarkably fine nose for a certain category of "surprises": I am now talking about such unanticipated consequences and side effects of new laws or reforms as might thwart or vitiate their original intent. The underlining of such negative side effects is, of course, part and parcel of fracasomania. It is therefore well for the analyst to be on his guard against possible exaggerations of these effects. For example, I strongly disputed the widespread notion that Colombia's progressive Land Law of 1936 (Law 200) had primarily had the effect of dispossessing tenant farmers and of converting crop lands to cattle pasture. In the first place, so I argued, there was very little real evidence of any widespread expulsion of tenant farmers. Secondly, and more important, exclusive focusing on this unforeseen

15. For a good analysis, see Stephen Krasner, "Business-Government Relations: The Case of the International Coffee Agreement," *International Organization* 27 (Fall 1973): 495–516.

and unfortunate side effect of the law has hidden from view its genuine achievement—the legalization of the breakup of certain large estates and plantations which had been invaded or taken over by squatters and tenants over many years of rural unrest (pp. 107–113).

Today we hear once again claims that land reforms that have taken place over the last decade are spawning some unfortunate side effects. This time the claim is that the beneficiaries of the reform are a minority of the peasantry and that other rural groups, the landless labourers in particular, may possibly be less well off than before the reform. The fact that the reform broke the power of an "oligarchy" which for decades had been held to be at the source of economic and political oppression in these societies is already forgotten.[16]

Interestingly enough, those who in Latin America stress the negative side effects of well-meaning reforms tend to be found among the more radical and revolutionary intellectuals who feel that "partial" reforms are bound to be ineffective. In the United States and Europe, to the contrary, those with the sharpest eye for such side effects are generally conservatives who have long argued that government interference with the market is futile at best, and usually perverse. In the last few years, in fact, a "new Conservatism" has emerged in the United States that stresses "The Limits of Social Policy" and the "Counter-intuitive Nature of Social Systems" and which warns against any such "simple-minded" attack on social problems as building houses when there is a housing shortage or providing welfare payments to people without means of support.[17] This literature argues not just that new problems emerge when old problems get solved, but that because of some "positive feedback loop" the old problem actually gets worse as a result of these well-meaning but hopelessly unsophisticated attempts at a cure.

16. A more contemporary example than Colombia's Land Law of 1936 is Latin America's post-war industrialization experience. Originally hailed as the only way out, industrialization has been found to spawn so many unfortunate side effects, from penetration of foreign capital to a reprieve and boost for lopsided income distribution, that it is widely regarded as yet another Latin American fracaso. For a discussion of some of these things, see *Bias for Hope*, Chapter 3 Chapters 1 and 5 of *Essays in Trespassing*, cit.
17. See Nathan Glazer's influential article "The Limits of Social Policy," *Commentary*, 1971, and Jay W. Forrester, "Counter-intuitive Nature of Social Systems," *Technology Review*, 73 (January 1971). As is well known, Forrester's ideas and methods formed the basis for the *Limits to Growth* report by Donella M. Meadows et al. (New York: Universe Books, 1972).

A related line of attack on social and political reform emphasizes that the beneficiaries of reform measures are frequently different from those for whom the measures were originally (or ostensibly) taken and intended. Agencies set up to regulate corporations operating in monopoly-prone sectors end up being captured by these corporations and making their monopoly profits more secure; low-cost housing projects, as other social programs intended for the poor and as expenditures on public goods in general, end up benefiting primarily the middle class.[18] This criticism is actually a close analogue to that made in Latin America of land reforms which was mentioned before.

The third and perhaps best known line of attack on man-made change in the United States concentrates on the indirect effects and "externalities" of technological advance. Here we are in the vast realm of environmental pollution and degradation. However, the groups who warn, with this experience in mind, against the further uncontrolled proliferation of technology overlap only in part with those who would caution against social and political engineering. The irony here is that a great deal of brand new social engineering would be necessary to keep technical progress from "running riot."

These various new insights and resulting concerns have generated a diffuse mood of distrust toward the activity that was so highly regarded and advertised a mere decade ago as "problem-solving" and "decision-making." As a result of this converging United States-Latin American mood, of this stress on the ominous consequences and side effects of social action and public policy, the policy analyst's task is today, in part at least, to redress the balance and to examine carefully for any given policy whether it has really "done more harm than good" or "created more problems than it has solved." In leaning somewhat against the prevailing wind, the analyst may discover some hitherto unnoticed *positive* side effects[19] or he may find that the negative side effects are not beyond correction through some

18. For a good survey of the literature in this area, see S. M. Miller and Martin Rein, "Can Income Redistribution Work?" *Social Policy* (May/June, 1975).
19. For example, Simon Kuznets has called attention to the positive effects of new technology, once it is widely applied, on the further progress of science: "The extensive application of a major invention, its diffusion in mass production, is bound to add further detail and information about the underlying forces, processes, and materials not contained in the scientific discovery or even in the invention before its spread in mass use.… This additional knowledge may, in turn, provide a base for new advances in basic science, often in unexpected directions and ways." *Economic Growth of Nations* (Cambridge, MA: Harvard University Press, 1971), p. 330.

new policymaking, so that one deals with a converging rather than a continually expanding series of problems. This may, for example, be the case for some of the much advertised defects of Latin American industrialization, such as excessive participation of foreign capital, failure to export, and to develop an indigenous technology.

Nevertheless, the detection of unanticipated effects of public policy will always remain one of the principal purposes of policy studies. Public discussion will often focus on some of the most glaring of these effects, but many others will remain to be discovered. Those that stand in the forefront of the discussion are typically either "good" or "bad," but it is important to realize that a number of important side effects cannot be easily classified in this fashion. As I pointed out elsewhere, an irrigation project may have the unanticipated consequence of provoking a conflict over limited water resources between established plantation owners and new settlers, but it may be anything but obvious whether such a conflict will make a positive or negative contribution to the country's development and history.[20]

In addition, there are a number of side effects which, though perhaps more easily classified as either good or bad or as either costs or benefits, will hardly ever be subjects of public discussion because they are highly speculative and, for that reason, do not make good debating points. Three years ago, I conducted a brief preliminary inquiry into the experience with national economic planning under the Presidency of Carlos Lleras Restrepo (1966–1970) in Colombia. Conversations with a number of key participants and observers brought out the following points:

1. There can be no doubt that for the first time in its tempestuous history[21] the Planning Office functioned properly: it played an important role in advising on basic economic policy and even more in contributing to public investment decisions, through the application of cost-benefit analyses;
2. Similarly, there is no doubt that the delegation of decision-making to a body of "cold" experts had a sizable political cost for President Lleras, the magnitude of which he probably did not perceive correctly. The fact that he recently lost the nomination for a second term on the Liberal

20. *Development Projects Observed*, pp. 186–187.
21. It would be interesting to inquire why most Planning Offices, set up to impart more stability and long-term perspective to economic policymaking, have themselves been among the most unstable of government agencies. See also Chapter 5, p. 120 of *Essays in Trespassing*.

ticket may in fact be related to enmities he incurred by curtailing traditional pork-barrel spending;

3. The orderly procedures for decision-making on investment projects that were established and the competent way in which they were analysed in the Planning Office made Colombia a very attractive country for the international lending agencies. As a result, the Government found itself flush with foreign finance and pressures for needed fiscal reforms eased considerably;
4. In general, these orderly procedures in which the Government took such pride may have made it impossible to attack some of the more basic tasks which the Colombian economy faced, and to which Lleras Restrepo was in principle committed, such as urban reform or vigorous prosecution of the land reform. Making progress in these conflict-ridden areas would have required a readiness to manoeuver and to surprise which was not easily compatible with the orderly decision-making in which the principal policymakers were revelling.

The last three propositions spell out some political and policy costs of economic planning in the Colombian environment. At this stage, they are, of course, the merest conjectures. But the possibility that the successes and the failures of the Lleras Administration are connected in these ways seems worth exploring.

This sort of connection is much more obvious in the case of Mexico where the policy of "development with stability" (*desarrollo estabilizador*) of the sixties, while highly successful in its own terms, resulted in greater income inequalities, larger foreign indebtedness, and a strengthened veto power of the domestic financial community over national policy.[22]

There is, of course, some danger that this sort of analysis leads right back into the swamp of fracasomania, but I would hope not. The point of the exercise is not to prove that planning in Colombia or economic growth with monetary stability in Mexico were just two more miserable failures even though they had been touted as big successes. Nor is it to admonish policymakers that they have to solve all problems—planning *and* structural reforms, monetary stability *and* income redistribution—at the same time or be damned for falling down on one of the

22. See, for example, the articles by Miguel S. Wionczek, Francisco Javier Alejo, and Jorge Eduardo Navarrete in M. S. Wionczek et al., *Crecimiento o desarrollo econòmico?* Secretaria de Education Publica, 1971. Also Carlos Bazdresch, "La politica econòmica" in *Plural*, No. 22 (July 1973).

tests an analyst sets up in retrospect. The purpose of unravelling the indirect and roundabout consequences of a given policy is rather to understand how certain policies, in spite of their apparent success, may run into decreasing returns, how from a "spur" they may turn or have already turned into a "fetter," to use Marxian terminology. In this way policy studies could serve to sensitize opinion to needed changes and turnarounds in policy-making. And even without this practical use, they would tell us something about changing biases, blindspots, and lapses in foresight that have been typical, from time to time, of different political actors and systems.

Concluding Lament

With the last two sentences I have touched upon the twin purpose of policy studies: (1) to learn more about the nature of policymaking and that means, in the last analysis, about the nature of state, society, and politics; and (2) to contribute to improvements ("reform") in policymaking in the specific area that is being studied. Clearly both motivations, the theoretical and the practical, are likely and ought to be present in the minds of researchers in the field, but the balance between the two will vary considerably with different social and political settings. Whenever reform is perceived to be within easy reach, the practical "reformist" component will come to the fore. When, on the other hand, reform proposals are beyond the political realities of the moment, policymaking studies will tend to dwell on the nature of the state and society that rules out these partial improvements. It is of course anything but easy to diagnose the conditions under which reform is feasible and *Journeys* was in large part meant to correct what seemed to me to be misperceptions of these conditions on the part of both conventional reformers and orthodox revolutionaries.

But a correct appraisal of the feasibility of reform is no longer enough. In a number of Latin American situations the policy analyst will want to ask an additional question: supposing partial reform is possible, what would be its effect on the further dynamics of state and society? To explain this point I must go back to the introductory paragraphs of this essay where the notion that "all good things go together" was held up to some ridicule. The practically minded policy analyst operates normally on a weaker, yet related assumption: he likes to think that, at a minimum, a possible improvement in policymaking he has discovered as a result of his research will leave the area of his specialized concern better off and the rest of the world unchanged so that the world as a whole would find itself in a somewhat improved state. But what if even this modest assurance is no longer to be had? What if improved policymaking in, say, public health or education, is likely to result in more widespread violations of human rights? What if, in sum, we inhabit not a Faustian, but a Quixote-Buñuel-type world where he who wills the good forever creates evil?

One possible reaction to so parlous a state of affairs is for the policy analyst to retreat from any attempt to put the results of his research to any immediate practical use and to concentrate entirely on the theoretical aspects and findings of his work. But such a self-denying ordinance is excessive, unnatural, and, therefore, unlikely to be effective. Another course seems therefore indicated: the analyst should add to his labours a concern about the possibly perverse consequences in other areas of public policy of an advance that might be achieved in his own.

Considerations of this sort are formally similar to the canvassing for negative side effects that is today part and parcel of any policy study. The explorations we have hinted at here are of course far more speculative. Formerly they could legitimately be neglected. Unhappily, they are today essential, both for practical policy advice and for the understanding of the singularly "cold monster" that the State has become in a large number of Latin American countries.

14

Varieties of Consumer Disappointment

Disappointment is so common and therefore so seemingly transparent an experience that no one appears to have bothered to explore its nature, components, and varieties in systematic fashion. My principal concern in this chapter is with disappointments incidental to the private consumption of goods and services. These are obviously not the only possible disappointments with one's private pursuits. A very important category of disappointment has to do with the job experience. One reason why it is not dealt with here is the existence of a large literature on job satisfaction and dissatisfaction in which economists have begun to take an active part.[1] Another is my suspicion that one potent reason for job dissatisfaction could be tied up not so much, as is generally assumed, with the characteristics of the job as with the general satisfaction workers experience as members of society and therefore also as consumers. Because jobs in our society are primarily considered as a means to the earning of income which in turn serves to pay for consumption, the quality of the consumption experience—or the quality of life experience in

1. See the papers on "Quality of Working Life," by Karl-Olof Faxém, Richard B. Freeman, and Lester C. Thurow, in *American Economic Review* 68 (May 1978), 131–148, and Graham L. Staines, "Is Worker Dissatisfaction Rising?" *Challenge* 2 (May/June 1979), 38–45.

general—could easily reflect on the quality of the job experience. This is in fact the conclusion reached in a recent study of the apparent drop in job satisfaction that took place in the course of the seventies in the United States. Having unsuccessfully tested explanations that relate the drop to various job characteristics, the author concludes: "… the recent decline in job satisfaction … may have very little to do with jobs or conditions of employment at all. We may instead be witnessing a much broader social malaise …."[2]

Without necessarily subscribing to this thesis, I shall focus here on the world of objects and consumption expenditures as possible and differential sources of disappointment and discontent. The idea that some goods may have more disappointment potential than others is present, albeit at a very high level of aggregation, in a brilliant passage of Georg Simmel's *Philosophy of Money* (1900). Simmel distinguishes between money, on the one hand, and all consumer goods, on the other, and notes that, insofar as money is desired purely for the purpose of accumulation (by the avaricious, for example), its possession is immune to disappointment.[3] The reason for this is the abstract character of money which is "a thing absolutely devoid of quality" and therefore totally known: a dollar is a dollar is a dollar, far more so than a rose is a rose is a rose. Here is the principal psychological difference between money and other goods which all are paradoxically *richer* than money as they "harbor either surprises or disappointments" that are experienced in the course of use.[4]

2. Staines, "Worker Dissatisfaction," p. 44.
3. *Philosophie des Geldes* (Leipzig: Duncker & Humblot, 1907, 2nd ed.), pp. 246–249. See also my comment on this passage in *Passions and Interests*, pp. 55–56.
4. From the context of this passage it is clear that Simmel was thinking almost exclusively in terms of *disappointments*: in the immediately preceding pages he talks at length about the "terrible discrepancy between desire and fulfillment" and again about the "often tragic, often comical incommensurability between desire and fulfillment." Another point: my earlier semantic observation [according to which in no language the opposite of disappointment exists] is confirmed by the passage quoted in the text; Simmel made here an attempt to be evenhanded as between disappointment and its opposite, but language did not collaborate since it does not have a compact term for the antonym of disappointment. Hence, Simmel is awkwardly reduced to using "surprise" (*Überraschung*), which is a strictly neutral term—a surprise can be either pleasant or unpleasant—as the opposite of the negative-valued "disappointment" (*Enttäuschung*).

In the present chapter, I shall attempt to carry forward the inquiry pioneered by Simmel and look at some reasons why, *within* the universe of goods, the disappointment potential of some categories of goods might be greater than that of others. My method will be inductive rather than deductive: I start with some well-established subdivisions among consumer purchases, such as durables vs. nondurables, or goods vs. services, and then inquire whether there inheres in some of these subcategories a characteristic that makes for particularly high (or low) propensity to disappointment. Once the characteristics that make for low or high propensity to disappointment have been identified, they are of course likely to define sets of goods that do not precisely overlap with the simple-minded, given categories that have been fashioned for quite different purposes. A good example of this procedure follows immediately.

The Privileged Position of Truly Nondurable Goods

In this section as well as in the next, I shall draw on some of the conceptual distinctions, taken from psychology, which Tibor Scitovsky has recently proposed to explain why our economy is "joyless." His point of departure is the notion of arousal of the nervous system: when *arousal* is too high, the result is discomfort in the form of hunger, thirst, or physical pain; and when it is too low, boredom—another, peculiarly human, kind of *discomfort*—sets in. When either of these two varieties of discomfort is relieved by various consumption activities designed to satisfy wants or to relieve boredom, the result is both pleasure and comfort: pleasure is the experience of traveling from discomfort to comfort while the latter is achieved at the point of arrival. Hence a contradiction between *pleasure* and *comfort*: for pleasure to be experienced, comfort must be sacrificed temporarily.

While contrasting comfort with pleasure in this manner, Scitovsky chooses largely to ignore the pleasures that have their origin in various drives (food, sex, sleep), and in the ensuing satisfaction of primary wants; he concentrates instead on those pleasures that come from keeping boredom at bay, on what he calls "stimulation."[5] His reason is that, in the affluent societies with which he is primarily concerned, want satisfaction may be taken for granted and is crowded out as a source of pleasure by stimulation. This focus on stimulation and on the different extent to which it is practiced through various devices by consumers in different affluent societies is central to Scitovsky's assertion that consumers in the

5. *Joyless Economy*, p. 79.

United States suffer from under stimulation in comparison to Western Europeans. However that may be, it seems a pity that he has almost wholly neglected the very considerable portion of our pleasures that still derive, no matter how affluent we may be, from catering to our physiological needs. As these needs are recurrent, comfort gives way automatically to discomfort with the passage of time so that the pleasure-yielding trip back to comfort can once again be undertaken. We are dealing here with truly paradigmatic pleasures—simple, familiar, yet intense and indefinitely renewable as long as we live. A closer look at the goods supplying these pleasures is useful as a first step toward evaluating the comparative disappointment potential of various consumer purchases.

We all know the adage: "The best things in life are free." Let me now propose the following, only slightly more complex variant: "Some of the most durable (that is, renewable) and least disappointment-prone pleasures in life are those to be gotten from nondurable goods that are literally *consumed*, that vanish in the act of consumption." The division of the universe of consumer goods that is implicit in this statement is somewhat different from the usual one between durables and nondurables. The latter category conventionally contains such items as clothing and shoes. But from the point of view of pleasure generation and disappointment potential, the important distinction is between the *truly* nondurable goods, primarily food and fuel, that must be used up to the greatest possible extent (i.e. except for waste products of which ideally there should be none) in the process of consumption, and all those goods where decay and impairment resulting from use or the passage of time are accepted only as inevitable imperfections. Food has a special ability to provide pleasure that is based on the body's recurring physiological need for the energy it supplies. Foodstuffs disappear precisely in the process of conveying their energy to the body, and their disappearance is essential to the pleasure felt in the act of consumption.[6] That disappearance also makes for the privileged position the truly nondurable commodities hold with regard to

6. In the twenties a Nobel-prize winning British chemist, Frederick Soddy, published a book, *Wealth, Virtual Wealth and Debt* (New York: Dutton, 1933, 2nd ed.), that caused a certain stir and went through several editions. The book is quite forgotten today and, on the whole, for good reasons. But on pp. 116–118 the author makes an interesting point which I amplify here for my own purposes: some basic goods, such as food and fuel, have the function to release energy for the use of humans and they *must* change, deteriorate, or perish in the performance of this function—this characteristic sets them off from all other consumer goods which are ideally unchanging. Annette Weiner who called my attention to the book also cites this point in her paper

the potential for disappointment: they are very different from the more durable goods, also known as "possessions," that are still there after disappointment has been experienced in the process of consumption and act thereby as reminders of such disappointments. Moreover, at the inevitable subsequent moments of discouragement and unhappiness, the "possessions" may well *compound* those feelings: we realize resentfully that these possessions have failed to bring the hoped-for private happiness, or experience self-reproach for feeling terrible when we should feel great, considering all these goods at our command.

There is then something both pleasure-intensive and peculiarly disappointment-resistant about goods that disappear in the process of consumption. The Roman emperors knew, so it seems, what they were doing when they took care to supply the masses with bread and circuses: *both* vanish once you have taken them in, without leaving behind a corporeal shape on which consumers can vent any disappointment, boredom, or anxiety they may have suffered or may yet suffer.

It is necessary to point out and to stress the privileged position, from our point of view, of those truly nondurable goods, for language is not at all cooperative in this endeavour: durable seems offhand so much preferable to nondurable and perishable. The Greeks invented the Midas myth to remind themselves that durability has a few drawbacks, but somehow the lesson has not sunk in. Language has no generic term with a positive connotation for those goods whose outstanding merits are wholly bound up with their *non*-durability.[7] Moreover, the low esteem in which perishable goods are held has been compounded, at least insofar as economists are concerned, by the well-known fact that income elasticity of demand for these goods is lower than for durables (and services). As a result, the important compensating virtues of our truly nondurables, the sturdiness of

"More Desired than Gold: A Study of Women, Their Wealth and Political Evolution in the Pacific," unpublished, 1981.

7. One reason may be that foodstuffs dominate the category of truly nondurable goods. Yet, there are others: fuel, soap, cosmetics, and pharmaceuticals, to cite just a few of some importance. A second reason is the modern alteration in the meaning of the term consumption. Originally we *consumed* turnips and candles whereas we *owned* and *used* gowns and carriages, but with time (and the progress of macroeconomics) consumption came to refer to *all* the goods and services people produced or purchased for their own use. "Consumables" would once have been an apt and reasonably positive term for the category of goods I have in mind, but it has by now been contaminated by the diluted meaning of consumption.

the pleasures purveyed by them and their resistance to disappointment, have been lost from view.

In extolling the truly nondurable goods as particularly disappointment-resistant I certainly do not wish to affirm that they are disappointment-*exempt*. They cannot wholly overcome that human incapacity for achieving fulfilment which was so well characterized by Kant: "give a man everything he desires and yet at this very moment he will feel that this *everything* is not *everything*"*. Actually, this incapacity was frequently illustrated in the age of Kant by reference to the very experience of eating and drinking: Edward Young in his enormously successful *Night Thoughts*, Samuel Johnson in *Rasselas* and Giacomo Leopardi in one of his major poems, all compare the total contentment sheep feel after grazing to the lingering dissatisfaction and *ennui* that is (so they allege) the lot of the shepherd after he has had *his* meal.[8] But the fact that eating is here singled out as being subject

*. see *Shifting Involvements*, page 11; Italics in the text.

8. Edward Young perhaps started this genre by writing in *Night Thoughts* (1742):

> Is it, that things terrestrial can't content?
> Deep in rich pasture, will thy flocks complain?
> Not so; but to their master is deny'd
> To share their sweet serene. (Night VII, lines 36–40)

Samuel Johnson is much more meticulous in *Rasselas* (1759):

> What … makes the difference between man and all the rest of the animal creation? Every beast that strays beside me has the same corporal necessities with myself; he is hungry and crops the grass, he is thirsty and drinks the stream, his thirst and hunger are appeased, he is satisfied and sleeps; he rises again and is hungry, he is again fed and is at rest. I am hungry and thirsty like him, but when thirst and hunger cease I am not at rest; I am, like him, pained with want, but am not, like him, satisfied with fulness. (Chapter II)

Finally, in Leopardi's "Canto Notturno di un pastore errante dell'Asia" (1830) the act of eating is no longer specifically mentioned, but it is implied to have just taken place in the following lines where the shepherd speaks to his flock:

> When in the shade you lie upon the grass,
> You are tranquil and content,
> And yet I sit upon the grass, and in the shade,
> And weariness invades my mind. (Translation by John Humphreys Whitfield, *Canti*, Naples: Scalabrini, 1962, p. 175.)

to disappointment, far from contradicting my thesis, rather serves to confirm it: to make their point about the basic, metaphysical incapacity of man to achieve happiness and fulfilment in the strongest possible terms, these writers focused on those human consumption activities that are comparatively least subject to disappointment. If even eating and drinking, so they argue implicitly, are followed by feelings of frustration and unhappiness, then it is verily man's condition never to be satisfied.

In the following, consumer experiences characteristic of our truly nondurable goods will *not* be compared, I hasten to add, to those of various animals with similar goods. Rather, these experiences will be compared to those made by humans with other categories of goods and services. It is in this manner that the differential, commodity-specific incidence of consumer disappointment can best be evaluated. Such comparisons will be attempted with respect to consumer durables in the next section, and with respect to various types of services in the one following.

Consumer Durables

If Scitovsky is right in holding that comfort is the enemy of pleasure, then any good that assures comfort or keeps discomfort at bay in a durable fashion, such as an automatic heating system or a refrigerator, will yield a comparatively low amount of pleasure. As long as it is in working order, such a good will satisfy a need once and for all, so that pleasure is experienced only once, when the good is first acquired and put to use ("turned on"). Thereafter, comfort is assured, but the pleasure that comes with traveling from discomfort to comfort is no longer available. There is a good expression for this state of affairs: we say that the particular good has come to be taken for granted. Implicit in this expression is a slight reproach or regret—we feel that we should be more happy, grateful, and freshly pleased about having the good than we really are. To achieve an appropriately appreciative state of mind we can either work on our imagination—try to get back, each time we use the good (or each time we remember it is in use) into the same state of mind as when we first acquired it—or, less commendably, we can work up feelings of relative superiority and think of the poor fellows who haven't got it quite yet. But these sorts of mental exercises are still unlikely to generate the acute pleasure that is experienced when a needed or useful good is first acquired and put to use. In truth, the refrigerator already comes close to yielding as little active pleasure as much older, similarly most useful objects and inventions such as plate glass or, for that matter, the wheel.

Actually when we say that we take certain of these permanently comfort-yielding durable goods for granted, we may well address a reproach not only to ourselves, but to the goods in question. We fault them precisely for being all comfort and hardly any pleasure, in sharp contrast to more traditional purchases of nondurables such as food. Goods that yield considerable pleasure along with comfort have taken up the bulk of consumer purchases for many centuries; they also stand in the centre of the consumption experience of childhood and youth. Hence, the drastic change in the *balance of pleasure and comfort* that comes with durables is unforeseen and the small amount of pleasure they yield is initially disconcerting.[9] As time passes consumers will presumably come to accept that in the case of durables the pleasure-comfort balance is different from that of nondurables: they will learn to trade off comfort against pleasure and otherwise adjust their expectations. To some extent, each generation may have to go through this process inasmuch as consumption experiences during adulthood are more heavily weighted with durables than those during childhood. But if our analysis is right, disappointment could be especially widespread in a society in which mass diffusion of durables first occurs. This is of course quite paradoxical, since one might expect a population to be in a fine mood when large parts of it accede for the first time to the much celebrated, Rostovian blessings of "high mass consumption." In actual fact both moods, general optimism and widespread disaffection, could be encountered in rapid succession. They also could exist side by side, as when the older generation successfully represses any disappointment with its life-style and emphasizes the material progress it has achieved, while the younger generation has no empathy for that experience and denounces the emptiness of the parents' lives. As a result of these contrasting moods, the period of transition to "high mass consumption" could be politically quite volatile.

Having made my major point with regard to durables I must qualify it. To divide all consumer goods into durables and nondurables exaggerates the difference in disappointment potential between these two categories. From the point of view of the pleasure-comfort balance it is useful to distinguish between three

9. The argument is somewhat analogous to, though hopefully less speculative and more convincing than, the notion of some anthropologists that *homo sapiens* is still primarily programmed by evolution as the hunter and gatherer he was for several hundreds of millennia and that his maladjustments are to be attributed to his having taken up sedentary occupations just a few thousand years ago.

subcategories of durables: (1) those that are in continuous use—the house or apartment, heating or air conditioning systems, refrigerators, etc.; (2) those that are in use at regular cyclical or generally predictable intervals because their use is tied in with the natural rhythm and structure of everyday life—the car (when it is used for utilitarian transportation such as driving to work, shopping, etc.), washing machines, dishwashers, etc.; (3) those that are used at irregular intervals in accordance with whether the owners "feel like" using them—hi-fi equipment, piano, camera, the car to the extent it is used purely for the sake of getting "driving pleasure," and so on.[10]

What has been said about the disappointment-generating characteristic of durables—that they are more weighted with comfort than pleasure in comparison with traditional purchases—applies most strongly to the first category of durables, somewhat less so to the second, and least to the third. Durable articles that are used at the owner's whim are in many ways like nondurables: whenever the owner decides to use them, this is so because he or she derives pleasure or stimulation from them, as well as some comfort after use—as when the desire to take pictures or to play the piano has been pacified (or when boredom has been temporarily contained).

The durables of the third category can best be considered as consumer capital, similar to children's toys, that yield a stream of services rather similar, from the point of view of the potential for disappointment, to such nondurable purchases as a ticket to the opera or the stadium, a pleasure trip, or even an ice-cream cone. An important difference is, however, that once the services dispensed by the durable are no longer desired, the durable good itself still "hangs around"; thus it reminds the owner that it has ceased providing enjoyment and therefore continues to provoke a certain amount of disappointment. Children are in a better position than adults in this respect, as any excessively durable toy that no longer yields pleasure and stimulation will be "made to disappear" by the parents or destroyed by the children.

More will be said in the next chapter of *Shifting Involvements* on the recurring hostility toward durable objects meant to provide pleasure and comfort. At this stage, however, I wish to argue that the first two categories of durables are especially prone to generating disappointment. These durables constitute the core of the modem household durable culture. That the pleasure-comfort balance is totally

10. As with any classification, there are difficulties with neatly arranging all durables into the three categories. For example, does television belong to the second or third category? For the majority of viewers, who have developed the "TV habit," to the second.

different from that normally experienced in conjunction with nondurables has already been noted for those durables (heating system, refrigerator, etc.) that are in continuous use. It is the characteristic homeostatic property of these articles that accounts for their ability to keep discomfort permanently at bay, with the counterpart that the pleasure-generating trip from discomfort to comfort is eliminated.

In the case of the second category of durables—those that are in use at regular intervals because their use is tied in with the rhythm and structure of everyday life—the homeostatic property is less pronounced as they still have to be set in motion and otherwise manipulated by their owners to yield their services. Washing machines and dishwashers, for example, still need to be at least "loaded," set in motion by their users, and unloaded, and some real if fleeting moment of pleasure is accordingly associated with such operations as well as with the pushing of the button. Also, the visible, effortless, and a bit wondrous transformation wrought by these machines—the turning of dirty objects into clean ones—produces some renewable pleasure. But what has been said about the peculiar comfort-pleasure balance of the first category of durables applies here too, if to a lower degree.

The most important modern durable good is the private automobile. It is of course still less homeostatic or automatic than the machines just noted. Also, there is no doubt that it can yield pleasure, "driving pleasure," either in connection with its utilitarian function or even in pure form as when people take—or rather, used to take—a "joyride." The fact is that the automobile provides, in Scitovsky's terms, "stimulation" as well as want satisfaction: this is perhaps its unique strength as a durable consumer good.[11] According to a well-known French critic, the car is a "sublime object": "The mobility without effort it provides makes for a kind of unreal happiness, with existence and responsibility in suspense."[12] All of this can be granted, especially for the first time when "person meets car." Nevertheless, the car's utilitarian function is eventually paramount; and its ability to carry out this function tends to be taken for granted almost as rapidly as that of the thermostat-equipped heating system to provide even heat. The reason is that the need for transportation—pressing though it may be—is very different from the body's need for food, sleep, or sex. Each time I am hungry I get genuine, indefinitely renewable pleasure from filling my stomach (a process well illustrated by the German proverb "appetite is the best cook"), but the excitement and pleasure I get from my car's ability to satisfy my (non-physiological) need for transportation

11. Some kitchen appliances have a similar ability to rise above pure utility and to provide stimulation, in particular the modern food processor.
12. Jean Baudrillard, *Le système des objets* (Paris: Gallimard, 1968), p. 94.

wanes rather rapidly. Here lies perhaps an important reason for the remarkable success of higher-priced and luxury cars. Such cars are precisely meant to enhance the stimulation function in relation to the want satisfaction function of the automobile. As a recent advertisement for a BMW blurts it out: "MEETING THE DEMANDS OF SOCIETY [read: safety and antipollution devices, fuel economy] IS NO EXCUSE FOR BUILDING A BORING CAR." Many consumers thus strive to fight the disappointment that they sense will be connected with the purely utilitarian aspect of the car by spending more on the vehicle than is strictly necessary for transportation purposes. In this manner, they obtain both a somewhat superior driving experience and the satisfaction of feeling superior to the great mob of motorists. They are willing to spend a substantial amount of money on tilting the pleasure-comfort balance of their purchase in the direction of more pleasure. For exactly the same reason, they have long tolerated—perhaps desired—a certain amount of "built-in obsolescence": a new automobile makes for a radical shift in the pleasure-comfort balance.

Another distinction may be made between durable goods that, when bought, are totally finished and are not supposed to be given any sort of individual touch by the consumer and those that permit or even require that touch. By far the most important item in the latter category is of course the individually owned house or apartment, while the conventional consumer durables, from car to washing machine, belong in the former. The difference between these two categories from the point of view of pleasure generation and maintenance is fairly obvious: when owners have the opportunity, as with a house, to furnish, arrange and rearrange it, to repair, improve, or even to add to it, they in effect make it into a reflection of themselves. The pleasure yielded by the house is immeasurably enhanced by the narcissistic contemplation of the result of their own efforts and choices. Here is an important way of counteracting the loss of pleasure that would otherwise follow upon the permanent-comfort-producing acquisition of a house.[13] However, this remedy against pleasure loss is typically not available to consumers in relation to

13. This is also true of personal belongings that undergo substantial change simply as a result of use. A marvellous account is in Diderot's essay "Regrets on an Old Robe or Advice to Those Who Have More Taste than Wealth": "Why did I not keep it? It was made for me; I was made for it.… When the thick ink would not flow from my pen, it offered its side. Long black streaks testified to the frequent service it had given me. These long streaks proclaimed the *littérateur,* the writer, the man who works. At present [in my new robe], I look like a rich *fainéant;* one does not know who I am." Diderot, *Oeuvres* (Paris: Pléiade, 1935), p. 733.

their more modern purchases that "come" complete and just have to be "plugged in." The only change which they can experience is not a further transformation or improvement in accordance with the special needs or tastes of the individual consumer, but a breakdown which, once again, does not permit the owner to intervene—by "fixing it" himself he would regenerate the pleasure received from the article—but obliges him to call in a specialist repairman at great cost. With the automobile, the second most important possession of the average citizen, there is at least the possibility of keeping up its appearance, and it is perhaps this desire to make it "one's own" and to derive from it the concomitant narcissistic pleasure, that pushes so many car owners to spend a large portion of their free weekend time on washing it and on shining it up. The case of sports cars and motorcycles comes close to that of the owner-occupied house in that the owners of these vehicles tend to take full and enthusiastic charge of maintenance as well as of all kinds of modifications and additions. Finally, an extraordinary instance of the propensity to make assembly-line standard objects into wholly personal creations is the phenomenon of the "Lowriders" in San Francisco and elsewhere in the West. Here the Chicano and other Spanish-speaking communities have invented a parade, held primarily on weekend evenings, of older, originally quite nondescript cars that have been totally transformed into outlandish, garish, highly personal vehicles that boast a special type of low suspension (hence "Lowriders") and are "customized" in many other respects. Such cars are part of a "life-style" that is an open protest against the "square," pleasure-poor world of the usual utility vehicle.

A closer look at various categories of durable goods leaves intact the point made earlier when all durables were contrasted with nondurables: the modern, mass-produced durable consumer good subverts the way in which consumers extracted pleasure from their purchases in the predurable era. Along with their extraordinarily useful services, these goods are likely to generate a great deal of vaguely felt disappointment, particularly at the time of their first massive diffusion in a society.[14]

14. An influential article by a British sociologist has pointed to another possible source of resentment against durables. In the case of workers, the acquisition of durables (including automobiles) precipitates and symbolizes a change in the "image of society" from a class-struggle *or* a traditional-reverential image to a privatized, pecuniary image of social relationships. Such a change brings with it a sense of loss, and some of the blame for that loss will attach to the newly acquired gadgets. See David Lockwood, "Sources of Variation in Working-Class Images of Society," *Sociological Review* 14 (Nov. 1966), 249–267, reprinted in Martin Bulmer, ed., *Working-Class Images of Society* (London: Routledge and Kegan Paul, 1975), pp. 16–31, particularly p. 23.

Services

In the advanced capitalist countries of the West, an important shift in the occupational structure has taken place in recent decades. Employment in the so-called service sector, that congeries of activities comprising not only finance and commerce, but educational, health, recreational, professional, and government services, has grown much faster than employment in industry and agriculture. As a consequence, so it has been proclaimed, our economy has become a "Service Economy" (Victor Fuchs) and our society a "Post-Industrial Society" (Daniel Bell).

The expansion of the service sector has as its counterpart an increase in consumers' expenditures on services, particularly in such fields as education, health, and recreation. To the extent that governments provide such services, actual expenditures are replaced by higher general and social security taxes (or stronger inflationary pressures); the direct link between the rendering of a service and the monetary quid pro quo is thereby severed. Nevertheless, the existence of these services and the fact that one has paid taxes (or suffered inflation) to support them create expectations of entitlement. Regardless of the institutional arrangement, it is therefore possible to speak of a new and increasingly important category of consumer purchases.[15] It will now be argued, as earlier with consumer durables, that the disappointment potential of these purchases is likely to be quite high.

The reasons, however, are very different. In the case of consumer durables, the trouble was not their performance, which on the whole is rather reliable, but their failure to yield "pleasure" to the extent consumers were expecting on the basis of their prior experience with nondurable purchases. In the case of health and educational services, on the other hand, performance itself is notably uneven and unpredictable; here one new and jarring experience, in comparison with more traditional purchases, is the high degree of variability in the quality and efficacy of

15. The shares in the consumer budget of actual spending on services remained constant in Great Britain, as was shown by J. I. Gershuny, in his study "The Self-Service Economy," *New Universities Quarterly* (Summer 1977), 50–66. But a proper accounting should include welfare state services that were received by the consumer without immediate cash counterpart. There can be no doubt that, with this sort of accounting, the share of expenditures for services would show a substantial increase particularly for those items—health and education—that are of major interest for the present study.

the thing acquired. As a result, the large numbers who lose out in this particular lottery are likely to be an unhappy and disappointed lot.

Once again, the likelihood of disappointment is greatest for the first generation of consumers of these services, that is, for consumers who approach these purchases with the expectations about reliability and predictability of the product that have been formed during the many years in which they purchased mostly apples, eggs, shoes, refrigerators, and such. Thus, it is again the upwardly mobile groups brimming over with new consumption ambitions who will bear the brunt of the disappointment as they painfully learn about the much higher degree of risk and uncertainty associated with services which they are now anxious to try out. Nevertheless, even after considerable experience with the risk involved in these service purchases, the disappointment potential remains high for the many who simply refuse to comprehend that educators, physicians, and psychiatrists are entitled to large payments (in fees or via taxes) in exchange for services whose efficacy can be so far off the mark.

The argument about the high disappointment potential of these services becomes a great deal stronger in times when a substantial effort is made to expand rapidly the supply of these services with the intention of making them more widely available. Under these conditions, their *average quality* is likely to drop substantially. This is so in part because it is difficult to assemble at the same time all the inputs needed for high quality performance—new school buildings are built faster than new teachers are formed, or vice versa. It is therefore precisely when a society makes a determined effort to widen access to certain services that the quality of these services will decline, with obvious negative effects on the morale of both new and old consumers.[16]

The drop in quality consequent upon expansion is a peculiar characteristic of certain services and does not apply to consumer durables or to other services, at least not nearly to the same extent. The principal reason is that the tolerance for quality decline is much wider, for example, in the case of educational services than for industrial goods such as refrigerators or for high-technology services, such as airplane travel. An expansion in airplane travel or in the production of refrigerators cannot take place unless all or most essential inputs are available in appropriate quantities, whereas newly expanded higher education services can be and

16. For a fuller treatment of this and the following points, see my article "The Welfare State in Trouble: Systemic Crisis or Growing Pains?" *American Economic Review* 70 (May 1980), 113–116.

typically are offered *in spite* of unresolved bottlenecks, that is, with unprepared teachers, impossibly crowded classrooms, or other such imbalances.

The likelihood of a disappointing performance of newly established or expanded services is reinforced by some further observations. In the first place, when certain social services like education are expanded so as to cater to newly emerging social groups, it may not be appropriate to offer exactly the same services as have been previously supplied to the traditional "educated class." Hence even without quality decline, and precisely because there has been no change or adaptation, the services might be ineffective and meet with resistance. Again, a period of learning and mutual adjustment will be needed.

Secondly, there is a class of services for which a strong demand may arise in advance of real knowledge about how to satisfy it; recent examples are day-care facilities and psychotherapeutic services. What happens in these situations is that, in response to an effective market demand, some members of society come forward proclaiming, like any good hustler, "We can handle this for you," but actually only begin to learn "on the job," in the process of rendering these newly popular services as best they can. A great deal has been written about consumer ignorance and the resulting asymmetrical situation of consumer and producer.[17] In the present case, producers are just as ignorant as consumers, at least during the earlier stages of their operation. It is the supplier's ignorance rather than his wiles that accounts for the poor quality of services rendered. Again, the resulting consumer disappointment is engendered by the peculiar marketability of certain services in spite of quality being much lower than expected.

Grounded as it is in a variety of converging situations and characteristics, the disappointment potential of certain newly expanded social services has by now assumed a rather formidable look. In fact, the argument here developed amounts to one way of understanding what is sometimes called "the Crisis of the Welfare State." The feeling is widespread today that the attempt at making capitalism compatible with the eradication of poverty and unemployment and with a more equal distribution of income and of life chances has been increasingly running into inflationary and other troubles in a number of countries. The explanation of this development has generally been sought in some deep-seated "structural" characteristics of Western societies. In this vein, James O'Connor has written

17. See Kenneth J. Arrow, "Social Responsibility and Economic Efficiency," *Public Policy* 21 (Summer 1973), 303–318, and George Akerlof, "The Market for 'Lemons': Quality Uncertainty and the Market Mechanism," *Quarterly Journal of Economics* 85 (August 1970), 488–500.

about the contradiction between the accumulation and the legitimation function of the capitalist state,[18] while Fred Hirsch has pointed to the impossibility of ever-increasing numbers of people acceding to what are strictly finite opportunities and types of enjoyment.[19] In contrast, the perspective here proposed does not look at the difficulties of the Welfare State as the reflection of "fundamental contradictions" or of absolute ceilings; rather, it sees these difficulties as serious, but quite possibly temporary growing pains. These pains may well cause considerable trouble when first encountered, but can eventually be brought under control as a result of various learning experiences and mutual adjustments. Hence our message on these matters is rather less dismal than other diagnoses that have achieved a great deal of notoriety.

What happens to the disappointment that is generated by the various unhappy experiences that have been reviewed? One possibility is that customers (or patients) will become angry at the institutions, firms, or individuals that supply disappointing goods or services, and will clamour for improvement and reform. Recent history indeed provides several illustrations of this outcome, for example, with respect to educational services in Western Europe.

But anger at the supplier is not the only conceivable reaction. In the case of psychotherapy, for example, the patient must complement the psychotherapist's services by some input of his own. Thus the reason for the meagre result of his visits to the therapist could well lie in the inadequacy of his own contributions. In this case, the disappointment the purchaser feels could well be turned against himself. This mutation of disappointment with the thing purchased and with the seller into *disappointment with oneself* could also occur in connection with other services that involve some collaboration on the part of the recipient—for example, in the case of educational and various professional services, as indeed with any purchase that requires discrimination on the part of the buyer.[20]

It is interesting to speculate whether paying for services directly or indirectly (through taxes) would influence the degree of disappointment that is likely to

18. See James O'Connor, *The Fiscal Crisis of the State* (New York: St. Martin's Press, 1975).
19. See Fred Hirsch, *Social Limits to Growth* (Cambridge, MA: Harvard University Press, 1976).
20. Some advertisements are meant to convince prospective buyers that they will become beautiful or lovable as a result of purchasing some product, but at the same time manage to intimate that, if the desired transformation does not take place, those buyers have only themselves to blame. See Arthur A. Leff, *Swindling and Selling* (New York: Free Press, 1975), pp. 157–175.

arise. On the one hand, direct payment should make the customers more critical and quality-conscious than if the service is supplied without an immediate cash quid pro quo. On the other hand, the very fact of payment often sets up the presumption that one *must* have received an adequate counter value, so that people will tend to blame themselves (and remain silent) if the outcome of the transaction is unsatisfactory. It is perhaps in part because of this strange psychological mechanism that publicly financed services are so much more frequently and strongly criticized than those rendered on a private basis.

It may be useful to review the argument that has been developed in this chapter. Consumption experiences, so it has been shown, yield dissatisfaction and disappointment along with satisfaction. It was first argued that the *truly* nondurable goods (such as food), which necessarily forfeit their physical shape through consumption, hold a privileged position as being peculiarly pleasure-intensive and disappointment-resistant. Then, the argument has focused on two specific categories of consumer purchases, durables and services, which have greatly gained in importance in recent decades, and whose disappointment potential is shown to be high. Quite different reasons apply in each case. With respect to durables, disappointment originates primarily in the fact that the balance between pleasure and comfort provided by these goods is tilted much more toward comfort (and against pleasure) than is the case for nondurables. With respect to services, disappointment arises out of the large number of cases—in comparison with goods purchases—in which there is a partial or total failure to achieve the purpose for which the services are acquired, particularly in the case of educational, medical, and other professional services. Moreover, if such services are suddenly offered—in response to social pressures—in much larger quantities than before, their average quality is likely to suffer and the intended beneficiaries of the expansion will be disgruntled rather than grateful.

It is a characteristic of all these findings that they apply with special force to periods when important progressive changes are taking place, with new groups gaining access to goods and services previously reserved for the few or not available at all. Disappointment arises typically because new types of purchases are undertaken with the kinds of expectations that consumers have come to associate with more traditional purchases.

15

From Private Concerns into the Public Arena

Collective Action and the Rebound Effect

The task of making the turn from private to public pursuits persuasive is not nearly completed. Thus far I have tried to show why the quest for happiness through the accumulation of consumer goods could yield various kinds of disappointments and discontents, making for a readiness to participate more actively than before in public or collective actions of various sorts.

The trouble with accepting this conclusion is that we have been schooled for some time now in the multiple obstacles standing in the way of collective in comparison to individual action. One of these obstacles consists in the possibility that the costs of participation in collective action would exceed the benefits the participating individual could expect to derive from it. This is, for example, said to be the case in elections where the benefit the individual can expect to derive from the marginal efficacy of his vote is small in relation to the cost (primarily in time spent) of voting. This is the so-called voters' paradox—the paradox or puzzle being why so many people bother to vote when they really shouldn't if they were behaving according to the canons of economic rationality. The paradox is not one of the more difficult to resolve, as has been shown by various writers—and as shall indeed be pointed out here also. But I shall first pass on to a more sophisticated argument on the obstacles to collective action. Drawing on the theory of public goods elaborated by a long line of economists from David Hume to Paul Samuelson, Mancur Olson came out in the mid-sixties with a forceful and influential formulation of this matter in his book *The Logic of Collective Action*[1] He showed how unlikely it is for individual citizens to participate in collective action even though the benefits of the prospective outcome of that action for the individual might *exceed* the costs of participation. The reason is the famous "free ride" phenomenon: since the outcome of the collective action (assuming it is successful) is a public good that can be enjoyed by all regardless of prior participation, the individual is tempted to withhold his contribution in the expectation that others will exert themselves on his behalf. As a result, everyone waits for the next person to jump first—and nothing happens. The only way in which collective action groups such as public interest associations, unions, political parties, etc. can build up and maintain a large membership is by distributing, along with the public goods, some "selective incentives" which are defined as privately appropriable benefits such as subscriptions to magazines, insurance services, and so on.

Now it must be recalled that Mancur Olson proclaimed the impossibility of collective action for large groups (just as Daniel Bell proclaimed the "end of ideology") at the precise moment when the Western world was about to be all but engulfed by an unprecedented wave of public movements, marches, protests, strikes, and ideologies. Olson's book was widely praised, as indeed it deserved to be for the lucidity of its analysis, but the inconsistency between the triumphant theory and the recalcitrant practice that followed in its wake has escaped attention. Here I shall venture a brief aside on the sociology of knowledge. It seems to me paradoxically conceivable that the success of Olson's book *owes* something to its having been contradicted by the subsequently evolving events. Once the latter had safely run their course, the many people who found them deeply upsetting could go back to *The Logic of Collective Action* and find in it good and reassuring reasons why those collective actions of the sixties should never have happened in the first place, were perhaps less real than they seemed, and would be most unlikely ever to recur. Thus the book did not suffer from being contradicted by

1. Harvard University Press, 1965. Some of the subsequent critique of Olson has been stimulated by Brian Barry's review article of my *Exit, Voice, and Loyalty (British Journal of Political Science* 4 [February 1974], 79–107) where he criticized me for not having adequately appreciated the force of Olson's argument in relation to my own, particularly with regard to the prospects for "voice," that is, for private citizens engaging in public action.

subsequent events; rather, it gained by actively contradicting them and became a great success among those who found these events intolerable and totally aberrant. In this manner, false prophecy can be the foundation stone of fame and reputation in the social sciences!

In contrast to *The Logic of Collective Action,* but aware of its strictures, I am trying to make sense of the periodic outbreaks of mass participation in public affairs and of collective action in general. In this enterprise the vantage point I have reached affords a first argument. A general criticism that can be levelled against the Olson analysis—and against much economic decision theory in general—is that its subjects, while efficient and often even ingenious and devious, are *without a history.* In fact, it is easy to think of situations in which the rule "bygones are bygones" is not likely to be, nor should be, observed. Take first the case where efforts and resources have been poured into policy A rather than B, and where the result, while none too promising, is not yet clearly apparent at the time when a new decision has to be made on whether to spend additional funds on A. Here the decision is likely to be biased in favor of continuing with A, so that, quite possibly, good money will be thrown after bad. Up to a point, this will be done for some quite valid reasons; in certain situations it can be important to maintain self-esteem and to avoid giving the appearance of not being steadfast, especially when outside observers, such as potential adversaries, friends, and allies, are watching.[2] By the same token, once course A has unequivocally proven disastrous, the opposite bias (favouring B over A) is likely to arise, once again for good reasons and in defiance of the economic theorem according to which "sunk costs" should be disregarded in making choices. This is why we so often overreact to the perceived lessons of history.

Returning to the argument here developed, take a group of people who have experienced a great deal of disappointment in their search for happiness through private consumption: they are infinitely more "ripe" for collective action than a group that is just setting out on that search. It is often possible to explain the choice of an amorous partner that is puzzling to outsiders on the grounds that one (or both) of the persons concerned was "on the rebound" from another involvement that ended unhappily. This sort of "rebound effect" can illuminate many of our social choices. It makes for an exaggeration of the benefits and an underestimate of the costs of the action that provides a counterpoint to the action

2. See Charles Wolf, Jr., "The Present Value of the Past," *Journal of Political Economy* 78 (July-August 1970), 783–792.

that has been taken previously and has turned sour. Another way of expressing the matter in the economist's language is to say that once a transaction that one has entered into has turned out badly, a transaction with opposite characteristics may have *negative transaction costs* (alternatively, one might speak of transaction benefits). The transaction will in effect be subsidized—by none other than the transactor himself.[3]

I apologize for using so many words in making plausible something that must seem obvious common sense to the general reader. But as a result of a long process of refinement, economic analysis has moved so far away from common sense that to re-establish contact between economics and common sense while still using the concepts of economics is sometimes no simple matter.

Actually the only area in which the "rebound effect" has been given its due in economic writings is in the analysis of migration. Here it was obviously impossible for any realistic description of the process to apply the famous "bygones-are-bygones" rule and to model the decision of the migrant solely on the basis of a cost-benefit calculation relating to the future without taking past experience into account. Hence, migration has long been analysed in terms of so-called push and pull factors, with the push factor corresponding roughly to what I have here called rebound effect. It is significant that this account of the migration decision dates from a time when benefit-cost analysis and decision theory were in their infancy and could therefore not choke off a realistic, if unrigourous, treatment of the subject matter.

I submit that a good portion of the so-called puzzle of collective action and participation in public affairs disappears when the rebound effect is taken into account. But by itself this effect only reduces the subjective costs and increases the benefits of any contemplated collective action and therefore does not do away with the logic of the free ride. Also, it may be argued that it is unsatisfactory to have the probability of the turn to public action rest on what are essentially

3. Benefit-cost analysis could of course be reformulated so as to include the rebound effect. The benefit of a certain action B coming after A would then include not only the direct positive consequence of B but also the satisfaction accruing from being no longer involved in action A. But this is of course no longer what is commonly understood by benefit-cost analysis, which would then come to be defined tautologically as a mode of decision-making covering every conceivable human action. For a similar critique of attempts to "broaden" the concept of maximization so as to include any human behaviour whatsoever, see Harvey Leibenstein, "'The Missing Link'—Micro-Micro Theory," *Journal of Economic Literature* 17 (June 1979), 493–496.

systematic estimating biases and errors on the part of the decision makers. I do not really agree with this objection, for, as already stated, mistake-making is one of the most characteristic of human actions, so that a good portion of the social world becomes unintelligible once it is assumed away.

Be that as it may, the rebound effect is only a partial way of accounting for the turn to public action. There remains the argument of the free ride, that is, the contention that a rational individual, motivated by self-interest, will ordinarily stand on the sidelines and expect others to "do the dirty work" as long as the result of their exertions can be enjoyed by him whether or not he has collaborated in bringing it about. The argument about the rebound effect already casts some doubt on this line of reasoning, for it implies that the satisfaction which disappointed consumers are seeking in turning toward public action derives not just from the expected results of such action. It is precisely this matter that needs to be dealt with at greater length.

Why Free Rides Are Spurned

I briefly return now to Scitovsky's *Joyless Economy* from which I have learned a great deal but which has stimulated me also—as frequently happens—through a number of "intimate disagreements" I have with its argument. In the second part of his book, Scitovsky comments on a number of novelty-intensive and stimulus-producing activities which could provide the pleasures no longer yielded by an environment saturated with identical mass-consumption goods. He comes up with cut flowers for the home, handcrafted goods, and cultural activities such as theater, concert going, and the visiting of cafes and bars. With the exception of the last activity, he directs attention to certain kinds of purchases that are based on the stimulation of pleasure through ever new types of private consumption, including the consumption of culture in its infinite varieties. While his critique of American consumption patterns is often acute, the kind of life-style he recommends for maximum satisfaction has a strangely breathless quality: it consists in the relentless search for ever new pleasures and reminds one of the early stage of Faust's compulsive and disastrous quest which Goethe's hero himself characterizes—and deprecates—by exclaiming:

> Thus I stagger from desire to rapture,
> And in rapture I die of new desire.
> (So tauml' ich von Begierde zu Genuss,
> und im Genuss verschmacht' ich nach Begierde.)

With their urge to seek out novel "trinkets and baubles" Scitovsky's ideal consumers similarly resemble Don Juan with his never-ending search for sensual-sexual adventures, excitements, and delights. Or, just as Italians under Mussolini were condemned, according to a contemporary quip, to permanent enthusiasm, so are these consumers condemned to permanent pleasure-seeking.

Scitovsky is actually aware that this sort of intense pleasure-seeking is not necessarily everybody's cup of tea, for he speaks at one point admiringly of "people who have one overwhelming passion in life—their work or their hobby—to which they subordinate all else" (p. 75). But he seems to see such people as a tiny elite group and their solution as one that is not available to the great majority. At no point in the book does he deal explicitly with an alternative that is open to the consumer-citizen quite apart from the choice between self-centred comfort and self-centred pleasure: participation in the public life by joining a movement, participating in a community, advocating a cause, etc.

It is both strange and easy to understand why this way out of the frustrations of the purely private and self-centred life should not have been dealt with in Scitovsky's otherwise comprehensive register of consumer choices: strange because the problem of choosing between the private and the public life has been a fundamental theme in Western thought on human conduct from Aristotle and Cicero via Hobbes, Rousseau, Benjamin Constant, and Marx to Hannah Arendt; easy to understand, on the other hand, because a very considerable portion of people's normal activities under modern conditions, during very long periods of their lives, is devoted to their private affairs—so that it *seems* safe to disregard public action and participation as a *real, ever present* potential alternative to private-centred action. The matter is perhaps best illustrated by a joke that was rather current during the "private" fifties. A married woman is asked who makes the decisions in the family and she answers, "My husband, of course, makes the important decisions and I make the unimportant decisions." "So, give me some examples of what's important and what's not." "Well, I decide where we go on our next vacation, whether the children should go to private or public school, whether we should buy a new car or a new house, etc." "And what then are the important decisions that your husband makes?" "Well, he decides what should be done about desegregation in the South, how to handle the conflict in the Middle East, whether we should recognize Red China, etc." In line with the "private" temper of the times, this story ridicules pompous and futile concern with public affairs in contrast to "cultivating one's garden"—but then the sixties came along and demonstrated, with their civil rights marches and the mass protest against the Vietnam war, that, even for a suburban family, the truly important decisions might very well turn out suddenly to be those dealing with public affairs. The joke could simply no longer be told; it had become unintelligible.

Actually, upon looking more closely at Scitovsky's examples of activities particularly rich in "stimulus" and "novelty" rather than comfort, it is possible to discern some elements of public concern and interest. In discussing important differences between patterns of consumption and leisure time uses in various countries, he shows very effectively that the French and English spend considerably more time than North Americans in cafés, pubs, or similar public places. Scitovsky attributes this difference to the greater desire of Europeans for "stimulus" and "novelty." But a different interpretation is possible: in congregating in these public places, the French and English escape from their purely private activities, discuss all kinds of matters of public concern, from current sports and scandals to rising prices and the forthcoming elections, and thereby engage in action that has some bearing on the public interest. In flocking to their cafes and pubs, the French and the English are therefore perhaps not so much manifesting a preference for pleasure over comfort as one for public over private activities. I believe that this is indeed so. But for this belief to carry conviction, the nature of public action and participation, in comparison to private-regarding activity, must be explored in some detail.

One of the major attractions of public action is the exact opposite of the most fundamental characteristic of private pleasures under modern conditions: while the pursuit of the latter through the production of income (work) is clearly marked off from the eventual enjoyment of these pleasures, there is no such clear distinction at all between the pursuit of the public happiness and the attainment of it. As I have put the matter on a previous occasion,[4] striving for the public happiness (in some concrete respect) and attaining it cannot be neatly separated. Indeed, the very act of going after the public happiness is often the *next best thing* to actually *having* that happiness (and sometimes not even the next best thing, but much the best thing of the whole process, because of the various disappointments over the results of public-oriented action—but more about that later).

Public-oriented action belongs, in this as in other respects, to a group of human activities that includes the search for community, beauty, knowledge, and salvation. All these activities "carry their own reward," as goes the somewhat trite

4. *Essays in Trespassing*, p. 216.

phrase, but what really goes on here still needs to be better understood. To regain a fresh perspective on the matter it is well, first of all, to cite an observation of Pascal on the nature of the search for God:

> The hope Christians have to possess an infinite good is mixed with actual enjoyment ... for they are not like those who would hope for a kingdom of which they have nothing, being subjects; rather, they hope for holiness, for freedom from injustice, and they partake of it. (*Pensées,* 540, Brunschvicg edition.)

Here the peculiar feature of these activities, that is, the fusion of—or confusion between—striving and attaining, is particularly well expressed.

Once this essential characteristic of participation in collective action for the public good is understood, the severe limitations of the "economic" view about such participation, and about the obstacles to it, come immediately into view. The implication of the confusion between striving and attaining is that the neat distinction between costs and benefits of action in the public interest vanishes, since striving, which should be entered on the cost side, turns out to be part of the benefit.[5]

This is a hard pill to swallow for our imperious bottom-line mentality. For what I am saying is that, at some stage in our cycle, the benefit of collective action for an individual is not the difference between the hoped-for result and the effort furnished by him or her, but the *sum* of these two magnitudes! And a

5. At the outset of his fine study "Two Concepts of Democracy: James and John Stuart Mill," Alan Ryan ventures the same thought by asking: "... [with respect to] participation, can we not simply add into our account such previously unthought of benefits as increased self-awareness, perhaps so many of them as to make it no longer a net expense but a net benefit, independently, that is, of its instrumental efficacy?" Sec Martin Fleisher, ed, *Machiavelli and the Nature of Political Thought* (New York: Atheneum, 1972), p. 80.
   A different formulation of the same point is made by James E. Krier and Edmund Ursin in *Pollution and Policy* (Berkeley and Los Angeles: University of California Press, 1977), 270–271. Showing how crises stimulate citizens' protest and thereby lead to policy-making, they note that in these crises citizens view participation no longer merely as an effort, costly in time and money, that is required for the *production* of a desired policy, but rather regard action in the public interest as part of their *consumption,* as directly pleasurable. Similarly, Allen Buchanan in "Revolutionary Motivation and Rationality" in *Philosophy and Public Affairs* 9 (Fail 1979), 71–73, speaks briefly of "in-process benefits" as a possible solution to the public goods problem.

further surprising consequence follows immediately: since the output and objective of collective action are ordinarily a public good available to all, the only way in which an individual can raise the benefit accruing to him from the collective action is by stepping up *his own input,* his effort on behalf of the public policy he espouses. Far from shirking and attempting to get a free ride, a truly maximizing individual will attempt to be as activist as he can manage, within the limits set by his other essential activities and objectives. It is in effect the need to restrain this activism that is at the source of some of the specific disappointments over action in the public interest, as will be shown ....

From the point of view adopted here, individuals who have developed a taste for a public good that has yet to be "produced" and who attempt to get a "free ride" by letting others exert themselves on their behalf do not just cheat the community as is implied in the "free ride" metaphor; *they cheat themselves first of all.*

The matter was neatly expressed by Golda Meir in an interview she gave in 1977. She said that life in Israel was so difficult when she first immigrated in 1921 that "people ask me why I came. And I say because I'm selfish ... when I heard what was being done here I decided that they're not going to do it by themselves. I won't have a share in it? No, I must be a part of it. Just pure selfishness, I suppose ...."[6]

My contention that free rides will be spurned in precisely this manner depends crucially on the claim that the confusion between striving and attaining is characteristic, at one stage, of public-regarding activity. That claim can perhaps become more persuasive if it is put into a somewhat different language. For this purpose, it is useful to return to the distinction between comfort and pleasure made in the preceding chapter. Comfort is defined as the absence of discomfort—a prime example is the feeling of satiation after the meal. Pleasure is experienced in the process of traveling from discomfort to comfort, that is, during the meal. While language is not totally consistent with this terminology—we speak of eating pleasure, but also of being "pleasantly full"—there is no doubt that the total utility of a meal has these two components, with the pleasure of eating being quite distinct from the comfort of satiation. But then there is yet another stage to be considered. Before the meal, time and effort must be expended on earning the income needed to pay for it: this is the cost to the individual of the ensuing dual benefits of pleasure and comfort. In private consumption activities, the state

6. Marilyn Berger, "Golda Meir Speaks Her Mind," *New York Magazine,* December 12, 1977, p. 12.

of satiation or comfort is thus preceded by a time stretch that is divided into a cost segment (during which income is earned to acquire a good) and a subsequent pleasure segment (during which the good is being gradually appropriated, experienced, and consumed).

What I called the confusion between striving and attaining with respect to public-regarding activities becomes easier to understand with this temporal representation of private consumption. In effect, I affirmed that the neat dividing point between the cost segment and the pleasure segment of presatiation time tends to disappear in the case of public-regarding activities. *Here the pleasure segment penetrates the cost segment and suffuses it with its own experience.* It is easy to visualize such a process which in fact is by no means rigidly confined to public-regarding activities. Even in the process of labouring away at our daily job we do on occasion "savor in advance" certain recurrent private delights that are going to be our reward once the monthly paycheck comes in. But the melting of the cost into the pleasure segment is far more typical of activities that are not concerned with routine private consumption even though they are not necessarily public-regarding. The best illustration is perhaps the phenomenon of *pilgrimage,* which traditionally consists of a lengthy journey to a remote holy site at which prayers are said and other devotional acts performed. "The point of it all is to get out, go forth, to a far holy place approved by all."[7] Obviously, it would make no sense to categorize the travel as the cost of the pilgrimage, and the sojourn and prayers at the holy site as benefit. The discomforts suffered and perils confronted during the trip were part and parcel of the total "liminal" experience sought by the pilgrim, and distance from the site often acted as a stimulant to the decision to go forth rather than as a brake.[8] Close parallels to this aspect of the medieval pilgrimage can be found today, mostly in nonreligious activities. For example, according to a survey of soccer fans in Brazil, attendance of Rio fans at the game is not related to the distance of the fans' homes to the city stadium, again presumably because a true fan considers traveling to the game as part of the fun and of his obligation to the team he is rooting for.[9]

It is not so easy to understand why activities usually considered as costs should become benefits in a different context. One way of approaching this problem is

7. Victor Turner and Edith Turner, *Image and Pilgrimage in Christian Culture* (New York: Columbia University Press, 1978), p. 7.
8. Turner and Turner, pp. 7–11.
9. Janet Lever, *Soccer Madness: Sport's Contribution to Social Integration in Brazil* (University of Chicago Press, 1982).

to distinguish between routine and non-routine undertakings. With regard to routine tasks, there is no doubt in the individual's mind that labour will yield the anticipated outcome—a given job, or an hour of labour, will either yield directly the well-known, sought-after result or entitle the worker to a certain sum of money which can be used for the purchase of a meal or of other desired goods. Under these conditions, the separation of the whole process into means and ends, or costs and benefits, occurs almost spontaneously. In the case of non-routine activities, such as exertion for a public policy, on the other hand, there is always much uncertainty as to whether the effort will be crowned with success. Strangely, such uncertainty produces not only anxiety. Undertakings that have no precedent and whose successful outcome is not assured are felt as peculiarly noble: effort now becomes "striving," and *as though in compensation for the uncertainty* it is this striving that is endowed with the feeling of already having a pleasurable experience.

But the fusion of striving and attaining that is so characteristic of public action when it is first undertaken can also be explained by two rather less speculative considerations. In the first place, public action is often the result of a radical cognitive change, akin to a revelation. Large numbers of people grow up with the feeling that the existing social and political order is not subject to change or that, in any event, they are powerless to bring such change about. The sudden realization (or illusion) that I can act to change society for the better and, moreover, that I can join other like-minded people to this end is in such conditions pleasurable, in fact intoxicating, in itself. To savour that pleasure, society does not have to be actually changed right away: it is quite enough to act in a variety of ways *as though* it were possible to promote change.[10] Obviously, if no change is achieved, disappointment will set in. But that reaction belongs to a later phase of the story.

Secondly, there is the opposite pleasurable experience: not that *I* can change society, but that my work and activities in the public arena change and develop *me,* regardless of any real changes in the state of the world that I might achieve. As Ryan shows in his already cited study of James and John Stuart Mill, this was the younger Mill's reason for considering participation in public affairs as a good in itself, rather than as a mere means to an end—that was his father's strictly utilitarian view. Participation would "guard against passivity, inertia, timidity and

10. See Aristide R. Zolberg, "Moments of Madness," *Politics and Society* (Winter 1972), 183–207. Zolberg defines such moments as those in which people suddenly feel that "all is possible," and draws for illustrations on various crisis points in the history of modern France from 1848 to 1968.

intellectual stagnation." The open, rather than secret, vote oddly favoured by John Stuart Mill was advocated by him as one element in an intensive participation that

> involves exposing yourself to new influences, competitive views of the world, new demands on your capacities. It thus seems quite unlike shopping for policies in your interest; it is a—on the face of it gruelling—piece of social and political education.[11]

The pleasures of political participation come rather hard here, in typically Victorian fashion. But to the extent that political activity does lead to self-development—and the twentieth-century observer must register considerable doubt about the generality of this experience—it will, in the end, be enjoyable.

The upshot of this discussion is that there is much fulfilment associated with the citizen's exertions for the public happiness. These exertions are in effect often compared with the pleasurable experiences of eating and drinking: we speak of citizens "hungering" or "thirsting" for justice,[12] and Tocqueville wrote about the "craving for liberty" that a "few of us" have durably developed.[13] It is in the very struggle for justice and liberty that the thirst is quenched and the craving is gratified. Who, then, would want to miss all that active pleasure and get a free ride to what is at best the comfortable and usually somewhat disappointing, outcome of these processes? To elect a free ride under the circumstances would be equivalent to declining a delicious meal and to swallow instead a satiation-producing pill that is not even particularly effective!

11. Ryan, "Two Concepts of Democracy," pp. 104–106.
12. Pascal speaks of the "hunger for justice" in *Pensées,* 264 (Brunschvicg edition).
13. The full sentence reads: "What's to be done about it? There just are a few of us stubborn old people who have developed a craving for human liberty … and who absolutely cannot give it up." Letter to Gobineau of February 19, 1854, *Oeuvres complètes* (Paris: Gallimard, 1959), Vol. 9, p. 212.

16

Against Parsimony: Three Easy Ways of Complicating Some Categories of Economic Discourse

Economics as a science of human behaviour has been grounded in a remarkably parsimonious postulate: that of the self-interested, isolated individual who chooses freely and rationally among alternative courses of action after computing their prospective costs and benefits. In recent decades, a group of economists has shown considerable industry and ingenuity in applying this way of interpreting the social world to a series of ostensibly noneconomic phenomena, from crime to the family, and from collective action to democracy. The "economic" or "rational-actor" approach has yielded some important insights, but its onward sweep has also revealed some of its intrinsic weaknesses. As a result, it has become possible to mount a critique which, ironically, can be carried all the way back to the heartland of the would-be conquering discipline. That the economic approach presents us with too simpleminded an account of even such fundamental economic processes as consumption and production is my basic thesis here.

I am not alone in this view. Schelling has noted that "the human mind is something of an embarrassment to certain disciplines, notably economics … that have found the model of the rational consumer to be powerfully productive." And in a well-known article, significantly entitled "Rational Fools: A Critique of the Behavioral Foundations of Economic Theory," Sen has asserted not long ago that "traditional [economic] theory has *too little* structure."[1] Noting that individual preferences and actual choice behaviour are far from being always identical, he introduced novel concepts, such as commitment and second-order preferences. Like any virtue, so he seemed to say, parsimony in theory construction can be overdone, and something is sometimes to be gained by making things more complicated. I have increasingly come to feel this way. Some years ago, I suggested that criticism from customers, or "voice," should be recognized as a force keeping management of firms and organizations on their toes, along with competition or "exit," and it took a book to cope with the resulting complications. Here I deal with various other realms of economic inquiry that stand similarly in need of being rendered more complex. In concluding, I examine whether the various complications have some element in common: that would in turn simplify and unify matters.

Two Kinds of Preference Changes

A fruitful distinction has been made, by Sen and others, between first-order and second-order preferences, or between preferences and meta-preferences, respectively. I shall use the latter terminology here. Economics has traditionally dealt only with (first-order) preferences, that is, those that are revealed by agents as they buy goods and services. The complex psychological and cultural processes that lie behind the actually observed market choices have generally been considered the business of psychologists, sociologists, and anthropologists.

There were some good reasons for this self-denying ordinance. Nevertheless, one aspect in the formation of choice and preference must be of concern to the economist, to the extent that he claims an interest in understanding processes of economic change. That aspect has nothing to do with the cultural conditioning of tastes and choice behaviour, at least at a first level of inquiry; its starting point is rather a very general observation on human nature (and should therefore be congenial to economics with its eighteenth-century moorings): men and women have the ability to step back from their "revealed" wants, volitions, and preferences, to ask themselves whether they really want these wants and prefer these preferences

1. See Schelling, Thomas C., *Choice and Consequence* (Cambridge, MA: Harvard University Press, 1984), p. 342, and Sen, Amartya K. "Rational Fools: A Critique of the Behavioral Foundations of Economic Theory", *Philosophy and Public Affairs* (1977), 6, p. 335.

and, consequently, to form metapreferences that may differ from their preferences. Unsurprisingly, it was a philosopher who first put matters this way. Harry Frankfurt argued that this ability to step back is unique in humans, but is not present in all of them. Those who lack this ability he called "wantons": they are entirely, unreflectively, in the grip of their whims and passions. (The terminology is quite apt as it conforms to common usage: wanton murder is precisely murder "for no good reason," that is, murder that has not been preceded by the formation of any metapreference for murder.)

It is easy to see that there is a close link between preference change and the concept of metapreferences; for, as I have pointed out before, certainty about the existence of metapreferences can only be gained through changes in actual choice behaviour. If preferences and metapreferences always coincide, so that the agent is permanently at peace with himself no matter what choices he makes, then the metapreferences hardly lead an independent existence and are mere shadows of the preferences. If, on the other hand, the two kinds of preference are permanently at odds, so that the agent always acts against his better judgment, then again, the metapreference cannot only be dismissed as wholly ineffective, but doubts will arise whether it is really there at all. In such cases, the situation is best characterized as a "tie-in purchase": along with the preferred commodity the consumer insists on acquiring unhappiness, regret, and guilt over having preferred it.

The notion of metapreference does not tell us much about the way actual change in choice behaviour comes about. The battle to impose the metapreference is fought out within the self and is marked by all kinds of advances and reverses as well as by ruses and strategic devices. I am not concerned here with this topic, which Schelling has made his own, only with pointing out that an occasional success in changing choice behaviour is essential for validating the concept of metapreferences.

Conversely, this concept illuminates the varied nature of preference change, for it is now possible to distinguish between two kinds of preference changes. One is the reflective and tortuous kind, preceded as it is by the formation of a metapreference at odds with the observed and hitherto practiced preference. But preference changes also take place without any elaborate antecedent development of metapreferences. Following Frankfurt's terminology, the unreflective changes in preferences might be called wanton. These are the preference changes economists have primarily focused on: impulsive, uncomplicated, haphazard, publicity-induced, and generally minor (apples vs. pears) changes in tastes. In contrast, the nonwanton change of preference is not really a change in tastes at all. A taste is almost defined as a preference about which you do not argue—*de gustibus non est disputandum*. A taste about which you argue, with others *or yourself*, ceases ipso facto being a taste—it turns into a *value*. When a change in preferences has been preceded by the formation of a metapreference, much argument has obviously gone on within the divided self; it typically represents a change in values rather than a change in tastes.

Given the economists' concentration on, and consequent bias for, wanton preference changes, changes of the reflective kind have tended to be downgraded to the wanton kind by assimilating them to changes in tastes: thus Becker ascribed patterns of discriminatory hiring to a "taste for discrimination," and Johnson similarly analysed increases in protectionism as reflecting an enhanced "taste for nationalism." Such interpretations strike me as objectionable on two counts: first, they impede a serious intellectual effort to understand what are strongly held values and difficult to achieve changes in values rather than tastes and changes in tastes; second, the illusion is fostered that raising the cost of discrimination (or nationalism) is the simple and sovereign policy instrument for getting people to indulge less in those odd "tastes."

There is a more general point here. Economists often propose to deal with unethical or antisocial behaviour by raising the cost of that behaviour rather than by proclaiming standards and imposing prohibitions and sanctions. The reason is probably that they think of citizens as consumers with unchanging or arbitrarily changing tastes in matters of civic as well as commodity-oriented behaviour. This view tends to neglect the possibility that people are capable of changing their values. A principal purpose of publicly proclaimed laws and regulations is to stigmatize antisocial behaviour and thereby to influence citizens' values and behaviour codes. This educational, value-moulding function of the law is as important as its deterrent and repressive functions.[2] Accordingly, as Kelman has shown, the resistance of legislators to the economists' proposals to deal with pollution exclusively through effluent charges and similar devices becomes intelligible and, up to a point, defensible.[3] The propensity to pollute of industrialists and corporations is not necessarily like a fixed demand schedule, so that all one can do is to make them pay their way for the pollution they are presumed to be bent on

2. "Lawgivers make the citizen good by inculcating [good] habits in them, and this is the aim of every lawgiver; if he does not succeed in doing that, his legislation is a failure. It is in this that a good constitution differs from a bad one." Aristotle. *Nicomachean Ethics*, translated by Martin Ostwald (Indianapolis: Bobbs-Merrill. 1962), 1103b.
3. See Kelman, Steven, *What Price Incentives? Economists and the Environment* (Boston, MA: Auburn House, 1981), pp. 44–53.

causing: that propensity is likely to be affected (the demand curve could shift) as a result of a general change in the civic climate that is signalled—in part—by the proclamation of laws and regulations against pollution.

In the light of the distinction between wanton and nonwanton preference changes, or between changes in tastes and changes in values, it also becomes possible to understand—and to criticize—the recent attempt of Becker and Stigler to do without the notion of preference changes for the purpose of explaining changes in behaviour. Equating preference changes to changes in what they themselves call "inscrutable, often capricious tastes," they find, quite rightly, any changes in those kinds of tastes (our wanton changes) of little analytical interest.[4] But in their subsequent determination to explain all behaviour change through price and income differences, they neglect one important source of such change: autonomous, reflective change in values. For example, in their analysis of beneficial and harmful addiction they take the elasticity of the individual's demand curve for music or heroin as given and, it would seem, immutable. May I urge that changes in values do occur from time to time in the lives of individuals, within generations, and from one generation to another, and that those changes and their effects on behaviour are worth exploring—that, in brief, *de valoribus est disputandum?*

Two Kinds of Activities

From consumption I now turn to production and to human activities such as work and effort involved in achieving production goals. Much of economic activity is directed to the production of (private) goods and services that are then sold in the market. From the point of view of the firm, the activity carries with it a neat distinction between process and outcome, inputs and outputs, or costs and revenue. From the point of view of the individual participant in the process, a seemingly similar distinction can be drawn between work and pay or between effort and reward. Yet there is a well-known difference between the firm and the individual: for the firm any outlay is unambiguously to be entered on the negative side of the accounts whereas work can be more or less irksome or pleasant—even the same work can be felt as more pleasant by the same person from one day to the next. This problem, in particular its positive and normative consequences for income differentials, has attracted the attention of a long line of economists starting

4. See Becker, Gary S., and Stigler, George. "De Gustibus Non Est Disputandum", *American Economic Review*, 67 (1977), p. 76.

with Adam Smith. Most recently Winston has drawn a distinction between "process utility" and "goal utility," making it clear that the means to the end of productive effort need not be entered on the negative side in a calculus of satisfaction.[5] At the same time, this distinction keeps intact the basic instrumental conception of work, the means-end dichotomy on which our understanding of the work and production process has been essentially—and, up to a point, so usefully—based.

But there is a need to go further if the complexity and full range of human activities, productive and otherwise, are to be appreciated. Once again, more structure would be helpful. The possible existence of wholly *non-instrumental* activities is suggested by everyday language, which speaks of activities that are undertaken "for their own sake" and that "carry their own reward." These are somewhat trite, unconvincing phrases: after all, any sustained activity, with the possible exception of pure play, is undertaken with some idea about an intended outcome. A person who claims to be working exclusively for the sake of the rewards yielded by the exertion itself is usually suspect of hypocrisy: one feels he is really after the money, the advancement, or—at the least—the glory, and thus is an instrumentalist after all.

Some progress can be made with the matter by looking at the varying predictability of the intended outcome of different productive activities. Certain activities, typically of a routine character, have perfectly predictable outcomes. With regard to such tasks, there is no doubt in the individual's mind that effort will yield the anticipated outcome—an hour of labour will yield the well-known, fully visualized result as well as entitle the worker, if he has been contracted for the job, to a wage that can be used for the purchase of desired (and usually also well-known) goods. Under these conditions, the separation of the process into means and ends, or into costs and benefits, occurs almost spontaneously and work appears to assume a wholly instrumental character.

But there are many kinds of activities, from that of a research scientist to that of a composer or an advocate of some public policy, whose intended outcome cannot be relied upon to materialize with certainty. Among these activities there are some—applied laboratory research may be an example—whose outcome cannot be predicted for any single day or month; nevertheless, success in achieving the intended result steadily gains in likelihood as the time of work is extended. In this case, the uncertainty is probabilistic, and one can speak of a certainty

5. See Winston, Gordon C., *The Timing of Economic Activities* (Cambridge: Cambridge University Press, 1982), pp. 193–197.

equivalent with regard to the output of the activity in any given period so that, once again, the separation of the process into means and ends is experienced, and work of this sort largely retains its instrumental cast. The combination of uncertainty about the result of work for a short stretch of time with near certainty of achievement over a longer period confers to these kinds of non-routine activities an especially attractive, "stimulating," "exciting" quality that tends to be absent both from wholly routine activities whose outcome never fails to materialize no matter how short the work period, and from very different kinds of non-routine activities, to be discussed presently.

From their earliest origins, men and women appear to have allocated time to undertakings whose success is simply unpredictable: the pursuit of truth, beauty, justice, liberty, community, friendship, love, salvation, and so on. As a rule, these pursuits are, of course, carried on through a variety of exertions for apparently limited and specific objectives (writing a book, participating in a political campaign, etc.). Nevertheless, an important component of the activities thus undertaken is best described not as labour or work, but as *striving*—a term that precisely intimates the lack of a reliable relation between effort and result. A means-end or cost-benefit calculus is impossible under the circumstances.

These activities have sometimes been referred to, in contrast to the instrumental ones, as "affective" or "expressive."[6] But labelling them does not contribute a great deal to understanding them, for the question is really why such activities should be taken up at all. It is important to note that by no means are these activities always pleasant in themselves; in fact, some of them are sure to be quite strenuous or highly dangerous. Do we have here, then, another paradox or puzzle, one that relates not just to voting (why do rational people bother to vote?) but to a much wider and most vital group of activities? I suppose we do—from the point of view of instrumental reason, non-instrumental action is bound to be something of a mystery. But I have proposed an at least semirational explanation: these non-instrumental activities whose outcome is so uncertain are strangely characterized by a certain fusion of (and confusion between) striving and attaining.

According to conventional economic thinking, utility accrues to an individual primarily upon reaching the goal of consumption, that is, in the process of actually consuming a good or enjoying its use. But given our lively imagination, things are really rather more complicated. When we become sure that some

6. See Smelser, Neil J. "Vicissitudes of Work and Love in Anglo-American Society." In *Themes of Work and Love in Adulthood*, edited by Neil J. Smelser and Erik H. Erikson (Cambridge, MA: Harvard University Press, 1980), and Parsons (cited by Smelser).

desired good is actually going to be ours or that some desired event is definitely going to happen—be it a good meal, a meeting with the beloved, or the awarding of an honour—we experience the well-known pleasure of *savouring* that future event in advance (the term *savouring* was suggested to me by George Loewenstein). Moreover, this premature hauling in of utility is not limited to situations where the future event is near and certain, or is believed to be so. When the goal is distant and its attainment quite problematic, something very much like savouring can occur, provided a determined personal quest is undertaken. He who strives after truth (or beauty) frequently experiences the conviction, fleeting though it may be, that he has found (or achieved) it. He who participates in a movement for liberty or justice frequently has the experience of already bringing these ideals within reach. In Pascal's formation:

> The hope Christians have to possess an infinite good is mixed with actual enjoyment … for they are not like those people who would hope for a kingdom of which they, as subjects, have nothing; rather, they hope for holiness, and for freedom from injustice, and they partake of both.[7]

This savouring, this fusion of striving and attaining, is a fact of experience that goes far to account for the existence and importance of non-instrumental activities. As though in compensation for the uncertainty about the outcome, and for the strenuousness or dangerousness of the activity, the striving effort is coloured by the goal and in this fashion makes for an experience that is very different from merely agreeable, pleasurable, or even stimulating: in spite of its frequently painful character it has a well-known, intoxicating quality.

The foregoing interpretation of non-instrumental action is complemented by an alternative view which has been proposed by the sociologist Pizzorno. For him, participation in politics is often engaged in because it enhances one's feeling of belonging to a group. I would add that non-instrumental action in general makes one feel more human. Such action can then be considered, in economic terms, as an *investment in individual and group identity*. In lieu of Pascal, those who advocate this alternative way of explaining non-instrumental action might invoke Jean-Paul Sartre as their patron saint, given the following lines from Sartre's posthumously published wartime diary:

7. See Pascal, Blaise, *Pensées* (Brunschvicg edition), 540.

> Throughout his enterprises [man] aims not at self-preservation, as has often been said, or at self-aggrandizement; rather, he seeks to *found* himself. And at the end of every one of these enterprises, he finds that he is back where he started: purposeless, through and through. Hence those well-known disappointments subsequent to effort, to triumph, to love.[8]

In other words, the feeling of having achieved belongingness and personhood is likely to be just as evanescent as the fusion of striving and attaining which I stressed earlier. The two views are related attempts at achieving an uncommonly difficult insight: to think instrumentally about the non-instrumental.

But why should economics be concerned with all this? Is it not enough for this discipline to attempt an adequate account of man's instrumental activities—a vast area indeed—while leaving the other, somewhat murky regions alone? Up to a point such a limitation makes sense. But as economics grows more ambitious, it becomes of increasing importance to appreciate that the means-end, cost-benefit model is far from covering all aspects of human activity and experience.

Take the analysis of political action, an area in which economists have become interested as a natural extension of their work on public goods. Here the neglect of the non-instrumental mode of action was responsible for the inability of the economic approach to understand why people bother to vote and why they engage from time to time in collective action. Once the non-instrumental mode is paid some attention, it becomes possible to account for these otherwise puzzling phenomena. It is the fusion of striving and attaining, as well as the urge to invest in individual or group identity, that leads to a conclusion exactly opposite to the "free ride" argument with respect to collective action: As I wrote in *Shifting Involvements*, "since the output and objective of collective action are … a public good available to all, the only way an individual can raise the benefit accruing to him from the collective action is by stepping up *his own input*, his effort on behalf of the public policy he espouses. Far from shirking and attempting to get a free ride, a truly maximizing individual will attempt to be as activist as he can manage."

The preceding argument does not imply, of course, that citizens will never adopt the instrumental mode of action with respect to action in the public interest. On the contrary, quite a few may well move from one mode to the other, and

8. See Sartre, Jean-Paul, *Les Carnets de la drôle de guerre* (Paris: Gallimard, 1983), p. 141; my emphasis.

such oscillations could help explain the observed instability both of individual commitment and of many social movements.

A better understanding of collective action is by no means the only benefit that stands to flow from a more open attitude toward the possibility of non-instrumental action. As I have argued earlier, a strong affinity exists between instrumental and routine activities on the one hand, and between non-instrumental and non-routine activities on the other. But just as I noted the existence of non-routine activities that are predominantly instrumental (in the case of an applied research laboratory), so can routine work have more or less of a non-instrumental component, as Veblen stressed in *The Instinct of Workmanship*. Lately the conviction has gained ground that fluctuations in this component must be drawn upon to account for variations in labour productivity and for shifts in industrial leadership. It does make a great deal of difference, so it seems, whether people look at their work as "just a job" or also as part of some collective celebration.

Contact can now be made with my earlier plea for complicating the analysis of choice behaviour with the concept of metapreferences. One important application of this concept can precisely be found in an individual's deliberation whether to devote more of his time and energy to instrumental activities at the expense of the non-instrumental ones, or vice versa. Shifts of this sort may mean an actual shift from one kind of activity to another (e.g. from public action to private pursuits); they will often involve a two-stage sequence in which an actor first decides to look, say, at some public involvement through instrumental rather than non-instrumental lenses, and then comes to feel that he should cut down on the public activity or give it up altogether. Quite possibly, what I was really after (or should have been after) in *Shifting Involvements* was to describe an oscillation between the instrumental and non-instrumental modes of action, with the pursuits of the private and of the public happiness serving as concrete manifestations of these two basic modes.

"Love": Neither Scarce Resource nor Augmentable Skill

My next plea for complicating economic discourse also deals with the production side, but more specifically with the role of one important prerequisite or ingredient known variously as morality, civic spirit, trust, observance of elementary ethical norms, and so on. The need of any functioning economic system for this "input" is widely recognized. But disagreement exists over what happens to this "input" as it is used.

There are essentially two opposite models of factor use. The traditional one is constructed on the basis of given, depletable resources that get incorporated into the product. The scarcer the resource the higher its price and the less of it will be used by the economizing firm in combination with other inputs. Arrow's more recent model recognizes the possibility of "learning by doing"; use of a resource such as a skill has the immediate effect of improving the skill, of enlarging (rather than depleting) its availability. The recognition of this sort of process—a considerable, strangely belated insight—also leads to important unorthodox policy conclusions, such as the desirability of subsidizing certain "scarce" inputs, since a subsidy-induced increase in their use will lead to the increased supply which, according to the more traditional model, was expected to be produced on the contrary by raising their price. I shall now attempt to show that neither of these two models is able to deal adequately with the nature of the factor of production that is under discussion here.

Because the "scarce resource" model has long been dominant, it has been extended to domains where its validity is highly dubious. Some thirty years ago, Robertson wrote a characteristically witty paper entitled "What Does the Economist Economize?" His often cited answer was: love, which he called "that scarce resource." Robertson explained, through a number of well-chosen illustrations from the contemporary economic scene, that it was the economist's job to create an institutional environment and pattern of motivation where as small a burden as possible would be placed, for the purposes of society's functioning, on this thing called "love," a term he used as a shortcut for morality and civic spirit. In so arguing, he was of course at one with Adam Smith, who celebrated society's ability to do without "benevolence" (of the butcher, brewer, and baker) as long as individual "interest" was given full scope. Robertson does not invoke Smith, quoting instead a telling phrase by Alfred Marshall: "Progress chiefly depends on the extent to which the *strongest* and not merely the *highest* forces of human nature can be utilized for the increase of social good."[9] This is yet another way of asserting that the social order is more secure when it is built on interest rather than on love or benevolence. But the sharpness of Robertson's own formulation makes it possible to identify the flaw in this recurrent mode of reasoning.

Once love and particularly public morality are equated with a scarce resource, the need to economize it seems self-evident. Yet a moment's reflection is enough

9. See Robertson, Dennis H. "What Does the Economist Economize?", *Economic Commentaries* (London: Staples Press, 1956), pp. 154, 148.

to realize that the analogy is not only questionable but a bit absurd—and therefore funny. Take, for example, the well-known case of the person who drives in the morning rush hour and quips, upon yielding to another motorist: "I have done my good deed for the day; for the remainder, I can now act like a bastard." What strikes one as funny and absurd here is precisely the assumption, on the part of our driver, that he comes equipped with a strictly limited supply of good deeds; that, in other words, love should be treated as a scarce resource—as Robertson claimed. We know instinctively that the supply of such resources as love or public spirit is not fixed or limited as may be the case for other factors of production. The analogy is faulty for two reasons: first of all, these are resources whose supply may well increase rather than decrease through use; second, these resources do not remain intact if they stay unused—like the ability to speak a foreign language or to play the piano, these moral resources are likely to become depleted and to atrophy if not used.

In a first approximation, then, Robertson's prescription appears to be founded on a confusion between the *use of a resource* and the *practice of an ability*. While human abilities and skills are valuable economic resources, most of them respond positively to practice, in a learning-by-doing manner, and negatively to non-practice. (Just a few skills—swimming and bicycle riding come to mind—seem to stay at the same level in spite of prolonged non-practice: once acquired, it is virtually impossible to lose or forget them. In counterpart, such skills often are not notably improved beyond one's level by practice.)

It was on the basis of this atrophy dynamic—the less the requirements of the social order for public spirit, the more the supply of public spirit dries up—that the United States' system for obtaining an adequate supply of human blood for medical purposes, with its only partial reliance on voluntary giving, was criticized by the British sociologist Richard Titmuss. And the British political economist Fred Hirsch generalized the point: once a social system, such as capitalism, convinces everyone that it can dispense with morality and public spirit, the universal pursuit of self-interest being all that is needed for satisfactory performance, the system will undermine its own viability, which is in fact premised on civic behaviour and on the respect of certain moral norms to a far greater extent than capitalism's official ideology avows.

How is it possible to reconcile the concerns of Titmuss and Hirsch with those seemingly opposite, yet surely not without some foundation, of Robertson, Smith, and Marshall? The truth is that, in his fondness for paradox, Robertson did his position a disservice: he opened his flank to easy attack when he equated love with some factor of production in strictly limited supply that needs to be economized.

But what about the alternative analogy that equates love, benevolence, and public spirit with a skill that is improved through practice and atrophies without it? This, too, has its weak points. Whereas public spirit will atrophy if too few demands are made upon it, it is not at all certain that the practice of benevolence will indefinitely have a positive feedback effect on the supply of this "skill." The practice of benevolence yields satisfaction ("makes you feel good"), to be sure, and therefore feeds upon itself up to a point, but this process is very different from practicing a manual (or intellectual) skill: here the practice leads to greater *dexterity*, which is usually a net addition to one's abilities, that is, it is not acquired at the expense of some other skill or ability. In the case of benevolence, on the other hand, the point is soon reached where increased practice does conflict with self-interest and even self-preservation: our quipping motorist, to go back to him, has not exhausted his daily supply of benevolence by yielding once, but there surely will be *some* limit to his benevolent driving behaviour, in deference to his own vital—perhaps even ethically compelling—displacement needs.

Robertson had a point, therefore, when he maintained that there could be institutional arrangements that make excessive demands on civic behaviour, just as Titmuss and Hirsch were right in pointing to the opposite danger: the possibility that society makes insufficient demands on civic spirit. In both cases, there is a shortfall in public spirit, but in the cases pointed to by Robertson et al., the remedy consists in institutional arrangements placing less reliance on civic spirit and more on self-interest, whereas in the situations that have caught the attention of Titmuss and Hirsch, there is need for increased emphasis on, and practice of, community values and benevolence. These two parties argue along exactly opposite lines, but both have a point. Love, benevolence, and civic spirit neither are scarce factors in fixed supply nor do they act like skills and abilities that improve and expand more or less indefinitely with practice. Rather, they exhibit a complex, composite behaviour: they atrophy when not adequately practiced and appealed to by the ruling socioeconomic regime, yet will once again make themselves scarce when preached and relied on to excess.

To make matters worse, the precise location of these two danger zones—which, incidentally, may correspond roughly to the complementary ills of today's capitalist and centrally planned societies—is by no means known, nor are these zones ever stable. An ideological-institutional regime that in wartime or other times of stress and public fervour is ideally suited to call forth the energies and efforts of the citizenry is well advised to give way to another that appeals more to private interest and less to civic spirit in a subsequent, less exalted period. Inversely, a regime of the latter sort may, because of the ensuing "atrophy of public meanings,"[10] give rise to anomie and unwillingness ever to sacrifice private or group interest to the public weal so that a move back to a more community-oriented regime would be called for.

Conclusion

I promised to inquire whether the various complications of traditional concepts that have been proposed have any common structure. The answer should be obvious: all these complications flow from a single source—the incredible complexity of human nature, which was disregarded by traditional theory for very good reason but which must be spoon-fed back into the traditional findings for the sake of greater realism.

A plea to recognize this complexity was implicit in my earlier insistence that "voice" be granted a role in certain economic processes alongside "exit," or competition. The efficient economic agent of traditional theory is essentially a silent-scanner and "superior statistician," as Arrow put it, whereas I argued that she also has considerable gifts of verbal and nonverbal communication and persuasion that will enable her to affect economic processes.

Another fundamental characteristic of humans is that they are self-evaluating beings, perhaps the only ones among living organisms. This simple fact forces the intrusion of metapreferences into the theory of consumer choice and makes it possible to distinguish between two fundamentally different kinds of preference changes. The self-evaluating function may be considered a variant of the communication or voice function: it also consists in a person addressing, criticizing, or persuading someone, but this someone is now the self rather than a supplier or an organization to which one belongs. But let us beware of excessive parsimony!

In addition to being endowed with such capabilities as communication, persuasion, and self-evaluation, humanity is beset by a number of fundamental, unresolved, and perhaps unresolvable tensions. A tension of this kind is that between instrumental and non-instrumental modes of behaviour and action. Economics has, for very good reasons, concentrated wholly on the instrumental mode. I plead here for a concern with the opposite mode, on the grounds that it is not wholly impervious to economic reasoning; and that it helps us understand

10. Taylor, Charles, *The Pattern of Politics* (Toronto: McClelland and Stewart, 1970), p. 123.

matters that have been found puzzling, such as collective action and shifts in labour productivity.

Finally, I have turned to another basic tension humanity must live with, this one resulting from the fact that we live in society.

It is the tension between self and others, between self-interest on the one hand, and public morality, service to community, or even self-sacrifice, on the other, or between "interest" and "benevolence" as Adam Smith put it. Here again, economics has concentrated overwhelmingly on one term of the dichotomy, while putting forward simplistic and contradictory propositions on how to deal with the other. The contradiction can be resolved by closer attention to the special nature of public morality as an "input."

In sum, I have complicated economic discourse by attempting to incorporate into it two basic human endowments and two basic tensions that are part of the human condition. To my mind, this is just a beginning.

17

The Concept of Interest: From Euphemism to Tautology

"Interest" or "interests" is one of the most central and controversial concepts in economics and, more generally, in social science and history. It is also extremely versatile, not to say ambiguous, and its meaning has been shifting a great deal. Since coming into widespread use, in various European countries around the latter part of the sixteenth century as essentially the same Latin-derived word (*intérêt*, *interesse*, etc.), the concept has stood for the fundamental forces, based on the drive for self-preservation and self-aggrandizement, that motivate or should motivate the actions of the prince or the state, of the individual, and, later, of groups of people occupying a similar social or economic position (classes, interest groups). When related to the individual, the concept has at times had a very inclusive meaning, encompassing interest in honour, glory, self-respect, and even afterlife, while, at other times, it became wholly confined to the drive for economic advantage. Correspondingly, "pursuing one's interests" can cover—to the point of tautology—all of human action while it will more usefully designate a specific manner or *style* of conduct, known variously as "rational" or as "instrumental" action.

The esteem in which interest-motivated behaviour is held has also varied drastically. The term was originally pressed into service as a euphemism serving, already in the late Middle Ages, to make respectable an activity, the taking of interest on loans, that had long been considered contrary to divine law and known as the sin of usury. In its wide meanings, the term achieved at times enormous prestige as key to a workable, peaceful, and progressive social order. But it has also been attacked as degrading to the human spirit and as dangerously disruptive and corrosive of the foundations of society. An inquiry into these multiple meanings and appreciations is in effect an exploration of much of economic history and in particular of the history of economic and political doctrine in the West over the past four centuries.

Moreover, the concept is still central in contemporary economics and political economy: the construct of the self-interested, isolated individual who chooses freely and rationally between alternative courses of action after computing their prospective costs and benefits to him- or herself, that is, while ignoring costs and benefits to other people and to society at large, underlies much of welfare economics; and the same perspective has yielded important, if disturbing, contributions to a broader science of social interactions, showing how the unfettered pursuit of private interest can lead to inefficient and harmful outcomes: examples are the decision problem known as the Prisoner's Dilemma, the obstacles to collective action because of free riding, and the problems of ensuring an adequate supply of public goods in general.

Two essential elements appear to characterize interest-propelled action: *self-centeredness,* that is, predominant attention of the actor to the consequences of any contemplated action for himself; and *rational calculation,* that is, a systematic attempt at evaluating prospective costs, benefits, satisfactions, and the like. Calculation could be considered the dominant or fundamental element: once action is supposed to be informed only by careful estimation of costs and benefits, with most weight necessarily being given to those that are better known and more quantifiable, it tends to become self-referential by virtue of the simple fact that each person is best informed about his or her *own* desires, satisfactions, disappointments, and sufferings.

Interest and Statecraft

Rational calculation was also preponderant in the emergence of the concept of interest-motivated action on the part of the prince in the sixteenth and seventeenth centuries. Self-centred-ness was then either hidden from view, as the interest of the prince was assumed to be identical with that of his subjects, or treated as a matter of course, rather than of choice; in relation to other princes, the absence of interests in common and the hazards of antagonistic coexistence were considered to be unalterable facts of nature.

It was probably this stress on rational calculation that accounts for the high marks that interest (interest-governed behaviour) received during the late sixteenth and early seventeenth century phases of its career in politics. The term actually did duty on two fronts. First, it permitted the emergent science of statecraft to assimilate the important insights of Machiavelli. The author of *The Prince* had almost strained to advertise those aspects of politics that clashed with conventional morality. He dwelt on instances where the prince was well-advised or even duty-bound to practice cruelty, mendacity, treason, and so on. Just as, in connection with money lending, the term interest came into use as a euphemism for the earlier term usury, so did it impose itself on the political vocabulary as a means of anesthetizing, assimilating, and developing some of Machiavelli's shocking insights. "Reason of state" was another such term, which as Meinecke later showed explicitly referred to the new practical rationality that came into favour.

But in the early modem age, "interest" was not only a label under which a ruler was given new latitude or was absolved from feeling guilty about following a practice he had previously been taught to consider as immoral: the term also served to impose new restraints, as it enjoined the prince to pursue his interests with a rational, calculating spirit that would often imply prudence and moderation. At the beginning of the seventeenth century, the interests of the sovereign were contrasted with the wild and destructive passions, that is, with the immoderate and foolish seeking of glory and other excesses involved in pursuing the by then discredited heroic ideal of the Middle Ages and the Renaissance. This disciplinary aspect of the doctrine of interest was particularly driven home in the influential essay *On the Interest of Princes and States of Christendom* by the Huguenot statesman, the Duke of Rohan (1579–1638).

The interest doctrine thus served to release the ruler from certain traditional restraints (or guilt feelings) only to subject him to new ones that were felt to be far more efficacious than the well-worn appeals to religion, morals, or abstract reason. Genuine hope arose that, with princely or national interest as guide, statecraft would be able to produce a more stable political order and a more peaceful world. A distinct nineteenth-century echo of these seventeenth-century notions is heard in various pronouncements of Bismarck, and particularly in a famous foreign policy speech of 1888 where he contrasted legitimate *Intere senpolitik* with arrogant *Machtpolitik,* which he defined as a policy "that seeks to influence and press upon the policy of other countries and to call the tune *outside* of one's own sphere of interests".[1]

Interest and Individual Behaviour

The early career of the interest concept with regard to statecraft finds a remarkable parallel in the role it played in shaping behaviour codes for individual men and women in society. Here also a new license went hand in hand with a new restraint.

The new license consisted in the legitimation and even praise that was bestowed upon the single-minded pursuit of material wealth and upon activities conducive to its accumulation. Just as Machiavelli had opened up new horizons for the prince, so did Mandeville two centuries later lift a number of don'ts for the commoner, in this case primarily in relation to moneymaking. Once again, a new insight into human behaviour or into the social order was first proclaimed as a startling, shocking paradox. Like Machiavelli, Mandeville presented his thesis on the beneficial effects on the general welfare of the luxury trades (which had long been strictly regulated) in the most scandalous possible fashion, by referring to the activities, drives, and emotions associated with these trades as "private vices." Here again, his essential message was eventually absorbed into the general stock of accepted practice by changing the language with which he had proclaimed his discovery. For the third time, euphemistic resort was had to "interest," this time in substitution for such terms as "avarice," "love of lucre," and so on. The transition from one set of terms to the other is nicely reflected by the first lines of David Hume's 1742 essay "On the Independency of Parliament":

> Political writers have established it as a maxim that, in contriving any system of government and fixing the several checks and balances of the constitution, every man ought to be supposed a *knave,* and to have no other end, in all his actions, than private interest. By this interest we must govern him, and, by means of it, make him, notwithstanding his insatiable avarice and ambition, cooperate to public good.[2]

Here interest is explicitly equated with knavishness and "insatiable avarice." But soon thereafter the memory of these unsavoury synonyms of interest was

1. Cited in Koselleck, Reinhart, "Der Interessebegriff im Wandel des sozialen und politische Kontexts", *Geschichtliche Grundbegriffe* (Stuttgart: Klett-Cotta, 1982), III, p. 349.
2. See Hume, David, *Essays Moral, Political and Literary*, 1742 (Edited by T. H. Green and T. H. Grose. London: Longmans, 1898), pp. 117–118.

suppressed, as in Adam Smith's famous statement about the butcher, the brewer, and the baker who are driven to supply us with our daily necessities through their interest rather than their benevolence. Smith thus did for Mandeville what the Duke of Rohan had done for Machiavelli. His doctrine of the Invisible Hand, which held that the general welfare is best served by everyone catering to his private interests, legitimated total absorption of the citizens in their own affairs and thereby served to assuage any guilt feelings that might have been harboured by the many Englishmen who were drawn into commerce and industry during the eighteenth century but had been brought up under the civic humanist code enjoining them to serve the public interest *directly*. They were now reassured that by pursuing their private gain they were doing so *indirectly*.

In fact, Adam Smith was not content to praise the pursuit of private gain. Prefiguring Milton Friedman's hostility to corporations contributing funds to charities and community improvements, he berated citizens' involvement in public affairs, by adding that he had "never known much good done by those who affected to trade for the public good." This may be just one of Smith's ill-humoured sideswipes, but ten years before Sir James Steuart, in his *Inquiry into the Principles of Political Oeconomy*, had supplied an interesting explanation for a similar aversion toward citizens' involvement in public affairs:

> ... were everyone to act for the public, and neglect himself, the statesman would be bewildered ... were a people to become quite disinterested, there would be no possibility of governing them. Everyone might consider the interest of his country in a different light, and many might join in the ruin of it, by endeavoring to promote its advantages.[3]

In counterpart to the new area of authorized and recommended behaviour, these statements point to the important restraints that accompanied the doctrine of interest. For the individual citizen or subject as for the ruler, interest-propelled action meant originally action informed by rational calculation in any area of human activity—political, cultural, economic, personal, and so on. In the seventeenth century and through part of the eighteenth, this sort of methodical, prudential, interest-guided action was seen as vastly preferable to actions dictated by the violent and unruly passions—the French liked to speak about *la violence et le désordre des passions*. Hope was held out that the steady, if self-centred, pull

3. See Steuart, Sir James, *Inquiry into the Principles of Political Oeconomy*, 1761 (Edited by A. S. Skinner. Chicago: University of Chicago Press, 1966), pp. 243–244.

of the interests might serve more efficiently as a brake on passionate behaviour than the traditional appeals to reason, duty, morals, and religion. At the same time, the interests of the vast majority of people, that is, of those outside of the highest reaches of power, came to be more narrowly defined as economic, material, or "moneyed" interests, probably because the non-elite was deemed to busy itself primarily with scrounging a living with no time left to worry about honour, glory, and the like. In this manner, the infatuation with interest helped to bestow legitimacy and prestige on commercial and related private activities that had hitherto ranked rather low in public esteem; correspondingly, the Renaissance ideal of glory, with its implicit celebration of the public sphere, was downgraded and debunked as a mere exercise in the destructive passion of self-love.[4]

Adam Smith and Sir James Steuart echo this feeling of mistrust toward, and disaffection from, activities that are aimed at achieving the public good directly. This change in attitude toward public involvement may have reflected a general mood: it is perhaps significant that only in the course of the eighteenth century did the verb "to meddle" firmly acquire its present-day derogatory sense.[5] The meaning of the French *se méler de* has had a similar evolution. Previously these terms had a neutral and sometimes even a positive connotation: after all, to meddle is to care for somebody or something outside of one's own immediate circle or area of interest, an attitude and activity that became offensive only in an era when to mind one's own business had become enthroned as a general rule of conduct.

The Political Benefits of an Interest-Based Social Order

The idea that the interests, understood as the methodical pursuit and accumulation of private wealth, would bring a number of benefits in the political realm took various distinct forms. There was, first of all, the expectation that they would achieve at the macro-level what they were supposed to accomplish for the individual: hold back the violent passions of the "rulers of mankind." Here the best known proposition, voiced early in the eighteenth century, says that the expansion of commerce is incompatible with the use of force in international relations and would gradually make for a peaceful world. Still more utopian—and therefore perhaps half-forgotten—hopes were held out for the effects of commerce on domestic politics: the web of interests delicately woven by thousands of transactions

4. See my *The Passions and the Interests*, pp. 31–42.
5. I owe this to a personal communication from Quentin Skinner.

would make it impossible for the sovereign to interpose his power brutally and wantonly through what was called "grands coups d'autorité" by Montesquieu or "the folly of despotism" by Sir James Steuart. This thought was carried further in the early nineteenth century when the intricacies of expanding industrial production compounded those of commerce: in the technocratic vision of Saint-Simon the time was at hand when economic exigencies would put an end, not just to *abuses* of the power of the state, but to any power whatsoever of man over man: politics would be replaced by administration of "things." As is well known this conjecture was taken up by Marxism with its prediction of the withering away of the state under communism. In this manner, an argument that a century earlier had been advanced on behalf of emergent capitalism was refurbished for a new, *anti*-capitalist utopia.

Another line of thought about the political effects of an interest-driven society looks less at the disciplines and constraints such a society will impose upon those who govern than at the difficulties of the task of governing. As already noted, a world where people methodically pursue their private interests was believed to be far more predictable, and hence *more governable,* than one where the citizens are vying with each other for honour and glory. There was thought to be a huge common gain here, quite apart from the proposition that voluntary acts of exchange necessarily imply the existence of mutual benefits.

The stability and lack of turbulence that were expected to characterize a country where men pursue single-mindedly their material interests were very much on the minds of some of the "inventors" of America, such as James Madison and Alexander Hamilton. The enormous prestige and influence of the interest concept at the time of the founding of America is well expressed in Hamilton's statement: "The safest reliance of every government is on man's interests. This is a principle of human nature, on which all political speculation, to be just, must be founded."[6]

Finally, at the most naïve level, a number of writers essentially extrapolated from the putative personality traits of the individual trader, as the prototype of interest-driven man, to the general characteristics of a society where traders would predominate. In the eighteenth century, perhaps as a result of some continuing, if unavowed, disdain for economic pursuits, commerce and moneymaking were often described as essentially innocuous or "innocent" pastimes, in contrast no

6. Cited in Ball, Terence, "The Ontological Presuppositions and Political Consequences of a Social Science", in *Changing Social Science,* edited by D. R. Sabia, Jr., and J. T. Wallulis (Albany: State University of New York Press, 1983), p. 45.

doubt with the more violent or more strenuous ways of the upper or lower classes. Commerce was to bring "gentle" and "polished" manners. In French, the term innocent appended to commerce was often coupled with *doux* (sweet, gentle), or *adoucir* (soften, render gentle), and what has been called the thesis of the *doux commerce* held that commerce was a powerful civilizing agent diffusing prudence, probity, and similar virtues within and among trading societies. Only under the impact of the French Revolution did some doubt arise on the direction of the causal link between commerce and civilized society: taken aback by the outbreak of social violence on a large scale, Edmund Burke suggested that the expansion of commerce depended itself on the *prior* existence of "manners" and "civilization" and on what he called "natural protecting principles" grounded in "the spirit of a gentleman" and "the spirit of religion."[7]

It was inevitable that the celebration of the interests should have enhanced the esteem accorded to those social groups that were primarily involved in commerce and industry. An early expression of this tendency is in *Robinson Crusoe* where Crusoe's father explains to his son—to dissuade him from his plans—that the "middle state" is "the most suited to human happiness, not exposed to the miseries and hardships, the labour and sufferings of the mechanic part of mankind, and not embarrassed with the pride, luxury, ambition and envy of the upper part of mankind."

Similar expressions of admiration for what was later often called the "middling rank of men" or simply "middle ranks" (rather than middle class) can be found in the writings of David Hume, Adam Smith, Adam Ferguson, and of the other exponents of the Scottish Enlightenment. In the nineteenth century James Mill waxed remarkably eloquent on this subject.[8] In France, the praise of the bourgeoisie as such was never quite so unreserved, but some of its constituent parts, such as the commercial community, rose in prestige as a result of the praise for the *doux commerce.*

7. Cited by Pocock, John G. A., "The Political Economy of Burke's Analysis of the French Revolution", *Historical Journal*, June 1982.
8. See Collini, Stefan; Winch, Donald and Burrow, John, *That Noble Science of Politics: A Study in Nineteenth-Century Intellectual History* (Cambridge: Cambridge University Press, 1983), p. 122.

The Invisible Hand

The capstone of the doctrine of self-interest was of course Adam Smith's Invisible Hand. Even though this doctrine, being limited to the economic domain, was more modest than the earlier speculations on the beneficent *political* effects of trade and exchange, it soon came to dominate the discussion. An intriguing paradox was involved in stating that the *general* interest and welfare would be promoted by the self-interested activities of numerous decentralized operators. To be sure, this was not the first nor the last time that such a claim of identity or coincidence or harmony of interests of a part with those of a whole has been put forward. Hobbes had advocated an absolute monarchy on the ground that this form of government brings about an identity of interests between ruler and ruled; as just noted, the writers of the Scottish Enlightenment saw an identity of interest between the general interests of British society and the interests of the middle ranks; such an identity between the interests of one class and those of society later became a cornerstone of Marxism, with the middling ranks having of course been supplanted by the proletariat; and finally, the American pluralist school in political science returned essentially to the Smithian scheme of harmony between many self-interests and the general interest, with Smith's individual economic operators having been replaced by contending "interest groups" on the political stage.

All these *Harmonielehren* (and I have probably been omitting some) have two factors in common: the "realistic" affirmation that we have to deal with men and women, or with groups thereof, "as they really are"; and an attempt to prove that it is possible to achieve a workable and progressive social order with these highly imperfect subjects, and, as it were, behind their backs. The mixture of paradoxical insight and alchemy involved in these constructs makes them powerfully attractive, but also accounts for their ultimate vulnerability. Perhaps social scientists ought to be advised to use caution in the construction of any further harmony-of-interests doctrines.

The Interests Attacked

The infatuation of the seventeenth and eighteenth centuries with the new insights offered by the concept of interest was remarkable. From the seventeenth-century English proverbs "Interest will not lie" or "Interest governs the world" to the late eighteenth-century dictum of the French *philosophe* Helvétius, "As the physical world is ruled by the laws of movement so is the moral universe ruled by the laws of interest," and to Hamilton's already noted similar pronouncement, interest was perceived as the key that unlocks the secrets of the social universe.

The seventeenth century was perhaps the real heyday of the interest doctrine. Governance of the social world by interest was then viewed as an alternative to the rule of destructive passions; that was surely a lesser evil, and possibly an outright blessing. In the eighteenth century, the doctrine received a substantial boost in the economic domain through the doctrine of the Invisible Hand, but it was indirectly weakened by the emergence of a more optimistic view of the passions: such passionate sentiments and emotions as curiosity, generosity, and sympathy were then given detailed attention, the latter in fact by Adam Smith himself in his *Theory of Moral Sentiments.* In comparison to such fine, newly discovered or rehabilitated springs of human action, interest no longer looked nearly so attractive. Here was one reason for the reaction against the interest paradigm that unfolded toward the end of the eighteenth century and was to fuel several powerful nineteenth-century intellectual movements, starting with romanticism.

Actually the passions did not have to be wholly transformed into benign sentiments to be thought respectable and even admirable by a new generation. Once the interests appeared to be truly in command with the vigorous commercial and industrial expansion of the age, a general lament went up for "the world we have lost." The French Revolution brought another sense of loss and Edmund Burke joined the two when he exclaimed, in his *Reflections on the Revolution in France,* "the age of chivalry is gone; that of sophisters, economists and calculators has succeeded; and the glory of Europe is extinguished forever." This famous statement came a bare fourteen years after the *Wealth of Nations* had denounced the rule of the "great lords" as a "scene of violence, rapine and disorder" and had celebrated the benefits flowing from everyone catering to his interests through orderly economic pursuits. Now Burke was an intense admirer of Adam Smith and took much pride in the identity of views on economic matters between himself and Smith. His "age of chivalry" statement, so contrary to the intellectual legacy of Smith, therefore signals one of those sudden changes in the general mood and understanding from one age to the next of which the exponents themselves are hardly aware. Burke's lament set the tone for much of the subsequent romantic protest against an order based on the interests which, once it appeared to be dominant, was seen by many as lacking nobility, mystery, and beauty.

This nostalgic reaction merged with the observation that the interests, that is, the drive for material wealth, were not nearly so "innocuous," "innocent," or "mild" as had been thought or advertised. To the contrary, it was now the drive for material advantage that suddenly loomed as a subversive force of enormous power. Thomas Carlyle thought that all traditional values were threatened by "that brutish god-forgetting Profit-and-Loss Philosophy" and protested that "cash payment is not the only nexus of man with man."[9] The phrase "cash nexus" was taken over by Marx and Engels, who used it to good effect in the first section of the *Communist Manifesto* where they painted a lurid picture of the moral and cultural havoc wrought by the conquering bourgeoisie.

In the same vein Proudhon saw property as a boundless revolutionary force. Trying to snatch good from evil, he conceived of the modern idea that the power of property might serve to check the equally terrifying power of the state: human liberty would be founded on this tension.[10] But such constructive or optimistic thoughts were exceedingly rare. Among the critics of capitalist society the accent was in general on the destructiveness of the new energies that were released by a social order in which the interests were given free rein. In fact, the thought arose that these forces were so wild and out of control that they might undermine the very foundations on which the social order was resting, that they were thus bent on self-destruction. In a startling reversal, feudal society, which had earlier been treated as "rude and barbarous" and was thought to be in permanent danger of dissolution because of the unchecked passions of violent rulers and grandees, was perceived in retrospect to have nurtured such values as honour, respect, friendship, trust, and loyalty, that were essential for the functioning of an interest-dominated order, but were relentlessly, if inadvertently, undermined by it. This argument was already contained in part in Burke's assertion that it is civilized society that lays the groundwork for commerce rather than vice versa; it was elaborated by a large and diverse group of authors, from Richard Wagner via Schumpeter to Karl Polanyi and Fred Hirsch.[11]

The Interests Diluted

While the interest doctrine thus met with considerable opposition and criticism in the nineteenth century, its prestige remained nevertheless high, particularly because of the vigorous development of economics as a new body of scientific thought. Indeed, the success of this new science made for attempts to utilize its

9. Carlyle, Thomas, *Past and Present*,1843 (New York: New York University Press, 1977), p. 187.
10. See my *The Passions and the Interests*, p. 120.
11. See my *Rival Views of Market Society*, 1982.

insights, such as the interest concept, for elucidating some noneconomic aspects of the social world. In his "Essay on Government" (1820), James Mill formulated the first "economic" theory of politics and based it—just as was later done by Schumpeter, Anthony Downs, Mancur Olson, and others—on the assumption of rational self-interest. But this widening of the use of the concept turned out to be something of a disservice. In politics, so Mill had to recognize, the gap between the "real" interest of the citizen and "a false supposition [i.e. perception] of interest" can be extremely wide and problematic. This difficulty provided an opening for Macaulay's withering attack in the *Edinburgh Review* (1829). Macaulay pointed out that Mill's theory was empty: interest "means only that men, if they can, will do as they choose ... it is ... idle to attribute any importance to a proposition which, when interpreted, means only that a man had rather do what he had rather do."

The charge that the interest doctrine was essentially tautological acquired greater force as more parties climbed on the bandwagon of interest, attempting to bend the concept to their own ends. Like so many key concepts used in everyday discourse, "interest" had never been strictly defined. While individual self-interest in material gain predominated, broader meanings were never completely lost sight of, as appears from the expression "narrow" self-interest, which is presumably distinguished from another kind of self-interest. An extremely inclusive interpretation of the concept was put forward at a very early stage of its history: Pascal's Wager—his demonstration that it is "rational" to act as though God existed, in the absence of certain knowledge about the matter—was nothing but an attempt to demonstrate that belief in God (hence, conduct in accordance with His precepts) was strictly in our (long-term) self-interest. Thus the concepts of *enlightened self-interest* or *intérêt bien compris* have a long history. But they received a boost and special, concrete meaning in the course of the nineteenth century. With the contemporary revolutionary outbreaks and movements as an ominous backdrop, advocates of social reform were able to argue that a dominant social group is well advised to surrender some of its privileges or to improve the plight of the lower classes so as to ensure social peace ("give up something not to lose everything"). "Enlightened" self-interest of the upper classes and conservative opinion was appealed to, for example, by the French and English advocates of universal suffrage or electoral reform at mid-century (the introduction of universal manhood suffrage in France after the 1848 Revolution was expected to "close the era of revolutions");[12] it was similarly invoked by the promoters of the early social-welfare legislation in Germany and elsewhere toward the end of the century, and again by Keynes and the Keynesians who favoured limited intervention of the state in the economy through countercyclical policy and "automatic stabilizers" resulting from welfare-state provisions. These appeals were often made by reformers who, while fully convinced of the intrinsic value and social justice of the measures they advocated, attempted to enlist the support of important groups by appealing to their "longer-term" rather than short-term and therefore presumably *short-sighted* interests. But the advocacy was not only tactical. It was sincerely put forward and testified to the continued prestige of the notion that interest-motivated social behaviour was the best guarantee of a stable and harmonious social order.

Whereas enlightened self-interest was something the upper classes of society were in this manner pressed to ferret out and to pursue, the lower classes were similarly exhorted, at about the same epoch but from different quarters, to raise their sights above day-to-day interests and pursuits. Marx and the Marxists invited the working class to become aware of its *real interests* and to shed the "false consciousness" from which it was said to be suffering as long as it did not throw itself wholeheartedly into the class struggle. Once again, the language of interests was borrowed for the purpose of characterizing and signifying a type of behaviour a group was being pressed to follow.

Here, then, was one way in which the concept of interest-motivated behaviour came to be diluted. Another was the progressive loss of the sharp distinction an earlier age had made between the passions and the interests. Already Adam Smith had used the two concepts jointly and interchangeably. Even though it became abundantly clear in the nineteenth century that the desire to accumulate wealth was anything but the "calm passion" as which it had been categorized and commended by some eighteenth-century philosophers, there was no return to the earlier distinction between the interests and the passions or between the wild and the mild passions. Perhaps this was so because moneymaking had once and for all been identified with the concept of interest so that all forms of this activity, however passionate or irrational, were automatically thought of as interest-motivated. As striking new forms of accumulation and industrial or financial empire-building made their appearance, new concepts were introduced, such as Schumpeter's entrepreneurial leadership and intuition or Keynes's "animal spirits"

12. See my *Shifting Involvements*, pp. 112–117.

(of the capitalists.) But they were not contrasted with the interests, and were rather assumed to be one of their manifestations.

In this manner the interests came to cover virtually the entire range of human actions, from the narrowly self-centred to the sacrificially altruistic, and from the prudently calculated to the passionately compulsive. In the end, interest stood behind anything people do or wish to do, and to explain human action by interest thus did turn into the vacuous tautology denounced by Macaulay. It so happened that, at about the same time, other key and time-honoured concepts of economic analysis, such as utility and value, became similarly drained of their earlier psychological or normative content. The positivistically oriented science of economics that flourished during much of this century felt it could do without any of these terms and replaced them by the less value- or psychology-laden "revealed preference" and "maximizing under constraints." And thus it came to pass that interest, which had rendered such long, faithful, and multiple services as a euphemism (for usury, for cruelty and other types of amoral princely behaviour, and for avarice and love of lucre), was now superseded by various even more neutral and colourless neologisms.

It may be conjectured that the development of the self-interest concept and of economic analysis in general in the direction of positivism and formalism was related to the discovery, toward the end of the nineteenth century, of the instinctual-intuitive, the habitual, the unconscious, the ideologically and neurotically driven—in short, to the extraordinary vogue for the non-rational that characterized virtually all of the influential philosophical, psychological, and sociological thinking of the age. It was out of the question for economics, all based on rationally pursued self-interest, to incorporate the new findings into its own apparatus. So that discipline reacted to the contemporary intellectual temper by withdrawing from psychology to the greatest possible extent, by emptying its basic concepts of their psychological origin—a survival strategy that turned out to be highly successful. It is of course difficult to prove that the rise of the non-rational in psychology and sociology and the triumph of positivism and formalism in economics were truly connected in this way. Some evidence is supplied by the remarkable case of Pareto: he made fundamental, *interrelated* contributions both to a sociology that stressed the complex "nonlogical" (as he put it) aspects of social action and to an economics that is emancipated from dependence on psychological hedonism.

Current Trends

Lately there have been signs of discontent with the progressive evisceration of the concept of interest. On the conservative side, there was a return to the orthodox meaning of interest and the doctrine of enlightened self-interest was impugned. Apart from the discovery, first made by Tocqueville, that reform is just as likely to unleash as to prevent revolution, it was pointed out that most well-meant reform moves and regulations have "perverse" side effects which compound rather than alleviate the social ills one had set out to cure. It was best, so it appeared, not to stray from the narrow path of narrow self-interest, and it was confusing and pointless to dilute this concept.

Others agreed with the latter judgment, but for different reasons and with different conclusions. They also disliked the manoeuver of having every kind of human action masquerade under the interest label. But they regarded as relevant for economics certain human actions and activities which cannot be accounted for by the traditional notion of self-interest: actions motivated by altruism, by commitment to ethical values, by concern for the group and the public interest, and, perhaps most important, the varieties of non-instrumental behaviour. A beginning has been made by various economists and other social scientists to take these kinds of activities and behaviour seriously, that is, to abandon the attempt to categorize them as mere variants of interest-motivated activity.[13]

One important aspect of these various forms of behaviour which do not correspond to the classical concept of interest-motivated action is that they are subject to considerable variation. Take actions in the public interest as an example. There is a wide range of such actions, from total involvement in some protest movement down to voting on Election Day and further down to mere grumbling about, or just commenting on, some public policy within a small circle of friends or family—what Guillermo O'Donnell has called "horizontal voice" in contrast to the "vertical" voice directly addressed to the authorities. The actual degree of participation under more or less normal political conditions is subject to constant fluctuations along this continuum, in line with changes in economic conditions, government performance, personal development, and many other factors. As a result, with total time for private and public activity being limited, the intensity of citizens' dedication to their private affairs is also subject to constant change.

13. Among many other works, reference should be made to writings by Boulding, Collard, Margolis, McPherson, Phelps, Pizzomo, Schelling, and Sen; see also chapter 16.

Near-total privatization occurs only under certain authoritarian governments, for, as Benjamin Constant acutely noted, "the art of oppressive government is to keep all its citizens separated from each other."[14] The most repressive regimes not only do away with the free vote and any open manifestation of dissent, but also manage to suppress, through their display of terrorist power, all *private* expressions of inconformity with public policy, that is, all those manifestations of "horizontal voice" that are actually important forms of public involvement.

An arresting conclusion follows. That vaunted ideal of predictability, that alleged idyll of a privatized citizenry paying busy and exclusive attention to its economic interests and thereby serving the public interest indirectly, but never directly, becomes a reality only under wholly nightmarish political conditions! More civilized political circumstances necessarily imply a less transparent and less predictable society.

Actually, this outcome of the current inquiries into activities not strictly motivated by traditional self-interest is all to the good: for the only certain and predictable feature of human affairs is their unpredictability and the futility of trying to reduce human action to a single motive—such as interest.

14. Cited in Holmes, Stephen, *Benjamin Constant and the Making of Modern Liberalism* (New Haven, CT: Yale University Press, 1984), p. 247.

Bibliography of Albert O. Hirschman's Work

Hirschman A. O. (1937) "La fecondità della donna italiana secondo l'età e il numero dei figli avuti. Osservazioni critiche"—mimeo.

Hirschman A. O. (1938a) "Note su due recenti tavole di nuzialità della popolazione italiana", *Giornale degli economisti*, January.

Hirschman A. O. (1938b) "Les finances et l'économie italienne: Situation actuelle et perspectives", *Supplément au bulletin quotidien* 123, n. 1, June.

Hirschman A. O. (1938c) *Il franco Poincaré e la sua svalutazione*. Dissertation. Università di Trieste, Facoltà di Economia e Commercio. Published by G. Gilibert, M. de Cecco e R. Finzi eds., Roma, Ed. Storia e Letteratura, 2004.

Hirschman A. O. (1938d) "Histoire de la lire de la rivalorization au controle des changes"—mimeo.

Hirschman A. O. (1939a) "Italie", *L'activité economique* n. 15, 16 and 17.

Hirschman A. O. (1939b) "Etude statistique sur la tendence du commerce extérieur vers l'equilibre et le bilateralisme"—mimeo; English tr. *Political Economy* 4, n. 1—1988.

Hirschman A. O. (1939c) "Mémoire sur le controle des changes en Italie"—mimeo; Italian tr. in A.O. Hirschman *Potenza nazionale*—1987.

Hirschman A. O. (1943a) "The Commodity Structure of World Trade", *Quarterly Journal of Economics*, August.

Hirschman A. O. (1943b) "On Measures of Dispersion for a Finite Distribution", *Journal of the American Statistical Association*, September.

Hirschman A. O. (1945) *National Power and the Structure of Foreign Trade*, Berkeley CA, University of California Press; third ed., with "Preface to the Expanded Edition"—1980.

Hirschman A. O. (1946a) "Bilateralism and 'Proportionalism'—Two Aspects of Trade Structure", *Review of Foreign Developments (RFD)*, December.
Hirschman A. O. (1946b) "Schuman's Devaluation Paradox", *RFD*, December.
Hirschman A. O. (1947a) "Conditions and Tests of Successful Devaluation: A Mathematical Note" *RFD*, January.
Hirschman A. O. (1947b) "Exchange Control in Italy", I and II, *RFD*, March and May.
Hirschman A. O. and Tamagna F. M. (1947c) "British-Italian Financial Settlement", *RFD*, May.
Hirschman A. O. (1947d) "France and Italy: Patterns of Reconstruction", *Federal Reserve Bulletin*, n. 4, April.
Hirschman A. O. (1947e) "Swiss Foreign Economic Policy", *RFD*, June.
Hirschman A. O. (1947f) "Public Finance, Money Markets, and Inflation in France", *RFD*, July.
Hirschman A. O. and Roberts M. J. (1947g) "Trade and Credit Arrangements between the Marshall Plan Countries", *RFD*, August.
Hirschman A. O. (1947h) "Trade Structure of the Marshall Plan Countries", *RFD*, August.
Hirschman A. O. and Lichtenberg C. (1947i) "French Exports and the Franc", *RFD*, September.
Hirschman A. O. and Lichtenberg C. (1947j) "French Foreign Trade: Customs vs. Exchange Control Statistics", *RFD*, December.
Hirschman A. O. (1947k) "Italian Exchange Rate Policy", *RFD*, December.
Hirschman A. O. (1948a) "The French Monetary Move", *RFD*, February.
Hirschman A. O. and Nixon F. (1948b) "Types of Exchange Rate Discrimination" *RFD*, February.
Hirschman A. O. (1948c) " 'Franco Valuta' Imports in France", *RFD*, March.
Hirschman A. O. (1948d) "Credit Restrictions and Deflation in Italy", *RFD*, April.
Hirschman A. O. (1948e) "Note on Offshore Procurement in Europe", *RFD*, June.
Hirschman A. O. and Lichtenberg C. (1948f) "Payments and Trade between ERP Countries in 1947", *RFD*, June.
Hirschman A. O. (1948g) "Inflation and Balance of Payment Deficit", *RFD*, August.
Hirschman A. O. (1948h) "Inflation and Deflation in Italy", *American Economic Review*, September.
Hirschman A. O. (1948i) "Dollar Shortage and Discrimination", *RFD*, September.
Hirschman A. O. and Roosa R. V. (1948j) "Some Recent Developments in French Finance and Credit Policy", *RFD*, October.
Hirschman A. O. (1948k) "Disinflation, Discrimination, and the Dollar Shortage", *American Economic Review*, December.
Hirschman A. O. (1948l) "Economic and Financial Conditions in Italy", *RFD*, December.
Hirschman A. O. (1949a) "The OEEC Interim Report on the European Recovery Program: A Summary", *RFD*, January.
Hirschman A. O. (1949ab) "Devaluation and the Trade Balance: A Note", *Review of Economics and Statistics*, February.
Hirschman A. O. and Rosa R. V. (1949c) "Credit Controls in the Postwar Economy of France", *RFD*, February.
Hirschman A. O. (1949d) "Proposal for a European Monetary Authority", mimeo.; Italian tr. in A. O. Hirschman, *Tre continenti*, 1990.
Hirschman A. O. (1949e) "Relaxation of Exchange Controls in Belgium and France", *RFD*, February.

Hirschman A. O. (1949f) "Intra-European Payments: A Proposal for Discussion", *RFD*, March.
Hirschman A. O. and Dembitz L. N. (1949g) "Movement toward Balance of International Transactions in the United States", *RFD*, April.
Hirschman A. O. and Rosa R. V. (1949h) "Postwar Credit Controls in France", *RFD*, April.
Hirschman A. O. (1949i) "International Aspects of a Recession", *RFD*, June.
Hirschman A. O. (1949j) "The New Intra-European Payment Scheme", *RFD*, July.
Hirschman A. O. (1949k) "The U.S. Recession and the Dollar Position of the OEEC Countries", *RFD*, September.
Hirschman A. O. (1949l) "Countries Notes on Recent Currency Adjustments", *RFD*, October.
Hirschman A. O. (1950) "Approaches to Multilateralism and European Integration", mimeo.; Italian tr. in A. O. Hirschman, *Tre continenti*, 1990.
Hirschman A. O. (1950a) "Liberalization of the ECA Dollar", *RFD*, January.
Hirschman A. O. (1950b) "European Payment Union—A Possible Basis for Agreement", *RFD*, February.
Hirschman A. O. (1950c) "Annex I: The EPU—A Short History", *RFD*, June.
Hirschman A. O. (1950d) "The Influence of U.S. Economic Conditions on Foreign Countries (Draft for Discussion)", *RFD*, June.
Hirschman A. O. (1951) "The European Payment Union: Negotiations and Issues", *Review of Economics and Statistics*, February.
Hirschman A. O. (1951a) "Types of Convertibility", *Review of Economics and Statistics*, February.
Hirschman A. O. (1951b) "Size and Distribution of the Public Debt in Selected Countries", *RFD*, February.
Hirschman A. O. (1951c) "Industrial Nations and Industrialization of Underdeveloped Countries", *Economia Internazionale*, August.
Hirschman A. O. (1951d) "Note on Hinshaw's Article on Currency Appreciation", *RFD*, September.
Hirschman A. O. (1951e) "The Problem of the Belgian Surplus in EPU". *RFD*. September.
Hirschman A. O. (1952) "Effect of Industrialization on the Markets of Industrial Countries", in B. F. Hoselitz ed. *The Progress of Underdeveloped Areas*, Chicago, Chicago University Press.
Hirschman A. O. (1954) "Guía para el análisis y la confecciòn de recomendaciones sobre la situación monetaria", *Economia Colombiana*, October.
Hirschman A. O. (1954a) "Economic and Investment Planning: Reflections Based on Experience in Colombia", in *Investment Criteria and Economic Growth*, mimeo, Cambridge MA, Center for International Studies, MIT; published by New York, Asia Publishing House, 1961.
Hirschman A. O. (1955a) "Diary of Survey Trip through Central America", mimeo, March-April.
Hirschman A. O. (1955b) "Study of the Present and of Prospective Financial Position of the Empresas Municipalities of Cali, with Recommendations", mimeo.
Hirschman A. O. and Kalmanoff G. (1955c) *Colombia Highlights of a Developing Economy*, Bogotà, Banco de la República Press.
Hirschman A. O. (1955d) "Survey of Executives Salaries in Colombia", mimeo.
Hirschman A. O. (1956a) "The Market for Paper and Pulp in Colombia", mimeo.
Hirschman A. O. (1956b) "La demanda para gas en Cali y en el Valle del Cauca", mimeo.
Hirschman A. O. and Kalmanoff G. (1956c) "Demanda de energia eléctrica para la C.V.C.", *Economìa Colombiana*, June.

Hirschman A. O. and Kalmanoff G. (1957a) *Investment in Central America: Basic Information for United States Businessmen*, Washington D.C., Dept. of Commerce.

Hirschman A. O. (1957b) "Economic Policy in Underdeveloped Countries", *Economic Development and Cultural Change*, July.

Hirschman A. O. (1957c) "Investment Policies and 'Dualism' in Underdeveloped Countries", *American Economic Review*, September.

Hirschman A. O. (1958a) *The Strategy of Economic Development*, New Heaven CT, Yale University Press.

Hirschman A. O. and Sirkin G. (1958b) "Investment Criteria and Capital Intensity. Once Again", *Quarterly Journal of Economics*, August.

Hirschman A. O. (1959) "Primary Products and Substitutes: Should Technological Progress Be Policed?", *Kyklos*, 7, 3.

Hirschman A. O. (1959–1960) "The Strategy of Economic Development", *Farm Policy Forum*, 12.

Hirschman A. O. (1960) "Invitation to Theorizing about the Dollar Glut" *Review of Economics and Statistics*, February.

Hirschman A. O. (1961a) "Preface to the Paperbound Edition" of *The Strategy* cit. 1958; sixth printing 1964.

Hirschman A. O. (1961b) "Exchange Controls and Economic Development: Comments", in H. S. Ellis ed. *Economic Development for Latin America,* International Economic Association, New York, St. Martin's Press.

Hirschman A. O. (1961c) "Second Thoughts on 'Alliance for Progress' ", The Reporter, May.

Hirschman A. O. ed. (1961d) *Latin American Issues: Essays and Comments*, New York, Twenties Century Fund.

Hirschman A. O. (1961e) "Ideologies of Economic Development in Latina America". In A. O. Hirschman ed. *Latin American Issues.*

Hirschman A. O. (1961f) "Abrazo vs. Coexistence: Comments on Ypsilon's Paper". In A. O. Hirschman ed. *Latin American Issues.*

Hirschman A. O. (1962a) "Analyzing Economic Growth: A Comment", in R. E. Asher et al. eds. *Development in Emerging Countries. An Agenda for Research,* Washington D.C. Brookings.

Hirschman A. O. and Lindblom C. E. (1962b) "Economic Development, Research and Development, and Policy-Making", *Behavioral Science*, April.

Hirschman A. O. (1962c) "Critical Comments on Foreign Aid Strategies", in R. E. Asher et al. eds. *Development in Emerging Countries. An Agenda for Research.* Washington D.C., Brookings.

Hirschman A. O. (1963a) *Journeys Toward Progress. Studies of Economic Policy-Making in Latin America*, New York, Twentieth Century Fund.

Hirschman A. O. (1963b) "Models of Reformmongering", *Quarterly Journal of Economics*, May.

Hirschman A. O. (1963c) "How Policy is Made", *Américas*, August.

Hirschman A. O. (1964a) "The Stability of Neutralism: A Geometrical Note", *American Economic Review*, September.

Hirschman A. O. (1964b) "The Paternity of an Index", *American Economic Review*, September.

Hirschman A. O. (1965a) "Obstacles to Development: A Classification and a Quasi-Vanishing Act", *Economic Development and Cultural Change*, July.

Hirschman A. O. (1965b) "Out of Phase", *Encounter*, September.

Hirschman A. O. (1967a) "The Principle of the Hiding Hand", *Public Interest*, Winter.
Hirschman A. O. (1967b) *Development Projects Observed*, Washington D.C., Brookings.
Hirschman A. O. (1968a) "The Political Economy of Import-Substituting Industrialization in Latin America", *Quarterly Journal of Economics*, February.
Hirschman A. O. and Bird R. M. (1968b) "Foreign Aid: A Critique and a Proposal", *Princeton Essays on International Finance*, July.
Hirschman A. O. (1968c) "Forward" to Judith Tendler *Electric Power in Brazil*, Cambridge MA, Harvard University Press.
Hirschman A. O. (1968d) "Underdevelopment, Obstacles to the Perception of Change, and Leadership", *Daedalus*, Summer.
Hirschman A. O. (1968e) "Industrial Development in the Brazilian Northeast and the Tax Credit Scheme of Article 34/18", *The Journal of Development Studies*, October.
Hirschman A. O. (1969) "How to Divest in Latin America, and Why", *Princeton Essays in International Finance*, November.
Hirschman A. O. (1970a) *Exit, Voice, and Loyalty: Responses to Decline in Firms, Organizations, and States*, Cambridge MA, Harvard University Press.
Hirschman A. O. (1970b) "The Search for a Paradigm as a Hindrance to Understanding", *World Politics*, March.
Hirschman A. O. (1971a) *A Bias for Hope. Essays on Development and Latin America*, New Haven CT, Yale University Press.
Hirschman A. O. (1971b) "Ideology: Mask or Nessus Shirt?". In A. Eckstein ed. *Comparative Economic System*, Berkeley, CA, University of California Press.
Hirschman A. O. (1973a) "Preface to the Norton Edition" of *Journeys Toward Progress*—1963.
Hirschman A. O. (1973b) "The Changing Tolerance of Income Inequality in the Course of Economic Development", *Quarterly Journal of Economics*, November.
Hirschman A. O. (1973c) "An Alternative Explanation of Contemporary Harriedness" *Quarterly Journal of Economics*, November.
Hirschman A. O. (1974) "Exit, Voice, and Loyalty: Further Reflections and a Survey of Recent Contributions", *Social Science Information*, February.
Hirschman A. O. (1975) "Policy Making and Policy Analysis in Latin America—A Return Journey", *Policy Sciences*, December.
Hirschman A. O., Geertz C. and Cardoso F. H. Conversation (1976a) "The Hungry, Crowded, Competitive World", mimeo; now in *The Tocqueville Review—La Revue Tocqueville* 2010, n. 2.
Hirschman A. O. (1976b) "On Hegel, Imperialism and Structural Stagnation", *Journal of Development Economics*, 3, March.
Hirschman A. O. (1976c) "Exit, Voice, and Loyalty: Comments", *American Economic Review*, Papers and Proceedings, May.
Hirschman A. O. (1977a) "A Generalized Linkage Approach to Development, with Special Reference to Staples", *Economic Development and Cultural Change*, supplement (essays in honor of B. F. Hoselitz).
Hirschman A. O. (1977b) *The Passions and the Interests. Political Arguments for Capitalism before its Triumph*, Princeton, NJ, Princeton University Press.
Hirschman A. O. (1978a) "Exit, Voice, and the State", *World Politics*, October.

Hirschman A. O. (1978b) “Beyond Asymmetry: Critical Notes on Myself as a Young Man and Some Other Old Friends”, *International Organization*, Winter; now in Hirschman A.O. *National Power*—1945; third ed., “Preface to the Expanded Edition”—1980.

Hirschman A. O. (1979a) “Foreword” to K. Q. Hill ed. *Toward a New Strategy for Development*, New York, Pergamon.

Hirschman A. O. (1979b) “The Turn to Authoritarianism and the Search for Its Economic Determinants”. In D. Collier ed. *The New Authoritarianism in Latin America*, Princeton NJ, Princeton University Press.

Hirschman A. O. (1979c) “Three Uses of Political Economy in Analyzing European Integration” mimeo. In A. O. Hirschman *Essays*, 1981.

Hirschman A. O. (1979d) “Private and Public Happiness: Pursuits and Disappointments”, mimeo.

Hirschman A. O. (1980a) “Morality and the Social Sciences: A Durable Tension”, Acceptance Paper, Memphis TN, P. K. Seidman Foundation.

Hirschman A. O. (1980b) “The Welfare in Trouble: Systemic Crisis or Growing Pains?”, *American Economic Review*, Papers and Proceedings, May.

Hirschman A. O. (1980c) “In difesa del possibilismo”. In R. Scartezzini et al. eds. *I limiti della democrazia*, Napoli, Liguori.

Hirschman A. O. (1981) *Essays in Trespassing: Economics to Politics and Beyond*, Cambridge UK, Cambridge University Press.

Hirschman A. O. (1982a) “The Rise and Decline of Development Economics”. In M. Gersowitz ed. *The Theory and Experience of Economic Development: Essays in Honor of Sir W. Arthur Lewis*, London, Allen.

Hirschman A. O. (1982b) “Rival Interpretations of Market Society: Civilizing, Destructive, or Feeble?”, *Journal of Economic Literature*, December.

Hirschman A. O. (1982c) *Shifting Involvements: Private Interest and Public Action*, Princeton NJ, Princeton University Press.

Hirschman A. O. (1983a) *Ascesa e declino dell’economia dello sviluppo ed altri saggi*, A. Ginzburg ed., Torino, Rosenberg.

Hirschman A. O. (1983b) “The Principle of Conservation and Mutation of Social Energy”, *Grassroots Development*, n. 2.

Hirschman A. O. (1984a) “University Activities Abroad and Human Rights Violations: Exit, Voice, or Business as Usual?”, *Human Rights Quarterly*, February.

Hirschman A. O. (1984b) “A Dissenter’s Confession: Revisiting *The Strategy of Economic Development*”, in G. M. Meier and D. Seers eds., *Pioneers in Development*, Oxford, Oxford University Press.

Hirschman A. O. (1984c) “Erinnerungen an das Französische Gymnasium”, mimeo.

Hirschman A.O. (1984d) *L’économie comme science sociale et politique*, F. Furet ed., Paris, Gallimard.

Hirschman A. O. (1984e) *Getting Ahead Collectively: Grassroots Experiences in Latin America*, New York, Pergamon.

Hirschman A. O. (1984f) “Against Parsimony: Three Easy Ways of Complicating Some Categories of Economic Discourse”, *American Economic Review*, May.

Hirschman A. O. (1984g) “Grassroots Change in Latin America”, *Challenge*, September-October.

Hirschman A. O. (1985) "Inflation: Reflections on the Latin American Experience". In L. Lindberg and C. S. Maier eds. *The Politics of Inflation and Economic Stagnation*, Washington D.C., Brookings.
Hirschman A. O. (1986a) "On Democracy in Latin America", *New York Review of Books*, April.
Hirschman A. O. (1986b) *Rival Views of Market Societies and Other Recent Essays.* New York, Viking.
Hirschman A. O. (1986c) *Vers une économie politique élargie*, Paris, Minuit.
Hirschman A. O. (1986d) "Out of Phase Again", *New York Review of Books*, December.
Hirschman A. O. (1987a) *Potenza nazionale e commercio estero. Gli anni Trenta, l'Italia e la ricostruzione*, P. F. Asso e M. de Cecco eds., Bologna, Il Mulino.
Hirschman A. O. (1987b) *L'economia politica come scienza morale e sociale*, with an essay by L. Meldolesi, L. Meldolesi ed., Napoli, Liguori.
Hirschman A. O. (1987c) "The Political Economy of Latin American Development: Seven Exercises in Retrospection", *Latin American Research Review*, n. 3.
Hirschman A. O. (1988a) "Berlin Festvortag", mimeo.
Hirschman A. O. (1988b) *Come complicare l'economia*, L. Meldolesi ed., Bologna, Il Mulino.
Hirschman A. O. (1989a) "Thomas Shelling". In R. Zeckhauser ed. "Distinguished Fellow: Reflections on Thomas Shelling", *Journal of Economic Perspectives*, Spring.
Hirschman A. O. (1989b) "Having Opinions: One of the Elements of Well-Being?", *American Economic Review*, Papers and Proceedings, May.
Hirschman A. O. (1989c) "Two Hundred Years of Reactionary Rhetoric: The Case of the Perverse Effect". In *The Tanner Lectures in Human Values*, Vol. 10.
Hirschman A. O. (1989d) "Reactionary Rhetoric", *Atlantic*, May.
Hirschman A. O. (1989e) "Opinionated Opinion and Democracy", *Dissent*, Summer.
Hirschman A. O. (1989f) "Statement of Dissent". In R. Dornbusch ed. *The Road to Economic Recovery. Report on International Debt.* New York: Priority Press.
Hirschman A. O. (1989g) "Comment on Chapter 6". In G. Di Tella and R. Dornbusch eds. *The Political Economy of Argentina 1946–83*, London, Palgrave.
Hirschman A. O. (1989h) "How the Keynesian Revolution Was Exported from America". In S. Bowles et al. eds. *Unconventional Wisdom: Essays in Honor of John Kenneth Galbraith*, Boston, Houghton.
Hirschman A. O. (1989i) "How the Keynesian revolution Was Exported from the United States, and Other Comments". In P. A. Hall ed. *The Political Power of Economic Ideas.* Princeton NJ, Princeton University Press.
Hirschman A. O. (1989j) "Reactionary Rhetoric: A Reply", *Atlantic*, September.
Hirschman A. O. (1989k) *Entwicklung, Markt und Moral*, Munchen, Hauser.
Hirschman A. O. (1990a) "Good News Is Not Bad News", *New York Review of Books*, October.
Hirschman A. O. (1990b) [Interview]. In R. Swedberg ed., *Economics and Sociology*, Princeton NJ, Princeton University Press.
Hirschman A. O. (1990c) "Tribute to Charles K. Kindleberger on His Eightieth Birthday", mimeo.
Hirschman A. O. (1990d) "The Case Against 'One Thing at a Time' ", *World Development*, n. 8.
Hirschman A. O. (1990e) "Remerciements", Paris, Institut d'études politiques.
Hirschman A. O. (1990f) ["Io, detective dell'economia fascista"] in A.O. Hirschman *Tre continenti*—1990.

Hirschman A. O. (1990g) *Tre continenti. Economia politica e sviluppo della democrazia in Europa, Stati Uniti e America Latina*, L. Meldolesi ed., Torino, Einaudi.

Hirschman A. O. (1990h) *Come far passare le riforme*, L. Meldolesi ed., Bologna, Il Mulino.

Hirschman A. O. (1991) *Rhetoric of Reaction. Perversity, Futility, Jeopardy*, Cambridge MA, Harvard University Press.

Hirschman A. O. (1992a) "Industrialization and Its Manyfold Discontents: West, East, and South", *World Development*, September.

Hirschman A. O. (1992b) "L'argument intransigeant comme idée reçue: En guise de réponse à Raymond Boudon", *Le Débat*, n. 69.

Hirschman A. O. (1992c) "Does the Market Keep Us out of Mischief or out of Happiness?", *Contemporary Sociology*, n. 6.

Hirschman A. O. (1993a) "Varian Fry in Marseilles", Preface to V. Fry, *Assignment Rescue*, New York, Scholastic.

Hirschman A. O. (1993b) "Exit, Voice, and the Fate of the German Democratic Republic: An Essay in Conceptual History", *World Politics*, January.

Hirschman A. O. (1993c) "Coimbra Talk", mimeo.

Hirschman A. O. (1993d) "Nanterre Talk", mimeo.

Hirschman A. O. (1993e) "La rhetorique progressiste et le reformateur", *Commentaire*, Summer.

Hirschman A. O. (1993f) "The Rhetoric of Reaction—Two Years Later", *Government and Opposition*, Summer.

Hirschman A. O. (1994a) "A Propensity to Self-Subversion". In L. Rodwin and D. A. Shön *Rethinking the Development Experience: Essays Provoked by the Work of Albert O. Hirschman*, Washington D.C., Brookings.

Hirschman A. O. (1994b) "The On-and-Off Connection between Political and Economic Progress", *American Economic Review*, Papers and Proceedings, May.

Hirschman A. O. (1994c) *Passaggi di frontiera*, C. Donzelli, M. Petrusewicz and C. Rusconi eds. Roma, Donzelli.

Hirschman A. O. (1994d) "Social Conflicts as Pillars of Democratic Market Society", *Political Theory*, June.

Hirschman A. O. (1994e) "A Hidden Ambition", New Preface of *Development Projects Observed*—1967.

Hirschman A. O. (1995a) *A Propensity to Self-Subversion*, Cambridge MA, Harvard University Press.

Hirschman A. O. (1995b) "Social Democracy Moves South", *Dissent*, Spring.

Hirschman A. O. (1996) "Meddling the Public and Private Spheres: Taking Commensality Seriously", *Critical Review*, Fall.

Hirschman A. O. (1997) "Fifty Years of the Marshall Plan: Two Posthumous Memoirs and Some Personal Recollection", *French Politics and Society*, Summer.

Hirschman A. O. (1998) *Crossing Boundaries. Selected Writings*, New York, Zone.

Index of Names

Index of Subjects